Paola Bassino
The *Certamen Homeri et Hesiodi*

TEXTE UND KOMMENTARE

Eine altertumswissenschaftliche Reihe

Herausgegeben von
Michael Dewar, Karla Pollmann, Ruth Scodel

Band 59

De Gruyter

The *Certamen Homeri et Hesiodi*
A Commentary

by

Paola Bassino

De Gruyter

ISBN 978-3-11-073687-8
e-ISBN (PDF) 978-3-11-058477-6
e-ISBN (EPUB) 978-3-11-058348-9
ISSN 0563-3087

Library of Congress Control Number: 2018957798

Bibliografische Information der Deutschen Nationalbibliothek
Die Deutsche Nationalbibliothek verzeichnet diese Publikation in der
Deutschen Nationalbibliografie; detaillierte bibliografische Daten sind im Internet
über http://dnb.dnb.de abrufbar.

© 2020 Walter de Gruyter GmbH, Berlin/Boston
This volume is text- and page-identical with the hardback published in 2019.
Satz: Michael Peschke, Berlin
Druck und Bindung: CPI books GmbH, Leck
www.degruyter.com

For my family

Acknowledgements

This book is a revised version of my Doctoral dissertation. I would like to thank the Department of Classics and Ancient History, the Faculty of Arts and Humanities, and Ustinov College at Durham University for providing me with financial support during my Ph.D. The final stages of research were carried out under the aegis of a large interdisciplinary project, directed by Prof. Barbara Graziosi at Durham University, generously funded by the European Research Council, and entitled *Living Poets: A New Approach to Ancient Poetry*: www.livingpoets.dur.ac.uk.

Prof. Barbara Graziosi has supervised my work with great competence, patience, and care, for which I will always be grateful to her. My second supervisor Prof. Johannes Haubold and Prof. Paola Ceccarelli read over my work and gave immensely useful advice during my Ph.D. Prof. Richard Hunter and Dr Ivana Petrovic examined my dissertation and offered several suggestions for improvement, which greatly helped me during the revision of my work.

I have benefitted from discussing my work with Giovanna Menci, who also shared with me the drafts of her *editio princeps* of P.Duk. inv. 665 while her work was in progress, and with the scholars who took part in the *Kyklos* teleconference (Harvard 2012) and the conference *Conflict and Consensus in Early Hexameter Poetry* (Durham 2012).

I would also like to thank David Speranzi and Filippomaria Pontani, who kindly offered comments on drafts of my section on Marcus Musurus, and with their expertise helped me improve it.

Table of Contents

Acknowledgements vii

Abbreviations of editions and works of reference xi

Introduction 1

Part 1: The tradition of the contest between Homer and Hesiod 5

   1. The origins 5
      Hesiod, *Works and Days* 648–62 5
      [Hesiod], fr. 357 MW 7
   2. Ancient scholarship on the *Works and Days*:
      Plutarch and Proclus 10
      The scholium to Hesiod's *Works and Days* 650–62 11
      Plutarch, *Table Talk* 674f–675a and *Dinner of the Seven Sages*
      153f–154a 13
      Proclus, *Life of Homer* 6 20
   3. Second Sophistic: Dio Chrysostom, Philostratus, and Lucian .. 23
      Dio Chrysostom, *Oration on Kingship* 2.7–12 24
      Philostratus, *Heroicus* 43.7–10 27
      Lucian, *True Story* 2.20–22 30
   4. Late antique rhetoric: Themistius and Libanius 34
      Themistius, *Oration* 30.348c–349a 34
      Libanius, *Defence of Socrates* 65–6 37
   5. The Byzantine age: John Tzetzes and Eustathius 40
      John Tzetzes 40
      Eustathius, *Commentary on Homer's Iliad* (I 6, 28–7, 1
      van der Valk) 45

Part 2: Textual tradition 47

   1. Manuscripts 48
      Florence, Biblioteca Medicea Laurenziana, Plut. 56.1 48
      Vienna, Österreichische Nationalbibliothek, Phil. gr. 187 52
   2. Papyri 60
      P.Petr. I 25 (1) (P.Lond.Lit. 191) 60
      P.Mich. inv. 2754 67
      P.Ath.Soc.Pap. inv. M2 75
      P.Freib. 1.1 b (inv. 12) 77
      P.Duk. inv. 665 (*olim* P.Duk. inv. MF75 6) 80

	Table of Contents
Part 3: Text and translation	83
Part 4: Commentary	115
Introductory remarks	115
1. Introduction (1–2); Hesiod's birthplace (2–6)	117
2. Homer's birthplace (7–17)	118
3. Homer's parents (18–27); Homer's name (27–32); Hadrian (32–43)	123
4. Homer's and Hesiod's chronology and genealogy (44–53)	131
5. Homer's oracle (54–62)	136
6. Introduction to the contest (62–74)	139
7. The 'riddles of the superlative' (74–89)	141
8. The reaction to Homer's performance (90–4); the 'insoluble challenge' (94–101)	144
9. The 'ambiguous propositions' (102–37)	147
10. The 'numerical problem' (138–48)	156
11. The 'philosophical questions' (148–75)	158
12. The 'finest passages' (176–204)	164
13. The verdict (205–14); Hesiod's oracle (215–23)	167
14. Hesiod's death (224–53)	170
15. Homer's *Thebaid* and *Epigoni* (254–60); the Midas epigram and the silver cup (260–74)	176
16. *Iliad* and *Odyssey* (275–6); Homer in Athens (276–85)	181
17. Homer in Corinth (286–7); Homer in Argos (287–314)	183
18. Homer in Delos (315–21); Homer's death (321–38)	188
Figures	195
Bibliography	199
General index	215
Index of Greek words	220
Index of passages	221

Abbreviations of editions and works of reference

Classical authors are abbreviated as in LSJ, journals as in the *Année Philologique*. All translations are my own. For the Lives of Homer I have used my own texts and translations (Bassino 2013a). All websites were last accessed on 28 June 2018.

Arnim = Arnim, I. von (ed.) (1905), *Stoicorum veterum fragmenta*, vol. 1. Stuttgart.
Bernabé = Bernabé, A. (ed.) (1987), *Poetae Epici Graeci: testimonia et fragmenta*, vol. 1. Leipzig.
Boissonade = Boissonade, J. F. (ed.) (1851), *Tzetzae Allegoriae Iliadis*. Paris.
CGFP = Austin, C. (ed.) (1973), *Comicorum Graecorum fragmenta in papyris reperta*. Berlin.
Cohoon = Cohoon, J. W. (ed.) (1932), *Dio Chrysostom*, vol. 1. *Dio Chrysostom, I, Discourses 1–11*. London.
Colonna = Colonna, A. (ed.) (1953), 'I Prolegomeni ad Esiodo e la Vita esiodea di G. Tzetzes', *BollClass* 2: 27–39.
Couvreur = Couvreur, P. (ed.) (1901), *Hermeias von Alexandrien. In Platonis Phaedrum scholia*. Paris.
Cribiore = Cribiore, R. (1996), *Writing, Teachers, and Students in Graeco-Roman Egypt*. Atlanta.
Davies = Davies, M. (ed.) (1988), *Epicorum Graecorum fragmenta*. Göttingen.
De Lannoy = De Lannoy, L. (ed.) (1977), *Flavii Philostrati Heroicus*. Leipzig.
DK = Diels, H., and Kranz, W. (eds) (1961, 10th ed.), *Die Fragmente der Vorsokratiker*. Berlin.
Downey = Downey, G., et al. (eds.) (1971), *Themistii Orationes quae supersunt*, vol. 2. Leipzig.
Drachmann = Drachmann, A. B. (ed.) (1927), *Scholia vetera in Pindari carmina*, vol. 3. Leipzig.
FGrHist = Jacoby, F. (ed.) (1923–), *Die Fragmente der Griechischen Historiker*. Berlin.
Fontenrose = Fontenrose, J. E. (1978), *The Delphic Oracle: Its Responses and Operations, with a Catalogue of Responses*. Berkeley.
Fowler = Fowler, R. L. (ed.) (2000), *Early Greek Mythography*, vol. 1. Oxford.
Förster = Förster, R. (ed.) (1909), *Libanius. Opera*, vol. 5. Leipzig.
Funaioli = Funaioli, H. (ed.) (1907), *Grammaticae Romanae fragmenta*, vol. 1. Leipzig.
Gaisford = Gaisford, Th. (ed.) (1823), *Poetae minores Graeci*, vol. 2. Leipzig.
Hubert = Hubert, C. (ed.) (1971 (1938)), *Plutarchi Moralia*, vol. 4. Leipzig.

ID = Dürrbach, F. (ed.) (1929), *Inscriptions de Délos: Comptes des Hiéropes (Nos. 372–498)*. Paris.

IG = (1873–), *Inscriptiones Graecae*. Berlin.

Keaney = Keaney, J. J. (ed.) (1991), *Harpocration: Lexeis of the Ten Orators*. Amsterdam.

Kindstrand = Kindstrand, J. F. (ed.) (1979), *Isaac Porphyrogenitus. Praefatio in Homerum*. Uppsala.

LDAB = *Leuven Database of Ancient Books*. Online resource: http://www.trismegistos.org/ldab/

LfrgE = Snell, B., et al (eds) (1955–2010), *Lexikon des frühgriechischen Epos*. Göttingen.

LIMC = Kahil, L., et al. (eds) (1994), *Lexicon iconographicum mythologiae classicae*, vol. 7.1. Zürich.

LSJ = Liddell, H. G., Scott, R., and Jones, H. (eds) (1940, 9th ed.), *A Greek-English Lexicon*. Oxford.

Macleod = Macleod, M. D. (ed.) (1972), *Luciani Opera*, vol. 1. Oxford.

Matthews = Matthews, V. J. (ed.) (1996), *Antimachus of Colophon, Text and Commentary*. Leiden.

Most = Most, G. (ed.) (2006), *Hesiod. Theogony. Works and Days. Testimonia*. Cambridge (MA).

MP^3 = *Mertens-Pack 3 online database*, online resource: http://cipl93.philo.ulg.ac.be/Cedopal/MP3/dbsearch.aspx

MW = Merkelbach, R., and West, M. L. (eds) (1967), *Fragmenta Hesiodea*. Oxford.

Paton = Paton, W. R., et al. (eds) (1974 (1925)). *Plutarchi Moralia*, vol. 1. Leipzig.

PCG = Kassel, R., and Austin, C. (eds) (1995), *Poetae Comici Graeci*, vol. 8. Berlin.

Pertusi = Pertusi, A. (ed.) (1955), *Scholia vetera in Hesiodi Opera et Dies*. Milan.

Powell = Powell, J. U. (ed.) (1925), *Collectanea Alexandrina: reliquiae minores poetarum Graecorum aetatis Ptolemaicae, 323–146 A.C.: epicorum, elegiacorum, lyricorum, ethicorum*. Oxford.

Rose = Rose, V. (ed.) (1886), *Aristotelis qui ferebantur librorum fragmenta*. Leipzig.

Sandbach = Sandbach, F. H. (ed.) (1969), *Plutarch's Moralia XV. Fragments*. Cambridge (MA).

Scheer = Sheer, E. (ed.) (1908), *Scholia in Lycophronem*, in *Lycophronis Alexandra*, vol. 2. Berlin.

Schneider = Schneider, O. (ed.) (1856), *Nicandrea: Theriaca et Alexipharmaca*. Leipzig.

SEG = Gieben, J. C., et al. (eds) (1923–), *Supplementum Epigraphicum Graecum*. Amsterdam.

SGDI = Collitz, H., et al. (eds) (1884–1915), *Sammlung der griechischen Dialekt-Inschriften*. Göttingen.

SM = Snell, B., and Maehler, H. (eds) (1987–89), *Pindari carmina cum fragmentis*, 2 vols. Leipzig.

Suppl. Hell. = Lloyd-Jones, P. H. (ed.) (1983), *Supplementum Hellenisticum*. Berlin.

Valk, M. van der = Valk, M. van der (ed.) (1971–87), *Eustathii Archiepiscopi Thessalonicensis ad Homeri Iliadem pertinentes*, 4 vols. Leiden.

Voigt = Voigt, E. M. (ed.) (1971), *Sappho et Alcaeus*. Amsterdam.

Wehrli = Wehrli, F. (ed.) (1969, 2nd ed.). *Die Schule des Aristoteles*, vol. 9. Basel.

West = West, M. L. (ed.) (1989–92, 2nd ed.), *Iambi et elegi Graeci*, 2 vols. Oxford.

Winiarczyk = Winiarczyk, M. (ed.) (1991), *Euhemeri Messenii reliquiae*. Stuttgart and Leipzig.

Wyss = Wyss, B. (ed.) (1936), *Antimachi Colofonii reliquiae*. Berlin.

Introduction

This book provides a comprehensive study of the *Certamen Homeri et Hesiodi*. It includes an analysis of the tradition of the contest between Homer and Hesiod, a study of the manuscript witnesses, a critical edition of the text, and the first commentary in English. My approach takes into account the peculiar nature and status of biographical material in antiquity: I aim to show that biographical traditions form a corpus that is open to variation, both in terms of the contents of the biographical episodes and of the textual tradition of the individual works. Through my analysis of the text, I hope to demonstrate that the *Certamen* was the product of a conscious and purposeful adaptation of its sources, and deals with material that was itself fluid and suitable for alteration.

Part 1 offers a discussion of the ancient Greek witnesses of the contest between Homer and Hesiod, from the *Works and Days* to the Byzantine Age, in order to present a picture of the wider tradition within which interpretation of the *Certamen* must be located. My treatment of this tradition is informed by recent studies on the value of biographical material as evidence for the early reception of a poet's work. It has long been acknowledged that ancient biographical accounts of the poets should not be considered reliable historical sources for reconstructing their actual lives. Claims such as those by Wilamowitz, who famously tried to produce a consistent and plausible biography of Homer from conflicting claims transmitted in the ancient sources, were criticised only a few years later by Jacoby.[1] More recently, in the first edition of her book *The Lives of Greek Poets* in 1981, Lefkowitz argued that most of the biographical material derives from statements included in the poets' own verses, and for this reason it can be disregarded as popular fiction.[2] Adopting an equally sceptical approach, Latacz entitled the chapter on the figure of Homer in his 1991 book *Homer: His Art and His Work* 'The Source Situation: Nothing Authentic'.[3] Scholars have subsequently proposed other ways of approaching these fictional accounts. In *Inventing Homer*, Graziosi suggested that early speculations regarding the author of the Homeric poems must ultimately derive from an encounter between the poems and their ancient audiences: seen in this light, biographical material becomes important not as a source for reconstructing a poet's real life, but as evidence for the re-

---

[1] Wilamowitz 1916: 397 suggested that the claims by Smyrna, Chios and Colophon could be cobbled together to fashion a plausible biography for Homer. The poet could have been born in Smyrna, been active as a teacher in Colophon and then settled in Chios. Jacoby 1933 suggested that these are independent local claims.
[2] Lefkowitz 1981: vii–xi.
[3] Latacz 1996: 23–30.

ception of his works.[4] Along similar lines, Hanink proposed that Euripides' biographies should be read in the context of the cultural and political forces within which the active imagination of biographers operated.[5] Beecroft, likewise, claimed that biographical anecdotes offer an 'implied poetics'.[6] In the second edition of her book, Lefkowitz herself acknowledged these new perspectives on biographical material, claiming that 'biographers could not tell their readers who Homer really was, but they could offer a portrait of the kind of person who might have written the *Odyssey*', and therefore biographies 'can provide clues to what ancient writers and audiences supposed the creative process to be, and can give us an impression of the kinds of poetry and subject matter that ancient people admired at different times and places'.[7]

My own work is located within this new wave of interest in biographical material: it treats the story of the contest between Homer and Hesiod as an ancient mode of literary reception. Part 1 demonstrates the longevity and adaptability of the story. I collect all the ancient Greek passages concerning the episode, grouping them into sections based on thematic connections and following an approximately chronological order, provide them with a new English translation, and discuss them. From my analysis it emerges that all versions of the story of the contest between Homer and Hesiod are equally authoritative in principle, for they testify to different acts of reception of the poets in different contexts, and were re-shaped, indeed re-created, accordingly. The only details of the contest that remained fixed were those given by Hesiod himself in his *Works and Days*. Flexibility at the level of contents is reflected in the textual fluidity of some of the sources discussed. It results, moreover, from the variety of contexts in which the story of the contest between Homer and Hesiod appeared: exegetical texts such as commentaries on the *Works and Days*, biographical texts such as the Lives of Homer and Hesiod and, importantly, rhetorical works. The fact that the competition between Homer and Hesiod was treated as a useful *exemplum* helps to explain why the text of the *Certamen* was copied alongside rhetorical works, as I argue in Part 2.

Part 2 provides a study of the textual transmission of the *Certamen*. Biographical texts were subject to variation and modification not only in terms of their contents, but also in terms of their textual transmission. West states that biographies are one of the categories of texts for which it is impossible to draw a standard *stemma codicum*; they were subject to embellishments, alterations and revisions, with the result that the high number of respect-

---

4 Graziosi 2002: 2–3.
5 Hanink 2008. See esp. p. 132.
6 Beecroft 2010. See esp. pp. 2 and 19.
7 Lefkowitz 2012: 2.

able-looking variants does not allow for the construction of an archetype.⁸ The number of variants found in the manuscripts of the Lives may reflect the fact that these stories were regarded as essentially fictional and, therefore, fluid and open to modification. This explains why it is impossible to find the correct or original version of a story about Homer or Hesiod; or even, in some cases, the correct or original reading of a version of such a story. Our aim should, rather, be to understand the value of variants as evidence for the flexibility of literary reception. Part 2, then, offers the first comprehensive study of the manuscript witnesses of the *Certamen* conducted on the basis of the considerations set out above. It opens with a discussion of the context of the transmission of the *Certamen* in a single manuscript (Florence, Biblioteca Medicea Laurenziana, Plut. 56.1), and then goes on to present a new important manuscript witness of our text (Vienna, Österreichische Nationalbibliothek, Phil. gr. 187). Part 2 continues with an analysis of five papyrus fragments, ranging in date from the third century BC to the seventh century AD, that are closely related to the manuscript text.

Part 3 provides a new edition and translation of the *Certamen*. The text I propose takes into account the 'open' tradition for which I have argued in Parts 1 and 2, and it does so by defending and accounting for the manuscript readings when possible. This is a deliberate response to the tendency, on the part of most editors, to propose emendations on the basis of other textual witnesses, and so create by force a unified tradition that never existed. The texts of the papyri, in the editions I propose in Part 2, are not emended on the basis of the manuscript unless strictly necessary; similarly, here I do not introduce or accept emendations (whether they are based on the papyrus texts or on editorial conjecture) unless these offer plausible solutions to what seem mere metrical or grammatical errors on behalf of the scribe, rather than the product of conscious adaptation.⁹ The same principle is adopted with respect to the other sources transmitting passages included in the *Certamen*, such as quotations from epic poems or other works,¹⁰ and the genealogy

---

8 West 1973: 16–17. It follows that a model such as that proposed by Allen 1924: 31–3 for the Lives of Homer, still considered valid by Esposito Vulgo Gigante 1996: 63, is in fact untenable. Allen suggests that all the extant Lives derive from a common lost source, of which the Anon. *Vit. Hom.* 1 preserves the fullest memory; the other texts are divided in two branches deriving from the Anon. *Vit. Hom.* 1. The situation seems to be similar for other *corpora* of ancient biographies, such as the *Vidas* of the Provençal troubadours: Boutière/Schutz in their edition of the *Vidas* (1950 and 1964) acknowledge that many of those texts are transmitted in different versions and claim that it is not possible to draw a *stemma* for them. Avalle 1960 in his edition of the *Vida* of Peire Vidal acknowledges the existence of different branches of manuscripts but, again, does not create a *stemma*.
9 See, e.g., at 82, with commentary *ad loc.*
10 See, e.g., at 176–204, with commentary *ad loc.*

of the two poets in the different forms transmitted by other authors.[11] The apparatus criticus is organised into two sections. The first section lists the sources transmitting verses or passages found in the *Certamen*, and indicates variations from the manuscript text in order to illustrate the diversity of the tradition. The second section collects modern editorial interventions on the text of the *Certamen*. I have taken into account all major editions of the text from Nietzsche onwards.[12] I have also considered noteworthy editorial interventions proposed in some of the more influential editions published before Nietzsche, and in various other studies that are relevant to the textual discussion of specific passages. The edition is followed by a new English translation of the text, essential not least because the most recent English translation is based on a Greek text that diverges from my own at several points.[13]

Part 4 offers the first systematic commentary in English on the *Certamen Homeri et Hesiodi*. The format of a commentary is ideally suited to the study of this work, given the number of issues that require individual attention, and the stratified composition of the text. Throughout this commentary, I focus on how the text constructs the biography and the characterisation of the two poets, and in particular the episode of their contest, as modes of reception of Homeric and Hesiodic poetry. I suggest that Homer is presented as the Panhellenic poet *par excellence*, in contrast with Hesiod's more local appeal; moreover, Homer is presented as divine, whereas Hesiod is associated with a more human form of wisdom. Not even defeat in the contest seems to weaken Homer's reputation, since the events that follow the contest compensate him for his loss. The commentary also addresses the role of Alcidamas as a source for the *Certamen* and identifies influences from other sources, especially those derived from fifth-century sophistic circles. Beginning with 'Introductory remarks', which includes a number of cross-references to the sections of the commentary in which specific aspects are discussed at length, the commentary is arranged over eighteen paragraphs, one for each paragraph of the text. Each paragraph includes: a) general entries, recognisible through the underlined titles, which discuss the main themes of a passage in relation to the text as a whole; b) more detailed entries for smaller sections of text; c) textual matters.

---

11 See, e.g., at 44–53, with commentary *ad loc.*
12 Nietzsche 1871. Nietzsche initiated modern scholarship on the *Certamen* with his studies published in 1870 and 1873, and was the first after Stephanus to base his edition of the text on an inspection of the manuscript. See Part 2.
13 West 2003a: 318–53.

Part 1: The tradition of the contest between Homer and Hesiod

1. The origins

Hesiod, *Works and Days* 648–62

The story of the poetic contest between Homer and Hesiod originated from *Works and Days* 648–62, the famous passage where Hesiod proclaims his victory in a poetic contest:

δείξω δή τοι μέτρα πολυφλοίσβοιο θαλάσσης,
οὔτέ τι ναυτιλίης σεσοφισμένος οὔτέ τι νηῶν·
650 οὐ γάρ πώ ποτε νηί γ' ἐπέπλων εὐρέα πόντον,
εἰ μὴ ἐς Εὔβοιαν ἐξ Αὐλίδος, ᾗ ποτ' Ἀχαιοὶ
μείναντες χειμῶνα πολὺν σὺν λαὸν ἄγειραν
Ἑλλάδος ἐξ ἱερῆς Τροίην ἐς καλλιγύναικα.
ἔνθα δ' ἐγὼν ἐπ' ἄεθλα δαΐφρονος Ἀμφιδάμαντος
655 Χαλκίδα τ' εἲς ἐπέρησα· τὰ δὲ προπεφραδμένα πολλὰ
ἆθλ' ἔθεσαν παῖδες μεγαλήτορος· ἔνθά μέ φημι
ὕμνῳ νικήσαντα φέρειν τρίποδ' ὠτώεντα.
τὸν μὲν ἐγὼ Μούσῃς Ἑλικωνιάδεσσ' ἀνέθηκα,
ἔνθά με τὸ πρῶτον λιγυρῆς ἐπέβησαν ἀοιδῆς.
660 τόσσόν τοι νηῶν γε πεπείρημαι πολυγόμφων·
ἀλλὰ καὶ ὣς ἐρέω Ζηνὸς νόον αἰγιόχοιο·
Μοῦσαι γάρ μ' ἐδίδαξαν ἀθέσφατον ὕμνον ἀείδειν. (ed. Most)

Now, I shall show you the measures of loud-roaring sea, although I am no expert on seamanship, nor on ships. For I have never sailed the broad sea in a ship, except to Euboea from Aulis, where once the Achaeans stayed during the winter, and assembled a great army to go from holy Greece to Troy of the lovely women. There, I crossed over to Chalcis for the funeral games of warlike Amphidamas; the sons of that great-hearted man had announced and set up many prizes. There, I say, having won with a hymn, I carried away a tripod with handles. I dedicated it to the Heliconian Muses, where for the first time they initiated me to sweet song. Such is my experience of well-riveted ships – but even so, I shall tell the mind of aegis-bearing Zeus, for the Muses have taught me to sing an unutterable hymn.

In this passage, Hesiod is not simply giving instructions on sailing, but also making programmatic statements. First of all, he aims to prove that he is a divinely inspired poet – an important claim present also in the *Theogony*.[14] He does not have much experience of sailing, as he himself admits,[15] but thanks to the Muses he is able to cover the topic with his song. Importantly, this passage also shows how Hesiod, a didactic poet, engages with the 'other' major Greek hexameter tradition represented by the heroic epic. Hesiod's sea-voyage starts from Aulis, just like the Homeric heroes' longer journey to Troy; furthermore, Hesiod employs Homeric diction in this passage by using the epic epithets καλλιγύναιξ ('of the lovely women') and ἱερή ('holy'), but reverses them in comparison with the Homeric poems.[16] As a result of these echoes of the heroic tradition, the name of Homer was naturally added as Hesiod's rival in the contest. Indeed, his name was even transmitted as a variant reading in some manuscripts of *Works and Days*, as a scholium to *Op.* 657 shows:

ὕμνῳ νικήσαντι· ἄλλοι γράφουσιν· ὕμνῳ νικήσαντ' ἐν Χαλκίδι θεῖον Ὅμηρον. (ed. Pertusi)

'having won with a hymn': others write 'when he defeated divine Homer in song at Chalcis'.

The verse as given in the scholium also forms part of the epigram allegedly inscribed on the tripod won by Hesiod.[17] We do not know whether the text of the epigram penetrated the text of *Works and Days*, or a variant reading present in *Works and Days* was later used as part of the epigram; nor do we know how widely attested this variant was.[18] But, importantly, it shows the extent and the power of the relationship between the Hesiodic text and the biographical story that originated from it.[19]

---

14 See the initiation scene at *Th.* 22–34, where the Muses transform Hesiod into a poet from a shepherd.
15 Between Aulis and Chalcis there are only 'some 65 metres of water' (West 1978: 320).
16 Canevaro 2015 (see esp. pp. 91, 130–2, and 199–200) offers the most recent and detailed discussion of these verses to date. See also Nagy 1982: 66 and 1990: 77–8; Rosen 1990 and 1997: 477–9; Graziosi 2002: 170, as well as Edwards 1971: 80 and West 1978: 320–1.
17 On the tripod and the epigram see Part 4, 210–14n.
18 West 1978: 321 suggests that the variant in *Works and Days* is an interpolation from the epigram; Nagy 1990: 78 and 2009: 304 claims that it may have reflected a genuine traditional alternative that was gradually ousted in the course of the poem's crystallisation into a fixed text. Cf. for discussion also Skiadas 1965: 10–13 and Debiasi 2012: 474.
19 This interaction is also shown by the fact that the authors who wanted to deny that the contest took place also denied the Hesiodic authorship of the related passage from

Hesiod's victory was proclaimed by the poet himself in his work, and therefore became a non-negotiable aspect of the story. But a fundamental role in sealing the verdict was played also by the material reception of the Hesiodic passage. A tripod bearing the epigram of Hesiod's victory was displayed in antiquity on Mt Helicon, in the place where Hesiod himself claims to have dedicated it (*Op.* 657–8), and was visible in Pausanias' time.[20] The tripod of Hesiod's victory against Homer was the visible and tangible evidence of Hesiod's success. As Manieri points out, this and other archaeological witnesses also seen by Pausanias guaranteed the immortal presence of Hesiod in the Valley of the Muses.[21] Its presence played an important part in the celebration of Hesiod's poetry on Helicon – a celebration that was made mainly in relation to Homer, as is confirmed by the absence of the statue of Homer from the statuary recorded in the sanctuary of the Muses on Helicon.[22] Because of the importance of the tripod, most writers were aware that treatment of the story involved almost by necessity a discussion of it.[23]

[Hesiod], fr. 357 MW

A fixed feature of the tradition of the contest between Homer and Hesiod is its location at Chalcis, in Euboea. It is Hesiod who authoritatively states that the contest happened there, a place full of metapoetic significance (see Part

---

Works and Days and proposed the athetesis of the passage. See Part 1, 'Plutarch'.

20 Paus. 9.31.3 = Hes. T40 Most: 'ἐν δὲ τῷ Ἑλικῶνι καὶ ἄλλοι τρίποδες κεῖνται καὶ ἀρχαιότατος, ὃν ἐν Χαλκίδι λαβεῖν τῇ ἐπ' Εὐρίπῳ λέγουσιν Ἡσίοδον νικήσαντα ᾠδῇ', 'On Mt Helicon there are many tripods, and the oldest is the one which Hesiod, they say, gained upon winning in song on the Euripus'.

21 Manieri 2009: 316 ('… le testimonianze archeologiche viste da Pausania, che garantivano l'immortale presenza di Esiodo nella Valle delle Muse…'). On the connection between the presence of Hesiod on Mt Helicon and the cult of the Muses, including the festival of the Mouseia, see: Vox 1980: 321; Lamberton 1988; Calame 1996: 51–2; Manieri 2009: 315–18 and 353, with further bibliography.

22 Hunter 2006: 19 notes that the tripod and the absence of a statue of Homer made the grove on Helicon 'not just explicitly Hesiod's mountain, but also, importantly, *not* Homer's'.

23 According to Varro (fr. 68 Funaioli, reported by Aulus Gellius in *Noctes Atticae* 3.11 = Hes. T3 Most), the tripod proved that the two poets were contemporaries and competed against each other: 'M. autem Varro in primo de imaginibus, uter prior sit natus, parum constare dicit, sed non esse dubium, quin aliquo tempore eodem vixerint, idque ex epigrammate ostendi, quod in tripode scriptum est, qui in monte Helicone ab Hesiodo positus traditur', 'But M. Varro says in the first book of his *Images* that it is hardly possible to establish which of the two was born first, but there is no doubt that they were contemporaries for some time, and that this is shown by the epigram which is inscribed on the tripod which has reportedly been set up by Hesiod on Mt Helicon'. For the use of the tripod in Greek sources see Part 1, esp. 'The scholium' and 'Dio Chrysostom'.

1, 'Hesiod'). However, the pseudo-Hesiodic fragment 357 MW reports that Homer and Hesiod sang together on another occasion as well: the two poets were once on Delos, engaged in the performance of a hymn to Apollo.[24] This is the text of our fragment:

ἐν Δήλῳ τότε πρῶτον ἐγὼ καὶ Ὅμηρος ἀοιδοί
μέλπομεν, ἐν νεαροῖς ὕμνοις ῥάψαντες ἀοιδήν,
Φοῖβον Ἀπόλλωνα χρυσάορον ὃν τέκε Λητώ.

On Delos, once, for the first time, I and Homer, the bards, stitching a song in new hymns, sang Phoebus Apollo with golden sword, whom Leto bore.

Some modern scholars have posited a connection between the meeting of the two poets on Delos and the meeting at Chalcis. West suggests that this fragment comes from a poem that told the story of the 'first' (πρῶτον) encounter between the two poets in which Homer won, followed by the Chalcidean episode which would be Hesiod's revenge. According to West, who argues that Alcidamas invented the story of the contest of Homer and Hesiod, such a work could not have existed before Alcidamas, or he would have set his story on Delos rather than at Chalcis, since Homer is not mentioned in *Works and Days* 648–62, whereas he is in this fragment.[25] However, the mere existence of the fragment and the presence of Homer's name do not prove its ability to become more influential than the *Works and Days* in determining the location of the contest between Homer and Hesiod for Alcidamas. Kivilo (who, unlike West, places the origins of the Delian fragment before Alcidamas) and Nagy believe that Delos was an alternative location for the episode of the contest between Homer and Hesiod that is usually situated at Chalcis.[26] But locating the contest on the island of Delos would contradict Hesiod's statement that he never sailed the sea except from Aulis to Chalcis (*Op.* 650–1). The tone of Hesiod's words in the fragment, the apparent collaboration between the two bards in order to create a single new song, the

---

24 This pseudo-Hesiodic fragment derives from a scholium to Pindar's *Nemean* 2.1 (3.31.7 Drachmann). The scholiast reports Philochorus' opinion on the etymology of the word 'rhapsode', which he connects to ῥάπτειν τὴν ᾠδήν: 'to stitch a song' (cf. 328 *FGrHist* 212). The fragment is quoted in support. This scholium contains information vital to our knowledge of ancient performative practices and touches on matters that are relevant to the *Certamen* too (e.g. the Homeridae, Cynaethus, and the *Hymn to Apollo*).
25 West 1967: 440.
26 Kivilo 2000: 3 and 2010a: 21; Nagy 2010: 70. Based on a doubtful passage of the *Certamen* (55), they also propose Aulis as a third possible location – although Kivilo 2010a: 19 seems to be open to the possibility, accepted in Part 4, 55n., that Aulis is mentioned as the place from which the two poets sailed to Chalcis.

mention of Apollo – aspects that are completely absent from the verses about Chalcis – are further reasons to look for the origins and the meaning of fr. 357 MW in other circumstances, independent from the Chalcidean episode.

Other, more convincing, circumstances have been proposed regarding the origins of this episode. Janko connects the fragment to a festival organised by Polycrates, tyrant of Samos, in 523–2 BC: this festival was held on Delos and was a joint celebration of Apollo of Delos and Apollo of Delphi, and it may have been a suitable occasion for the first joint performance of the two parts of the *Hymn to Apollo*, the Delian and the Pythian.[27] Fr. 357 MW worked therefore as an attempt to give ancient and authoritative roots to this festival, by attributing the proto-performance of the joint parts of the *Hymn* to Homer and Hesiod respectively.[28] If this suggestion is correct, it also accounts for the emphasis on the cooperation between the two bards that seems to emerge from the verses, and that makes the episode look quite different from the story told in the *Certamen*.[29]

Another famous story about Homer (this time Homer alone) performing this *Hymn* is told by Thucydides (3.104). The historian gives an account of the purification of Delos carried out by the Athenians in 426 BC, the first purification of the island after Peisistratus' time. He remarks that the action taken by his fellow citizens in 426 BC included the revival of the festival of the *Delia*, which, he recalls, in ancient times saw Homer himself reciting the *Hymn to Apollo*. Each of these two versions of the story emphasises different aspects of the performance, and this can be explained, at least in part, as a response to the different political contexts in which the story was told. Furthermore, some elements of the Thucydidean version seem to suggest that the two traditions were, to some extent, engaging and competing with each other. Since the story told in [Hes.] fr. 357 MW is likely to have its origins in a festival in honour of both Delian and Pythian Apollo, which hosted the joint performance of the Delian and Pythian parts of the *Hymn*, the presence of Hesiod in the story may have been determined by the Delphic element. The Thucydidean version, by contrast, focuses only on the Delian elements: the Athenians revived the festival called *Delia*, all the quoted verses come from the Delian part of the *Hymn* and are strictly connected to the figure of

---

27 Janko 1982: 113–14. On Polycrates' festival and the joint performance of the hymn see also Burkert 1979: 58–62.
28 For the Delian part as 'Homeric' and the Pythian as 'Hesiodic' see, e.g., Janko 1982: 113.
29 Graziosi 2002: 182 notes that when the two poets are presented together as religious experts the emphasis is on their cooperation rather than on their rivalry; Collins 2004: 181 stresses that the two are said to produce one single song (ἀοιδήν). The emphasis on their cooperation does not exclude that the context in which the performance was set was a competitive one (see Koning 2010: 246 n. 27 who criticises Heldmann 1982: 16–17).

Homer (esp. 165–72), who is the only poet to be mentioned. All this underlines the Athenian connection with Delos, with all the political and symbolic meaning that the island had for the Athenian empire; furthermore, Athens' relationships with Delphi were difficult at the time of the Peloponnesian War because of the pro-Spartan sympathies of the oracle.[30] Therefore, it is not surprising that Thucydides does not refer to the Delphic, that is Hesiodic, part of the *Hymn*. Interestingly, then, an element in the Thucydidean account seems to show that there was a certain degree of engagement among these different traditions: on the occasion of the festival to which fr. 357 MW is connected, Polycrates spectacularly dedicated the island of Rheneia to Apollo by binding it with a chain to Delos. Thucydides, before mentioning the Athenians' own revival of the Delian festival in 426 BC, relates that the Athenians during the purification of Delos brought the corpses to Rheneia, and then remarks that the two islands were so close to each other that Polycrates could bind Rheneia to Delos with a chain (3.104.2). The effect of this claim is to minimise the impact of an event that must have been important to Polycratean propaganda.

The version given in the *Certamen* (315–21) is similar to Thucydides'. Although not all details are the same, in both accounts Homer emerges as a Panionian poet. The *Certamen* seems to take inspiration from the tradition attested by Thucydides, according to which the process of Panhellenisation of Homer is connected to the image of the blind bard from Chios presented in the *Hymn to Apollo*: this was the image of the poet accepted and promoted by the Athenians, and thus became predominant.[31]

In conclusion, fr. 357 MW has no relation with the Chalcidean contest: the joint performance of Homer and Hesiod on Delos may have been inspired, or supported, by the Chalcidean tradition, but it does not represent an alternative version of it. Rather, it is connected to the story of the first performance of the *Hymn to Apollo* which, like the story of the contest at Chalcis, was adapted to suit different circumstances.

2. Ancient scholarship on the *Works and Days*: Plutarch and Proclus

Following on the above discussion of the Hesiodic passage that inspired the tradition of the contest between Homer and Hesiod, the present section analyses the ways in which ancient scholars approached it. It begins by looking at the ancient scholium to *Works and Days* 650–62. Authored by Proclus Di-

---

30 See Hornblower 1991: 517–31 for a detailed discussion of the political background behind the Thucydidean passage.
31 See also Part 4, 315–21n.

adochus (fifth century AD), it transmits the opinions that Plutarch (first-second century AD) expressed on the story of the contest in his commentary on the *Works and Days*. According to Proclus, Plutarch held extreme views on the contest tradition: he thought that it contained 'nothing of value', and went as far as to athetise the related Hesiodic passage.

As well as discussing the possible reasons for the Plutarchan athetesis, this section illustrates how Plutarch's opinion may have influenced Proclus' (and, later, that of another commentator, John Tzetzes – see Part 1, 'The Byzantine Age') and how their activity as commentators on the *Works and Days* influenced all the other mentions of the contest found in their works. Importantly, this series of connections between commentators and texts reveals that a number of passages by Plutarch and Proclus that at first sight seem (and have been generally regarded as) unrelated due to their differences in terms of chronology, purpose and literary genre, in fact derive from the same strand of ancient exegesis on the Hesiodic text.

Understanding the connections among these passages sheds further light not only on the ways in which the tradition of the contest was transmitted and shaped, but also on issues of interpretation and attribution concerning individual passages, such as the presence of Lesches in Plutarch's *Dinner of the Seven Sages* and the authorship of the *Chrestomathy*.

The scholium to Hesiod's *Works and Days* 650–62

Hesiod's *Works and Days* received a great deal of scholarly attention in antiquity. Traces survive in the corpus of the *scholia vetera*, which preserve most of what we know about two important exegetical works on our poem: the commentaries by Plutarch and Proclus.[32] In the scholium to the Hesiodic passage on the contest, Proclus informs us of Plutarch's opinion on the matter:

οὐ γὰρ πώποτε νηί γ' ἐπέπλων· ταῦτα πάντα περὶ τῆς Χαλκίδος <καὶ> τοῦ Ἀμφιδάμαντος καὶ τοῦ ἄθλου καὶ τοῦ τρίποδος ἐμβεβλῆσθαί φησιν

---

32 Useful introductions to ancient scholarship on Hesiod are Dickey 2007: 40–2 and Montanari 2009. Plutarch's commentary survives only in fragmentary form, mostly in the *scholia vetera*. Aulus Gellius (20.8.7 = Hes. T147 Most) informs us that it was in (at least) four books. Proclus' commentary, too, survives for the most part in the scholia, and preserves information from Plutarch and other commentaries. The *scholia vetera* are edited in Pertusi 1955. Studies of the two commentaries include: Sandbach 1969 (edition and translation of Plutarch's fragments); Faraggiana di Sarzana 1978 and 1987; Hunter 2014: 167–226 (on the relationships between Plutarch and Proclus); Marzillo 2010 (edition, German translation, and commentary on Proclus' fragments).

ὁ Πλούταρχος <ὡς> οὐδὲν ἔχοντα χρηστόν. [ἀθετοῦνται δέκα στίχοι διὰ τὸ τῆς ἱστορίας νεώτερον.] τὸν μὲν οὖν Ἀμφιδάμαντα ναυμαχοῦντα πρὸς Ἐρετριέας ὑπὲρ τοῦ Ληλάντου ἀποθανεῖν, ἆθλα δὲ ἐπ' αὐτῷ καὶ ἀγῶνας θεῖναι τελευτήσαντι τοὺς παῖδας, νικῆσαι δὲ ἀγωνιζόμενον τὸν Ἡσίοδον καὶ ἆθλον μουσικὸν τρίποδα λαβεῖν καὶ ἀναθεῖναι τοῦτον ἐν τῷ Ἑλικῶνι—ὅπου καὶ κάτοχος ἐγεγόνει ταῖς Μούσαις—καὶ ἐπίγραμμα ἐπὶ τούτῳ θρυλοῦσι. πάντα οὖν ταῦτα ληρώδη λέγων ἐκεῖνος, ἀπ' αὐτῶν ἄρχεται τῶν εἰς τὸν καιρὸν τοῦ πλοῦ συντεινόντων· ἤματα πεντήκοντα. (ed. Pertusi)

'For I have never sailed in a ship': Plutarch says that all this about Chalcis, Amphidamas, the funeral games and the tripod has been interpolated, since it contains nothing of value. [Ten lines are athetised because the story is more recent.] So, they babble that Amphidamas died in a naval battle against the Eretrians over the Lelantine plain, and his sons set up funeral games and contests for the deceased, and Hesiod in the competition won the musical game, carried away a tripod and dedicated it on Helicon – where he was also inspired by the Muses – and also the epigram on it. So, saying that all this is nonsense, he starts from the verses that concern the right time for sailing: 'for fifty days'.

According to Plutarch, the passage about Chalcis, Amphidamas, the funeral games and the tripod is an interpolation, on the grounds that 'it contains nothing of value' (<ὡς> οὐδὲν ἔχοντα χρηστόν): in one word, all that is 'nonsense' (ληρώδη). Plutarch rejects the story of the contest *and* the Hesiodic passage from which it derives. From a philological point of view, it is not easy to understand precisely which verses the Plutarchan athetesis concerns. The scholium refers to 650–62, that is, the whole section of the Hesiodic text that tells of how Hesiod never sailed the sea (650) except for his trip to Chalcis to participate in a poetic contest, up to the programmatic statement in which he explains that, thanks to the Muses, he is able to talk about navigation despite his lack of direct experience (660–2); accordingly, the scholium informs that for Plutarch the 'authentic' text started at 663: ἤματα πεντήκοντα. But a sentence attested in one manuscript reports that the athetesis concerned only ten verses (ἀθετοῦνται δέκα στίχοι διὰ τὸ τῆς ἱστορίας νεώτερον, 'ten lines are athetised because the story is more recent'). Pertusi brackets that sentence and, with a similarly sceptical attitude, West remarks that it 'sits rudely in the middle of Proclus'.[33] Although it does not help to identify the precise extent of the Plutarchan athetesis, the sentence is nonetheless interesting. First, if West is right in saying that it may be a frag-

---

33 Pertusi 1955 *ad loc*; West 1978: 319.

ment of the *scholia vetera*, and therefore may go back to Hellenistic times,[34] this would show that criticism on the tradition of the contest started earlier than its first attestation in Plutarch, and indicate where Plutarch may have found the authority for his athetesis. Second, it helps to explain the reasons behind Plutarch's athetesis, otherwise left to the phrases <ὡς> οὐδὲν ἔχοντα χρηστόν and ταῦτα ληρώδη λέγων ἐκεῖνος. The verses, the sentence says, should be rejected because the story is 'more recent': that is, while usually an autobiographical statement inspires accounts of an episode of the poet's life, in this case a piece of poetry is seen as a later interpolation that made its way into a poet's corpus because of a biographical episode already in circulation. It is indeed in this direction that recent interpretations of Plutarch's athetesis have tended: Lamberton suggests that Plutarch considered these verses as a later interpolation because he knew or thought that the tripod that was on display on the valley of the Muses, and that Pausanias saw (see Part 1, 'Hesiod'), was a forgery, which was created to give ancient and respectable roots to the *Mouseia*, the festival of Thespiae, and that the passage was in turn a later forgery to justify the existence of that tripod.[35]

As for Proclus, his position on the matter is not explicity stated in the scholium;[36] but, as we shall see below, there are reasons to think that he agreed with Plutarch that the Hesiodic verses were the object of misguided interpretations.

Plutarch, *Table Talk* 674f–675a and *Dinner of the Seven Sages* 153f–154a

Plutarch mentions the story of the contest in two other passages, from *Table Talk* (674f–675a) and *Dinner of the Seven Sages* (153f–154a) respectively. Both passages reflect Plutarch's opinion on the contest expressed in the scholium, and seem therefore to have been directly influenced by his exegetical activity on the Hesiodic text. In *Table Talk*, Plutarch refuses to use the contest between Homer and Hesiod as an example in support of the idea that poetry competitions are ancient – all that is, he says, 'babbles of the grammarians':

> ἐνίοις μὲν οὖν ἐπίδοξος ἤμην ἕωλα παραθήσειν πράγματα, τὰς Οἰολύκου τοῦ Θετταλοῦ ταφὰς καὶ τὰς Ἀμφιδάμαντος τοῦ Χαλκιδέως ἐν αἷς Ὅμηρον καὶ Ἡσίοδον ἱστοροῦσιν ἔπεσι διαγωνίσασθαι. καταβαλὼν δὲ ταῦτα τῷ διατεθρυλῆσθαι πάνθ' ὑπὸ τῶν γραμματικῶν [...] (ed. Hubert)

---

34 West 1978: 319.
35 Lamberton 1988.
36 See Marzillo 2010: 356.

According to some people, I was expected to mention, as well-worn events, the funerals of Oeolycus of Thessaly, and of Amphidamas of Chalcis, at which, it is narrated, Homer and Hesiod competed in verses. But rejecting all those as babbles of the grammarians [...]

The passage from the *Dinner*, then, sheds further light on Plutarch's attitude towards this story: since he believes it is fictional, he feels free to modify it and creatively retell its key features in different contexts. As we shall see, Plutarch's account is unique in many respects, but its most peculiar feature is the textually disputed mention of Lesches; the following analysis justifies the presence of Lesches as a competitor, rather than – as often suggested – the narrator or creator of the story.[37] In the *Dinner of the Seven Sages*, Plutarch tells the story of a dinner hosted by Periander and attended by the Sages and others. At the point of the text where mention of the contest occurs, the king of the Egyptians, Amasis, enlists the help of Bias, one of the Sages, to solve a riddle proposed by the king of the Ethiopians: how to drink up the ocean. Bias offers a suitable solution for the challenge (blocking the rivers flowing into the ocean), and Chilon suggests that Amasis should learn from Bias how to improve his government instead of how to play such silly games. After the Sages have engaged in political discussions and exchanged some riddles in turn, Cleodorus says that this game, too, is a waste of time. At this point, Periander refers to the story of the famous poetic contest in which Hesiod gained victory and a tripod. Below is the text in the Teubner edition:[38]

> ἀκούομεν γὰρ ὅτι καὶ πρὸς τὰς Ἀμφιδάμαντος ταφὰς εἰς Χαλκίδα τῶν τότε σοφῶν οἱ δοκιμώτατοι [ποιηταὶ] συνῆλθον· ἦν δ' ὁ Ἀμφιδάμας ἀνὴρ πολεμικός, καὶ πολλὰ πράγματα παρασχὼν Ἐρετριεῦσιν ἐν ταῖς περὶ Ληλάντου μάχαις ἔπεσεν. ἐπεὶ δὲ τὰ παρεσκευασμένα τοῖς ποιηταῖς ἔπη χαλεπὴν καὶ δύσκολον ἐποίει τὴν κρίσιν διὰ τὸ ἐφάμιλλον, ἥ τε δόξα τῶν ἀγωνιστῶν [Ὁμήρου καὶ Ἡσιόδου] πολλὴν ἀπορίαν μετ' αἰδοῦς τοῖς κρίνουσι παρεῖχεν, ἐτράποντο πρὸς τοιαύτας ἐρωτήσεις, καὶ προύβαλε μέν, ὥς φασι, Λέσχης·
> Μοῦσά μοι ἔννεπε κεῖνα, τὰ μήτ' ἐγένοντο πάροιθε μήτ' ἔσται μετόπισθεν,
> ἀπεκρίνατο δ' Ἡσίοδος ἐκ τοῦ παρατυχόντος·
> ἀλλ' ὅταν ἀμφὶ Διὸς τύμβῳ καναχήποδες ἵπποι

---

37 Part of what follows is published in Bassino 2013b.
38 Paton/Wegehaupt/Pohlenz 1974 (1925). This text is essentially the same as that in Wilamowitz 1929 (1916): 55, in the Belles Lettres edition of Plutarch by Defradas/Hani/Klaerr 1985: 213 and in Most 2006: 186 (Most gives the text προέβαλ' ὁ μέν, ὥς φασι, Λέσχης and translates it as follows: 'Lesches, as they say, proposed the following').

ἅρματα συντρίψωσιν ἐπειγόμενοι περὶ νίκης.
καὶ διὰ τοῦτο λέγεται μάλιστα θαυμασθεὶς τοῦ τρίποδος τυχεῖν.

For we hear that the most famous [poets] among the wise men of the time went together to Chalcis for the funeral of Amphidamas. Amphidamas was a warrior, and died during the wars over Lelantus after causing many troubles to the Eretrians. Since the verses that had been prepared by the poets, being of the same quality, made the judgement hard and troublesome, and the fame of the contestants [Homer and Hesiod] caused much difficulty, along with embarrassment, to the judges, they turned to questions of the following kind, and Lesches, as they say, proposed this:
> Muse, tell me those things which did not happen in the past, nor will happen in the future.

And Hesiod answered offhand:
> When around the tomb of Zeus loud-hoofed horses will shatter chariots, eager for victory.

And for this reason, it is said that he was deeply admired and gained the tripod.

Here Lesches is presented as one of the contestants: he proposes a riddle that Hesiod solves, thus winning the contest. But the presence of Lesches, indeed that of any poet other than Homer and Hesiod, is not attested elsewhere in the tradition of the contest, and scholars have therefore proceeded to expel Lesches from the event. Following one of the variants attested in the manuscript tradition, Allen published a text in which Lesches is not a competitor, but the narrator of the story: καὶ προύβαλ' ὁ μέν, ὥς φησι Λέσχης ('and he [*scil.* Homer], as Lesches asserts, proposed the following').[39] According to Allen, Lesches might have written about the contest story either in the *Little Iliad*, or in a poem that Lesches wrote about Homer's life. Allen's text was

---

39 Allen 1912: 136, 218 and 1924: 25–6. The text is accepted in the Loeb edition of Plutarch by Babbitt 1928: 390 (καὶ προέβαλ' ὁ μέν, ὥς φησι Λέσχης). For the sake of clarity, I reproduce here the relevant parts of the apparatus as it appears in the Teubner edition:
15 secl. Larsen   **19** secl. Wil.   **21** προύβαλε (–βαλλε **P**) **PQB** προυβάλομεν ν προυβάλλομεν O   φασι **QhJ nwB** φησί O.
Some of the scholars who have dealt with the manuscript tradition of this passage have misunderstood it because of the presence of an ambiguous *siglum* in the apparatus. Kirk 1950: 150 n. 1 claims that O is alone in transmitting the reading φησί, and he is followed by West 1967: 439 and Kivilo 2000: 4 and 2010a: 23. In fact, the *siglum* present in this section of the apparatus, **O** (Greek letter omicron), stands for *codices omnes praeter citatos*, while it is O (Latin alphabet) that represents a manuscript, the Ambr. 528 s. (cf. *conspectus siglorum* at p. XLVI in the Teubner edition), which is not mentioned here. It follows that the manuscripts **QhJ nwB** give the reading φασι; all the others (except for those mentioned and including O) give φησί.

recently defended by O'Sullivan, Kivilo and Koning.[40] However, it is improbable that a poet closely associated with Homer, such as Lesches, would have told a story in which Hesiod defeated Homer. The poems attributed to Lesches, such as the *Little Iliad*, are set in the heroic age, to which the story of the contest does not belong.[41] More fundamentally, the very attempt to discover the original author of such a story seems misguided, since most of the biographical episodes related to the lives of the archaic poets circulated anonymously at an early stage.

It has been argued in defence of Allen's reading that we have no evidence for a contest of singers with three or more contestants competing at the same time.[42] But in fact the last part of Periander's introductory sentence does seem to imply more than two participants. Furthermore, other witnesses of the story such as the *Certamen* and even Hesiod's *Works and Days* appear to set no explicit limits on the number of competitors who took part in the event as a whole. Even if such a version of the contest did not exist before Plutarch, he may, in any case, have invented further competitors to suit his own rhetorical purposes. The mention of the competition between the poets occurs in the context of advice given to kings. In the *Dinner*, Plutarch suggests a connection between riddle solving and the ability to rule well, two talents which have σοφία in common. The Sages, who can solve riddles, are also engaged in enlightened political discussions, and a female character in the work, Cleobulina, who improved the government of her father, is also famous for her riddles. Amasis, by contrast, does not excel in either ability. It stands to reason that, when telling of one of the most famous competitions in riddle solving, Plutarch wants to draw as close a parallel as possible between the σοφοί who took part in that competition and the σοφοί at his banquet; that may well be why he suggests, by mentioning Lesches, that more than two wise poets competed in the contest. Lesches is an appropriate choice for extra competitor for several reasons: he was an epic poet and even shared with Homer the attribution of the *Little Iliad*.[43] But the latter work could

---

40 O'Sullivan 1992: 80–1; Kivilo 2000: 4–5 and 2010a: 23–4 (cf. also Kivilo 2010b: 90); Koning 2010: 259–62.
41 In this respect, it is useful to remark, with West 1967: 439, that 'we know of a considerable number of early hexameter poems that were current in antiquity, and not one of them was about post-Dark Age personalities. "Biographical" poetry did not exist, to the best of our knowledge'. Kivilo's attempts to identify the 'trace of an archaic biographical poem here' (2010a: 24 n. 72) do not seem convincing. In order to argue for an early date for the origins of the story of the contest between Homer and Hesiod, we do not necessarily need a connection with Lesches or any other specific name. Another, more convincing attempt to trace the earliest developments of the legend in archaic times is in Debiasi 2012, according to whom the story originated in connection with the Lelantine war.
42 Kivilo 2010a: 23.
43 Collection of *testimonia* in Davies 1988: 49–52.

not compete with the real *Iliad* in terms of perceived poetic quality; and Lesches was nowhere near as famous as Homer.⁴⁴ Unlike the *Certamen*, where Hesiod defeats Homer solely on the basis of Panedes' verdict, here the poetic skills of Hesiod do not leave room for disagreement over his victory: Plutarch can thus safely use this episode to make his point about the importance of riddle solving. Lesches was also known to have participated in another poetic contest, against Arctinus, and that may have been at the back of Plutarch's mind when he included him in this story.⁴⁵

A related textual problem in this passage is posed by the words τῶν ἀγωνιστῶν Ὁμήρου καὶ Ἡσιόδου. These have almost unanimously been thought to contradict the presence of Lesches at the contest. Some scholars use them as evidence for the fact that Plutarch refers to a contest between Homer and Hesiod only.⁴⁶ Others solve this apparent problem by athetising Ὁμήρου καὶ Ἡσιόδου, and suggesting that it was a marginal gloss that made it into the text at an early stage of transmission.⁴⁷ This latter suggestion seems plausible, but the alleged gloss is attested in all our manuscripts,

---

44 As Graziosi 2002: 172 suggests, he is 'the perfect substitute in that he is traditionally very close to Homer, but less authoritative'. This remark does not necessarily contradict the claim that at the contest τῶν τότε σοφῶν οἱ δοκιμώτατοι ποιηταὶ συνῆλθον (*pace* Koning 2010: 260 n. 85). Important, here, is the fact that the *Dinner of the Seven Sages* mentions several obscure names of sages and other guests: clearly, Plutarch is displaying his erudition by revealing surprising and generally unknown elements of both the tradition of the Seven Sages and the tradition of the poetic contest. Comparing his version against other accounts of the Seven Sages (Pl. *Prt.* 343a; D. L. 1.40; Stob. 3.1.172), we find differences in the names of the Sages and in the place of their meeting.
45 Phaenias fr. 33 Wehrli. Other tentative explanations have been offered: Milne 1924: 57 suggests that the name of Lesches replaced Homer's in the Hellenistic period or later because of the chronological problem of making Homer and Hesiod contemporaries; Richardson 1981: 2 argues that Plutarch's account may reflect an earlier version of the story; Erbse 1996: 313–14 suggests emending the name of Lesches to Panedes. Among the attempts to account for the role of Lesches as the narrator of the story in the Plutarchan passage, Fowler's remarks (in Kivilo 2010a: 23 n. 71) seem the most reasonable: he claims that 'Plutarch may not necessarily have quoted first hand and there could be false inference behind his reference'. That is, even if Plutarch was indeed presenting Lesches as a narrator, he could have been wrong and this passage alone cannot prove Allen's and Kivilo's theory that Lesches was the creator of the contest story. More recently, Stamatopoulou 2014 suggests that the fact that Hesiod wins against Lesches, rather than against Homer, contributes to the 'marginalisation' of Hesiod and the self-definition of the Sages as a group that has surpassed the great authoritative figures of the past (see esp. pp. 538–43).
46 Koning 2010: 260 n. 84; Kivilo 2000: 4 and 2010a: 23.
47 The athetesis was first proposed by Wilamowitz 1879: 161. See also Wilamowitz 1929 (1916): 55 and 1916: 405. It was later accepted in the Teubner and Belles Lettres editions and by West 1967: 439.

which means that we should be careful about suggesting an athetesis.⁴⁸ In fact, it is possible to make sense of the text as it stands: the text says that the quality of Homer's and Hesiod's performance made it difficult for the judges to issue a verdict; hence they asked for the competition to go on and Hesiod, able to solve Lesches' riddle, was eventually awarded the victory. The fact that Hesiod replies 'offhand' (ἐκ τοῦ παρατυχόντος) may also mean that Hesiod was the first to reply to a riddle proposed to all the contestants: Lesches poses a riddle, and Hesiod solves it first – thus winning the competition.

Another explanation for the presence of Lesches that has gathered some consensus among modern scholars, and deserves attention here, is West's. He claims that 'if Lesches has any relevance here at all', the only possibility is that the name of Lesches replaced the name of Homer in the text: Homer would be the contestant who actually proposes the challenge, but a reader may have been reminded of Lesches by the verses of the question, and his name written in the margin of a copy of Plutarch's text would then have penetrated the text.⁴⁹ If the presupposition of West's statement is right, namely that these or similar verses may have reminded an ancient reader of Lesches' poetry, Plutarch, too, must have been aware of this connection: there is no need to postulate that he gave Homer verses reminiscent of another poet, when we consider that the tradition offered an alternative version for the question, which Plutarch may well have known.⁵⁰ It seems more probable that Lesches was present in Plutarch's account from the very beginning. In

---

48 However, from my remark it does not follow that the presence of these words in all the manuscript guarantees their genuineness. The fact that the readings φασι and φησί, that allow Lesches two completely different roles in the passage, are both well represented in the manuscript tradition shows that this passage was not perceived as straightforward by those who copied it, and it would not be surprising that an attempt made by someone to specify the names of the most canonical contestants successfully entered the text and was then transmitted unanimously.

49 West 1967: 438–40. More recently, West claimed that he 'can make nothing of the appearance of Lesches' name' in this passage (West 2013: 35 n. 76).

50 On a general level, it should be noted that Plutarch was without doubt well aware of the tradition of the contest, since he mentions it in three passages. He also commented on the relevant passage from the *Works and Days*, which must have involved some research on the topic. Moreover, he mentions details that are not found anywhere else, e.g. the fact that Amphidamas died in a naval battle during the Lelantine war. More specifically on this exchange of question and answer: in the relevant section of the manuscript of the *Certamen* (f. 16v), the words καναχήποδες ἵπποι are missing. Plutarch's text was used to complete the hexameter by the earliest editors of the *Certamen,* and P.Petr. I 25 (1), published in 1891 (see Part 2), confirmed that Plutarch's reading was current already in the third century BC (cf. ll. 44–7). In both the *Certamen* (97–8) and the aforementioned papyrus (ll. 38–41) the question is different from the one in Plutarch, and since he was well informed about the tradition of the answer, he may also have been aware of the alternative question with which it circulated.

any case, there is no definitive proof that the lines were ever associated with poems attributed to Lesches, and this makes it particularly unfortunate that they are often included in collections of fragments from the lost works of Lesches.[51] This is not to argue that the verses pronounced by Lesches in this passage are a creation of Plutarch: rather, it is to suggest that they could well derive from another source, for example a now-lost *corpus* of hexameters used in poetic contests similar to the collection of verses in the *Certamen* or indeed fluid oral epic performances. The fact that the Muses are asked *not* to sing a particular topic reverses the traditional epic invocation to the Muses, and in itself suggests a riddling or agonistic context for their creation, which is precisely the kind of context in which Plutarch mentions them.

There is one further peculiarity to this exchange of verses: the second verse in the question is left incomplete. Lesches is asking his opponent to talk about something that never was in the past and never shall be in the future; the second verse is then abruptly interrupted. Anyone familiar with the formulae of epic poetry will notice that the present is not mentioned: the couplet recalls the famous epic formula τά τ' ἐόντα τά τ' ἐσσόμενα πρό τ' ἐόντα ('the things that are, shall be and were'), which is also used in the corresponding question in the *Certamen* and in P.Petr. I 25 (1).[52] Most remarkably, because of the absence of the present, the question in Plutarch does not contain an obvious difficulty: if asked not to sing of the past or the future, Hesiod could refer, in his answer, to anything happening in the present.[53] Again it is instructive to see how this fits the context in which the verses appear, in particular by looking at Plutarch's conception of time as a philosophical issue in the *Dinner*. In the passage described at the beginning of this section, Bias solves the riddle posed to Amasis by referring to the present time: Amasis should ask the king of the Ethiopians to stop the rivers which are emptying into the ocean *at the present time*, because he is drinking up the ocean as it is at the present time; the question, Bias explains, concerns the ocean as it is now, not the ocean as it will be in the future (151d). In an-

---

51 Because of the mention of Lesches these verses have sometimes been connected with the *Little Iliad* and interpreted as its incipit (fr. 1 Bernabé: see Bernabé 1984 and 1987: 76). But the poem is more likely to have started with another couplet, transmitted in Ps.-Hdt. *Vit. Hom.* 16 and explicitly glossed as the beginning of the poem (fr. 1 Davies: see Davies 1989a: 60 and 1989b: 6; Burgess 2001: 24). Furthermore, fr. 1 Davies is more ancient than the Plutarchan couplet can be proved to be, as it is found in an inscription from the fifth century BC (Vinogradov 1969: 142–3; Vinogradov and Zolotarev 1990: 109 and 119 fig. C = *SEG* 1990: 612). For another hypothesis see Scafoglio 2006.
52 The formula is found at: *Il.* 1.71, Hes. *Th.* 38, *Th.* 32 (here in the shortened form τά τ' ἐσσόμενα πρό τ' ἐόντα which again leaves out the present).
53 The reference to the tomb of Zeus, something that can never exist because of the immortality of the god, well responds to the question formulated in the *Certamen* (see Part 4, 94–101n.). Strictly speaking, it is not appropriate in this context.

other passage (153b), time is defined as partaking of past, present and future; in another work (*On Common Conceptions against the Stoics* 1081c–1082d) Plutarch criticises the Stoic doctrine according to which time partakes only of past and future. In Lesches' question the importance of the present is demonstrated by its very absence: a verse is left incomplete and thus the couplet contains no difficulty to solve. The curtailed couplet suits Plutarch's philosophical discourse on time better than any corresponding verse transmitted in the rest of the tradition.

What can be concluded without controversy is this. First of all, Plutarch's account of the contest differs considerably from the version of the contest we know from the *Certamen*, however we read and edit his text. Secondly, it is clear that his version of the story was variously discussed and altered, so that some of the manuscripts have Lesches as narrator of, rather than participant in, the contest. The role of Lesches as narrator aligns Plutarch's version more closely with the *Certamen*, and may be the result of ancient or medieval attempts at harmonising the story. But it must be said that Lesches' role as narrator does not accord with Plutarch's own take on the story of the contest in other works: his *Table Talk* and the scholium to *Op.* 650–62 count against it. Finally, the manuscript reading that makes Lesches the narrator of the contest has the knock-on effect of creating one more epic fragment, which is then sometimes included in collections of Lesches' work. On that basis, some scholars argue for a very early origin of the story of the contest, ascribing its creation to a sixth- or seventh-century Lesches. That seems a conclusion of very dubious standing. Beyond the uncertainties, the present discussion of the Plutarchan passage shows how flexible the story of the contest was, and how often it was manipulated, in antiquity and in modern times, through the work of editors. Plutarch, the scrupulous critic of literature, rejects the authenticity of the contest story; and, precisely because he regards it as essentially fictional, he feels free to adapt it to his own creative purposes, in suitable contexts such as the *Dinner of the Seven Sages*.

Proclus, *Life of Homer* 6

The scholium discussed earlier does not indicate explicitly the extent to which Proclus agreed or disagreed with Plutarch's opinion on *Op.* 650–62, but a passage from the *Life of Homer*, originally part of the first book of Proclus' *Chrestomathy*,[54] suggests that Proclus may have found that Plutarch's

---

54 The *Chrestomathy* is now lost, but its contents can be in part reconstructed thanks to Photius' summary (Bibliotheca cod. 239) and to a few manuscripts transmitting the Life of Homer and a summary of the Epic Cycle. Photius informs us that the *Chrestomathy* also included a Life of Hesiod. For the manuscript tradition of Photius

criticism fitted well his own views on the episode, and on the two poets more generally:

τυφλὸν δὲ ὅσοι τοῦτον ἀπεφήναντο αὐτοί μοι δοκοῦσι τὴν διάνοιαν πεπηρῶσθαι· τοσαῦτα γὰρ κατεῖδεν ἄνθρωπος ὅσα οὐδεὶς πώποτε. εἰσὶ δὲ οἵτινες ἀνεψιὸν αὐτὸν Ἡσιόδου παρέδοσαν, ἀτριβεῖς ὄντες ποιήσεως· τοσοῦτον γὰρ ἀπέχουσι τοῦ γένει προσήκειν ὅσον ἡ ποίησις διέστηκεν αὐτῶν. ἄλλως δὲ οὐδὲ τοῖς χρόνοις συνεπέβαλον ἀλλήλοις. ἄθλιοι δὲ οἱ τὸ αἴνιγμα πλάσαντες τοῦτο·
   Ἡσίοδος Μούσαις Ἑλικωνίσι τόνδ' ἀνέθηκεν,
   ὕμνωι νικήσας ἐν Χαλκίδι θεῖον Ὅμηρον.
ἀλλὰ γὰρ ἐπλανήθησαν ἐκ τῶν Ἡσιοδείων Ἡμερῶν· ἕτερον γάρ τι σημαίνει.

All those who have claimed that he was blind were themselves, in my opinion, intellectually blind. For that man saw more than anyone else ever. There are some who claimed that he was Hesiod's cousin, but they are only amateurs in matters of poetry, for they are as distant in lineage as their poetry is different. Besides, they were not contemporaries either. Wretched were those who invented this riddle:
   Hesiod dedicated this to the Heliconian Muses when he defeated
   divine Homer in song at Chalcis.
They were, in fact, misled by the Hesiodic *Days*; for the verses have a different meaning.

Proclus' account of the life of Homer, based on extensive research that he carried out for his pupils,[55] is particularly encomiastic and often refutes some of the most famous features of the Homeric biographical tradition. The poet, for example, was not blind, nor poor, nor did he write anything that could be considered inferior to the *Iliad* and the *Odyssey*.[56] Along similar lines, Proclus also maintains that Homer was never defeated by Hesiod in a poetic contest, for 'they are as distant in lineage as their poetry

---

   and the other fragments of the *Chrestomathy* see Severyns 1938–1963 and Ferrante 1957. For the discussion of its authorship see below.
55 Par. 5: ἀλλὰ δὴ ταῦτα μὲν πολλῆς ἔχεται ζητήσεως, ἵνα δὲ μηδὲ τούτων ἄπειρος ὑπάρχῃς, διὰ τοῦτο εἰς ταῦτα κεχώρηκα, 'these matters certainly require a lot of research – however, I have explored them so that even here you may not be uninformed'.
56 For Proclus on Homer's blindness see par. 6 quoted above. On his poverty, see par. 8: τούτῳ δὲ προσυπονοητέον καὶ πλούτου πολλὴν περιουσίαν γενέσθαι· αἱ γὰρ μακραὶ ἀποδημίαι πολλῶν δέονται ἀναλωμάτων, 'One may also assume that he had significant financial resources; for long journeys entail great expenses'. On the attribution of works, see par. 9: γέγραφε δὲ ποιήσεις δύο, Ἰλιάδα καὶ Ὀδύσσειαν, 'He has written two poems, the *Iliad* and the *Odyssey*'.

is different. Besides, they were not contemporaries either' (τοσοῦτον γὰρ ἀπέχουσι τοῦ γένει προσήκειν ὅσον ἡ ποίησις διέστηκεν αὐτῶν. ἄλλως δὲ οὐδὲ τοῖς χρόνοις συνεπέβαλον ἀλλήλοις). Consequently, those who created the epigram of Hesiod's victory were 'wretched' (ἄθλιοι) and misinterpreted the Hesiodic passage. Given his views on Homer's life, Proclus may have found Plutarch's criticism of the story, which he knew and transmitted to us, very convenient, and may have used it as the very basis for his statement in the *Life of Homer*. There is, of course, a difference between Plutarch and Proclus in the treatment of the Hesiodic text: Plutarch athetises the Hesiodic passage; Proclus, as the *Life* shows, suggests that it needs to be reinterpreted (ἀλλὰ γὰρ ἐπλανήθησαν ἐκ τῶν Ἡσιοδείων Ἡμερῶν· ἕτερον γάρ τι σημαίνει, 'They were, in fact, misled by the Hesiodic *Days*; for the verses have a different meaning'). But the attitude towards the tradition that arose from it remains virtually identical to that found in the scholium on *Op.* 650–62, thus showing that the mention of the contest in the *Life* was influenced by Proclus' exegetical activity and knowledge of Plutarch's work: both texts link the discussion of the contest to the analysis of the related Hesiodic passage, show awareness of the contest tradition that arose from it, and go on to dismiss the credibility of the story itself.

This detail helps us set out the controversy concerning the authorship and date of the *Chrestomathy*. The ancient sources unanimously attribute this work to Proclus Diadochus, the Neoplatonic philosopher who lived in the fifth century AD.[57] But some modern scholars have attributed it to Eutychius Proclus, a grammarian of the second century AD.[58] Scholars who study the attribution of the *Chrestomathy* often overlook the *Life of Homer*, but, as we have seen, scholium and *Life* take the same approach to the story of

---

57 Suda s.v. 'Proclus' attributes to him the *Chrestomathy* and commentaries on Hesiod's *Works and Days*; the manuscript Ottobonianus gr. 58 (15th century AD) attributes explicitly the Life of Homer to Proclus Diadochus; a scholium to Gregory of Nazianzus Or. 43 attributes a treatise on the Epic Cycle to Proclus Πλατωνικός.

58 Eutychius Proclus is mentioned in the *Historia Augusta* (e.g. Aemil. Tyr. 22.13): he was a Latin grammarian; he was advanced to a proconsulship; he was the most learned man of his time; and the author of a work about foreign countries. Welcker 1835: 3–7 was one of the first scholars to question the traditional attribution. Hillgruber 1990 identifies points of contacts between the Pseudo-Plutarchan treatise *De Homero* and the *Chrestomathy*, and dated both works to the second century AD. Kuisma 1996: 57 denies the presence of explicit Neoplatonic features in the *Chrestomathy*. Most recently, West 2013: 7–11 has argued that there are good reasons to think that the *Chrestomathy* is the work of a scholar earlier than Proclus Diadochus, perhaps of the second century AD. In defence of the traditional attribution, Ferrante 1957: 10–13 underlined that the wide range of Proclus Diadochus' cultural interests also included the study of literature. Ferrante, in addition, points out that, according to the *Historia Augusta*, Eutychius Proclus was not a Greek but a Latin grammarian. More recently, Longo 1995 questioned Hillgruber's theory about the derivation of the Pseudo-Plutarchan *De Homero* from the *Chrestomathy*.

the contest, and therefore seem to belong to the same author – Proclus Diadochus. Furthermore, the *Life* offers other pieces of evidence in support of Proclus Diadochus' authorship. At par. 2 Homer is said to be κοσμοπολίτης, a 'citizen of the world': this word seems to define the dispute over Homer's birthplace in philosophical terms, since the word is remarkably rare in extant Greek texts, and apparently belongs exclusively to philosophical discourse;[59] as such, it may have been used by a philosopher such as Proclus Diadochus. Furthermore, Lamberton identifies a point of strong agreement between this *Life* and Proclus Diadochus' *Commentary on Plato's Republic*.[60] In that work (1.174.4–5), Proclus claims that Homer's blindness was a metaphor for his inner vision. In the *Life* (par. 6 quoted above), Proclus says that Homer was not blind, but able to see 'more than anyone else ever': those who invented this story were in fact mentally blind. In both passages, the ability to see is not simply a physical issue, and this, again, supports the attribution of the *Chrestomathy* to Proclus Diadochus.

3. Second Sophistic: Dio Chrysostom, Philostratus, and Lucian

The present section is devoted to three passages by authors belonging to the so-called Second Sophistic: Dio Chrysostom, Philostratus, and Lucian. These authors insert mention of the contest between Homer and Hesiod in fictional contexts: Dio places it in a dialogue between Alexander the Great and his father Philip; in Philostratus' work the story is told by the Homeric hero Protesilaus; Lucian makes it part of his imaginary visit to the Island of the Blessed, a few lines after his meeting with Homer.

These three authors are perplexed at the outcome of the competition, either because Homer's defeat in a poetic contest does not fit their view on his

---

59 The idea of 'cosmopolitanism' was current in the Classical era (Goulet-Cazé 2006), but the word κοσμοπολίτης does not appear to have been used before the Hellenistic period. The Cynic philosopher Diogenes (404–323 BC) seems to have been the first to use the word (see D. L. 6.63: ἐρωτηθεὶς πόθεν εἴη, 'κοσμοπολίτης', ἔφη, 'when he was asked where he was from, he said "I am a citizen of the world"'. A search on the TLG reveals that the word appears only 22 times in the entire corpus of extant Greek literature, and only in philosophical (Cynic and Stoic) and religious texts, ranging from the Hellenistic age to the late Byzantine period: Chrysippus (3rd BC), Philo Judaeus (1st BC–1st AD), Didymus Caecus (4th AD), the *Constitutiones Apostolorum* (4th AD), Eustathius (12th AD). The phrase κόσμου πολίτ- appears only 3 times and always in philosophical texts from the Imperial age: Epict. *Dissertationes ab Arriano digestae* 2.10.3; Lucianus *Vit. Auct.* 8.4; Heraclit. *Ep.* 9.2.11. The only author other than Proclus to use the word with reference to Homer is Janus Lascaris (1445–1535), in *Epigram* 64. On cosmopolitanism see also Montiglio 2005: ch. 8 and 9; Moles 1996; Richter 2011.
60 Lamberton 1986: 177–8.

poetry, or because they wish to make a parodic allusion to this feature of the story. However, unlike Plutarch, they do not athetise the Hesiodic passage. They rather downplay the impact of Homer's defeat by questioning the way in which the final verdict was issued. In so doing, they launch a strategy that will later be exploited by several authors.

Two of these passages also offer the earliest extant references to the two 'finest passages' that the poets perform during the contest (cf. *Cert.* 176–204) – another detail which is not mentioned by Hesiod, but is very common among later writers. The selected passages are never exactly the same in the various accounts of the story – authors manipulated them, by adding or cutting verses, or making only vague references to a passage from the two poets' works – but show what was considered as most representative of Homeric and Hesiodic poetry when staged against each other.

Finally, these passages contain a large amount of biographical material on Homer (e.g., information on his chronology and place of birth). The biography of the poet was a matter of interest to the Second Sophistic, and this explains the popularity of the story of the contest during that period.

Dio Chrysostom, *Oration on Kingship* 2.7–12

In Dio Chrysostom's second oration *On Kingship* (first-second century AD), Alexander the Great and his father Philip are on their way home from Chaeronea when they engage in a conversation about Homer – a conversation that is, in fact, mainly about kingship (see par. 1). In the first few paragraphs Alexander puts forward the idea that lies at the heart of the oration: kings should read Homer, because his poetry alone is suited to a king (esp. par. 6). His father then asks what he thinks of other poets, including Hesiod, and this provides the opportunity for a reflection on the story of the contest between Homer and Hesiod that also resembles a 're-enactment' of it,[61] with Philip and Alexander performing Hesiodic and Homeric verses respectively.

(7) [...] πάνυ οὖν ὁ Φίλιππος αὐτὸν ἠγάσθη τῆς μεγαλοφροσύνης, ὅτι δῆλος ἦν οὐδὲν φαῦλον οὐδὲ ταπεινὸν ἐπινοῶν, ἀλλὰ τοῖς τε ἥρωσι καὶ τοῖς ἡμιθέοις παραβαλλόμενος. (8) ὅμως δὲ κινεῖν αὐτὸν βουλόμενος, Τὸν δὲ Ἡσίοδον, ὦ Ἀλέξανδρε, ὀλίγου ἄξιον κρίνεις, ἔφη, ποιητήν; Οὐκ ἔγωγε, εἶπεν, ἀλλὰ τοῦ παντός, οὐ μέντοι βασιλεῦσιν οὐδὲ στρατηγοῖς ἴσως. Ἀλλὰ τίσι μήν; καὶ ὁ Ἀλέξανδρος γελάσας, Τοῖς ποιμέσιν, ἔφη, καὶ τοῖς τέκτοσι καὶ τοῖς γεωργοῖς. τοὺς μὲν γὰρ ποιμένας φησὶ φιλεῖσθαι ὑπὸ τῶν Μουσῶν, τοῖς δὲ τέκτοσι μάλα ἐμπείρως παραινεῖ πηλίκον χρὴ τὸν ἄξονα τεμεῖν, καὶ τοῖς γεωργοῖς, ὁπηνίκα ἄρξασθαι πίθου. (9) Τί

---
61 Koning 2010: 263.

οὖν; οὐχὶ ταῦτα χρήσιμα, ἔφη, τοῖς ἀνθρώποις, ὁ Φίλιππος; Οὐχ ἡμῖν γε, εἶπεν, ὦ πάτερ, οὐδὲ Μακεδόσι τοῖς νῦν, ἀλλὰ τοῖς πρότερον, ἡνίκα νέμοντες καὶ γεωργοῦντες Ἰλλυριοῖς ἐδούλευον καὶ Τριβαλλοῖς. Οὐδὲ τὰ περὶ τὸν σπόρον, ἔφη, καὶ τὸν ἀμητόν, ὁ Φίλιππος, ἀρέσκει σοι τοῦ Ἡσιόδου μεγαλοπρεπῶς οὕτως εἰρημένα;
 Πληιάδων Ἀτλαγενέων ἐπιτελλομενάων
 ἄρχεσθ' ἀμητοῦ, ἀρότοιο δὲ δυσομενάων.
(10) Πολύ γε μᾶλλον, εἶπεν ὁ Ἀλέξανδρος, τὰ παρ' Ὁμήρῳ γεωργικά. Καὶ ποῦ περὶ γεωργίας εἴρηκεν Ὅμηρος; ἤρετο ὁ Φίλιππος, ἢ τὰ ἐν τῇ ἀσπίδι μιμήματα λέγεις τῶν ἀρούντων καὶ θεριζόντων καὶ τρυγώντων; Ἥκιστά γε, εἶπεν ὁ Ἀλέξανδρος, ἀλλὰ ἐκεῖνα πολὺ μᾶλλον·
 οἱ δ' ὥστ' ἀμητῆρες ἐναντίοι ἀλλήλοισιν
 ὄγμον ἐλαύνωσιν ἀνδρὸς μάκαρος κατ' ἄρουραν
 πυρῶν ἢ κριθῶν· τὰ δὲ δράγματα ταρφέα πίπτει·
 ὣς Τρῶες καὶ Ἀχαιοὶ ἐπ' ἀλλήλοισι θορόντες
 δῄουν, οὐδ' ἕτεροι μνώοντ' ὀλοοῖο φόβοιο.
(11) Ταῦτα μέντοι ποιῶν Ὅμηρος ἡττᾶτο ὑπὸ Ἡσιόδου, ὁ Φίλιππος εἶπεν· ἢ οὐκ ἀκήκοας τὸ ἐπίγραμμα τὸ ἐν Ἑλικῶνι ἐπὶ τοῦ τρίποδος·
 Ἡσίοδος Μούσαις Ἑλικωνίσι τόνδ' ἀνέθηκεν
 ὕμνῳ νικήσας ἐν Χαλκίδι θεῖον Ὅμηρον;
(12) Καὶ μάλα δικαίως, εἶπεν ὁ Ἀλέξανδρος, ἡττᾶτο· οὐ γὰρ ἐν βασιλεῦσιν ἠγωνίζετο, ἀλλ' ἐν γεωργοῖς καὶ ἰδιώταις, μᾶλλον δὲ ἐν ἀνθρώποις φιληδόνοις καὶ μαλακοῖς. τοιγαροῦν ἠμύνατο τοὺς Εὐβοέας διὰ τῆς ποιήσεως Ὅμηρος. [...] (ed. Cohoon)

(7) [...] Philip, then, admired him (i.e., Alexander) greatly for his magnanimity, since he clearly did not put his mind to anything unworthy or mean, but was interested in heroes and demigods. (8) But since he wanted to challenge him anyway, he said: 'Then, Alexander, do you consider Hesiod little worthy as a poet?' 'Not at all', he said, 'I consider him definitely worthy – but not for kings, nor for leaders either'. 'Then, for whom?'. And Alexander, laughing, said: 'For shepherds, carpenters, and farmers; for he says that shepherds are loved by the Muses, and with great expertise advises the carpenters on how large they should cut an axle, and the farmers on when to broach a cask. (9) 'What, then? Are these things not useful to men?' said Philip. And he replied: 'Not to us, father, not to the Macedonians who live now, but to those who lived in the past, at the time when they were slaves, herding and farming for the Illyrians and the Triballians'. 'Do you not like', said Philip, 'even the verses that Hesiod so magnificently spoke about sowing and reaping?
 When the Atlas-born Pleiades rise, start the harvest; the ploughing, when they set'.

(10) 'Much more', said Alexander, 'I like the verses on agriculture in Homer'. 'And where has Homer spoken about agriculture?', asked Philip, 'Or do you mean the representations on the shield of the people ploughing and gathering grain and grapes?'. 'Absolutely not', said Alexander, 'but much rather these:

> As when reapers march opposite each other in the field of barley or wheat of a rich man, and handfuls fall thick, so Trojans and Achaeans, leaping upon each other, slay each other, and neither are mindful of ignominious fear'.

(11) 'However, even though he composed these lines, Homer was defeated by Hesiod', Philip said, 'or have you not heard of the epigram on the tripod on the Helicon?

> Hesiod dedicated this to the Heliconian Muses when he defeated divine Homer in song at Chalcis'.

(12) 'And rightly indeed was he defeated', said Alexander, 'for he did not compete before kings, but farmers and common people, or rather, before people who were lovers of pleasure and weak. And for this reason Homer pays back the Euboeans through his poetry'.

In this oration the story of the contest *between* Homer and Hesiod is presented within another quasi-competitive context, a contest *over* Homer and Hesiod acted out by Philip and Alexander. Through the way he develops the narrative of both competitions, Dio shows a good degree of awareness of certain common features of the tradition of the contest between Homer and Hesiod: the outcome, the tripod, and the epigram celebrating Hesiod's victory. At the same time, however, the selection of passages recited and the account of the final verdict are shaped to suit Dio's specific aims.

Alexander insists that Homer's is the only poetry suitable for kings, while the rest is for 'shepherds, carpenters, and farmers' (par. 8): Hesiod gives useful advice to such people, but not to a ruler like him. To this, Philip replies by asking his son what he thinks about the magnificent (cf. μεγαλοπρεπῶς, par. 9) lines by Hesiod about seed-time and harvest; a performance of *Works and Days* 383–4 follows. These verses are the beginning of the passage that Hesiod selects as his finest in several versions of the contest. According to Philip too, it seems, these verses stand out in the Hesiodic production. Alexander replies that he prefers what Homer says about agriculture, and performs a passage from the *Iliad*, as in the rest of the tradition of the contest. In this case, however, the selected verses are *Il.* 11.67–71, a simile in which warriors of the Trojan and Achaean side are said to leap on each other like reapers who 'march opposite each other in the field of barley or wheat of a rich man, and handfuls fall thick'. This simile is chosen because it uses a spectacular agricultural simile to represent a battle, thereby revealing the kind of agricultural work Alexander favours – and Homer's expertise on typically Hesiodic matters.⁶²

At this point, the story of the contest between Homer and Hesiod enters the narrative. Philip remarks that 'even though he composed these lines' (par. 11) Homer was defeated by Hesiod, and offers as evidence the epigram of the victory and the tripod on which it was inscribed. The tripod and its epigram are important pieces of evidence and it is difficult to ignore them: indeed, these details come from Hesiod himself (*Op.* 657–8).⁶³ Therefore Alexander, in order to defend his thesis of Homer's superiority over Hesiod, works with another detail of the story: the final verdict. In Alexander's version the people who judged the performance were not 'kings, but farmers and plain folk, or, rather, people who were lovers of pleasure and effeminate', and these are the people, as Alexander pointed out earlier, who can find useful advice in Hesiod's poetry and prefer it to Homer's. A king, Alexander seems to claim implicitly, could not have issued such a verdict. Consequently, the existence of a character such as Panedes is completely omitted. Dio may well have known about the name of that king, because it was already circulating by the third century BC;⁶⁴ but a king who prefers Hesiod over Homer would be a threat for the main argument of the oration: kings should like Homer.

Philostratus, *Heroicus* 43.7–10

In his *Heroicus*, Philostratus (second-third century AD) stages a dialogue, that takes place in the Thracian Chersonesus, between a local vinedresser and a Phoenician merchant who had to interrupt his navigation because of unfavourable winds.⁶⁵ The vinedresser turns out to be a friend of Protesilaus,

---

62 See also Koning 2010: 264 and n. 95.
63 See Part 1, 'Hesiod'.
64 P.Petr. I 25 (1), l. 4. As has been noted (Richardson 1984; Koning 2010: 264 n. 97), this confutes Heldmann's theory that the scene of Panedes is a late addition to the contest story made precisely in response to Dio's account (see Heldmann 1982: 45–53).
65 The attribution and dating of the *Heroicus* is debated. The Suda (φ 421–3) mentions three authors named Philostratus and attributes the *Heroicus* to Philostratus II (son of Philostratus I the son of Vero), whose death is placed in 244–9 AD. Although inconsistencies between some of the information given in the Suda entries and internal evidence from the works of the Philostrati have raised doubts about the reliability of the Suda entries themselves, the majority of modern scholars accept the attribution of the *Heroicus* to Philostratus II: for the debate see esp. Solmsen 1940; Anderson 1986: 294–5; De Lannoy 1997: 2391; Berenson Maclean/Bradshaw Aitken 2001: xlii–xlv.

the first Greek hero to die at Troy.[66] Together they cultivate the vines and discuss the Homeric poems. At 43.5 the Phoenician claims that the level of knowledge of the Trojan deeds shown in the Homeric epics is more appropriate for a god than for a mortal. In response to this, to prove that Homer was in fact a man, albeit a divinely inspired one, the vinedresser offers a brief survey of biographical information about Homer, which includes the episode of his contest with Hesiod:

γέγονε γάρ, ξένε, γέγονε ποιητὴς Ὅμηρος καὶ ᾖδεν, ὡς μέν φασιν ἕτεροι μετὰ τέτταρα καὶ εἴκοσιν ἔτη τῶν Τρωικῶν, οἱ δὲ μετὰ ἑπτὰ καὶ εἴκοσι πρὸς τοῖς ἑκατόν, ὅτε τὴν ἀποικίαν ἐς Ἰωνίαν ἔστειλαν· οἱ δὲ ἑξήκοντα καὶ ἑκατὸν ἔτη γεγονέναι μετὰ τὴν Τροίαν ἐπὶ Ὅμηρόν τέ φασι καὶ Ἡσίοδον, ὅτε δὴ ᾆσαι ἄμφω ἐν Χαλκίδι, τὸν μὲν τὰ ἑπτὰ ἔπη τὰ περὶ τοῖν Αἰάντοιν καὶ ὡς αἱ φάλαγγες αὐτοῖς ἀραρυῖαί τε ἦσαν καὶ καρτεραί, τὸν δὲ τὰ πρὸς τὸν ἀδελφὸν τὸν ἑαυτοῦ Πέρσην, ἐν οἷς αὐτὸν ἔργων τε ἐκέλευεν ἅπτεσθαι καὶ γεωργίᾳ προσκεῖσθαι, ὡς μὴ δέοιτο ἑτέρων μηδὲ πεινῴη. καὶ ἀληθέστερα, ξένε, περὶ τῶν Ὁμήρου χρόνων ταῦτα· ξυντίθεται γὰρ αὐτοῖς ὁ Πρωτεσίλεως. δύο γοῦν ποιητῶν ὕμνον ποτὲ εἰπόντων ἐς αὐτὸν ἐνταυθοῖ καὶ ἀπελθόντων, ἤρετό με ὁ ἥρως ἀφικόμενος ὅτῳ αὐτῶν ψηφιζοίμην· ἐμοῦ δὲ τὸν φαυλότερον ἐπαινέσαντος (καὶ γὰρ μᾶλλον ἔτυχεν ᾑρηκώς), γελάσας ὁ Πρωτεσίλεως «καὶ Πανίδης» εἶπεν, «ἀμπελουργέ, ταὐτόν σοι πέπονθε· Χαλκίδος γὰρ τῆς ἐπ' Εὐρίπῳ βασιλεὺς ὢν ἐκεῖνος Ἡσιόδῳ κατὰ Ὁμήρου ἐψηφίσατο, καὶ ταῦτα τὸ γένειον ἔχων μεῖζον ἢ σύ.» (ed. De Lannoy)

For he existed, my guest, the poet Homer existed and sang, some say, twenty-four years after the Trojan War, others say one hundred and twenty-seven years later, at the time of the Ionian colonisation; others say that, after Troy, a hundred and sixty years passed until the time of Homer and Hesiod, when they both sang at Chalcis – one the seven epics on the two Ajaxes, and how the the battle lines were compact and strong, while the other, the verses for his brother Perses, in which he encourages him to work and devote himself to agriculture, so that he will not need others' help or be hungry. And, my guest, these things about Homer's times are definitely true, for Protesilaus agrees on them. Well, once, when two poets were here performing a song for him and had left, the hero came and asked me for which of them I would vote. Since I commended the least skilled (and indeed he happened to have won by a large margin), Protesilaus, laughing, said: 'The same thing happened to Panides too, vinedresser. He, as the king of Chalcis on the Euripus,

---

66 See *Il.* 2.695–710.

voted for Hesiod against Homer, and did this although he had a beard that was longer than yours'.

Philostratus' discussion of the life of Homer shows that he was familiar with the Homeric biographical tradition, and he may have had access to sources similar to the extant Lives of the poet.[67] As is typical of the Lives, several possible solutions for the date of the poet are listed and attributed generically to 'some people'; Homer's date is measured in relation to his chronological proximity to events such as the Trojan war and the Ionian migration, or to poets such as Hesiod;[68] in the passage that follows the mention of the contest, Homer is said to travel to several places, including Ithaca;[69] finally, Homer emerges from the discussion of his birthplace as being ἄπολις, a person claimed by all cities because he belongs to none.[70] In the same or similar sources Philostratus must have also found information on the story of the contest between Homer and Hesiod, about which he seems to be well informed. As in the *Certamen* (44–55), the episode of the contest is introduced in connection with the discussion of Homer's chronology, with explicit reference to the issue of his contemporaneity with Hesiod. The passages that the poets recite are clearly taken from the same sections of the *Works and Days* and the *Iliad* as in most witnesses of the contest (although no verse is quoted), but the specific selection is peculiar to this account: the description of Hesiod's performance suggests that

---

67 Kim 2010: 208 n. 86 also briefly mentions the similarity between this biographical interlude and some of the extant Lives of Homer.
68 In particular, that Homer was born twenty-four or one hundred and twenty-seven years after the Trojan war is known from no other source; his contemporaneity to the Ionian colonisation is mentioned in Ps.-Plu. *Vit. Hom.* 1.3, Ps.-Plu. *Vit. Hom.* 2.3 and Procl. *Vit. Hom.* 7, but in the last two sources (where the information is said to go back to the school of Aristarchus) the Ionian migration is dated one hundred and forty years after the Trojan war, rather than one hundred and twenty-seven as in the *Heroicus*; that Homer was born one hundred and sixty years after the Trojan war is known also from Suda s.v. 'Homer' 4. For more discussion on Homer's dating in antiquity see also Part 4, 44–53n. and cross-references therein, with bibliography.
69 For biographical traditions on Homer and Ithaca, including attempts to establish genealogical connections between the poet and some characters from the *Odyssey*, see Part 4, 23–4n. and 25–6n.
70 For the diffusion of this idea in antiquity see Part 4, 7–17n.

the poet is reciting *Op.* 384–404;[71] Homer recites the 'seven epics' on the two Ajaxes and their ranks of battle.[72]

Philostratus also knew the outcome of the contest, but the verdict in favour of Hesiod does not fit the *Heroicus* and, more specifically, the opinion of Homer expressed by Protesilaus (to whom Philostratus entrusts the report of the competition): at 24.1–25.17, Protesilaus' opinion on Homer is reported, and the hero claims, among other things, that Homer proved better than all the poets he met, in all subject matters, and more pertinently that the poet talked about peace, agriculture, and the appropriate time for performing each agricultural tasks: these are famously and typically Hesiodic areas of expertise, which granted him victory in some versions of the contest.[73] Therefore Philostratus, through the mouth of Protesilaus, accuses the judge Panides of having chosen the simpler of the two poets – a strategy often used to justify Homer's defeat.

Philostratus' account has many points in common with Dio's: for instance, both insert the contest between Homer and Hesiod within another contest (a dispute between Alexander and Philip in Dio, one between two poets singing hymns to Protesilaus in Philostratus),[74] and both claim that Homer's verses on agriculture are as fine as Hesiod's – if not better. But the two different contexts require different narrative details. Hence, according to Dio, Hesiod is awarded the victory by the common people because of the connection between Homer's poetry and kingship established in that work. That connection is not present in Philostratus, who can thus make use of the figure of the incompetent king Panides.

---

71 The expression ὡς μὴ δέοιτο ἑτέρων, μηδὲ πεινῴη ('so that he will not need others' help or be hungry') sums up the content of *Op.* 395–404, where Hesiod explains that agriculture makes a man self-sufficient. This leads West 1967: 442 n. 3 to suggest that in the *Certamen*, too, 'originally the extract may have gone on to v. 404'. But it seems safer to conclude that the length of the selected passages was one of the 'semi-fixed' features of the story that could be, at least partially, modified, rather than postulate the existence of an 'original' extract – impossible to verify – and several 'variations' from it.

72 It is not entirely clear what τὰ ἑπτὰ ἔπη ('seven epics') refers to. Some manuscripts omit ἑπτά (see De Lannoy's apparatus *ad loc.*), perhaps because this number creates a difficulty: such selection must include at least eight verses to reach a syntactical stop (*Il.* 13.126–33) as in *Cert.* 191–8, rather than seven.

73 For discussions of Philostratus' general attitude towards Homer and Homeric poetry see: Berenson Maclean/Bradshaw Aitken 2001: lx–lxxvi; Kim 2010: 175–215, with further bibliography.

74 Plutarch too inserts the story of the contest between Homer and Hesiod within another contest (*Dinner of the Seven Sages* 153f–154a).

3. Second Sophistic: Dio Chrysostom, Philostratus, and Lucian

Lucian, *True Story* 2.20–22

Lucian (second century AD) alludes to the story of the contest between Homer and Hesiod in his *True Story*: at 2.22 he relates that the two poets competed on the occasion of the Θανατούσια, the 'Games of the Dead' on the Island of the Blessed, and 'Homer was far the best, in truth, but Hesiod won anyway'. This playful comment, concise as it may be, clearly shows Lucian's awareness of the tradition of the contest and some of its main features, in particular in its echo of the reaction of surprise and disappointment that often caught both the public who attended the contest and later readers of the story. The allusion to the contest follows one of the most famous and entertaining episodes of the whole *True Story*, the interview with Homer. Helpfully for us, this passage displays Lucian's knowledge of ancient Homeric scholarship and biography, thus offering the background against which we should read his reference to the contest:

(20) Οὔπω δὲ δύο ἢ τρεῖς ἡμέραι διεληλύθεσαν, καὶ προσελθὼν ἐγὼ Ὁμήρῳ τῷ ποιητῇ, σχολῆς οὔσης ἀμφοῖν, τά τε ἄλλα ἐπυνθανόμην καὶ ὅθεν εἴη, λέγων τοῦτο μάλιστα παρ' ἡμῖν εἰσέτι νῦν ζητεῖσθαι. ὁ δὲ οὐδ' αὐτὸς μὲν ἀγνοεῖν ἔφασκεν ὡς οἱ μὲν Χῖον, οἱ δὲ Σμυρναῖον, πολλοὶ δὲ Κολοφώνιον αὐτὸν νομίζουσιν· εἶναι μέντοι γε ἔλεγεν Βαβυλώνιος, καὶ παρά γε τοῖς πολίταις οὐχ Ὅμηρος, ἀλλὰ Τιγράνης καλεῖσθαι· ὕστερον δὲ ὁμηρεύσας παρὰ τοῖς Ἕλλησιν ἀλλάξαι τὴν προσηγορίαν. ἔτι δὲ καὶ περὶ τῶν ἀθετουμένων στίχων ἐπηρώτων, εἰ ὑπ' ἐκείνου εἰσὶ γεγραμμένοι. καὶ ὃς ἔφασκε πάντας αὐτοῦ εἶναι. κατεγίνωσκον οὖν τῶν ἀμφὶ τὸν Ζηνόδοτον καὶ Ἀρίσταρχον γραμματικῶν πολλὴν τὴν ψυχρολογίαν. ἐπεὶ δὲ ταῦτα ἱκανῶς ἀπεκέκριτο, πάλιν αὐτὸν ἠρώτων τί δή ποτε ἀπὸ τῆς μήνιδος τὴν ἀρχὴν ἐποιήσατο· καὶ ὃς εἶπεν οὕτως ἐπελθεῖν αὐτῷ μηδὲν ἐπιτηδεύσαντι. καὶ μὴν κἀκεῖνο ἐπεθύμουν εἰδέναι, εἰ προτέραν ἔγραψεν τὴν Ὀδύσσειαν τῆς Ἰλιάδος, ὡς οἱ πολλοί φασιν· ὁ δὲ ἠρνεῖτο. ὅτι μὲν γὰρ οὐδὲ τυφλὸς ἦν, ὃ καὶ αὐτὸ περὶ αὐτοῦ λέγουσιν, αὐτίκα ἠπιστάμην· ἑώρα γάρ, ὥστε οὐδὲ πυνθάνεσθαι ἐδεόμην [...] (22) προϊόντος δὲ τοῦ χρόνου ἐνέστη ὁ ἀγὼν ὁ παρ' αὐτοῖς, τὰ Θανατούσια [...] ποιητῶν δὲ τῇ μὲν ἀληθείᾳ παρὰ πολὺ ἐκράτει Ὅμηρος, ἐνίκησεν δὲ ὅμως Ἡσίοδος. τὰ δὲ ἆθλα ἦν ἅπασι στέφανος πλακεὶς ἐκ πτερῶν ταωνείων. (ed. Macleod)

(20) Two or three days had barely passed, and going up to the poet Homer when both of us had some spare time, I asked him, among other things, where he came from, saying that this was a matter of particular enquiry among us even to the present day. He said that he was not unaware that some thought he was a Chian, some a Smyrnaean, many a Colophonian; but actually, he said, he was a Babylonian, and among his fellow citizens he was not called Homer, but Tigranes; later on he changed his name, after

he was taken hostage among the Greeks. And then I also asked about the athetised lines, whether they had been written by him, and he said that they are all his own. I therefore condemned the work of Zenodotus' and Aristarchus' followers as pure nonsense. When he had responded to these questions adequately, I asked him why he had started with the wrath (of Achilles), and he said that it came to him like this, with no specific reason. And I also wanted to know this: whether he had written the *Odyssey* before the *Iliad*, as most people say. He said he had not. That he was not blind, which also is said about him, I understood at once: for he could see, and therefore I did not need to ask [...] (22) After some time had passed the local games took place, the Games of the Dead. [...] Among the poets, Homer was far the best, in truth, but Hesiod won anyway. The prize for every contest was a crown made of intertwined peacock feathers.

The *True Story*, as Lucian himself points out in the prologue, invites readers to take part in a game of allusion. In order for this game to work, Lucian must refer to works or passages that are famous enough to be recognised by his audience.[75] The fact that he mentions Homer's superiority over Hesiod and his unexpected defeat means that these features were common enough in the tradition of the contest to be recognised by Lucian's readership; and by choosing this as the object of one of his parodic allusions, Lucian is making fun of all the scholarly efforts that had been made to cope with it, just as in chapter 20 he ridicules the debates over other famous controversies of Homeric scholarship.[76]

Before referring to the contest, Lucian fills the episode with learned allusions to many other details of the ancient Homeric biographical tradition.[77] First, Lucian refers to the dispute about Homer's birthplace by mentioning the three contenders generally recognised in antiquity as having the strongest and most ancient claims to Homer's origins: Smyrna, Chios and Colophon.[78] Homer's own surprising assertion of his Babylonian origins, then, works well as a parody of the many outlandish solutions that had been proposed in

---

75   Some studies on this allusive method and the proem of the *True Story* are: Georgiadou/Larmour 1998: 22–4 and 51–9; Möllendorff 2000.
76   Georgiadou/Larmour 1998: 205 suggest that Homer does not win the contest because this would not be consistent with all the criticism and parodies Lucian has made of him. But this seems secondary: first and most importantly, Lucian is making a playful allusion to a widespread tradition.
77   Detailed studies of this episode are: Jones 1986: 54–5; Georgiadou/Larmour 1998: 200–3; Möllendorff 2000: 367–73; Nesselrath 2002; Ní-Mheallaigh 2009; Kim 2010: 162–8. Together with the allusions to the Homeric biographical tradition that will be discussed below, Lucian in this passage also refers to ancient textual exegesis: the chronological priority of the *Iliad* over the *Odyssey*, the athetised verses, the first word of the *Iliad*. On these, see bibliography above.
78   See Part 4, 7–17n.

antiquity to the famous question concerning his birthplace.[79] But Lucian, as well as making a preposterous suggestion, is also alluding to the doctrines of a specific Homeric school: we know from some ancient scholia on *Il.* 23.79 that scholars of the school of Pergamum such as Crates and Zenodotus of Mallos argued that Homer was a Chaldaean.[80] Homer's claim also allows for a series of interrelated allusions to other biographical anecdotes.

The fact that Homer's original name Tigranes recalls the name of the Tigris, a river associated with his alleged birthplace Babylon, echoes the tradition according to which Homer took his original name Melesigenes from the Meles, the river that runs through another alleged Homeric birthplace, Smyrna.[81] Lucian then reports that Homer changed his name after being taken hostage; this, too, echoes a well-attested biographical anecdote.[82] Moreover, a historical king of the same name, Tigranes II the Great of Armenia (140–55 BC), was likewise taken hostage, and this creates the possibility for further levels of allusion.[83] Finally, the feature of Homer's *persona* that is perhaps best known is his blindness: Lucian reverses this too by claiming that it was absolutely clear that Homer could see very well.[84]

Lucian's encounter with Homer is filled with parodic allusions to specific texts, and more general references to biographical anecdotes that were known during the author's time. In the case of the contest between Homer and Hesiod, it is difficult to establish whether Lucian is alluding to a specific text or version of it. However, his mention of the contest in this parodic pas-

---

[79] See for example Suda s.v. 'Homer' 2 for a list of no fewer than twenty cities that had claims on the poet, many of which were outside the Greek world. See also Heath 1998.

[80] See, e.g.: Bompaire 1998: 110 n. 76; Georgiadou/Larmour 1998: 201; Broggiato 2001: 181 n. 161. The parody of the school of Pergamum is balanced later on in the text by the mention of the other main centre of Homeric studies, the Alexandrian school, of which Zenodotus and Aristarchus were the most famous exponents. For further discussion of Homer's Babylonian origins see also Matteuzzi 2000–2002 who suggests that, by making Homer a Babylonian, Lucian, who is a Syrian by origin, wanted to make him his 'fellow-citizen' and his alter ego as an Eastern Greek; see also: Zeitlin 2001: 246 and n. 76; Nesselrath 2002: 155; Kim 2010: 165–6.

[81] For the Smyrnean tradition and its features see Part 4, 8–12n. and cross-references therein. That the name Tigranes is a parody of Melesigenes has been suggested only by Möllendorf 2000: 368–9. But it is only to be expected that Lucian, when inventing an alleged original name for Homer, plays with the existing traditions on the topic. That Lucian was aware of such traditions, and more specifically of the name Melesigenes, is proved by another passage in his *Dem. Enc.* (par. 9).

[82] See Part 4, 29–32n.

[83] Str. 11.14.15. As Allen 2006: 151–4 points out, the name Tigranes, combined with hostageship, became an opportunity for sarcasm for Lucian. Tigranes II, moreover, is actually mentioned in a work of the Lucianic corpus, although this is unanimously considered spurious (*Macr.* 15).

[84] On Homer's blindness see Part 4, 11–12n.

sage shows the wide circulation of the story, as well as a common reaction to Hesiod's victory.

4. Late antique rhetoric: Themistius and Libanius

The popularity of the contest between Homer and Hesiod continued in Late Antiquity. The story is narrated in two rhetorical works from the fourth century AD: Themistius' *Oration* 30 and Libanius' *Defence of Socrates*. Both works show how the story of the contest could be fruitfully used as an *exemplum* to support the author's argument: Themistius mentions it to prove that agriculture is the best activity for men, while Libanius draws on it to show that criticising poets, one of the charges put forward against Socrates, has never been a crime.

These passages show that, if authors could not change the outcome of the competition, they were still free to change the other details concerning the final verdict: Themistius claims that Hesiod was considered the best by all the judges, thus giving the widest support to the poet who, like him, promotes agriculture; Libanius, on the other hand, mentions as a source for the episode a text that does not offer any information on how the verdict was issued, which gives him a valuable opportunity to construct his argument in a convincing and rhetorically effective way.

Themistius, *Oration* 30.348c–349a

Themistius refers to the story of the poetic contest between Homer and Hesiod at the beginning of his *Oration* 30, known by the title θέσις εἰ γεωργητέον (*On whether one should engage in farming*). This work belongs to the group of Themistius' so-called private orations, a miscellaneous group of rhetorical pieces.[85] It is a brief but enthusiastic text in praise of agriculture, described as the primary activity for human beings from which all good things derive.[86]

---

[85] The modern numbering of Themistius' orations and the division of his corpus in two parts (private and public speeches) have no manuscript support. They were first proposed in Harduinus' edition of Themistius in 1684. See Penella 2000: 6–9 for a detailed history and discussion of the modern classification of the speeches in the different editions.

[86] Many reasons have been proposed for Themistius' passionate encomium of agricultural activities: it may have autobiographical significance; it may be due to sociopolitical purposes such as encouraging agricultural productivity; or it may be related to a specific historical event such as Theodosius' Visigothic treaty of 382 AD

Because of the topic and the rhetorical aim of this *Oration*, Themistius can conveniently include the story of the triumph of Hesiod, the poet of agriculture, over Homer: Hesiod's victory is here a matter of celebration rather than of controversy or disappointment. That such an episode was considered particularly useful by Themistius is indicated by the fact that he puts it at the very beginning of the work, after a few introductory words that underline how for Hesiod, just as much as for Themistius himself, agriculture and virtue are one and the same thing.

> δεῖ δὲ ἤδη καὶ ἡμᾶς Ἡσιόδῳ καὶ Μούσαις ἀκολουθοῦντας ἐπιδεῖξαι διὰ πλειόνων ὡς ἄρα οὐ μάτην Ἡσίοδος σοφὸς ἐνομίσθη, ἀλλ' εἰς τοσοῦτον εὐκλείας διὰ τοὺς εἰς γεωργίαν λόγους προῆλθεν, ὥστε καὶ Ὁμήρῳ περὶ σοφίας καὶ μουσικῆς ἐν ταφαῖς Ἀμφιδάμαντος εἰς ἀγῶνα ἐλθὼν παρὰ τῶν κριτῶν τὸν στέφανον καὶ τὴν νίκην ἔχειν. ὁ μὲν γὰρ πολέμους καὶ μάχας καὶ τὸν συνασπισμὸν τοῖν Αἰάντοιν καὶ ἄλλα τοιαῦτα προσῇδεν, ὁ δὲ γῆς τε ὕμνησεν ἔργα καὶ ἡμέρας, ἐν αἷς τὰ ἔργα βελτίω γίνεται· καὶ διὰ ταῦτα πᾶσι τοῖς κριταῖς κρατεῖ. (ed. Downey)

But now it is necessary that we, being followers of Hesiod and the Muses, show at length that Hesiod is not without reason thought to be wise, but he gained so much fame through his verses on agriculture, that he won the crown and the victory from the judges against Homer, when he participated in a contest in wisdom and poetry at Amphidamas' funeral. For one sang of wars and battles and the two Ajaxes fighting close and other such things, the other of the works of the earth and the days in which the works are best done. And for this reason, he was considered the best by all the judges.

For Themistius, agriculture is virtue, and one should be learned from the other. The setting of the victory of the wise Hesiod is presented accordingly as a contest 'in wisdom and poetry' (περὶ σοφίας καὶ μουσικῆς). Of all the various types of challenges in which Homer and Hesiod are said to engage in the sources, then, Themistius chooses the one that best emphasises the traditional image of Hesiod as the poet of agriculture, in contrast to that of Homer as the poet of war: the recitation of the two finest passages from the poets' works. As in most versions of the contest that include this scene, Homer 'sang of wars and battles and the two Ajaxes fighting close and other such things' (πολέμους καὶ μάχας καὶ τὸν συνασπισμὸν τοῖν Αἰάντοιν καὶ ἄλλα τοιαῦτα προσῇδεν).[87] Hesiod is said to sing, more generically, 'of the

---

    that secured peace for the farmers of the Balkans. Discussion in Maisano 1995: 935 and Penella 2000: 33–4.

87 From what Themistius says here, it is not possible to understand just how many verses he thought were included in Homer's performance. If Penella 2000: 184

works of the earth and the days in which the works are best done' (ὁ δὲ γῆς τε ὕμνησεν ἔργα καὶ ἡμέρας, ἐν αἷς τὰ ἔργα βελτίω γίνεται), apparently referring not to a specific passage of the *Works and Days* but to the entire work – and at the same time underlining the positive and constructive effects of Hesiod's poetry on human life (a view that is echoed in the *Oration* as a whole), as opposed to the destructive results of 'war and battles', the topic of Homer's song.

Due to the importance that this work gives to agriculture and to Hesiod as its poet *par excellence*, Themistius cannot but express agreement with the outcome of the competition that favoured Hesiod. To emphasise the success of Hesiod's performance as far as possible, Themistius claims that the poet 'was considered the best by all the judges' (πᾶσι τοῖς κριταῖς κρατεῖ): unlike in other versions, there is no need to single out the figure of an individual judge on whom to blame a questionable verdict, or a group of people who do not have the necessary skills to judge such a competition. On the contrary, thanks to the impact of his songs on human life, Hesiod wins unanimously and deservedly.

There is another passage from Themistius' works that describes the same sharp opposition between Homer and Hesiod on the basis of the subject matter of their poems: *Or.* 15.184c–d. In that passage there is no explicit reference to the poetic contest between Homer and Hesiod, but, interestingly, Themistius seems to be using the same elements featuring in the contest story. Specifically, the description of the poets' works echoes the two passages that they traditionally perform when competing against each other:

> Ἡσιόδῳ δὲ τῷ Ἀσκραίῳ δόρατα μὲν φρίττοντα καὶ ἀσπίδας συνερειδούσας καὶ ὀλλύντας τε καὶ ὀλλυμένους καὶ αἵματι ῥεομένην τὴν γῆν οὐκ ἐδόκει εἰσενεγκεῖν εἰς τὴν ποίησιν, τὰ δὲ χαμαίζηλα ταῦτα καὶ εἰρηνικὰ καὶ ἀσπαστότερα τοῖς ἀνθρώποις, ὁπηνίκα μὲν χρὴ ἀροῦν, ὁπηνίκα δὲ σπείρειν, ὁπηνίκα δὲ κλᾶν τὰς ἀμπέλους καὶ ἡλίκον τὸν ἄξονα τέμνειν καὶ ἡλίκην σφῦραν. καὶ ταῦτα ᾄδοντι αὐτῷ ἐκ τοῦ Ἑλικῶνος τὰ ὦτα ὑπεῖχον οἱ Ἕλληνες καὶ ἐκηλοῦντο καὶ ᾤοντο ὠφελίμους οὐχ ἧττον εἶναι τὰς Ἡσιόδου νουθεσίας ἢ τὰς Ὁμήρου ἀνδροκτασίας.

> It did not seem appropriate to Hesiod the Ascrean to bring into his poetry bristling spears, shields overlapping with each other, people killing and killed by other people, and the earth covered in blood – but rather the following topics that are humble, peaceful, and more friendly for men:

---

is right in identifying the 'συνασπισμὸν τοῖν Αἰάντοιν' with *Il.* 13.701 ff., rather than *Il.* 13.126 ff. (the passage most commonly presented as Homer's finest, with mention of the two Ajaxes), we would have yet another piece of evidence for the fluidity of this tradition. Unfortunately, though, Penella does not investigate further this issue at p. 184 n. 3, where he mentions the *Certamen*.

when it is necessary to plough, when to sow, when to cut the vines, how large to cut an axle, and how a hammer. And the Greeks listened to him singing these things from Helicon, and were charmed, and thought that Hesiod's admonitions were not less beneficial than Homer's slaughters.

What Hesiod is said *not* to sing (and is rather attributed to Homer, mentioned in the previous lines) paraphrases *Il.* 13.130–1 (*Cert.* 195–6):

φράξαντες δόρυ δουρί, σάκος σάκει προθελύμνῳ·
ἀσπὶς ἄρ' ἀσπίδ' ἔρειδε, κόρυς κόρυν, ἀνέρα δ' ἀνήρ.

joining spear close to spear, shield to overlapping shield; shield pushed on shield, helmet on helmet, man on man.

The expression δόρατα μὲν φρίττοντα used by Themistius recalls the Homeric φράξαντες δόρυ δουρί, while ἀσπίδας συνερειδούσας reads as a prose version of ἀσπὶς ἄρ' ἀσπίδ' ἔρειδε, and ὀλλύντας τε καὶ ὀλλυμένους has the same meaning as ἔρειδε ἀνέρα δ' ἀνήρ. Here, therefore, we clearly have a precise verbal correspondence between the story of the contest – and the Homeric passage often featured in it – and its rhetorical reworking in Themistius. When Themistius lists the topics that interested Hesiod, the references to his finest passage (*Op.* 383–92) seem less pointed, but two main features of his poetry are emphasised in both texts: Hesiod teaches the main agricultural activities, and the right moment for each. This passage does not mention the story of the contest between Homer and Hesiod explicitly, but the fact that the author does use features of it when drawing an opposition between Homer and Hesiod testifies to the great resonance of this story in antiquity.[88]

Libanius, *Defence of Socrates* 65–6

The next account of the story of the contest is part of another rhetorical piece, the *Defence of Socrates* by Libanius. This *Defence* is the longer and more elaborate of the two extant Socratic pieces by Libanius: in this work, an anonymous advocate defends Socrates from the two traditional charges

---

[88] This is shown also by Maximus of Tyre (second century AD), who set up a contrast between Homer and Hesiod in similar terms, again without referring to the story of their contest. In his *Dissertation* 13, in which he argues that a farmer is more useful to the city than a soldier, and in *Dissertation* 14, in which he argues for the opposite thesis, Maximus quotes from Homer and Hesiod to support the superiority of agriculture and that of war respectively; and at the end of *Dissertation* 14, in order to describe the activities of 'he who is wise in agriculture', he quotes *Op.* 383–4, the verses that start Hesiod's finest passage in, e.g., the *Certamen* (180–1).

brought against him: corruption of the young and impiety.[89] Part of the accusation is based on the fact that Socrates criticised poets such as Hesiod, Theognis, Homer and Pindar, who had always been respected in Athens. In order to show that 'we are perfectly free' to do so, Libanius introduces the poetic competition of Homer and Hesiod as an example.[90]

> (65) ἠγωνίσατό ποτε Ὁμήρῳ Ἡσίοδος καὶ τοῦτο αὐτὸς Ἡσίοδος ἐν ἐπιγράμματι διδάσκει φιλοτιμούμενος καὶ λέγων νενικηκέναι τὸν Ὅμηρον. οὐκοῦν εἰ μὲν ἀπάσαις Ἡσίοδος ἐνίκα, πάντες δήπου ληρεῖν ἡγοῦντο τὸν Ὅμηρον· εἰ δ' οἱ μὲν τοῦτον ἡγοῦντο βελτίω, παρὰ δὲ τοῖς πλείοσιν εὐδοκίμει τὰ τοῦ Ἡσιόδου, τῶν οὐκ ἐπαινούντων ἑκάτερος ἐτετυχήκει καὶ δῆλον ὡς τοῦ συλλόγου διαλυθέντος οἱ μὲν τούτῳ θέμενοι τὸν Ἡσίοδον ἐκάκιζον, οἱ δὲ ἐκείνῳ τοῦτον. αὐτοῖς γὰρ οὕτω γε ἐβοήθουν ἄν. (66) εἶπεν οὖν τις τῶν τὰς ἱστορίας συντεθεικότων, ὅτι δίκην τις ἔδωκεν ἐν Χαλκίδι διὰ τὸν Ἡσιόδου ψόγον ἢ τὸν Ὁμήρου; οὐδείς. πῶς οὖν οὐ δεινὸν τοῖς μὲν πάλαι τῶν ποιητῶν αὐτῶν λεγόντων ἀκηκοόσιν ἐξεῖναί τι καὶ ἐπιτιμῆσαι, τῶν δ' ὕστερον τοὺς οὐ χρηστόν <τι> παρ' ἐκείνοις ὁρῶντας ἢ σιγᾶν ἢ ἀπολωλέναι; (ed. Förster)

> (65) Once Hesiod competed against Homer, and Hesiod himself relates this with pride in an epigram, and says that he defeated Homer. So then, if Hesiod won with the support of all the people, presumably everyone thought Homer was talking nonsense; but if some people thought that he was the best, and Hesiod's verses were held in esteem among the majority, then each had some people who did not praise him, and it is clear that, after the meeting had been dissolved, those people who had supported Homer abused Hesiod's supporters, and those who had supported Hesiod abused Homer's supporters. So they would have defended themselves. (66) Now, has any of those who related the events said that anyone in Chalcis has punished the blame given to Hesiod, or to Homer? Nobody. How, then, is it not incongruous that those who in ancient times attended the performances of the poets themselves were allowed to criticise, and those who in later times see something not valuable in the poets' work either have to keep silent or will be put to death?

Like Themistius, Libanius uses the story of the contest as an *exemplum* that contributes to the development of his argument, but the argument itself is different: Libanius argues that criticising poets is not, and never has been, against the law. Indeed, he explains, no historian has ever written of any

---

89 The second Socratic work is a shorter declamation in which Socrates' accusers propose that, whilst in prison, he should be forbidden to speak as an additional punishment. Translation in Russell 1996: 58–66.
90 Cf. parr. 62–3.

punishments inflicted on those members of the audience who, during the competition in Chalcis, found fault with either poet's performance. In this account, Libanius mentions, as the source for the story of the contest, an epigram in which Hesiod proclaims his victory against Homer: the reference must be to the epigram allegedly inscribed on the tripod that Hesiod won at the contest and dedicated to the Muses, although the text is not quoted.[91] The epigram gives only very basic information about the contest: the name of the two participants, the location and the winner. Accordingly, Libanius does not add any further details to the narrative.

If we ask what reasons might be behind the choice of naming merely the epigram as a witness of the contest, there are at least two possible answers. One is that the epigram was the only source known to Libanius: we know that this short text had independent circulation, and was transmitted in school books.[92] It may, therefore, have been in a similar context that Libanius learned of the story of the contest between Homer and Hesiod. However, Libanius' decision to mention the epigram alone may also reflect the fact that he thought this text to be a particularly suitable rhetorical ally: its scarcity of details allows him to build up his argument in the way that best suits him. The epigram fails to mention details that are vital to Libanius' argument, namely how Hesiod was proclaimed the winner, and how the public reacted to the performances and to the verdict. Libanius, therefore, endeavours to present all the possible options. Hesiod, he explains, must have been supported either by everyone, or by the majority of the people. The first option, however, implies that everyone thought Homer talked nonsense. Therefore, he goes on, some must have favoured Hesiod and some Homer, and conversely both poets found some who did not praise them. Consequently, criticising the poets must be an ancient habit and must have happened on that occasion already. Since there is no evidence that this was considered a crime at that time, there is no reason why it should be so for Socrates. In conclusion, by choosing the epigram as his source, and taking its silence as an opportunity to develop a sophisticated argument as he does, Libanius makes his point in a way that displays his rhetorical skills effectively: his source did not provide any information concerning the specific aspect of the story that interested him, yet he has successfully turned it into a compelling piece of evidence.

---

91 On the tripod and the epigram see Part 1, 'Hesiod', and Part 4, 210–14n.
92 See *AP* 7.53 and P.Freib. 1.1b (on which see Part 2).

5. The Byzantine age: John Tzetzes and Eustathius

Scholars of the Byzantine age took a keen interest in the story of the contest between Homer and Hesiod – and, more generally, in the biographies of the two poets. Discussions of the contest tradition are found in exegetical works on Homeric and Hesiodic poetry: Tzetzes' *Commentary on Hesiod's Works and Days* and Eustathius' *Commentary on the Iliad* (twelfth century AD). Tzetzes and Eustathius mention the story as part of the biographical introductions on Hesiod and Homer at the beginning of their commentaries. Tzetzes also mentions it in several points of his commentary, most notably on *Op.* 652. The outcome of the competition causes some embarrassment for our authors: Eustathius makes only a cursory reference to the story and invites readers interested in the topic to find more information in other works; Tzetzes makes more impassioned comments, and also claims that the two poets were not contemporaries in order to suggest that Hesiod in fact competed with a later Homer, not with the poet of the *Iliad*.

The present analysis shows that Tzetzes drew on the works of earlier commentaries on *Works and Days*, including and especially those by Plutarch and Proclus, which he knew and used extensively. Furthermore, an understanding of the connections existing between scholars in antiquity sheds further light on the issue of the authorship of the *Life of Hesiod*, which is disputed, in the manuscripts and in modern scholarship, between Proclus and Tzetzes. Finally, like his predecessors, Tzetzes exported the results of his scholarly activity to other works, as shown by his dismissal of the contest on the ground of its chronological implausibility in his *Allegories of the Iliad*.

John Tzetzes

John Tzetzes refers several times to the story of the poetic competition between Homer and Hesiod in his works: *Commentary* on Hesiod's *Works and Days* 268ter, 274bis, 280bis, 652; *Life of Hesiod*, prolegomenon to his *Commentary* 123–42 Colonna; *Allegories of the Iliad* Prol. 89–92 Boissonade. Tzetzes denies that the contest ever took place, on the grounds that the two poets were not contemporaries. As a commentator on Hesiod's *Works and Days*, when developing his approach to this episode, he was certainly influenced by the earlier exegetical tradition (i.e., Plutarch's and Proclus' commentaries), where the contest tradition was already denied (see Part 1, 'Ancient scholarship'). Tzetzes' comment on *Op.* 652 is particularly informative in this respect:

5. The Byzantine age: John Tzetzes and Eustathius

(652) ΑΜΦΙΔΑΜΑΝΤΟΣ. Οὗτος ὁ Ἀμφιδάμας Εὐβοίας ὢν βασιλεὺς πρὸς Ἐρετριέας ναυμαχῶν ἀνηρέθη· καὶ οἱ παῖδες αὐτοῦ ἐπ' αὐτῷ προεκήρυξαν ἀγῶνας παντοίους, καὶ ἆθλα, ὅπερ τὸ ΠΡΟΠΕΦΡΑΔΜΕΝΑ δηλοῖ, ἤγουν προκεκηρυγμένα. Οὖ νικήσας Ἡσίοδος, ὡς ληροῦσι, τὸν ἡμίθεον Ὅμηρον, τρίποδα ἔλαβε, καὶ ταῖς Ἑλικωνίτισι Μούσαις ἀνέθετο, ὅπου πρῶτος ἐπαιδεύετο· ἢ καὶ κόπῳ καὶ μόχθῳ ἀνυπερβλήτῳ χρησάμενος ἐμεμαθήκει, ἅπερ μεμάθηκεν. Ὅτι δὲ ὕστερος ἦν Ἡσίοδος τοῦ παλαιοῦ Ὁμήρου, καὶ πρότερον εἰρήκειν, κἂν καὶ ὁ Ἡρόδοτος, ὁ ἐν πολλοῖς ἐμοὶ ἐλεγχθεὶς ὡς ψευδηγορῶν, ὁμοχρόνους τούτους φησί. Καὶ εἰ ὁμόχρονος ἦν Ἡσίοδος, ὁ θεῖος ἐκεῖνος ἀνὴρ ἡττήθη ἂν εὖ οἶδα, καὶ οὐκ ἐνδοιάζων φημί. Αἰεὶ γὰρ κατὰ τοῦτον τὰ χερείονα νικᾷ. (ed. Gaisford)

'Of Amphidamas': this Amphidamas, who was the king of Euboea, was killed in a naval battle against the Eretrians; and his sons announced contests and funeral games of all sorts for him, as shown by ΠΡΟΠΕΦΡΑΔΜΕΝΑ, that is, 'announced'. And there, as they say (but it is nonsense), Hesiod defeated the demigod Homer, carried away a tripod, and dedicated it to the Heliconian Muses, where he was first trained in the poetic art – or rather, with unsurpassed trouble and distress he had learned what he used to know. I have already said that Hesiod was later than the Homer who lived in the ancient past, although even Herodotus, who has been said to be a liar in many works of mine, says that they were contemporaries. And if Hesiod had been contemporary of Homer, I know well that that divine man would have been defeated, and I am not in doubt when I say that. For, according to him, always 'the worse wins'.

Tzetzes' text draws explicitly on Plutarch's/Proclus' scholium on *Op.* 650–62. In addition to the (already mentioned) common rejection of the story, both passages give the same biographical information on Amphidamas, king of Euboea, who died in a naval battle against the Eretrians, and explain that his sons organised funeral games for him. Moreover, Hesiod's victory is mentioned and denied in the two scholia in similar terms: Plutarch, according to Proclus, says that all this information about the contest is ληρώδη, 'nonsense'; Tzetzes too claims that those who created this story ληροῦσι, that is, talked nonsense.

Tzetzes' use of the earlier exegetical material is also confirmed by a comparison with other extant scholia.[93] A scholium to *Op.* 655 runs:

---

93 The scholia mentioned here are fragments of ancient commentaries transmitted in the manuscripts together with fragments from Plutarch and Proclus in the scholia vetera (Pertusi 1955; Marzillo 2010). Thus, Tzetzes probably read Proclus' commentary in a form similar to the one we know: marginal comments transmitted alongside the text of Hesiod, and drawn from various commentaries.

ΤΑ ΔΕ ΠΡΟΠΕΦΡΑΔΜΕΝΑ. Τὰ ἆθλα, τῶν ἀγωνιζομένων δηλονότι, προκεκηρυγμένα ἦσαν.

'The (prizes) announced': the prizes – those for the competitors, obviously – had been announced in advance.

Tzetzes seems to insert this comment into his own work by saying: ὅπερ τὸ ΠΡΟΠΕΦΡΑΔΜΕΝΑ δηλοῖ, ἤγουν προκεκηρυγμένα ('as shown by ΠΡΟΠΕΦΡΑΔΜΕΝΑ, that is, 'announced''). Other scholia read:

(658a) ΤΟΝ Τρίποδα ἐγὼ φησὶν ἀνέθηκα εἰς τὸν τόπον, ὅπου ἐποίησάν με ἐκ ποιμένος ἀοιδὸν αἱ Μοῦσαι.
(659a) ΕΝΘΑ ΜΕ ΤΟ ΠΡΩΤΟΝ. Ἢ ἐν Χαλκίδι, ἢ ἐν ἄλλῳ τόπῳ, ὅπου πρῶτον ὑπήντησαν αὐτῷ αἱ Μοῦσαι.

(658a) I dedicated the tripod, he says, in the place where the Muses made me a bard from a shepherd.
(659a) 'where for the first time (they initiated) me': either in Chalcis or in another place, where for the first time the Muses met him.

Tzetzes seems to have borrowed the notion that Hesiod 'dedicated it (i.e., the tripod) where he was first trained in the poetic art' (ἀνέθετο, ὅπου πρῶτος ἐπαιδεύετο) precisely from these scholia. Tzetzes' original contribution, then, enables us to understand the reasons of his agreement with previous commentators about the rejection of the story: for him, Homer's poetry is better than Hesiod's. He ends with a witty reflection based on *Il.* 1.576 and claims that, had the contest ever taken place, Hesiod would have certainly defeated Homer, since Homer himself claimed that 'the worse wins'.

Other references to the contest in Tzetzes' commentary are always linked to his criticism of Hesiod's poetry, which often relates, in turn, to Proclus' criticism. The instance that deserves a closer look is found in the so-called *Vita Hesiodi,* included in the *Prolegomena.* This is the section of the text concerning the contest (123–42 Colonna):

οἱ δὲ συγχρόνους αὐτοὺς εἶναι λέγοντες ἐπὶ τῇ τελευτῇ Ἀμφιδάμαντος τοῦ βασιλέως Εὐβοίας φασὶν αὐτοὺς ἀγωνίσασθαι, καὶ νενικηκέναι Ἡσίοδον, ἀγωνοθετοῦντος καὶ κρίνοντος τὰ μέτρα Πανείδου τοῦ βασιλέως τοῦ ἀδελφοῦ Ἀμφιδάμαντος καὶ τῶν υἱῶν Ἀμφιδάμαντος Γανύκτορός τε καὶ τῶν λοιπῶν. ἐξηρωτηκέναι γὰρ αὐτοὺς πολλὰ πρὸς ἀλλήλους φασὶ δι'ἐπῶν αὐτοσχεδίων καὶ ἀποκρίνασθαι, καὶ πᾶσι τὸν Ὅμηρον τὰ πρωτεῖα λαμβάνειν· τέλος τοῦ βασιλέως Πανείδου εἰπόντος αὐτοῖς τὰ κάλλιστα τῶν ἑαυτῶν ἐπῶν ἀναλεξαμένους εἰπεῖν, Ὅμηρος μὲν ἄρχεται λέγειν τουτὶ τὸ χωρίον ἀπὸ πολλῶν ἐπῶν ἀρξάμενος ὄπισθεν·

ἀσπὶς ἄρ' ἀσπίδ' ἔρειδε, κόρυς κόρυν, ἀνέρα δ' ἀνήρ,
ψαῦον δ' ἱππόκομοι κόρυθες λαμπροῖσι φάλοισι
νευόντων· ὡς πυκνοὶ ἐφέστασαν ἀλλήλοισι,
καὶ περαιτέρω τούτων. Ἡσίοδος δὲ τοῦ·
Πληιάδων Ἀτλαγενέων ἐπιτελλομενάων
ἀπάρχεται καὶ ὁμοίως Ὁμήρῳ προβαίνει μέχρι πολλοῦ τῶν ἐπῶν. καὶ πάλιν ἐπὶ τούτοις οἱ παρεστῶτες πάντες τῶν ἐλλογίμων καὶ στρατιωτῶν τὸν Ὅμηρον ἐστεφάνουν, ὁ δὲ Πανείδης ἔκρινε νικᾶν τὸν Ἡσίοδον, ὡς εἰρήνην καὶ γεωργίαν διδάσκοντα, καὶ οὐ καθάπερ ὁ Ὅμηρος πολέμους καὶ σφάγια. ἀλλὰ ταῦτα μὲν ληρήματα τῶν νεωτέρων εἰσὶ καὶ πλάσεις τῶν πρὸς ἀλλήλους ἐρωτημάτων καὶ τῶν ἐξ Ὁμήρου παρεκβεβλημένων ἐπῶν καὶ ὑπ' ἐκείνου δῆθεν ῥηθέντων. Ὅμηρος γὰρ ὁ χρυσοῦς, ὡς ἐγῷμαι, μᾶλλον δὲ ἀκριβεστάτως ἐπίσταμαι, πολύ τε παλαιότερος Ἡσιόδου ὑπῆρχε.

Those who say that they were contemporaries say that they competed against each other upon the death of Amphidamas king of Euboea, and that Hesiod won at the contest established and judged by King Paneides, Amphidamas' brother, and Amphidamas' sons, Ganyctor and the others. They say that they exchanged many challenges and responses with each other by means of improvised verses, and Homer was in all of them ahead of the game; at the end, since King Paneides asked them to select and perform the finest of their own verses, Homer starts performing the following passage, after (performing) several of the previous verses:

> joining spear close to spear, shield to overlapping shield; shield pushed on shield, helmet on helmet, man on man, and the horsehair crests on the bright helmet-ridges touched as they were bending forward; so compact they stood against each other.

and the verses following these. Hesiod started from:

> When the Atlas-born Pleiades rise

and, like Homer, carried on with many verses. And also in this case, all those present among the well-thought-of people and soldiers wanted to crown Homer, but Paneides decided for Hesiod to win, since he taught peace and agriculture, and not wars and slaughters, like Homer. But that is all nonsense invented by more recent writers, and the challenges they exchanged, the fact that Homer excerpted these verses from his work and performed them are, in truth, all made up. For golden Homer, as I believe – no, as I know with absolute precision – was much more ancient than Hesiod.

There are several problems related to the history of the transmission of this text, and a serious lack of scholarly attention. All we can understand from the existing studies is that it was transmitted in forms of differing length, and that the attribution is disputed, in the manuscripts, between Proclus and Tzetzes.[94] However, a comparison between this piece of the text and other passages, deriving both from the same work and from Proclus' *Life of Homer*, may offer some clarification. The episode of the contest is here, as in Proclus' *Life of Homer*, connected to the discussion of the chronology of the two poets, and dismissed on the grounds that the two poets were not contemporaries. Furthermore, Proclus and Tzetzes give similar accounts of other biographical episodes, such as Homer's meeting with Creophylus,[95] and Homer's death after slipping on mud and falling on a stone.[96] Given the many points in common between Proclus' and Tzetzes' biographical narratives, and Tzetzes' extensive use of Proclus' exegetical work, it seems plausible that the confusion in the manuscripts concerning the authorship of the *Life of Hesiod* has arisen because two similar *Lives of Hesiod* existed, one by Proclus contained in the *Chrestomathy* (as testified by Photius) and one – which comprehensively draws on the Proclean one – by Tzetzes. The lost *Life of Hesiod* written by Proclus must, therefore, have been similar in content to the extant one circulating under Tzetzes' name.

Like Proclus and Plutarch, Tzetzes uses the work he has undertaken for the *Commentary* in other contexts as well. In his *Allegories of the Iliad* (Prol. 89–92 Boissonade) he claims:

Οἱ μάτην γράφειν θέλοντες ἱστορικὰ βιβλία
90   ὁμόχρονον τὸν Ὅμηρον λέγουσιν Ἡσιόδου,
ἐπὶ τῷ Ἀμφιδάμαντος τάφῳ δοκιμασθέντας.
Ἀλλ'οὗτοι μὲν ἠγνόησαν εἶναι πολλοὺς Ὁμήρους.

---

94 Gaisford 1823 included the same *Vita Hesiodi* in both Proclus' and Tzetzes' Prolegomena, and did not offer any detail on the attribution in the manuscripts. Wilamowitz 1929 (1916): 47 on this matter claims that the manuscripts provide two recensions of the text ('*duas codices praebent recensiones*'); Pertusi 1951 considered the attribution to Proclus in some manuscripts as arbitrary and reached the conclusion that Tzetzes was the original author of this text, which was later shortened, inserted in the manuscripts of the scholia and wrongly attributed to Proclus. Following Pertusi's studies, Colonna 1953 attempted to establish the original text of Tzetzes' *Vita Hesiodi*. The results of these studies are reflected in Marzillo's recent edition of Proclus' commentary (Marzillo 2010), which does not include the *Vita Hesiodi*. A new critical edition, in preparation by Marta Cardin, will offer a much-needed reassessment of the textual tradition of Tzetzes' scholia ('Ἰωάννου γραμματικοῦ τοῦ Τζέτζου ἐξήγησις τῆς βίβλου τῶν Ἔργων καὶ ἡμερῶν Ἡσιόδου, introduzione e testo critico a cura di Marta Cardin').
95 Procl. *Vit. Hom.* 5; Tz. *Alleg.* Prol. 119; Tz. *H.* 13. 658. Cf. also *Cert.* 321–3.
96 Procl. *Vit. Hom.* 5; Tz. *Alleg.* Prol. 131–2; Tz. *H.* 13.664–5. Cf. also *Cert.* 323–38. This account is transmitted also in P.Mich. 2754 – for its relationship to the *Certamen* see Part 2.

Those who want to write futile historical books say that Homer was a contemporary of Hesiod, and that they competed at Amphidamas' funeral. But those people did not know that there are many Homers.

Eustathius, *Commentary on Homer's Iliad* (I 6, 28–7, 1 van der Valk)

Eustathius discusses the contest between Homer and Hesiod in an account of the life of Homer that forms part of the introduction to his *Commentary on Homer's Iliad*. In this section, he presents Homer's poetry as a source of wisdom and knowledge, and claims that all writers receive inspiration from Homer just as all rivers receive their water from the ocean.[97]

The discussion of the life of Homer is included in Eustathius's work only as a brief introduction to Homer's poetry rather than as the focus of his attention in its own right. When approaching the topic, Eustathius claims that he is not embarking on new research; instead, he is collecting the results of the studies that had been conducted by his predecessors, and had crystallised into traditional forms by his time. Eustathius begins with the standard remark that, despite the importance of Homer's poetry, nothing certain is known about his life because there is no biographical information in his works; as a result of this, the poet is claimed as a fellow citizen by every city. As in many other biographies, a list of the contender cities follows, with a few comments. After mentioning the names of poets allegedly older than Homer, the poet's blindness, change of name, and works, Eustathius comments on the tradition of the poetic competition between Homer and Hesiod:

εἰ δὲ καὶ ἤρισεν Ὅμηρος Ἡσιόδῳ τῷ Ἀσκραίῳ καὶ ἡττήθη, ὅπερ ὄκνος τοῖς Ὁμηρίδαις καὶ λέγειν, ζητητέον ἐν τοῖς εἰς τοῦτο γράψασιν, ἐν οἷς ἔκκεινται καὶ τὰ ῥητὰ τῆς ἔριδος.

Whether or not Homer also competed against Hesiod the Ascraean and was defeated, which the Homeridae hesitate even to mention, is to be researched in the works that have been written about this topic, in which one can also read the verses exchanged during the competition.

As with the other biographical anecdotes, Eustathius offers scarce detail on the story of the contest, and invites the reader to search for more information on it in other works. Similarly, he does not offer his own opinion on the episode, although his positive attitude towards Homer would probably suggest that, like the Homeridae, he must have hesitated to pronounce. Eustathius' mention of the Homeridae seems to confirm the idea, advanced by

---

97 On this metaphor see Cesaretti 1991: 135–6; 180–1; 213–15.

recent scholars, that they had an active role in the transmission, and perhaps selection, of Homeric biographical material – although, given our lack of information on Eustathius' knowledge on the topic, he may have used their name as a general reference to Homer's admirers and the keepers of his reputation.[98]

Perhaps the most interesting detail in this passage is the fact that the author encourages his readers to find information on the contest ἐν τοῖς εἰς τοῦτο γράψασιν ('in the works that have been written about this topic'). Eustathius elsewhere uses εἰς with the title of a work in the accusative to refer to line-by-line commentaries,[99] and here, therefore, he seems to be pointing to the existence of works on the story of the contest of Homer and Hesiod accompanied by detailed exegetical notes, arguably for use in school environments, rather than generically referring to works about that story. The phrase ἐν οἷς ἔκκεινται καὶ τὰ ῥητὰ τῆς ἔριδος ('in which one can also read the verses exchanged during the competition'), then, suggests that, although we have only one manuscript transmitting the *Certamen* and reference to the so-called finest passages in a few literary works, the verses that the two poets exchanged circulated more widely right into the Middle Ages.

---

98 On the Homeridae see Part 4, 13–15n.
99 *Il.* I 3, 34; I 46, 26; I 80, 14; I 94, 22.

Part 2: Textual tradition

Part 2 offers the first comprehensive and up-to-date study of the extant manuscript witnesses for the *Certamen*. By analysing each witness individually, the present study identifies the main features of the textual tradition through which the *Certamen* was transmitted.[100]

The study of the only manuscript transmitting the text in its entirety (MS Florence, Biblioteca Medicea Laurenziana Plut. 56.1, henceforth **L**) is followed by the first edition of a new manuscript witness of the text: unpublished notes by the Renaissance scholar Marcus Musurus, contained in one of his personal manuscripts (MS Vienna, Österreichische Nationalbibliothek, Phil. gr. 187, **M**), are here identified as extracts from the *Certamen*. Five papyrus fragments preserve sections of texts that can be variously related to the *Certamen*: three of them testify to works that can be seen as the literary sources of it and are attributed to Alcidamas (P.Petr. I 25 (1), P.Mich. inv. 2754, P.Ath.Soc.Pap. inv. M2); the other two papyri transmit some of the epigrammatic material used in the *Certamen* (P.Freib. 1.1 b and P.Duk. inv. 665). In the case of P.Petr. I 25 (1) and P.Mich. inv. 2754, I propose new editions of the text. In the other three cases, making a new edition was not possible or not necessary: there is no workable image of P.Ath.Soc.Pap. inv. M2 available in the public domain or for purchase; only two lines of the text of P.Freib. 1.1 b are relevant here, and they do not contain any textual problems; P.Duk. inv. 665, finally, was published for the first time while this study was in progress.

From the context of transmission of the *Certamen* in manuscript **L** and some features of the papyri, it emerges that the story of the contest between Homer and Hesiod was probably taught in schools and used for rhetorical exercises, and thereby made its way into several literary works. The fact itself that it was considered as material of such sort indicates a somewhat innate susceptibility to adaptation, as suggested in Part 1. By comparing the texts of the papyri with the corresponding passages of the *Certamen*, moreover, we can see that a tendency to compress and alter emerges as a characteristic feature of the textual transmission of this material.

This invites reflection on the practice of textual criticism on this material. Undoubtedly the contribution of the papyri is often useful to our understanding of the text transmitted in **L** and vice-versa; but ultimately the *Certamen* is the product of conscious and purposeful acts of adaptation, and contains material that is itself fluid and suitable for alterations. Each case

---

100 Some preliminary remarks in Bassino 2012.

of divergence between the textual witnesses should therefore be considered individually.

1. Manuscripts

Florence, Biblioteca Medicea Laurenziana, Plut. 56.1

This manuscript (**L**) was bought and brought from Crete to Florence in 1492 by Janus Lascaris on behalf of Lorenzo de' Medici, where it became part of the Medicean Library.[101] Among the documents attesting the purchase of manuscripts by Lascaris, one mentions a manuscript containing *Polienus de stratagematibus et Polux in uno volumine*: this volume is to be identified with **L**.[102] One of its readers was Angelo Poliziano,[103] and it was also used by Giovanni Pico della Mirandola.[104] Henricus Stephanus copied it in the first half of the sixteenth century (MS Leiden, University Library, Vossianus gr. qu. 18, **S**), and in 1573 he published some material from **L** in a miscellaneous book: that was the *editio princeps* of the *Certamen*.[105] After Stephanus, traces of the manuscript seem to have been lost, and Westermann stated that the only extant manuscript of the text, from which Stephanus had made his *editio princeps*, was a manuscript held in Paris, rather than in Florence.[106]

---

101 URL: http://opac.bml.firenze.sbn.it/Manuscript.htm?Segnatura=Plut.56.1. Fryde 1996 is a recent and exhaustive summary of the known information about the manuscript; see esp. p. 784, with cross-references therein. See also Daneloni/ Martinelli 1994: 311–12. Images are available from the URL above.

102 Piccolomini 1874 publishes the documents which attest to Lascaris' trips to Greece. See also Desmed 1974: 316 n. 20; Fryde 1983: 223 n. 11 and 1996: 127; Rubinstein 1990: 20 n. 38; Gentile 1997: 490 and n. 85; Cameron 2004: 336; Pagliaroli 2004: 218 n. 1 (with further bibliography); Daneloni 2005: 185.

103 The manuscript even seems to have been found in Poliziano's scriptorium after his death (Daneloni/Martinelli 1994: 311). Poliziano mentions the story of the contest between Homer and Hesiod in his *Silvae* (*Nutricia*, 388–90) published in 1486, but he cannot have been influenced by the *Certamen*, since **L** reached Florence only in 1492. Poliziano was interested in the text of the *Paradoxographus Florentinus* (Daneloni/Martinelli 1994: 311–12; Fryde 1996: 394 and 729–30) and of Pollux (Fryde 1996: 127 and 382). For Poliziano and this manuscript more generally, see also Desmed 1974: 316 n. 20; Bausi 1996: 203; Harsting 2001: 16 n. 17; Daneloni 2005: 185–9.

104 Gentile 1997: 490 with n. 85.

105 The full title of the publication is *Homeri et Hesiodi Certamen. Matronis et aliorum parodiae. Homericorum heroum epitaphia*. Digital images of the book are available at the following URL: http://www.e-rara.ch/gep_g/content/pageview/1777967.

106 Westermann 1845: vii: 'Hesiodi et Homeri certamen [...] ex unico qui restat, ut videtur, libro Parisino edidit Henr. Stephanus Paris. 1573 [...]'.

The manuscript was rediscovered in 1864 in Florence by Rose,[107] and it is only in 1871 that the text of the *Certamen* was edited again, for the first time after Stephanus, on the basis of the text of the Florentine manuscript, inspected and collated for Nietzsche by Rohde.[108]

L is a paper codex made up of 292 pages, written by several hands and dated to the twelfth to fourteenth century AD.[109] The codex contains mainly rhetorical works and seems to have been used as a school book.[110] The opening pages are lost and the title of the first work is missing. The *Certamen* is copied at 15*v*–19*r*, by the first identifiable hand of the book. It belongs to a group of pages running from 1–83*v*, which constitute the first of four codicological units which make up the book.[111]

This is a detailed list of the contents of the first section of the manuscript:

1*r*: excerpts from the works of Menander Rhetor.
11*r*: a series of anonymous works among which is the *Certamen*:
11*r*: κρῆναι καὶ λίμναι καὶ πηγαὶ καὶ ποταμοὶ ὅσοι θαυμάσιά τινα ἐν ἑαυτοῖς ἔχουσι. This is a catalogue of springs, lakes and rivers which are said to be marvellous by ancient authors. Sources are often quoted. It ends with a treatise about the flooding of the Nile. The work is also known as the *Paradoxographus Florentinus*.
13*r*: γυναῖκες ἐν πολεμικοῖς συνεταὶ καὶ ἀνδρεῖαι. This text, also known by the title *De mulieribus*, contains short *exempla* of women who distinguished themselves for courage and ability in war. Here too, sources are often mentioned.
14*v*: τίνες οἶκοι ἀνάστατοι διὰ γυναῖκας ἐγένοντο. List of families ruined by a woman; the name of the family is usually accompanied by the name of the woman who destroyed it. This and the remaining texts listed below contained in 14*v*–15*v* are also known as *Anonymus Florentinus*.
14*v*: φιλάδελφοι. List of brothers who loved each other.
14*v*: φιλέταιροι. List of friends who loved each other.

---

107 Rose 1864: 1–26.
108 See also Latacz 2014: 12.
109 The different parts seem to belong to different periods: Canart 2002: 41; Cameron 2004: 336. The website of the Biblioteca Laurenziana dates the whole manuscript to 1301–1400 AD: see http://teca.bmlonline.it/TecaRicerca/showMag.jsp?RisIdr=TECA0000647661.
Russell/Wilson 1981: xli have dated the hand that copied Menander's works to the second half of the 12th century. The same period has been proposed by Rubinstein 1990: 20 n. 38; Fryde 1996: 127, 382, 409 n. 384; Cavallo 2000: 231. 13th–14th c.: Giannini 1965: 315; Desmed 1974: 316 n. 20; Daneloni/Martinelli 1994: 311–12. 14th c.: Allen 1912: 188; Rzach 1913: 234; Colonna 1959: 74.
110 Cavallo 2000: 231.
111 Daneloni/Martinelli 1994: 311.

15r: short notice on Cleobis and Biton, with no title. The pair seems to be cited as an example of people who loved their mother, which would not be out of place after examples of brothers and friends who loved each other. For this reason, Westermann supplied the title φιλομήτορες.[112]

15r: a text telling the story of the Phrygian Lityerses. Without title in the manuscript, Westermann proposed ἀσεβεῖς, as Lityerses seems to be an *exemplum* of impiety.[113] The passage includes a quotation from *Daphnis*, a lost drama by Sositheus.[114]

15r: a list of people struck by thunderbolts. Included under the heading ἀσεβεῖς in early editions, it was first distinguished from the previous list of 'impious people' by Wilamowitz, who suggested the title κεραυνωθέντες.[115]

15r: a collection of mythical *exempla* of metamorphoses brought about by the will of some gods or goddesses. Again, there is no title in the manuscript; Westermann proposed μεταμορφωθέντες.[116]

15v: the stories of Leucone, wife of Cyanippus, and Polyhymnus of Argos. L gives no title.[117]

15v: περὶ Ὁμήρου καὶ Ἡσιόδου καὶ τοῦ γένους καὶ ἀγῶνος αὐτῶν. This is our *Certamen*.

19r: ποῦ ἕκαστος τῶν Ἑλλήνων τέθαπται καὶ τί ἐπιγέγραπται ἐπὶ τῷ τάφῳ. A collection of epigrams inscribed on the tombstones of some Greek heroes.

20v: four orations by Theophylact of Bulgaria.

43r: Polemo's epitaph for Callimachus and Cynaegeirus.

52r: extracts from a commentary on Hermogenes' rhetorical writings by Gregory of Corinth.

82r: *Hypotheseis* to seven of Demosthenes' orations.

83v: a list of Demosthenes' orations.

---

112 Westermann 1843: 346. The suggestion is accepted by Cameron 2004: 338.
113 *Ibid.* (see note above).
114 *TrGF* 99 F 2–3.
115 Wilamowitz 1875: 181 n. 4. This suggestion too is accepted by Cameron 2004: 338.
116 Westermann 1843: 347. See also Cameron 2004: 338.
117 Early editions of the texts that precede the *Certamen* in L (except for Menander) are Heeren 1789; Westermann 1839: 213–23 and 1843: 345–8. Landi 1895 provided a new transcription of these texts on the basis of L. For more recent work on the *Paradoxographus Florentinus* see Öhler 1913 and esp. Giannini 1965: 315–29; on the *De Mulieribus* see Gera 1997 and also Brodersen 2010; on the *Anonymus Florentinus* see Cameron 2004: 240–2, 245, 286–303; with new edition of the text at 335–9. L was the antigraph for the other three main manuscripts transmitting these texts, two of which were copied by Michael Apostoles in Crete: Öhler 1913: 28–33; Dain 1950: 425–39; Gera 1997: 5–6; Cameron 2004: 335–6.

The rest of the manuscript contains:

84r: books 5–10 of Pollux's *Onomasticon*.
163r: an anonymous fragment on geometry.
165v: Polyaenus' *Stratagems*.
284r: another anonymous fragment, on the origin of dreams, capped by an investigation of the winds.[118]

L was a school book which in its first section contains, after excerpts from Menander's rhetorical works, a series of anonymous texts including the *Certamen*. These texts are mainly lists with little or no narrative content: they give several examples of marvellous springs, lakes and rivers; courageous women; families ruined by women; and so on. The very context of transmission suggests that the *Certamen* was, like the texts that accompany it, unlikely to be protected by a desire to preserve one authentic version; those who copied and read the text clearly envisaged adaptation to specific rhetorical aims and different narrative contexts. This may be due ultimately to the fact that our text originated, and was used, in a school environment, as a didactic piece or a rhetorical exercise. Moreover, the very nature of the biographical material may have had a role in making the text inherently adaptable to new contexts and purposes. The contribution of the papyrus witnesses will confirm these hypotheses.

The nature and purpose of the *De mulieribus* and the *Anonymus Florentinus* have recently received close scholarly attention.[119] It is therefore useful to look at these works in order to understand the editorial plan behind the section of the manuscript that contains the *Certamen*. Both the *De mulieribus* and the *Anonymus Florentinus* are sub-literary works: they were not meant to have a literary integrity of their own, but rather drew on existing literary texts. Their lack of literary ambition can be seen in a tendency to employ simple sentences and a very plain style. More specifically, Gera points out that in the *De mulieribus* the sentences are usually short, with few subordinate clauses or participles.[120] The *exempla* given in this work are all summaries, or brief encyclopaedic notices, whose contents turn out to be less elaborate than their literary sources arguably were. Similar points apply to the *Anonymus Florentinus*: Cameron remarks that the list of metamorphoses goes back to an earlier and fuller text, either a dictionary or a series of narratives.[121] We are therefore presented with texts that are collected from fuller sources, selected and then elaborated. These texts may have been used for

---

[118] The content of the manuscript is also listed in Bandini 1768: 289–94; Daneloni/Martinelli 1994: 311–12; Cameron 2004: 335–6.
[119] Gera 1997; Cameron 2004.
[120] Gera 1997: 26–8.
[121] Cameron 2004: 287.

rhetorical exercises, and may be defined as collections of 'memorable precedents to be quoted or copied when occasion arises':[122] that is, they provide readers with the necessary material to construct arguments when *exempla* of fraternal love, courageous women etc. are needed.[123]

The *Certamen* shares some of the characteristics of these texts. Already at a first glance, the dry style of its prose signals the same pronounced tendency toward concision. This is particularly evident in the agonistic section, where there is little or no description of how the competition unfolds, besides the mere exchange of verses. The verses themselves are only rarely attributed to either interlocutor. At the beginning of the section we learn that Hesiod asks the questions and Homer replies to each of them (72–4). After that, only a few words indicate changes of speaker (77, 80, 83). A similar introduction is given to another section of the contest, that containing the 'ambiguous proposition' (102–37), and the verses that follow are not attributed explicitly to either poet. The same concise approach is also evident in the second last section of the contest (esp. 161–75). Some of the papyri studied in the next pages show a more complex and ornate text, suggesting that the author of the *Certamen* adopted a similar attitude towards his sources to that of the *De mulieribus*, the *Anonymus Florentinus* and the other texts in this part of **L**: they all involve simplification, abridgment, and adaptation. The *Certamen* was copied among texts that were not 'sacrosanct literary entities',[124] and appears not to have been one itself.

Vienna, Österreichische Nationalbibliothek, Phil. gr. 187

This manuscript is a composite codex produced between 1490 and 1510, and now held in the Österreichische Nationalbibliothek in Vienna. At 48*r* (see Figure 1) it contains information on the origins of Homer, more specifically on his birthplace and his parents.[125] The author of these notes has been identified by David Speranzi in Marcus Musurus (Crete *ca*. 1470–Rome 1517), 'probably the greatest Greek Classical scholar of the Renaissance along with

---

122 This expression is borrowed from Momigliano 1993: 72.
123 Practical examples of how this might have worked are provided by Cameron 2004: 245, who compares the list of examples of families ruined by women to a similar list found in a novel, and argues that the source for that literary work must have been somewhat similar to what we find in the *Anonymus Florentinus*. Later (pp. 286–303) he suggests that the collection of metamorphoses goes back to the same source as Ovid's *Metamorphoses*.
124 Cf. West 1973: 16.
125 Information on the manuscript is available in the online catalogue of the Österreichische Nationalbibliothek at the URL http://data.onb.ac.at/rec/AL00232328. See also Hunger 1961: 295; Speranzi 2013: 370–3.

his teacher Janos Laskaris'.[126] The texts transmitted on that page, as yet unpublished, are catalogued by Hunger as 'Anthol. Pal. XIV 102. Stammbaum Thoosa-Apollon bis Homer' (i.e., the epigram on Homer given to the emperor Hadrian by the Pythia, and a genealogy listing characters from Apollo and Thoosa to Homer).[127] However, that is not a complete description of the contents of the page. The text of the epigram is preceded by two and a half lines in prose, which are not mentioned in the catalogue. Furthermore, to the best of my knowledge, there has been no attempt to identify the provenance of this material, or to analyse the possible relationships between the texts. The present study shows that the texts at 48*r* are extracts from the *Certamen*. The individuation of the origins of these materials offers a glimpse of the impact the *Certamen* had upon its arrival in the West, and of the ways in which Renaissance scholars approached and used it. More specifically, it makes Musurus the first attested reader of the *Certamen*. Furthermore, this is the earliest known case in which the Florentine manuscript was used as an antigraph for the text of the *Certamen*, thus constituting an important new chapter of the history of the transmission of our text. Apart from the copy made by Henri Estienne in preparation for his *editio princeps* of the text (**S**), this is the only extant textual witness of the *Certamen* copied from the Florentine manuscript.

Some background information on the manuscript will be useful to introduce the discussion of the notes at 48*r*. The manuscript is made up of I+147 pages and, judging from the type of texts it contains and the presence of sporadic annotations, as well as from its codicological and palaeographical characteristics, it was made for personal use and study purposes. The contents are detailed below. Attribution and dating of the individual sections are those proposed by Speranzi.[128]

---

126 The quotation is from F. Pontani 2002–2003: 175. 'Bibliografia critica' on Musurus is collected by Ferreri 2014: 75–83; on Musurus' life and works see especially Bietenholz/Deutscher 1986: 472–3; Wilson 1992: 148–56; Pagliaroli 2004; Speranzi 2013; Ferreri 2014: 33–67. See also the *Repertorium der griechischen Kopisten* I n. 265; II nn. 359, 379; III nn. 433, 454. Musurus was a major collaborator of Aldus Manutius; for Aldus' press he edited, among others, the works of Aristophanes (1498), Plato (1513), Hesychius (1514), Athenaeus (1514), and Pausanias (1516); see Ferreri 2014: 84–425. He also taught Greek at University in Padua and Venice: on his teaching activity see Ferreri 2014: 429–54. Among his own works are the *Ode to Plato*, published in 1513 in Musurus' own edition of Plato (text in Ferreri 2014: 140–6); hexameter paraphrases of the Creed and of the Hail Mary (see F. Pontani 2002–2003 and 2014); other poems and epigrams (F. M. Pontani 1973–1974 and 1978; F. Pontani 2002–2003: 176 and nn. 2 to 5 with further details and bibliography; Speranzi 2010a: 375; Cavarzeran 2014).
127 Hunger 1961: 295.
128 Proposed 'su base codicologica, testuale e grafica': see Speranzi 2013: 370–3.

I. Copied in Northern Italy at the end of the fifteenth/beginning of the sixteenth century AD by Michael Suliardus.
1r–11v: Manuel Moschopulus' *Erotemata*.

II. Copied in Florence in 1492–1494/5 by Marcus Musurus.
12r–22v: scholia to Aeschylus' *Seven Against Thebes*.
23r–30v: scholia to Aeschylus' *Persians*.
31v: anonymous short poem.
32r: anonymous on libations.

III. Copied in Florence in 1492–1494/5 by Marcus Musurus.
33r–43v: extracts from Aelian's *The Nature of Animals*.
44v–45r: notes, and *schemata* of three virtues: justice, prudence, and manly spirit (δικαιοσύνη, σωφροσύνη, ἀνδρεία).
46r–47v: anonymous treatise on plants (*Mythographi de plantis*).
48r: catalogued by Hunger as 'Anthol. Pal. XIV 102. Stammbaum Thoosa-Apollon bis Homer',[129] these texts are extracts from the *Certamen Homeri et Hesiodi*.
48v has been left blank.
49r–51r: extracts from Euripides' *Hippolytus* and *Andromache*.
52r: extracts from Polyaenus' *Stratagems*.
52v: extracts from Aristotle's *On the Soul*.
53r: extracts from Plato's *Apology of Socrates*.
54v–56v: notes, verses, and sentences in Greek, Latin, and vulgar.

IV. Copied in Carpi, Padua, or Venice in 1500–1510 by Marcus Musurus.
57r–90v: anonymous commentary on Aelius Aristides' *Panathenaic*.

V. Copied in Carpi, Padua, or Venice in 1502–1510 by Marcus Musurus.
91r–106r: Demetrius Phalereus' *On Elocution*.

VI. Copied in Florence in 1492–1494/5 by Aristobulus Apostolius and Marcus Musurus.
109v–118r: scholia to Aeschylus' *Prometheus*.

It is now time to present the text on 48r:[130]

---

129 Hunger 1961: 295.
130 This edition is based on an inspection of a digital image of the manuscript.

1. Manuscripts

Διαφωνίας πολλῆς οὔσης περὶ τῶν τοῦ Ὁμήρου γονέων καὶ πατρίδος καὶ αὐτοκράτορος Ἀδ<ρ>ιανοῦ χρήσαντος πόθεν εἴη, ἀπεφοίβασε ἡ Πυθία τάδε·

   ἄγνωστόν μ' ἔρεαι γενεὴν καὶ πατρίδα γαῖαν·
   Τηλέμαχος δὲ πατὴρ καὶ Νεστορέη Ἐπικάστη
   μήτηρ ἥ μιν ἔτικτε βροτῶν πολὺ πάνσοφον ἄνδρα.

Ἀπόλλων Θόωσα
Λίνος
Πιέρων
Οἴαγρος
Ὀρφεύς
Ὄρτης
Ἁρμονίδης
Φιλοτέρπης
Εὔφημος
Ἐπιφράδης
Μελάνωπος

Δῖος   Ἀπελλαῖος

Ἡσίοδος   Πέρσης
            Μαίων
            Μέλης
            Ὅμηρος

As there was much disagreement about Homer's parents and fatherland, and the emperor Hadrian asked the oracle about Homer's provenance, the Pythia, inspired, uttered the following:
> You ask me the forgotten descent and fatherland; Telemachus is his father and Epicaste, daughter of Nestor, the mother who bore him, most wise man among mortals.

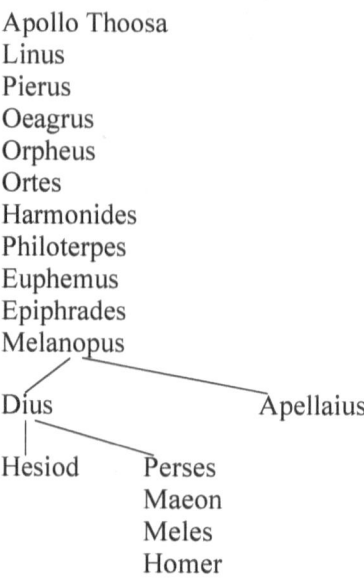

Apollo Thoosa
Linus
Pierus
Oeagrus
Orpheus
Ortes
Harmonides
Philoterpes
Euphemus
Epiphrades
Melanopus

Dius   Apellaius

Hesiod Perses
        Maeon
        Meles
        Homer

A comparison between Musurus' notes and the following passages from the *Certamen* will show immediately strong similarities and connections.

(19–20) περὶ δὲ τῶν γονέων αὐτοῦ πάλιν πολλὴ διαφωνία παρὰ πᾶσίν ἐστιν. (32–40) ὅπερ δὲ ἀκηκόαμεν ἐπὶ τοῦ θειοτάτου αὐτοκράτορος Ἀδ<ρ>ιανοῦ εἰρημένον ὑπὸ τῆς Πυθίας περὶ Ὁμήρου, ἐκθησόμεθα. τοῦ γὰρ βασιλέως πυθομένου πόθεν Ὅμηρος καὶ τίνος, ἀπεφοίβασε δι' ἑξαμέτρου τόνδε τὸν τρόπον·
ἄγνωστόν μ' ἔρεαι γενεὴν καὶ πατρίδα γαῖαν
ἀμβροσίου σειρῆνος. ἕδος δ' Ἰθακήσιός ἐστιν,
Τηλέμαχος δὲ πατὴρ καὶ Νεστορέη Ἐπικάστη
μήτηρ, ἥ μιν ἔτικτε βροτῶν πολὺ πάνσοφον ἄνδρα.

(46–53) Ἀπόλλωνός φασι καὶ Θοώσης τῆς Ποσειδῶνος γενέσθαι Λίνον, Λίνου δὲ Πίερον, Πιέρου δὲ καὶ νύμφης Μεθώνης Οἴαγρον, Οἰάγρου δὲ καὶ Καλλιόπης Ὀρφέα, Ὀρφέως δὲ Ὄρτην, τοῦ δὲ Ἁρμονίδην, τοῦ δὲ Φιλοτέρπην, τοῦ δὲ Εὔφημον, τοῦ δὲ Ἐπιφράδην, τοῦ δὲ Μελάνωπον, τούτου δὲ Δῖον καὶ Ἀπέλλαιον, Δίου δὲ καὶ Πυκιμήδης τῆς Ἀπόλλωνος θυγατρὸς Ἡσίοδον καὶ Πέρσην· Πέρσου δὲ Μαίονα, Μαίονος δὲ θυγατρὸς καὶ Μέλητος τοῦ ποταμοῦ Ὅμηρον.

(19–20) About his parents, again, there is much disagreement among all. (32–40) We shall now reveal what we have heard about Homer from the Pythia in the time of the most divine emperor Hadrian. For when the ruler enquired about Homer's provenance and parentage, she, inspired, those spoke in hexameter:
> 'You ask me the forgotten descent and fatherland of the immortal Siren. He is an Ithacan by origin, Telemachus is his father and Epicaste, daughter of Nestor, the mother who bore him, most wise man among mortals'.

(46–53) From Apollo and Thoosa, daughter of Poseidon, they say Linus was born, from Linus Pierus, from Pierus and the nymph Methone Oeagrus, from Oeagrus and Calliope Orpheus, from Orpheus Ortes, from him Harmonides, from him Philoterpes, from him Euphemus, from him Epiphrades, from him Melanopus, from this man Dius and Apellaius, from Dius and Pycimedes, daughter of Apollo, Hesiod and Perses; from Perses Maeon, from the daughter of Maeon and the river Meles Homer.

It is clear that the Viennese notes are heavily indebted to the *Certamen*; but in the process of making extracts from its contents, Musurus ultimately produced a different, unique work. For him, the text of the *Certamen* was a source from which to select, excerpt, and reorganise useful and interesting information, rather than a literary text to be copied faithfully. Musurus starts off his series of extracts with a short sentence that contextualises the poem that follows. The two brief statements in the genitive absolute (διαφωνίας πολλῆς οὔσης ... καὶ αὐτοκράτορος Ἀδ<ρ>ιανοῦ χρήσαντος) summarise the contents of the sections of the *Certamen* immediately preceding the epigram. The first subordinate clause introduces the διαφωνία ('disagreement') surrounding Homer's origins, which is clearly inspired by *Cert.* 18–9. But Musurus twists the sentence found in his source to suit his own version of the text: while the *Certamen* mentions the idea of 'disagreement' as the prelude to its list of Homer's alleged parents in the next lines (περὶ δὲ τῶν γονέων αὐτοῦ πάλιν πολλὴ διαφωνία παρὰ πᾶσίν ἐστιν), Musurus uses it to introduce an epigram on Homer's parents and birthplace (cf. *Cert.* 37: γενεὴν καὶ πατρίδα γαῖαν), and therefore applies it to both matters (διαφωνίας πολλῆς οὔσης περὶ τῶν τοῦ Ὁμήρου γονέων καὶ πατρίδος). The second genitive absolute presents the episode of the emperor Hadrian consulting the oracle told at *Cert.* 32–6, but in a much more concise and impersonal way: in the *Certamen*, this is the only episode in which the authorial voice comes out (ἀκηκόαμεν ... ἐκθησόμεθα); Musurus, more interested in the information given than in the literary features of the text, leaves no trace of it. A peculiarity of this section of Musurus' text is the misspelling Ἀδιανοῦ, which has clearly been taken wholesale from **L**. These introductory sentences are followed by the epigram. Musurus follows the text given in the *Certamen*, with all the unique variant readings that distinguish it from the version transmitted in the *Anthologia Palatina* – another piece of evidence of the derivation of these notes from the *Certamen*.[131] The only visible difference is that Musurus omits the second line transmitted in **L**. The reason is unknown, but the omission is all the more striking if we think that that line contains indication of Homer's birthplace (ἕδος δ' Ἰθακήσιός ἐστιν), a topic in which, as we have seen above, Musurus showed interest by adding 'καὶ πατρίδος' in his introductory sentence. There follows a graphic representation of the genealogy found in the *Certamen*. Musurus reports the names in the same sequence as in the manuscript **L**, and writes the names one under the other; the straight genealogical line is divided into two branches after Melanopus and Dius, the two characters said to have more than one child. One difference between the two genealogies is the form Πιέρων found in Musurus, instead of Πίερος. Another difference in the genealogy by Musurus is the sequence 'Maeon – Meles – Homer' in place of the *Certamen*'s 'Maeon – Maeon's daughter + Meles – Homer': Musurus may have misread his source, but the difference may simply be due to the fact that, as a general rule, he reports exclusively the male line of the poet's descent. There are only two exceptions to this: Thoosa, a female character who is included (perhaps because her union with the god Apollo makes her an important figure), and Poseidon, a male character who is not included (perhaps because the way he is mentioned in the *Certamen* makes it difficult to include him in the linear representation of the genealogy which Musurus may have sketched at the same time as reading the text: Ἀπόλλωνός φασι καὶ Θοώσης τῆς Ποσειδῶνος γενέσθαι Λίνον, 'from Apollo and Thoosa, daughter of Poseidon, they say Linus was born'). One last remark on the text gives an idea of how Musurus worked with his source. The form Μαίων, in the nominative, is a correction made by Musurus himself over his own writing. As in the case of the name of Hadrian, Musurus seems to have been copying the text mechanically from his source: he read the name in the genitive form given in the *Certamen* (Μαίονος – 'from the daughter of Maeon and the river Meles Homer'), and copied it straightaway, with an *omicron* instead of an *omega*, and the ending –ος above the line. Subsequently, upon realising that a nominative is needed in

---

131 At line 37: ἐρέεις γενεῆς καὶ πατρίδος αἴης in place of ἔρεαι γενεὴν καὶ πατρίδα γαῖαν; 38: Ἰθάκη τις Ὁμήρου in place of Ἰθακήσιός ἐστιν; 39: Πολυκάστη in place of Ἐπικάστη; 40: πολυπάνσοφον ἄλλων in place of πολὺ πάνσοφον ἄνδρα. See also Part 3, apparatus *ad loc.*, and Part 4, 37–40n.

order to achieve consistency with the rest of the genealogy, he changed the *omicron* into an *omega*, deleted the ending above the line, and introduced (or so it seems) an accent.

Let us now look at the events that led to Musurus' encounter with the *Certamen* in its only surviving manuscript. In 1490 Janus Lascaris embarked on a journey to the East in order to acquire manuscripts for the library of Lorenzo de' Medici and bring to Florence talented young Greek scholars – βίβλια διζέμεναι παῖδας θ'ἑλλαδικούς, to use Lascaris' own words; Musurus and the manuscript of the *Certamen* both arrived in Florence as part of this Medicean programme of acquisition of new knowledge and intellectual resources from the Greek world.[132] There is direct evidence that Musurus read the manuscript **L**, and used it for his studies upon his arrival in Florence. **L** contains three marginal annotations by the hand of Musurus; palaeographical evidence indicates that they should be ascribed to his Florentine period (1492–1495) – like the extracts he copied from it into the Viennese manuscript.[133] Furthermore, Musurus seems to have used **L** as an antigraph for the extracts of Polyaenus he copied into the same Viennese manuscript, at 52*r* – that is, in the same section that contains the extracts from the *Certamen*.[134]

Having identified the origins of the Viennese notes, it is important to put them into the wider context of Musurus' intellectual activity, in order to understand the reasons for his interests in the *Certamen*. From various sources, it is possible to reconstruct Musurus' lifelong interest in Homer and the Homeric poems: to mention but the most relevant facts, he lectured on Homer both in Padua and in Venice, and a copy of the *editio princeps* of Homer testifies to the important exegetical activity that he carried out on the Homeric poems.[135] When, as a young man, he had access to **L** in Florence and read the hitherto unknown *Certamen*, he must have been struck by the text, and decided to take notes from it. Indeed, the sections of the *Certamen* excerpted by Musurus trans-

---

132 See Pagliaroli 2004; Speranzi 2013: 43–8. The Greek quotation is part of an epigram (vv. 22–3) by Lascaris found in the MS Paris, Bibliothèque nationale de France, gr. 2248. The epigram can be dated to the 1530s and its full text can be found in A. Pontani (Meschini) 1976: 84–7.
133 Musurus' marginal annotations in **L** refer to the text of Menander (6*r*, 7*r*), and of Polyaenus (206*v*). They were identified for the first time by Speranzi 2010b: 345 n. 110; see also Speranzi 2013: 82–3 and 263.
134 Speranzi 2013: 372–3. Musurus may have used **L** also for the text of Polyaenus copied in his Marc. gr. vii. 9. For the debate see Dain 1940: 51 and Schindler 1973: 108–10.
135 He taught Homer in 1508 in Padua, and in 1514 in Venice (Ferreri 2014: 438, 449). An incunable (Vatican City, Biblioteca Apostolica Vaticana Inc. I 50) contains marginal scholia compiled by Musurus between 1503 and 1509 (F. Pontani 2005a: 481–5 *et passim*; Speranzi 2013: 258; Ferreri 2014: 558–60). Musurus also annotated the *Vita Homeri* and the Ps.-Plutarchan *De Homero* contained in the same incunable, which confirms his interest in the life, as well as the works, of Homer.

mit information on the life of Homer that is rarely, or never, attested in other texts. The episode of the emperor Hadrian asking the Pythia about Homer's origins and receiving an epigrammatic response is narrated to some length only in the *Certamen*; the only other hint to the tradition is the lemma ἐκ τῆς Πυθίας τῷ βασιλεῖ Ἀδριανῷ, that introduces the epigram in the *Anthologia Palatina*. The epigram itself was transmitted, before the discovery of the *Certamen*, only in the *Anthologia Palatina*. The rarity of the epigram and of the tradition it represents, together with Musurus' more general interest in epigrammatic texts, explain his decision to report the epigram in his personal manuscript.[136] Finally, an extensive genealogy of Homer and Hesiod was known through Proclus and the Suda lexicon, but in different forms.[137] The version that Musurus found in **L** may not have been known to the Western world before the arrival of the manuscript in Florence – an arrival that, as suggested by these notes, scholars must have greeted with keen curiosity and interest.

2. Papyri

P.Petr. I 25 (1) (P.Lond.Lit. 191)

Catalogues: London British Library Pap. 500; MP³ 0077; LDAB 178.

Editions and critical studies mentioned in the apparatus: Mahaffy 1891; Allen 1912; Rzach 1913; Milne 1927; Wilamowitz 1929 (1916); Colonna 1959; Avezzù 1982; Cavallo/Maehler 2008.

P.Petr. I 25 (1) contains, after a few introductory words, an account of the first stages of the poetic competition between Homer and Hesiod – a text that closely resembles *Cert*. 69–102. This papyrus was discovered in Gurob (Fayyum, Egypt), and comes from the cartonnage of a mummy. It was published for the first time by Mahaffy in 1891, and was acquired by the British Library, where it is now held, in 1895. It was originally part of a papyrus roll and transmits on the *recto* forty-eight lines of text on two columns. It is unanimously dated on palaeographic grounds to the second half of the third century BC.[138]

---

136 For Musurus' poetic production, see above. He taught a course on the *Anthologia Planudea* in Padua in the academic year 1505–1506 (Ferreri 2014: 430–4), and may have been involved in the Aldine edition of that work in 1503 (A. Pontani 2002a and 2002b; Ferreri 2014: 349–55).
137 See Proclus *Vit. Hom.* 4 and Suda s.v. 'Homer' 1. Details and commentary in Part 4, 45–53n.
138 For more information on the papyrus see also Mahaffy 1891: 70–3; Milne 1927: 157; Cavallo/Maehler 2008: 59, 62 (nr 30); for a palaeographical analysis see also

This papyrus shows that a text similar to the *Certamen* was in circulation at least as early as the third century BC. It also confirms that Panedes was included in the narrative among the judges already in very early stages of the tradition,[139] and features the same exchanges of verses that we find in the *Certamen*. Furthermore, it includes a couplet, quoted by Stobaeus as coming from Alcidamas' *Museum*, on the basis of which Nietzsche was able to identify Alcidamas as one of the sources for the *Certamen*.[140] Accordingly, the papyrus has been attributed to Alcidamas, thus becoming the earliest extant piece of evidence for the literary sources used by the author of the *Certamen*.

The papyrus confirms what has been argued above about the nature of the text preserved in **L**: it shows that the short and cursory sentences of the manuscript version are the product of a process of abbreviation and re-elaboration of a fuller and more sophisticated text found in a literary source. The passages indicating the changes of speaker show that the papyrus text pays more attention to literary form than the *Certamen*, where we are often left with the sole name of the new speaker, or little more than that. Furthermore, we find changes to the word order and different syntactical structures. Some of the verses are reported in, or quoted from, other literary works: in these cases, too, comparison with **L** reveals a tendency toward textual variation. Here I propose a new edition of the text:[141]

Cavallo/Maehler 2008: 1–26, esp. 9, 14, 19. An image of the papyrus is available in Mahaffy 1891 and Cavallo/Maehler 2008: 59.

139 Heldmann 1982: 45–53 suggests that the presence of King Panedes in the *Certamen* is an addition from the second century AD (see also Part 1, 'Dio Chrysostom') but the presence of the king's name at line 4 in the papyrus, underestimated by Heldmann because the text does not read exactly as in **L**, clearly proves this suggestion wrong.

140 See Part 4, 78–9n.

141 This edition is based on a direct inspection of the papyrus. Supplements to hexameter lines have been proposed on the basis of **L** merely to give a readable text (Allen's and others' choice to leave most lines unsupplemented ultimately limits the utility of the text) but the possibility that the papyrus contained different readings needs to be borne in mind. The apparatus is divided into two registers: the first collects sources that transmit some of the verses included in the *Certamen* and notes variants between them, the papyrus (Π) and the manuscript (**L**); the second collects modern editorial interventions (relevant differences in reading, supplements).

1   ...τὸ]ν τρόπ[ον τοῦτο]γ·   θ[ωσι τράπεζαι σίτου καὶ κρειῶν, μέ-
        ...τοῦ δὲ ἀγῶνο]ς ἁπάντων   θυ δ'ἐ[κ κρητῆρος ἀφύσσων] οἰν[ο-   25
                    ]των κριτῶν   χό-
        ...Π]ανήδου προε-   ος φορέηι[σι]καὶ ἐγχε[ίηι δεπάεσσιν
5   ]παρελθόν-   τοῦτο <τί> μοι κάλλιστ[ον ἐνὶ φρεσὶ
        τα....φασὶν μὲν τὸν] Ἡσίοδον ἐρω-   φαί-
        τῆσαι τούσδε τοὺς στίχου]ς· υἱὲ   νεται εἶναι. ῥηθέν[των δὲ καὶ τού-
        Μέλητος Ὅμηρε θεῶν ἀ]πὸ μήδεα   των τῶν ἐπῶν ο[ὕτω σφοδρῶς
        εἰδώς, εἴπ' ἄγε μοι πάμπρω]τα, τί   φασὶν θαυμασθῆν[αι τοὺς στί-   30
10   φέρτατόν ἐστι βροτοῖσι]ν; τὸν   χου`ς´ ὑπὸ τῶν Ἑλλήν[ων ὥστε χρυ-
        δ' Ὅμηρον...   ἀ]ποκρί-   σοῦς αὐτοὺς προσα[γορεύσαντες
        νασθαι... τάδε τὰ ἔ]πη· ἀρ-   πρὸ τῶν δείπνων καὶ [τῶν σπον-
        χὴν μὲν μὴ φῦναι ἐ]πιχθονίοισι-   δῶν προκατεύχοντα[ι πάντες.
        ν ἄριστον, φύντα δ']ὅπως ὤκισ-   ἀχθεσθεὶς δὲ ὁ Ἡσίοδος ἐ[35
15   τα πύλας Ἀίδαο περῆσ]αι. ἐπιβα-   ἐ]πὶ τὴν ἀπορίαν τῆς ἀ[ποκρίσεως
        λόμενος δ' ὁ Ἡσίοδ]ος ἐρωτᾶι τὸ   ὥρμησεν καὶ λέγει τ[οὺς στίχους
        δεύτερον· εἴπ' ἄγε μοι καὶ τ]οῦτο θε-   τούσδε· Μοῦσ' ἄγε μοι τ[ὰ τ'ἐόντα
        οῖς ἐπιείκελ' Ὅμηρε, τί θν]ητοῖς κάλ-   τά τ'ἐσσόμενα πρό τ'ἐ[όντα
        λιστον οἴεαι ἐν φρεσὶν ε]ἶναι; ὁ δ'   τῶν μὲν μηθὲν ἄειδ[ε, σὺ δ'ἄλλης   40
                                         Ὅμη- μνῆσαι ἀοιδῆς. ὁ δ' Ὅμ[ηρος βουλό-
20   ρος ἀποκρίνεται] τοὺς στίχους   μενος λῦσαι τὴν ἀπο[ρίαν τῆς ἐ-
        [τούσδε· ὁππότ' ἂν εὐφροσύνη μὲν]   ρωτήσεως ἀποφθ[έγγεται τοὺς
        [ἔχηι κατὰ δῆμον ἅπαντα, δα]ιτυ-   στίχους τούσδε· [οὐδέποτ'ἀμφὶ
        μόνες δ'ἀνὰ δώματ' ἀκουάζ]ωνται   Διὸς τύμβον κἀν[αχήποδες ἵπ-   45
23b   [ἀοιδοῦ ἥμενοι ἑξείης, παρὰ δὲ πλή-]   ποι ἅρμα[τα συντρίψουσιν ἐρί-
                                                ζοντες [περὶ νίκης.
                                                Ὁμήρου.[

---

4 π]ανηδου Π Πανοίδης L 12–15 Thgn. 425 et 427, Stob. 4.52.22 14 ὅπως Π Thgn. Stob. ὅμως L 18–19 κάλ- / [λιστον] Π ἄριστον L 21–8 Od. 9.6–11 27–8 φαί-] / νεται Π εἴδεται L Od. 30–1 [τοὺς στί- /]χου`ς´ Π τὰ ἔπη L 40 μηθὲν Π μηδὲν L 44–7 Plu. Conv. Sept. Sap. 154a 45 τύμβον Π τύμβῳ L Plu. 46–7 ἐρίζοντες Π L ἐπειγόμενοι Plu.

1–7 τὸν] τρό[πον / τοῦτον φασὶν] ἁπάντων / κρατῆσαι] τῶν κριτῶν / ἐν ἀγῶνι, τοῦ Π] ανήδου προε- / στηκότος·] παρελθόν- / τα γὰρ τὸν] Ἡσίοδον ἐρω- / τῆσαι τὸν Ὅμη- ρον οὕτ]ως· υἱὲ Colonna τοῦ δὲ ἀγῶνος ἁπάντων τῶν ἐπισήμων ὄντων κριτῶν τῶν Χαλκιδέων μετὰ Πανήδου, πρὸς τοὺς κριτὰς πρότερον παρελθόντα φασὶν τὸν Ἡσίοδον ἐρωτῆσαι τοὺς στίχους τούσδε Avezzù 4–5 π]ανηδου προε / [... Milne Allen Rzach προε / [στηκοτος Mahaffy Allen 6–7 ἐρω- / [τῆσαι Wilamowitz ερω- / [ταιν κατα τοιαδε Mahaffy Allen Rzach 8 απο] Mahaffy Allen Rzach ἀπ]ὸ Wilamowitz 11 δ' Ὅμηρον Mahaffy δὲ Ὅμηρον Wilamowitz δὲ Ὅμηρον καλῶς Colonna 11–12 ?σοιπ / ...] η αρ Mahaffy σοιπ / ...επ]η αρ[χην Allen σοιπ / ...επ]η αρ[Rzach ἀποκρί- / νασθαι

2. Papyri

... in this way ... the contest ... all ... the judges ... Panedes, they say that Hesiod came forward and asked these lines:

> Son of Meles, Homer, you who know the counsel of the gods; come, tell me first of all, what is the best thing for mortals?

And Homer ... answered with these verses:

> Not to be born at all is the best thing for people on earth, and once born, to pass through the doors of Hades as soon as possible.

Adding another question, Hesiod asked for the second time:

> Come, tell me this, then, godlike Homer, what do you reckon in your heart to be the finest thing for mortals?

Homer replied with these lines:

> When good cheer spreads over all the people, and the guests in the house listen to a bard, sitting in rows, and nearby there are tables full of bread and meat, and drawing wine from a large bowl, the cupbearer carries it around and pours it into the beakers. This, in my heart, seems to me to be the finest thing.

And after these verses were spoken, they say that the lines were so deeply admired by the Greeks that they were called 'golden', and all people perform them before meals and libations. Hesiod, annoyed ..., turned to posing insoluble challenges and spoke these lines:

> Come, Muse, the things that are, shall be and were – sing nothing to me of those: but remember another song.

And Homer, desiring to solve the difficulty of the challenge, uttered these lines:

> Never around the tomb of Zeus will loud-hoofed horses shatter chariots, striving for victory.

Homer...

τοῦτον τὸν τρό]πον Milne Colonna **14** ἄριστον: φέριστον Wilamowitz Avezzù **15–16** ἐπιβα- / λομενος δ ο ησιοδ]ος Allen Rzach ἐπιβα- / λῶν δὲ Ἡσίοδ]ος Wilamowitz Colonna (δ' ὁ Colonna) Avezzù **17** δεύτερον Wilamowitz Colonna Avezzù δε Rzach; το]υτο θε[οις Allen **19–21** ὁ δ' Ὅμη- / ρος ἀποκρίνεται τοὺς] στίχους / [τούσδε Wilamowitz Colonna Avezzù **22** υ Mahaffy δαιτ]υ[μονες δ Allen Rzach δαιτ]ύ- Wilamowitz Colonna **23b** om. Π **25** δ'ἐ[κ κρ]ητῆρ[ος Colonna **27–8** φαί-] / νεται Wilamowitz Colonna εἶδ-] / εται Allen Rzach φαιν-] / εται Mahaffy **28** δὲ καὶ Wilamowitz **32** προσα[γορεύσαντες Rzach προσα[γορευουσι και ετι Mahaffy προσα[γορευθηναι Allen προσα[γορεύοντες Wilamowitz Colonna Avezzù **35–6** ε[? / πι την απορίαν της [ερωτησεως Mahaffy Allen Rzach ἐ[πὶ τούτοις ἐ- / πὶ ... ἀ[ποκρίσεως Wilamowitz ἐ- / πὶ ἀ[ποκρίσεως Colonna ἐπὶ τῇ Ὁμήρου εὐημερίᾳ Avezzù **38** Μοῦσ' ἄγε Wilamowitz Avezzù μουσα γε Mahaffy Allen Rzach Colonna Cavallo/Maehler **43** ἀποφθ[έγγεται Wilamowitz Colonna Avezzù αποφε[υγειν προφερει Mahaffy αποφε[τους] Allen Rzach αποφε Cavallo/Maehler **45** δυος Π **46** ποι αρμα[τα ερι] Allen **47–8** Καλῶς δὲ τοῦ] / Ὁμήρου Wilamowitz Colonna καλως δε] / ομηρου Mahaffy] / ομηρου Allen Rzach **48** κ[αὶ ἐν τούτοις Colonna [καὶ ἐν τούτοις ἀπαντήσαντος Avezzù

From the very first lines of the papyrus, despite their poor state of preservation, it is possible to identify variations of several kinds between the text on the papyrus and the text on the manuscript L. To start with, the two texts organise some of the narrative material in different ways, and present some features of the episode in altered order, or with different details. For example, the first papyrus line contains what looks like the end of an introductory statement to the effect that Hesiod won, or that the contest went, 'in this way' (1: τὸ]ν τρόπ[ον τοῦτο]ν); then, at 2–4, Panedes and the other judges make their appearance. In the *Certamen* the presentation of Panoides (as his name is spelled in L, see Part 4, 69n.) and the other judges (68–70) comes before the phrase that parallels the first line of the papyrus (71–2). Furthermore, while *Cert.* 68–9 states that 'some of the distinguished Chalcideans' were sitting as judges of the contest (ἄλλοι τέ τινες τῶν ἐπισήμων Χαλκιδέων), at 2–3 the papyrus mentions 'all ... the judges' (ἁπάντων ... κριτῶν). Despite the lacuna, the papyrus text seems to be giving a slightly different detail than L: it may be that the papyrus presents all the Chalcideans, as well as Panedes, as judges of the contest, and this would make the contest between the two poets look similar to one of the public performances of rhapsodes or orators which Alcidamas could see on display in his times.

The section of the papyrus that transmits the exchanges of challenge and response, and in particular the descriptions of the changes of speaker, is the most revealing of the manuscript's tendency to abbreviate its sources. As a general rule, the papyrus presents longer and more elaborate sentences, with only one exception: before introducing Hesiod's question, the *Certamen* adds a sentence that finds no correspondence in the papyrus and explains how the contest will develop (72–4: πυνθάνεσθαι τοῦ Ὁμήρου καθ' ἓν ἕκαστον, τὸν δὲ Ὅμηρον ἀποκρίνασθαι, '[Hesiod] challenged Homer with one question after another, and Homer answered each one'). The expansion, however, is merely apparent: by giving this information at the beginning of the contest, L can be much more concise in its handling of individual speech introductions. A first example of this occurs in *Cert.* 74, where L has φησὶν οὖν Ἡσίοδος ('So, Hesiod said') against the papyrus' more expansive φασὶν μὲν τὸν] Ἡσίοδον ἐρω[τῆσαι τούσδε τοὺς στίχου]ς (6–7, 'they say that Hesiod ... asked these lines'). The same happens at 10–12, where the introduction to Homer's answer is again more elaborate than in the *Certamen* (77: Ὅμηρος, 'Homer'); and at 15–17, of which τὸ δεύτερον ('for the second time') at *Cert.* 80 appears as a shortened version, if the reconstruction ἐπιβαλόμενος δ' ὁ Ἡσίοδος ἐρωτᾶι τὸ δεύτερον ('adding another question, Hesiod asked for the second time') is correct. An extreme instance of abbreviation is *Cert.* 83, where the introduction to Homer's answer transmitted in the papyrus at 19–21 is summarised in ὁ δέ.

The papyrus and the manuscript give texts that differ in terms of their syntax too. At the beginning of the papyrus text, the three words in the genitive απαντων, κριτων and Π]ανηδου (2–4) suggest the presence of a genitive absolute, as opposed to *Cert*. 68–70: τοῦ δὲ ἀγῶνος ἄλλοι τέ τινες τῶν ἐπισήμων Χαλκιδέων ἐκαθέζοντο κριταὶ καὶ μετ' αὐτῶν Πανοίδης, ἀδελφὸς ὢν τοῦ τετελευτηκότος ('some of the distinguished Chalcideans were sitting as judges of the contest, and with them was Panoides, brother of the dead man'). Furthermore, the audience's reaction to Homer's verses at 28–34 has inspired *Cert*. 90–4, but each text has a different syntactical structure: while the *Certamen* has two coordinated infinitives (προσαγορευθῆναι ... καὶ ... προκατεύχεσθαι, 'they were called 'golden', and ... all people perform them'), in the papyrus the second verb seems compatible with an indicative present, προκατεύχοντα[ι. (Reasonable supplements for the first verb, of which fewer traces are left on the papyrus, are Rzach's προσαγορεύσαντες, or Wilamowitz's προσα[γορεύοντες. Allen's προσαγορευθηναι seems incompatible with the indicative form of the other verb in the sentence). As a last example, the introduction to Homer's last answer is presented in the papyrus (41–4) in an elaborate phrasing, while the corresponding text at *Cert*. 99 resorts to more common words and simpler syntax: τὸ ἄπορον λῦσαι instead of the papyrus' τὴν ἀπορίαν τῆς ἐρωτήσεως λῦσαι, and φησίν ('said') for ἀποφθέγγεται τοὺς στίχους τούσδε ('uttered these lines'; ἀκολούθως has no correspondence in the papyrus).

Other differences between the two texts concern individual words or phrases. While describing the audience's reaction to Homer's performance of the Odyssean passage, the *Certamen* (92) adds a detail that is not present in the corresponding papyrus text (28–34), namely that these verses are performed 'even now' (καὶ ἔτι καὶ νῦν): this may be an attempt by the author of the *Certamen* to make his sources seem relevant to his own time. In some cases, the papyrus readings can be used to improve the text of the manuscript: at 30–1 the papyrus gives τοὺς στίχους, which seems a better reading than L's τὰ ἔπη (after ὑπὸ τῶν Ἑλλήνων). L's reading does not agree with the words that follow, χρυσοῦς αὐτούς, and may well owe its existence to τῶν ἐπῶν earlier in the sentence. Other attempts to emend L are less legitimate. For example, there is no need to insert τούτων at *Cert*. 90 on the basis of lines 28–9 of the papyrus. Changing the word order at *Cert*. 91 on the basis of lines 30–1 of the papyrus is not necessary either; e.g., Allen: θαυμασθῆναι τοὺς στίχους ὑπὸ τῶν Ἑλλήνων, instead of θαυμασθῆναι ὑπὸ τῶν Ἑλλήνων τοὺς στίχους (L: τὰ ἔπη). See apparatus and commentary on *Cert*. 90–4 for more details.

The hexameter material present in the text too seems to have been subject to variations. For example, at the end of line 18 of the papyrus the letters ΚΑΛ lead us to supplement κάλλιστον ('the finest thing'), whereas *Cert*.

82 reads ἄριστον ('the best thing'). In this case the papyrus helps us to understand what seems to be a problematic passage of the manuscript text: in the papyrus text the second exchange of verses presents a question and an answer which are both about the κάλλιστον for human beings (18–9 and 27); in the corresponding sequence in the *Certamen* as transmitted in **L**, Hesiod asks what the ἄριστον is (82), and Homer replies by defining the κάλλιστον (89) (note that Homer had already defined the ἄριστον in his previous answer, 78). An emendation of the manuscript on the basis of the papyrus text allows it to have in the *Certamen* too an exchange on the 'best' and one on the 'finest' thing. In the *Certamen*, the reading ἄριστον may be due to the influence of the same word at 78 (in Homer's first answer). See also Part 4, 81–2n. At least one instance of variation is visible also in the passage from the *Odyssey*: at 27–8 the papyrus gives the reading φαίνεται, while the Homeric manuscripts and the *Certamen* read εἴδεται. Some of the editors of the papyrus print εἴδεται on the basis of the *Odyssey*, but ΝΕΤΑΙ at the beginning of line 28 makes the reading φαίνεται inevitable.

Notes to the text

2–3. Colonna's supplement ἁπάντων κρατῆσαι τῶν κριτῶν is based on the passage about the contest from Themistius' *Oration* 30 (see Part 1), where Hesiod πᾶσι τοῖς κριταῖς κρατεῖ, but that is a different version of the story that fits other specific purposes, and therefore this supplement cannot be accepted.

2. τοῦ δὲ ἀγῶνο]ς: a fairly clear trace of Σ can be read and this gives some support to Avezzù's τοῦ δὲ ἀγῶνος.

10–12. At the end of line 11, there are traces which seem to be compatible with the letters ΠΟΚΡΙ, and could be part of the verb ἀποκρίνασθαι sometimes used in the *Certamen* too to introduce Homer's answers (*Cert.* 104, 142). Mahaffy's tentative identification of these traces with the letters ΣΟΙΠ was already questioned by Wilamowitz (see his apparatus). Only Colonna, on the basis of Milne's reading, proposes the supplement ἀποκρίνασθαι, but his reading of the rest of the line as τοῦτον τὸν τρό]πον cannot be correct: the letters ΑΡ indicating the beginning of Homer's answer are at the end of line 12 rather than at the beginning of line 13, as he suggests; before them, Η is visible, possibly following Π, which may lead us to supplement ἔ]πη, and hence the phrase ἀποκρίνασθαι [...] τάδε τὰ ἔπη.

23b. This line is missing in the papyrus, seemingly at the bottom of the first column.

35. The end of the line is difficult. Wilamowitz proposed the supplement ἐπὶ τούτοις] ἐ[/πὶ τὴν ἀπορίαν ('vexed at these [verses, he turned] to [asking perplexing questions]'). Colonna connected ε with the following line as if it were the last letter of line 35, but there is actually room after it for some more letters.

36. τῆς ἀ[ποκρίσεως: the supplement τῆς ἐρωτήσεως proposed by some of the earliest editors allows some correspondence with ἐπὶ τὴν τῶν ἀπόρων ὥρμησεν ἐπερώτησιν (*Cert.* 95), but the last visible letter of the line almost certainly is A rather than E. Wilamowitz's τῆς ἀποκρίσεως should therefore be accepted.

43. ἀποφθ[έγγεται: the last letter before the lacuna can be identified with a good degree of confidence with a θ. The only Greek verb which fits the context is the one proposed by Wilamowitz, ἀποφθέγγομαι.

44–7. [οὐδέποτ'ἀμφὶ ... [περὶ νίχης: these verses are mentioned also in Plu. *Dinner of the Seven Sages* 154a, in connection with the same contest story (see Part 1, 'Plutarch'). Plutarch's text, however, reads ἐπειγόμενοι where the manuscript of the *Certamen* and the papyrus transmit ἐρίζοντες. The words κἀναχήποδες ἵπποι are missing in **L** and in Stephanus' copy, and they have been integrated by Barnes on the basis of Plutarch's text. The traces of the letters present in the papyrus fit these words, and confirm the soundness of Barnes' supplement.

P.Mich. inv. 2754

Catalogues: MP³ 0076; LDAB 177.

Editions and critical studies mentioned in the apparatus: Winter 1925; Hunt (in Winter 1925); Körte 1927; Solmsen 1932; Page 1936 (appendix to revised edition of Evelyn-White 1936 (1914)); Kirk 1950; Dodds 1952; West 1967; Koniaris 1971; Renehan 1971 and 1976; Richardson 1981; Avezzù 1982.

P.Mich. inv. 2754 transmits, in lines 1–14, an account of the death of Homer in a version which is similar to *Cert.* 327–38; lines 15–23 contain a section in praise of the poet that is not found in the *Certamen* or indeed in any other source; a *subscriptio* giving the name of Alcidamas closes the text. This papyrus was discovered in 1924 during an excavation conducted by the University of Michigan at the Egyptian site of Karanis (Arsinoite nome). It is the final column of a papyrus roll, written both on the *recto* and on the *verso*. While the *recto* is covered by accounts, the *verso* contains twenty-three lines of text and ends with a *subscriptio*. Its 'small well-formed book-hand' has been dated to the second-third century AD.[142]

P.Mich. inv. 2754 offers important insights into our understanding of the textual tradition of the *Certamen*, and sheds light on the more general issue of the relationship between Alcidamas and the *Certamen*. As in the case of the text transmitted by P.Petr. I 25 (1), a comparison between papyrus (1–14) and manuscript shows that they give virtually the same account of the story. However, the papyrus text is more elaborately phrased, and presents its own peculiar details. Here I propose a new edition of the text:[143]

1   οἱ δὲ ὁρῶντε[ς αὐ]τὸν ἐσχεδίασαν τόνδε [τὸ]ν
     στίχον· ὅσσ' ἔλομεν λ[ι]πόμεσθ' ὅσσ' οὐκ ἔλομεν
     φερόμε[σ]θα. ὁ δὲ οὐ δυνάμενος εὑρεῖν τὸ λε-
     χθὲν ἤρετο αὐτοὺς [ὅτι] λέγοιεν. οἱ δὲ ἔφασαν ἐ-
5   φ' ἁλιείαν οἰχόμενο[ι ἀγρ]εῦσαι μὲν οὐδέν, καθή-
     μενο`ι´ [δ]ὲ φθειρ[ί]ζεσ[θ]αι· τῶν δὲ φθειρῶν οὓς ἔλα-
     βον αὐτοῦ κατα[λ]ιπεῖν, οὓς δ' οὐκ ἔλαβον ἐν
     τοῖς τρίβωσιν ἐ[.]ναποφέρειν. ἀναμνησθεὶς δὲ
     τοῦ μαντε[ίο]υ [ὅτι] ἡ καταστροφὴ αὐτῶι το[ῦ]
10   βίου ἧκεν, π[οι]εῖ εἰς ἑαυτὸν ἐπίγραμ[μ]α τό[δ]ε·
     ἐνθάδ[ε] τὴν ἱε[ρὴ]ν κεφαλὴν κατὰ γαῖα κάλυ-
     ψε, ἀνδρῶν ἡρώων κοσμήτορα θεῖον Ὅμηρ[ο]ν.
     καὶ ἀν[α]χωρῶ`ν´ πηλοῦ ὄντος ὀλισθάνει καὶ πε-
     σὼν ἐ[π]ὶ πλευρὰν οὕτως, φασίν, ἐτελεύτησεν.
15   περὶ τούτου μὲν οὖν †ποιεῖσθαι τὴν ἀρετὴν ποι-
     ήσομεν†, μάλιστα δ' ὁρῶν τοὺς ἱστορικοὺς θαυ-
     μαζομένους. Ὅμηρος γοῦν διὰ τοῦτο καὶ ζῶν
     καὶ ἀποθανὼν τετίμηται παρὰ πᾶσιν ἀνθρώ-
     ποις. ταύτῃ[.] οὖν αὐτῷ τῆς παιδιᾶς χάριν ἀ-
20   ποδίδω[μι, τό τε γ]ένος αὐτοῦ καὶ τὴν ἄλλη[ν] ποί-
     ησιν διὰ β[ραχ]είας μνήμης τοῖς βουλομέ-
     νοις φι[λοκαλ]εῖν τῶν Ἑλλήνων εἰ`ς´ τὸ κοινὸν
     παραδο]ύς.
                [Ἀλκι]δάμαντος
                Περὶ Ὁμήρου

---

2 ἔλομεν ... ἔλομεν: ελ[αβ]ον et ελαβον Π corr. Winter 5 οἰχόμενο[ι Hunt 6 μενο⟦υ⟧`ι´ Π 7 κατα[.]ιποιεν Π corr. Winter 8 ε[ν]θ αποφερειν Winter ἐναποφέρειν Körte Page

---

142 An image and more information are available at the following URL: http://www.papyri.info/apis/michigan.apis.1622. The quotation is from Winter 1925: 120.

143 This edition is based on an inspection of the digital image of the papyrus available online at the URL above.

And on seeing him, they improvised this line:
> All that we caught we left behind, all that we did not catch we carry with us.

Since he had not been able to understand what had been said, he asked them what they meant. They said that, having gone to fishing, they had not caught anything, but, sitting, they deloused themselves, and they had left there the lice that they had caught, while those that they had not caught they were carrying with them in their cloaks. And remembering the oracle, that the conclusion of his life had come, he composed this epigram for himself:
> Here the earth covers the sacred head, adorner of warrior heroes, divine Homer.

Having departed that place, since it was muddy, he slipped and, having fallen on his side, they say, died in that way.

Therefore, about him †we will make our reputation…†, especially since we see that the historians are admired. For this reason, then, Homer has been honoured by all people both during his lifetime and after he died. So, I thank him for his entertainment, after having shortly narrated his life and the rest of his poetry to the benefit of all those who wish to become lovers of literature.

Alcidamas, On Homer.

The account of Homer's death given on the papyrus starts with the young fishermen proposing a riddle to Homer. Although it is not possible to know whether in the papyrus text Homer asked the boys if they had caught anything during the fishing expedition (cf. *Cert.* 325–6), this papyrus and the manuscript **L** give virtually the same version of the story of Homer's death from the episode of the riddle onwards. This shows that the author of the *Certamen* used Alcidamas' text as his source for the final section of his text.

Kirk Koniaris Renehan   **12** ανθ`δ΄ρων Π   **13** παληου Π corr. Winter   **15** ποιεῖσθαι: πονεῖσθαι Dodds secl. Körte lac. post ποιεῖσθαι West **15–16** ποιεῖσθαι … ποιήσομεν inter cruces Renehan ποιήσομεν: πειρασόμεθα Page πειράσομεν Solmsen fort. ποιήσομαι Dodds πειράσομαι Avezzù   **16** ορων⟨τες⟩ Winter ὁρῶ Dodds   **19** ταύτη[ν] Winter Kirk Dodds West ταύτη[ς] Körte Koniaris; παιδείας Körte Dodds Renehan   **19–20** ἀποδίδω[μι, τό τε γ]ένος Avezzù ἀποδιδῶ[μεν αγ]ῶνος Winter ἀποδιδό[ντες, τὸ γ]ένος Page Koniaris ἀποδιδό[ντες   ].νος Kirk ἀποδιδο[ύς τὸ γ]ένος Dodds ἀποδιδο[ύς, ἀφέμ]ενος West ἀποδιδό[   ]νος Renehan ἀποδιδό[……]ενος Richardson   **21** διὰ β[ραχ]είας West Koniaris δι'ἀκ[ριβ]είας Körte Kirk Dodds Avezzù δι αγ[χιστ]ειας Winter αγ.[   ]ειας Renehan   **22** φι[λοκαλ]εῖν Hunt   **23** παραδο]ύς Avezzù παραδώ[σω West, παραδῷ[μεν Winter Kirk Koniaris Renehan, παραδῶ Dodds   **25** [Ἀλκι]δάμαντος Winter

However, as in the case of P.Petr. I 25 (1), the *Certamen*'s text appears as a simplification of the papyrus'. To start with, the *Certamen* introduces the text of the riddle with fewer words (327: εἰπόντων δὲ ἐκείνων, 'and as they said in reply') than the corresponding one in the papyrus (1–2). Again, when it comes to inform us that Homer asked about the meaning of the riddle, the papyrus and the *Certamen* use the same words; but the *Certamen*'s οὐ νοήσας τὸ λεχθέν (329: 'since he did not understand what had been said') seems a concise form of the papyrus' ὁ δὲ οὐ δυνάμενος εὑρεῖν τὸ λεχθέν (3–4: 'since he had not been able to understand what had been said'). Then, in both texts the explanation of the riddle is based on the contrast, indicated by μέν and δέ, between the two actions of fishing and killing the lice (with minimal lexical variations). But the participles that in the papyrus further characterise these actions, οἰχόμενο[ι and καθήμενοι (5–6, 'they said that, having gone to fishing, they had not caught anything, but, sitting, they deloused themselves'), are dropped in the *Certamen* (329–30) οἱ δέ φασιν ἐν ἀλείᾳ μὲν ἀγρεῦσαι μηδέν, ἐφθειρίσθαι δέ, 'they said that during the fishing they had not caught anything, but deloused themselves'). The *Certamen* simplifies the papyrus text (6–8) also in the continuation of the explanation of the riddle (cf. *Cert*. 330–2: καὶ τῶν φθειρῶν οὓς ἔλαβον καταλιπεῖν, οὓς δὲ οὐκ ἔλαβον ἐν τοῖς ἱματίοις φέρειν, 'and they had left behind the lice that they had caught, while those that they had not caught they were carrying with them in their clothes'): it eliminates αὐτοῦ ('there') and gives φέρειν instead of a compound of φέρω (though it is difficult to identify the verb used in the papyrus, line 8: ἐ[.]ναποφέρειν). The *Certamen* also offers a variation: ἐν τοῖς ἱματίοις ('in their clothes') for the papyrus' ἐν τοῖς τρίβωσιν (8: 'in their cloaks'); it may be relevant that this is a context where variations were indeed common (cf. ἐν τῇ ἐσθῆτι Ps.-Plu. *Vit. Hom*. 1.4, Anon. *Vit. Hom*. 3.5; εἰς οἴκους Ps.-Hdt. *Vit. Hom*. 35). After the riddle, the story develops in the same way in the *Certamen* and in the papyrus (8–12): Homer remembers the oracle, its content is briefly summarised, and the poet then writes his tomb epigram (cf. *Cert*. 332–3: ἀναμνησθεὶς δὲ τοῦ μαντείου ὅτι τὸ τέλος αὐτοῦ ἥκοι τοῦ βίου, ποιεῖ τὸ τοῦ τάφου αὐτοῦ ἐπίγραμμα, 'and remembering the oracle, that the end of his life had come, he composed an epigram for his tomb'). The oracle is however summarised with different words in the two texts: ἡ καταστροφή (9) becomes τὸ τέλος in the *Certamen*; different verbal forms are used (ἥκοι, ἧκεν); the personal pronoun is used in different cases (dative and genitive); τοῦ βίου is in different positions. Compare also τὸ τοῦ τάφου αὐτοῦ ἐπίγραμμα and εἰς ἑαυτὸν ἐπίγραμ[μ]α τό[δ]ε. In the papyrus the epigram is reported straightaway and is introduced by τόδε; whereas the author of the *Certamen* puts it at the very end of his work, after saying that Homer slipped on mud and died. (For the position of the epigram in the *Certamen* see Part 4, 336–8n.) Furthermore, as in P.Petr. I 25 (1), there are differences in syntax, as can be seen in the scene of the very death of Homer (cf. *Cert*. 334–5: ἀναχωρῶν δὲ ἐκεῖθεν, ὄντος πηλοῦ ὀλισθὼν καὶ πεσὼν ἐπὶ τὴν πλευράν, τριταῖος ὥς φασι τελευτᾷ, 'Having departed that place, since it was muddy, after having slipped and fallen on his side, he died, they say, on the third day'). The *Certamen* short-circuits the balanced syntax of the papyrus texts (13–14: ἀν[α]χωρῶ`ν´ ... ὀλισθάνει καὶ πεσὼν ... ἐτελεύτησεν, 'Having departed that place ... he slipped and, having fallen on his side ... died') by assimilating ὀλισθάνει to πεσών. It also introduces some new ideas: τριταῖος ('on the third day') and καὶ ἐτάφη ἐν Ἴῳ ('and he was buried in Ios').

The second part of the papyrus (15–23) is not transmitted in the *Certamen*, and therefore it is not possible to compare it with the text of the manuscript. However, those lines are very important as they shed light on the issue of the sources used by the author of the *Certamen*. It has been suggested on various grounds that the *subscriptio* giving the name of Alcidamas refers only to the text at 15–23, while 1–14 are not by the same author; as a consequence, Alcidamas should not be seen as the source for the *Certamen*'s section on the death of Homer. No indisputable argument has, however, yet been offered as to why we should dissociate Alcidamas from 1–14.

The first editor, Winter, had no doubts that the whole text on the papyrus was to be attributed to Alcidamas and that the sophist was one of the sources for the *Certamen*.[144] Soon after that, however, Körte claimed that lines 1–14 were not by Alcidamas because they contain seven instances of hiatus, which Alcidamas avoided in his *On Sophists*: according to Körte, the lines may have been quoted by Alcidamas in his work, but were not written by him.[145] Kirk later built on these considerations and argued that the lines in question are an interpolation from an anonymous Life of Homer into two consecutive sentences of Alcidamas' Περὶ Ὁμήρου. He based his argument on a perceived lack of continuity between 1–14 and 15–23, on the traces of Koiné Greek in 1–14 (ἐσχεδίασαν, ἁλιείαν, φθειρίζεσθαι and the parenthetic use of φασίν), on the fact that the *Certamen* does not mention Alcidamas as the source for that specific section, while on other occasions it does, and on the fact that a 'circumstantial prose biography of Homer' is not likely to have existed 'as early as in the fifth century'.[146] Dodds accepted Kirk's objections to the unity of the papyrus text, but proposed yet another scenario for its transmission: according to him, the roll contained a number of *excerpta* περὶ

---

144 Winter 1925: 124–5 claims that 'the new fragment proves conclusively the validity of the Alcidamas tradition' because the text at ll. 1–14 'agrees so closely with the *Certamen* ... that the relationship is apparent', and the *subscriptio* proves it 'as conclusively as anything can'.
145 Körte 1927.
146 Kirk 1950: 149–57.

Ὁμήρου, and after a quotation on the death of Homer from an anonymous work the compiler quoted an extract from the preface of Alcidamas' *Museum* to close his collection in a suitably grand manner.[147] By contrast, Koniaris suggested that the papyrus fragment was part of a roll which contained the *Certamen* approximately as we have it, followed by a series of quotations about Homer; in his view, a quotation from Alcidamas started the series.[148]

The attempts to deny Alcidamas' authorship of 1–14 were not, however, completely successful. Renehan, building on West's studies, has shown that the forms considered by earlier scholars to contain traces of Koiné Greek are not exclusively postclassical. As for hiatus, Renehan suggests that the avoidance of it in the only treatise by Alcidamas that has reached us in its entirety may be coincidence, rather than conscious practice. In fact, he argues on the basis of another fragment, Alcidamas did not always avoid hiatus.[149]

Other arguments can be added. First, the restoration [Ἀλκι]δάμαντος, on the basis of which lines 15–23 are unanimously attributed to Alcidamas, is ultimately due precisely to the contents of lines 1–14. In these lines the account of the death of Homer is very similar to that in the *Certamen*, whose connection with Alcidamas is proved by other independent pieces of evidence.[150]

The sentence at 15–16 (περὶ τούτου ... ποιήσομεν†) has often been used as evidence for the fact that the papyrus contains two separate texts, since several scholars have received the impression of an abrupt transition between the text at 1–14 and that at 15–23. This sentence is slightly obscure in meaning and style, and may be corrupt. However, it still seems possible to make some sense of the text, and to recognise some connections with the previous lines. Indeed, τούτου in this context can be seen as a masculine pronoun (instead of neuter, as it has so far been interpreted): in this case it would be referring to Homer ('about him'), resulting in a clearer meaning to the sentence and a better link to the previous one.[151]

As for the last five lines (19–23: ταύτη[.] ... παραδο]ύς), these are fundamental to our understanding of the papyrus but, like 15–16, they present a very complicated text. Several supplements have been proposed, and different supplements have led to very different views on the relations between 1–14 and 15–23. In the first part of the sentence, Alcidamas thanks Homer (χάριν ἀποδίδ.[ ) while the second part refers to his account of Homer's life and poetry (γ]ένος ...καὶ τὴν ... ποίησιν ...παραδ.] – on the supplement

---

147 Dodds 1952.
148 Koniaris 1971.
149 West 1967: 434–8; Renehan 1971 and 1976: 144–59.
150 Renehan 1971: 104 concludes that 'if only lines 15–25 of the papyrus had survived no one would be calling it, as it is commonly called, the Alcidamas papyrus'.
151 See also Renehan 1971: 104 n. 22.

γ]ένος see below). In the papyrus the ending of both verbs is unreadable, and there is no agreement among previous editors on the identification of the last letter (ο or ω) before both lacunae. Scholars have suggested a range of verbal forms and, as a consequence, the syntax of the whole passage has been variously interpreted. The most plausible supplements for the two verbs are those proposed by Avezzù: ἀποδίδω[μι and παραδο[ύς. He seems right in identifying the traces of the last visible letter of each verb respectively with Ω and Ο, which makes some of the other supplements that have been proposed altogether impossible (see below). Even more importantly, though, Avezzù's reading gives a plausible general meaning to the whole fragment: Alcidamas is giving thanks to Homer (now, in the last few lines), after having written (in the previous section of the text, i.e. 1–14) about his life and his poetry. That Alcidamas gives thanks to Homer *after* discussing the poet's life and poetry sits well with the text of the papyrus, for 1–14 look like the end of a biographical account. The alternatives proposed are less convincing. Page read the lines as meaning 'let us then thank (χάριν ἀποδιδό[ντες) him thus ... and as for his origins and the rest of his poetry, let us hand them down (τὸ γ]ένος αὐτοῦ καὶ τὴν ἄλλη[ν] ποίησιν ... παραδῶ[μεν) ...'. Page's supplements were accepted by Kirk and Koniaris (who however did not propose a translation). Dodds' text and translation are similar: 'offering him this tribute (ταύτη[ν] ... χάριν ἀποδιδο[ύς), let me publish ... an accurate account of where he came from and what else he wrote (τὸ γ]ένος αὐτοῦ καὶ τὴν ἄλλη[ν] ποίησιν ... παραδῶ)'. None of these texts is paleographically likely (see above, on omega and omicron before the two lacunas) or results in a plausible overall interpretation, for they suggest that Alcidamas' account of Homer's life and poetry is yet to come. Other interpretations seem even less likely: Winter proposes 'let us then give him these thanks for the amusement of the contest itself (ταυτη[ν] ουν αυτω της παιδιας χαριν αποδιδω[μεν αγ]ωνος αυτου) ... and the rest of his poetry let us hand down (την αλλη[ν] ποιησιν παραδω[μεν)...' but this rests on an incorrect reading (αγ]ωνος at 20 cannot be right); while West's 'offering him this return (ταύτη[ν] ... χάριν ἀποδιδο[ύς) ... I will leave him (ἀφέμ]ενος αὐτοῦ) and go on to make other poets available too (τὴν ἄλλη[ν] ποίησιν ... παραδώ[σω)' makes the passage overly convoluted.[152]

At a more general level, the two passages definitely seem to be linked thematically. The papyrus does not directly connect Homer's death to his inability to solve a riddle, and therefore does not call his wisdom into question. In this version, the riddle seems to work as no more than a *terminus post quem* for Homer's death. This seems to be in line with the content of 15–23,

---

[152] See also Koniaris 1971: 123.

in which Homer is praised: separating Homer's death from an event that could cast doubt on his wisdom seems to reinforce his educational value.[153]

Furthermore, the text is copied continuously, with no sign of separation or space between lines 14 and 15: this suggests that the text was copied as a unity, rather than as a collection of separate sections. The *subscriptio*, then, because of its size and its position at the bottom margin of the papyrus, seems to refer to the whole text rather than only to its final section. In conclusion, there seem to be good reasons for thinking that Alcidamas is the author of the whole text on the papyrus, and that both it and the *Certamen* go back to Alcidamas as their ultimate source.

Notes to the text

5. οἰχόμενο[ι: this form, supplemented by Hunt, is not attested in other accounts of the story but has been unanimously accepted by all editors: as Winter points out, it accords with the traces and gives the necessary contrast with καθήμενοι.

7. κατα[λ]ιπεῖν: Winter's emendation κατα[λ]ιπεῖν for the papyrus' reading ΚΑΤΑ[.]ΙΠΟΙΕΝ is here accepted, since it provides a syntactical parallel to the infinitive ἐ[.]ναποφέρειν. The papyrus' spelling may be partially explained through iotacism.

16. ὁρῶν: there is no reason to propose either ὁρῶν<τες> (Winter) or ὁρῶ (Dodds). The first person singular does not seem to be problematic (and is used later in the text too, if the supplements ἀποδίδω[μι and παραδο[ύς are correct); the participle may function as a reason clause.

τοὺς ἱστορικούς: it has been suggested that Alcidamas either sees Homer as a historian (Kirk 1950: 154, who however finds this 'quite untypical of the Greek assessment of Homer') or that he sees himself as one, and Homer as a good subject on which to build his own reputation for excellence (Koniaris 1971: 122). But it seems that Alcidamas rather sets himself and Homer against the historians: the particles μέν and δέ and the gist of the passage, as far as it can be reconstructed, seem to suggest this contrast. It is impossible to know more precisely what Alcidamas meant by 'historians' and how he viewed them, because this is the only occurrence of the word in his extant works.

17–19. Ὅμηρος ... ἀνθρώ/ποις: the idea of Homer being honoured by all people is repeatedly emphasised in the *Certamen* (see also Richardson 1981: 4–5).

---

[153] See also Part 4, 323–38n.

19. ταύτη[.]: both ταύτη[ν] and ταύτη[ς] seem possible.

τῆς παιδιᾶς: the papyrus reading has sometimes been emended in παιδείας, which results in Alcidamas thanking Homer for his 'educational value' rather than for the 'entertainment' he provides. The papyrus reading is not problematic in itself (and it may mean, as suggested by one of the press' anonymous readers, that Alcidamas is implicitly defining his own text as a παίγνιον, which would be a significant move), although the emendation would be in line with the general gist of the passage and its praise of Homer. It is interesting to note that other sources too show that Homer could be associated with both concepts: in Ps.-Plu. *Vit. Hom.* 1.5, the manuscripts give both παιδείας and παιδιᾶς.

20. γ]ένος: the letter after the lacuna can be identified, with a good degree of certainty, with E: Winter's αγ]ῳνος is therefore to be rejected. γένος and ποίησις are the subject of many ancient treatises on the poets, including the extant Lives of Homer.

P.Ath.Soc.Pap. inv. M2

Catalogues: MP³ 0077.01; LDAB 6838.

Edition: Mandilaras 1990; reprinted in Mandilaras 1992.

This papyrus fragment transmits, on the *verso*, thirteen lines of a text that has been identified, on the basis of a few visible words on the first lines, as an account of the death of Hesiod similar to that attributed to Alcidamas in the *Certamen* (226–35). The fragment was found in the cartonnage of a mummy, probably in the Fayyum, and it was part of a roll. On palaeographical grounds it has been dated to the second century BC.

The papyrus text does not correspond completely to that transmitted in the manuscript, and reveals once again how the literary sources used by the author of the *Certamen* were subjected to a process of compression and adaptation. Mandilaras has shown that in at least two cases (at 1–2 and 7–8) the text of the manuscript is too short to fill the lacunae in the papyrus. Furthermore, the papyrus seems to transmit a somewhat more elaborate text than the manuscript.

Below is Mandilaras' edition of the text. He recognises that the papyrus differs from the manuscript text at several points, although he extensively supplements the former on the basis of the latter.

[εἰς δὲ] Ο[ἰνόην] τῆς Λοκρίδος[ἔρχεται καὶ κατα-
[λύει παρ'] Ἀμφιφάνει καὶ Γανύ[κτορι] τοῖς [Φηγέως

[παισὶν ἀ]γνοήσας τὸ μαντεῖον. Ὁ γὰρ [τόπος οὗτος
[ἅπας ἐκαλε]ῖ[το] Διὸς Νεμείου ἱερόν. [Δι]α[τριβῆς
[δ'αὐτῷ πλείονος γε]νομένης ἐν τοῖς Ο[ἰνοεῦ]σιν
[ὑπονοήσαντες] οἱ νεανίσκοι τὴν ἀδελ[φὴν αὐτῶ]ν
[παρθένον οὖσαν αἰσχῦναι τὸν Ἡσίο]δον[
[ἀποκτείναντε]ς αὐτὸν εἰς τὸ μεταξὺ [τῆς ἀκτῆ]ς
[τῆς Λοκρίδος καὶ] τῆς Εὐβοίας [πέλαγος κατεπόν-
[τισαν. Ὕστερον δὲ] τοῦ νεκροῦ τρ[ι]τα[ίου πρὸς τὴν
[γῆν ὑπὸ δελφίνων] προσενεχθέντ[ο]ς [ἑ]ορτῆς [τινος
[ἐπιχωρίου παρ' αὐτοῖς οὔ]σ[ης Ἀριαδνείας πάντες
[ἐπὶ τὸν αἰγιαλὸν ἔδραμον καὶ τὸ] σ[ῶμα γνωρίσαν-
[τες κτλ.]

[Hesiod] arrived at Oenoe in Locris and stayed with Amphiphanes and Ganyctor, the sons of Phegeus, having misunderstood the oracle. For that entire area is called sacred to Nemean Zeus. After he had spent some considerable time among the inhabitants of Oenoe, the young men, suspecting that Hesiod dishonoured their sister, who was a virgin, killed him and threw him in the sea between Locris and Euboea. When later, on the third day, his corpse was brought back to land by dolphins during a certain local festival in honour of Ariadne, everyone ran to the shore and, recognising the body [...]

The first lines of the papyrus are fundamental for identifying the text on the papyrus, because they contain some key elements of the episode: the names Locris (1), Amphiphanes and (partially) Ganyctor (2), and a reference to the misunderstood oracle (3). However, these lines also show that the papyrus text is slightly different from the text of **L**. The *Certamen*'s ἐλθὼν καταλύει ('upon arriving ... he stayed') is too short to fit the lacuna between lines 1 and 2. Mandilaras proposes ἔρχεται καὶ καταλύει ('[Hesiod] arrived...and stayed'), and this suggestion is certainly attractive: we have seen that **L** makes a more extensive use of subordination than earlier texts, especially through participles (see, e.g., P.Mich. inv. 2754, 13–14). Another key phrase for the identification of the text is at line 4: Διὸς Νεμείου ('(sacred) to Nemean Zeus') (cf. *Cert.* 228–9: ὁ γὰρ τόπος οὗτος ἅπας ἐκαλεῖτο Διὸς Νεμείου ἱερόν, 'for that entire area is called sacred to Nemean Zeus'). The text is slightly more complicated in the following line: the reading γε]νομένης (5) is only taken for granted by Mandilaras on the basis of the manuscript text (cf. *Cert.* 229–30), but it is not clearly legible on the papyrus. The end of line 5 would be of great interest if it were better preserved, as it overlaps with a difficult word in the manuscript: Οἰνῶσιν (on which see Part 4, 230n.). Once again in lines 6–7 the text must have been longer than the corresponding text of the *Certamen* (230–1). Based on the position of the words νεανίσκοι (which seems to be the only entirely visible word in line 6) and Ἡσίοδον (reasonable supplement for the only visible letters in line 7: ΔΟΝ), and the space available for additional letters around these, Mandilaras proposes the supplement παρθένον οὖσαν αἰσχῦναι ('dishonoured (their sister), who was a virgin'), which gives an idea of how much is missing in the papyrus text. Judging from the extent of the lacunae and the visible traces of letters, lines 8–10 too give a more elaborate text than *Cert.* 231–2, and also contain a personal pronoun (8: ΑΥΤΟΝ) that is not attested in the manuscript. The space between εἰς τὸ μεταξύ and τῆς Εὐβοίας shows that, unlike in the manuscript, something is missing between these words: it is possible that some of the space was occupied by τῆς Λοκρίδος, as Mandilaras suggests, so that we would have the two geographical names in reverse order. Εὐβοίας (9) is a very significant reading: it confirms, against all attempts to emend the corresponding passage in the *Certamen*, that according to Alcidamas the place of Hesiod's death was Eastern Locris (see Part 4, 226n. and 231–2n.). Unfortunately, lines 10–14 are very poorly preserved, and the only relevant words that seem to be visible are τοῦ νεκροῦ (10) and προσενεχθέντ[ο]ς (11). Everything else is supplemented to give a readable text (cf. *Cert.* 232–4).

P.Freib. 1.1 b (inv. 12)

Catalogues: MP³ 1577; LDAB 2729; Cribiore 248.

Edition: Aly 1914.

P.Freib. 1.1 b transmits the epigram of Hesiod's victory against Homer (*Cert.* 213–4) as the third in a group of four texts written on the *recto* of the papyrus.[154] The papyrus belonged to a roll that was used as a school book; on the *recto* there are traces of mathematical exercises that were washed out to write the anthology of verses, and the *verso* contains a lexicon of Homeric words.[155] It is dated to the second or first century BC.[156]

The text of the epigram as transmitted on the papyrus is identical to that in the manuscript of the *Certamen* and in most of the other sources. The context in which the epigram is cited, however, makes the contribution of this papyrus very interesting, since it proves that the contest story was used

---

[154] See below for details on the other texts.
[155] P.Freib. 1.1 a Ro: MP3 2658 ('Exercices de fractions') = LDAB 6902 ('exercise in fractions'); P.Freib. 1 c: MP3 1219 ('Homerica, Lexique alphabétique de mots homériques en ou-') = LDAB 5266 ('Lexicon Homericum, alphabetic').
[156] For more information on the papyrus see also Cribiore 1996: 232. An image is available from the URL: http://www.ub.uni-freiburg.de/index.php?id=882.

in schools. Furthermore, the texts copied along with the epigram may give some suggestions as to how the story could have been used. Below is Aly's edition of the text.

A. – – – – σαυτῷ λα/λεῖς;
δοκεῖς τι παρέχειν/ἔμφασιν λυπουμένῳ;
5 B. ἐ/μοὶ προσανάθου· λαβέ με//σύμβουλον. [τί δ'οὐ;]
μὴ καταφρο/νήσῃς οἰκέτου συμβουλί/αν.
πολλάκις ὁ δοῦλος τοὺς/τρόπους χρηστοὺς ἔχων/
10 τῶν δεσποτῶν ἐγένετο//σωφρονέστερος.
εἰ δ'ἡ τύ/χῃ τὸ σῶμα κατεδου/λώσατο,
ὅ γε νοῦς ὑπάρχει/τοῖς τρόποις ἐλεύθερος./

15 ὡς δ'ἁλιεὺς ἀκτῇ ἐν//ἁλιρράντῳ ἐπὶ πέτρῃ/
ἀγ(κ)ίστρου δ' ἕλικος τε/λιουχίδα μάστακ' ἀεί/ρας,
ὧδ'– – – – – – – – – – –
20 οὔραχος (?) ἐγ λο/[φιῆς ἁ]παλὴν τρίχα // — ˘˘ πῶυ/.

Ἡσίοδος Μούσαις Ἑλικωνίσι/τόνδ' ἀνέθηκεν
ὕμνῳ/ν(ι)κήσας ἐν Χαλκίδι θεῖον/Ὅμηρον. //

25 χαλκέῳ δ' ἐν κεράμῳ δέ/δετο τρεισκαίδεκα μῆν(α)ς/
καί νύ κεν ἔνθ' ἀπόλοιτο Ἄρης/ἄατος πολέμοιο,/
30 εἰ μὴ μητρυιὴ περικαλλὴς //Ἠερίβοια/
Ἑρμείᾳ 'ξήγγειλεν· ὁ δ' ἐξέκλε/ψεν Ἄρηα/
ἤδη τειρόμενον, χαλεπὸς/δέ ἑ δεσμὸς ἐδάμνα.

...talking to yourself? You seem to give the impression of torment. Take counsel with me, and take me as an adviser. Why not? Do not scorn a servant's advice. Often the earnest slave is more prudent than the masters. Even if Fate has enslaved the body, the mind that serves his manners is free.

Like a fisherman on a promontory washed by the sea, on a cliff, lifting up the fulfilment-bringing nourishment on the curved fish-hook, so ... tang ... soft hair from the mane ... flock...

Hesiod dedicated this to the Heliconian Muses when he defeated divine Homer with a hymn at Chalcis.

And he was bound in a brazen jar for thirteen months; and then Ares, insatiate of war, might have perished, had not the stepmother (of Aloeus' sons), the very beautiful Eëriboea, reported to Hermes; and he released Ares, now weakened, because of the grievous chains.

On this papyrus, the epigram of the *Certamen* is the third in a series of four texts. The verses that open the sequence are from a lost drama from New Comedy in which a slave encourages his master to accept his counsel.[157] The second text (four epic hexameters) is a simile in Homeric style.[158] The second part of the simile is badly preserved, but the verses seem to 'compare, somewhat uneasily, a fisherman's rod, baited hook and line with the notch of a spear or arrow dragging out the thin thread from a helmet's plume through which it has passed'.[159] The epigram of the *Certamen* is then followed by *Iliad* 5.387–91, where Dione tells the story of Ares bound by Otus and Ephialtes and helped by Eëriboia. In the *Iliad*, Dione mentions this story to her daughter Aphrodite, who has just been wounded by Diomedes, while recounting other episodes of gods wounded by mortals.

The relationship between these four texts and the presence of such a sequence of material in a schoolbook are not clearly explained, but a recent study argues that three of those passages (i.e., except for the simile) describe people of inferior status who advise or overcome a person of superior status: in these texts there would be a slave who offers advice to his master, a mortal who hurts a god, and an inferior poet who wins against a superior one. This suggests that the papyrus contains a list of *exempla*, which was possibly to be used for rhetorical exercises in schools.[160] If this suggestion is right, the presence of the epigram of Hesiod's victory against Homer in this context becomes significant of the way Hesiod's victory was commonly perceived. On a general level, the papyrus gives an idea of the ways in which the story of this poetic contest could enter the repertoires of rhetoricians such as Dio Chrysostom, Themistius, and Libanius. More specifically, the fact that the story is placed among examples of inferior people who overcome their superiors shows that Hesiod's victory was seen as a problematic, if crucial, feature of the episode. It was the final verdict, perhaps more than anything else, that encouraged and challenged rhetoricians and other authors to take up the story and shape it to their own purposes.

---

157 *PCG* VIII 1027 = *CGFP* 297. See also Arnott 1999: 78–9 and 2000: 486–9; attributed to Philemon or Menander. The most recent study of these lines is in Pernigotti 2015: 46–8, who finds a parallel with a passage from the *Comparatio Menandri et Philistionis*.
158 Bernabé 1987: 203 (nr 21). See also Powell 1925: 251; Huxley 1969: 25–6; attributed to Antimachus of Theos or Choirilus.
159 Huxley 1969: 25. Aly 1914: 11 admits that the interpretation of οὔραχος and πῶυ remains 'ganz unsicher'.
160 Pordomingo 2010: 52.

P.Duk. inv. 665 (*olim* P.Duk. inv. MF75 6)

Catalogues: MP³ 0077.02 (*antea* 2860.01); LDAB 5947.
Edition: Menci 2012.

A new papyrus has recently been added to the group of known fragments related to the *Certamen*. In 2012, Giovanna Menci (Istituto Papirologico 'Girolamo Vitelli', Florence) discovered that P.Duk. inv. 665, which was previously thought to transmit some 'marginal scholia',[161] contains part of an epigram transmitted in the *Certamen*. The lines in question are *Cert.* 309–12, that is, the first four lines of the epigram inscribed on the statue of Homer dedicated by the Argives. The fragment, of unknown origin, transmits the text in five lines of script, the first of which is occupied by a short title (Ο]μηρου εν Αργει, 'of Homer, in Argos'). The text is on the *recto*. Menci has dated it to the sixth-seventh century AD.[162]

This papyrus is particularly interesting, and its contribution especially welcome, because it is the only witness of the Argive epigram other than the *Certamen*. The fact that we can now compare two versions of the epigram helps us draw some conclusions on the selection, use and transmission of the epigrams contained in the *Certamen*, and indeed of the *Certamen* itself. Below is Menci's edition of the text. The supplements she proposes are based on Allen's text of the *Certamen*.

```
1                    Ο]μηρου εν Αργει
                     Vacuum
    θειος Ομηρος οδ εστιν ος Ε]λλαδα την [μεγα
    λαυχον πασαν εκοσμησ]εν καλλιεπι[σοφιηι
                     ]ˎ
                     ].δ..ριαυχεα Τροιην [η
5   ρειψαν ποινην ηυ]κομου Ελενης > > –[
                     Vacuum vel margo?
```

Of Homer, in Argos.
This is divine Homer, who adorned all proud Hellas with his beautifully expressed wisdom ... destroyed greatly glorious Troy as satisfaction for the conduct of fair-haired Helen.

---

[161] Cf. Menci 2012: 43 n. 3, who reports that in LDAB 5957 the content of the papyrus was catalogued as 'marginal scholia' and in MP³ 2860.01 as 'Scholies [avec mention d'Argos, Troie et Hélène]'. LDAB and MP³ have now been updated.

[162] An image (72 and 150 dpi) is available at the following URL: http://library.duke.edu/rubenstein/scriptorium/papyrus/records/665.html. A reproduction is available in Menci 2012.

For the sake of clarity and following Menci's example, I reproduce here the corresponding text in the *Certamen*:

θεῖος Ὅμηρος ὅδ' ἐστὶν ὃς Ἑλλάδα τὴν μεγάλαυχον
   πᾶσαν ἐκόσμησεν καλλιεπεῖ σοφίῃ,   310
ἔξοχα δ' Ἀργείους, οἳ τὴν θεοτειχέα Τροίην
   ἤρειψαν ποινὴν ἠυκόμου Ἑλένης.

This is divine Homer, who adorned all proud Hellas with his beautifully expressed wisdom, and especially the Argives, they who destroyed Troy with its wall built by gods as satisfaction for the conduct of fair-haired Helen.

The main peculiarity of the papyrus text is that at line 4 it transmits a variant reading: while the *Certamen* reads θεοτειχέα (311: 'built by gods'), the papyrus gives the reading ..ριαυχεα that has been supplemented by the editor as ἐριαυχέα ('greatly glorious'). This case of variation is especially interesting because both words seem to be attested nowhere else.[163] The two variants show how the epigram could be adapted to different contexts and respond to different traditions. On the one hand, the papyrus reading ἐριαυχέα seems to be suitable for a school context. If the papyrus too transmitted the reading μεγάλαυχον, then ἐριαυχέα would create a balance between the two sides of the Trojan war, each qualified with a compound of αὔχη, 'pride' (i.e., Ἑλλάδα τὴν μεγάλαυχον and τὴν ἐριαυχέα Τροίην), and the correspondence between ἐριαυχέα, a *hapax*, and μεγάλαυχον, an attested adjective, may aim to explain the meaning of the former on the basis of the latter. Moreover, ἐριαυχέα is very similar in sound to a Homeric word, ἐριαύχην ('with large neck', an epithet for horses): this similarity may have had a role in the creation of the *hapax* and we may see this as a didactic game on Homeric vocabulary.

But on the other hand, the creation of this double reading may also be due to reasons that are not strictly linguistic and didactic. In the manuscript, θεοτειχέα puts the maximum emphasis on the achievement of the Argives by saying that the walls they destroyed were a creation of the gods, and this makes the epigram fit the encomiastic context of the corresponding passage

---

163 Menci 2012: 46: 'L'alternativa al tràdito θεοτειχέα («con le mura costruite da un dio»), che è *hapax legomenon*, sembra proprio un altro *hapax*, ἐριαυχέα («grandemente gloriosa»)'. Menci 2012: 45: 'in un papiro che conserva soltanto sei parole pressoché intere, di cui tre nomi propri, è presente sicuramente una variante di un *hapax* (θεοτειχέα), che è a sua volta *hapax* (r. 4, ἐριαυχέα); ciò potrebbe dunque accordarsi con l'impressione che si ha da almeno tre degli altri quattro papiri testimoni del *Certamen*, e cioè la libertà di trattamento che caratterizza testi di questo genere, appartenenti alla letteratura di consumo o scolastica'.

in the *Certamen*.[164] However, some readers may have objected that what is built by the gods cannot be destroyed by men: ἐριαυχέα in the papyrus may therefore have worked as a corrective reading. Furthermore, the presence of ἐριαυχέα in place of θεοτειχέα may also correspond to a tradition about the Trojan walls according to which they were not built entirely by the gods. In *Il.* 6.433–4 Andromache mentions a point on the wall that is particularly vulnerable and open to assault; Pindar (*Ol.* 8.31–46), referring perhaps to this very tradition, says that a portion of the wall was built by a human, and not by gods.[165]

The papyrus also shows that the epigram could circulate in longer or shorter versions. The editor suggests that the quotation of the epigram on the papyrus may be limited to the first four lines.[166] The longer version of the *Certamen* may be an innovation designed to emphasise the quasi-divine status that Homer has achieved at this point in the narrative.

The fragment may have been part of a roll containing a collection of epigrams.[167] Although it is later than the assumed time of the composition of the *Certamen*, it suggests how biographical compilations such as the *Certamen* may have come into being: authors used material that was available in collections and anthologies, on which they could draw in order to enrich and reshape the text. The fact that P.Duk. inv. 665 was probably meant for school use suggests that much of this process took place in school environments.

---

164 In the *Certamen* the Argives feel honoured by a passage which Homer performs at Argos and pay him back with signs of divine respect. See esp. Part 4, 302–8n.
165 See further Graziosi/Haubold 2010: 33 and 202.
166 Menci 2012: 43: '…il r. 5 termina con due *diplai* e un tratto orizzontale la cui funzione potrebbe essere, oltre che riempitiva, indicativa della fine del testo'.
167 Menci 2012: 45: 'Le peculiarità paleografiche di P.Duk. inv. 665 suggeriscono una copia ad uso privato; la particolare *mise en page* indirizza verso l'ipotesi di un frammento di rotolo contenente una raccolta di passi, in particolare di epigrammi, destinata alla scuola; tuttavia non si può escludere la possibilità di un foglio isolato'.

Part 3: Text and translation

This edition is based on a direct inspection of the manuscript **L**.

The line numbers are taken from Allen 1912, the paragraph numbers from Wilamowitz 1929 (1916).

Sigla

L = MS Florence, Biblioteca Medicea Laurenziana, Plut. 56.1 (see Part 2)

M = MS Vienna, Österreichische Nationalbibliothek, Phil. gr. 187 (see Part 2)

S = MS Leiden, University Library, Vossianus gr. qu. 18 (copy of parts of **L** by Henri Estienne)

The papyrus fragments are indicated with their full names.

Editions

Stephanus = Estienne, H. (ed.) (1573), *Homeri et Hesiodi Certamen. Matronis et aliorum parodiae. Homericorum heroum epitaphia. Excudebat Henr. Stephanus.* Geneva (*editio princeps*).

Barnes = Barnes, J. (ed.) (1711), *Ilias et Odyssea, et in easdem scholia, sive interpretatio, veterum.* [...] *Accedunt Batrachomyomachia, Hymni et Epigrammata, una cum fragmentis, et gemini indices*, vol. 1. Cambridge.

Boissonade = Boissonade, F. (ed.) (1824), *Hesiodus. Curante Jo. Fr. Boissonade.* Paris.

Westermann = Westermann, A. (ed.) (1845), *Biographoi: Vitarum scriptores Graeci minores.* Braunschweig.

Nietzsche = Nietzsche, F. (ed.) (1871), 'Certamen quod dicitur Homeri et Hesiodi. E codice florentino post Henricum Stephanum denuo edidit Fridericus Nietzsche Numburgensis', *Acta societatis philologae Lipsiensis* 1: 1–23.

Goettling = Goettling, C. W. (ed.) (1878), *Hesiodi Carmina. Recensuit et commentariis instruxit Carolus Goettlingius. Editio tertia quam curavit Ioannes Flach.* Leipzig.

Allen = Allen, T. W. (ed.) (1912), *Homeri Opera*, vol. 5. Oxford.

Rzach = Rzach, A. (ed.) (1913), *Hesiodi Carmina recensuit Aloisius Rzach. Editio tertia. Accedit Certamen quod dicitur Homeri et Hesiodi.* Leipzig.

Evelyn-White = Evelyn-White, H. G. (ed.) (1936 (1914)), *Hesiod, the Homeric Hymns, and Homerica.* Cambridge (MA).

Wilamowitz = von Wilamowitz-Moellendorff, U. (ed.) (1929 (1916)), *Vitae Homeri et Hesiodi in usum scholarum.* Bonn.

Colonna = Colonna, A. (ed.) (1959), *Hesiodi Opera et dies. Recensuit Aristides Colonna.* Milan.

Avezzù = Avezzù, G. (ed.) (1982), *Alcidamante. Orazioni e frammenti.* Rome.

West = West, M. L. (ed.) (2003), *Homeric Hymns, Homeric Apocrypha, Lives of Homer.* Cambridge (MA).

Colbeau = Colbeau, A.-M. (ed.) (2005), *Raconter la vie d'Homère dans l'Antiquité: Edition commentée du traité anonyme, Au sujet d'Homère et d'Hésiode, de leurs origines et de leur joute, et de la Vie d'Homère attribuée à Hérodote.* Thèse soutenue à l'Université de Lille 3, le 1er décembre 2005. PhD Dissertation.

Other critical studies mentioned in the apparatus are cross-referenced to the Bibliography.

Περὶ Ὁμήρου καὶ Ἡσιόδου καὶ τοῦ γένους καὶ ἀγῶνος αὐτῶν

[1] Ὅμηρον καὶ Ἡσίοδον τοὺς θειοτάτους ποιητὰς πάντες ἄνθρωποι πολίτας ἰδίους εὔχονται λέγεσθαι. ἀλλ' Ἡσίοδος μὲν τὴν ἰδίαν ὀνομάσας πατρίδα πάντας τῆς φιλονεικίας ἀπήλλαξεν εἰπὼν ὡς ὁ πατὴρ αὐτοῦ

    εἴσατο δ' ἄγχ' Ἑλικῶνος ὀιζυρῇ ἐνὶ κώμῃ
    Ἄσκρῃ, χεῖμα κακῇ, θέρει ἀργαλέῃ, οὐδέ ποτ' ἐσθλῇ.

[2] Ὅμηρον δὲ πᾶσαι ὡς εἰπεῖν αἱ πόλεις καὶ οἱ ἔποικοι αὐτῶν παρ' ἑαυτοῖς γεγενῆσθαι λέγουσιν. καὶ πρῶτοί γε Σμυρναῖοι Μέλητος ὄντα τοῦ παρ' αὐτοῖς ποταμοῦ καὶ Κρηϊθίδος νύμφης κεκλῆσθαί φασι πρότερον Μελησιγενῆ· ὕστερον μέντοι τυφλωθέντα Ὅμηρον μετονομασθῆναι διὰ τὴν παρ' αὐτοῖς ἐπὶ τῶν τοιούτων συνήθη προσηγορίαν. Χῖοι δὲ πάλιν τεκμήρια φέρουσιν ἴδιον εἶναι πολίτην λέγοντες καὶ περισῴζεσθαί τινας ἐκ τοῦ γένους αὐτοῦ παρ' αὐτοῖς Ὁμηρίδας καλουμένους. Κολοφώνιοι δὲ καὶ τόπον δεικνύουσιν, ἐν ᾧ φασιν αὐτὸν γράμματα διδάσκοντα τῆς ποιήσεως ἄρξασθαι καὶ ποιῆσαι πρῶτον τὸν Μαργίτην·

5–6 Hes. *Op.* 639–40 **5** νάσσατο Hes.

2 λεγέσθαι L corr. S: γενέσθαι Barnes Nietzsche Rzach Evelyn-White **3** φιλονικίας West **5** εἴσατο L corr. S **7** ἄποικοι Hermann (1835: 282) Nietzsche Evelyn-White **8** γεγεννῆσθαι … τε L corr. S **10** Κριθηίδος Barnes Κρηθηίδος edd. cett.; Μελησιγένη edd. **15** αὑτοῖς Westermann edd. praeter Wilamowitz

On Homer and Hesiod, their life, and their contest.

[1] All people desire Homer and Hesiod, the most divine poets, to be called their fellow citizens. But Hesiod, by mentioning his own fatherland, prevented all argument when he said that his father
> settled near Helicon in a dreary village, Ascra, bad in winter, troublesome in summer, and never good.

[2] As for Homer, though, virtually all the cities and their inhabitants claim that he was born among them. And first, the Smyrneans say that he was the son of the Meles, their local river, and of the nymph Creithis, and that he was called Melesigenes at first; but later on, after becoming blind, he changed his name to Homer because of the name usually given to such people among them. The Chians, again, bring evidence that he was their fellow citizen, by saying in addition that some of his offspring, called Homeridae, survive among them. The Colophonians even show the place where, when he was a teacher of letters, they say he started his poetic activity and first composed the *Margites*.

[3] περὶ δὲ τῶν γονέων αὐτοῦ πάλιν πολλὴ διαφωνία παρὰ
πᾶσίν ἐστιν. Ἑλλάνικος μὲν γὰρ καὶ Κλεάνθης
Μαίονα λέγουσιν, Εὐγαίων
δὲ Μέλητα, Καλλικλῆς δὲ †Μασαγόραν, Δημόκριτος δὲ <ὁ>
Τροιζήνιος Δαήμονα ἔμπορον, ἔνιοι δὲ Θαμύραν, Αἰγύπτιοι
δὲ Μενέμαχον ἱερογραμματέα, εἰσὶ δ' οἳ Τηλέμαχον τὸν
Ὀδυσσέως· μητέρα δὲ οἱ μὲν Μῆτιν, οἱ δὲ Κρηθηίδα,
οἱ δὲ Θεμίστην, οἱ δὲ Εὐγνηθώ, ἔνιοι δὲ Ἰθακησίαν τινὰ
ὑπὸ Φοινίκων ἀπεμποληθεῖσαν, οἱ δὲ Καλλιόπην τὴν Μοῦσαν, τινὲς δὲ Πολυκάστην τὴν Νέστορος. ἐκαλεῖτο δὲ
Μέλης, ὡς δέ τινές φασι Μελησιγενής, ὡς δὲ ἔνιοι
Αὐλητής. ὀνομασθῆναι αὐτόν φασί τινες Ὅμηρον διὰ τὸ
τὸν πατέρα αὐτοῦ ὅμηρον δοθῆναι ὑπὸ Κυπρίων Πέρσαις, οἱ
δὲ διὰ τὴν πήρωσιν τῶν ὀμμάτων· παρὰ γὰρ τοῖς Αἰολεῦσιν
οὕτως οἱ πηροὶ καλοῦνται. ὅπερ δὲ ἀκηκόαμεν ἐπὶ τοῦ
θειοτάτου αὐτοκράτορος Ἀδ<ρ>ιανοῦ εἰρημένον ὑπὸ τῆς Πυθίας
περὶ Ὁμήρου, ἐκθησόμεθα. τοῦ γὰρ βασιλέως πυθομένου
πόθεν Ὅμηρος καὶ τίνος, ἀπεφοίβασε δι' ἑξαμέτρου τόνδε
τὸν τρόπον·

ἄγνωστόν μ' ἔρεαι γενεὴν καὶ πατρίδα γαῖαν
ἀμβροσίου σειρῆνος. ἕδος δ' Ἰθακήσιός ἐστιν,
Τηλέμαχος δὲ πατὴρ καὶ Νεστορέη Ἐπικάστη
μήτηρ, ἥ μιν ἔτικτε βροτῶν πολὺ πάνσοφον ἄνδρα.
οἷς μάλιστα δεῖ πιστεύειν διά τε τὸν πυθόμενον καὶ τὸν
ἀποκρινάμενον, ἄλλως τε οὕτως τοῦ ποιητοῦ μεγαλοφυῶς
τὸν προπάτορα διὰ τῶν ἐπῶν δεδοξακότος.

18–19, 32–40 cf. M 37–40 *AP* 14.102 37 ἐρέεις γενεῆς καὶ πατρίδος αἴης *AP* 38 Ἰθάκη τις Ὁμήρου *AP* om. M 39 Πολυκάστη *AP* 40 πολυπάνσοφον ἄλλων *AP*

19 Νεάνθης Arnim (1905: 133) Colonna 20 Μαίονα: μ in ras. L rest. Sturz (1787: fr. 171): βίωνα Stephanus; Εὐγαίων: γ in ras. L rest. Meineke (1843: 61): Εὐμαίων S Stephanus 21 †Μασαγόραν Wilamowitz: Δμασαγόραν Barnes Allen Colonna West Colbeau (coll. Eust. *Od.* 1713.20) Μαιαγόραν Nietzsche Μνασαγόραν Rzach Evelyn-White; Δημοκρίνης in app. Allen (coll. Anon. *Vit. Hom.* 1.3) 23 ἱερογραμματέα: ιε in ras. L rest. Nauck (coll. Tz. *Alleg.* Prol. 60): προγραμματέα S in marg. Nietzsche 25 Θεμιστώ Barnes (coll. Paus. 10.24); Εὐγνηθώ: Ὑρνηθώ Westermann edd. (coll. Anon. *Vit. Hom.* 3.1) praeter Nietzsche Evelyn-White; Ἰδακησίαν Rzach 28 Μελησιγένης edd. 29 αὐλητήν L Ἄλτης Welcker (1835: 149) edd. (coll. Schol. T *Il.* 22.51) 33 ἀδιανοῦ L corr. S in marg. 39 νεστορίη L; Πολυκάστη Nietzsche in app. West (coll. *Od.* 3.464 et *Cert.* 27) 40 πέρι πάνσοφον West

[3] About his parents, again, there is much disagreement among all. For Hellanicus and Cleanthes say he was Maeon, Eugaeon Meles, Callicles †Masagoras, Democritus of Troezen the merchant Daemon, some Thamyras, the Egyptians Menemachus the sacred scribe, and there are also those who say he was Telemachus the son of Odysseus; his mother, some say, was Metis, some Cretheis, some Themiste, some Eugnetho, some an Ithacan woman sold by the Phoenicians, some the Muse Calliope, some Polycaste the daughter of Nestor. He was called Meles, as some say Melesigenes, as others say, Auletes. Some say he took the name Homer because his father was given as a hostage to the Persians by the Cypriots; others because of his disabled eyesight, for this is what the disabled are called among the Aeolians. We shall now reveal what we have heard about Homer from the Pythia in the time of the most divine emperor Hadrian. For when the ruler enquired about Homer's provenance and parentage, she, inspired, thus spoke in hexameter:

> You ask me the forgotten descent and fatherland of the immortal Siren. He is an Ithacan by origin, Telemachus is his father and Epicaste, daughter of Nestor, the mother who bore him, most wise man among mortals.

And this above all we must believe, because of the enquirer and the respondent, and not least because the poet has so grandly glorified his forefather through his verses.

[4] ἔνιοι μὲν οὖν αὐτὸν προγενέστερον Ἡσιόδου φασὶν
εἶναι, τινὲς δὲ νεώτερον καὶ συγγενῆ. γενεαλογοῦσί τε
οὕτως· Ἀπόλλωνός φασι καὶ Θοώσης τῆς Ποσειδῶνος
γενέσθαι Λίνον, Λίνου δὲ Πίερον, Πιέρου δὲ καὶ νύμφης
Μεθώνης Οἴαγρον, Οἰάγρου δὲ καὶ Καλλιόπης Ὀρφέα,
Ὀρφέως δὲ Ὄρτην, τοῦ δὲ Ἁρμονίδην, τοῦ δὲ Φιλοτέρπην,
τοῦ δὲ Εὔφημον, τοῦ δὲ Ἐπιφράδην, τοῦ δὲ Μελάνωπον,
τούτου δὲ Δῖον καὶ Ἀπέλλαιον, Δίου δὲ καὶ Πυκιμήδης τῆς
Ἀπόλλωνος θυγατρὸς Ἡσίοδον καὶ Πέρσην· Πέρσου δὲ Μαίονα, Μαίονος δὲ θυγατρὸς καὶ Μέλητος τοῦ ποταμοῦ Ὅμηρον.
[5] τινὲς δὲ συνακμάσαι φασὶν αὐτοὺς ὥστε καὶ ἀγωνίσασθαι
ὁμόσε <γενομένους> ἐν Αὐλίδι τῆς Βοιωτίας. ποιήσαντα γὰρ τὸν Μαργίτην
Ὅμηρον περιέρχεσθαι κατὰ πόλιν ῥαψῳδοῦντα, ἐλθόντα δὲ
καὶ εἰς Δελφοὺς περὶ τῆς πατρίδος αὐτοῦ πυνθάνεσθαι τίς
εἴη, τὴν δὲ Πυθίαν εἰπεῖν·
    ἔστιν Ἴος νῆσος μητρὸς πατρίς, ἥ σε θανόντα
    δέξεται· ἀλλὰ νέων παίδων αἴνιγμα φύλαξαι.
τὸν δὲ ἀκούσαντα περιίστασθαι μὲν τὴν εἰς Ἴον ἄφιξιν,
διατρίβειν δὲ περὶ τὴν ἐκεῖ χώραν. [6] κατὰ δὲ τὸν αὐτὸν

46–53 cf. Charax (103 *FGrHist* 62) apud Suda s.v. Ὅμηρος 1 **M 49–53** cf. Hellanicus (4 *FGrHist* 5b = fr. 5 Fowler), Damastes (5 *FGrHist* 11b = fr. 11 Fowler), Pherecydes (3 *FGrHist* 167 = fr. 167 Fowler) apud Procl. *Vit. Hom.* 4 **59–60** *AP* 14.65, Paus. 10.24.2, Procl. *Vit. Hom.* 5, St. Byz. s.v. Ἴος, Ps.-Plu. *Vit. Hom.* 1.4 **60** παίδων: ἀνδρῶν Ps.-Plu. Procl.

45 γενεαλογοῦσι δὲ vel δ' edd. praeter Wilamowitz Colbeau **46** Αἰθούσης Nietzsche Rzach Evelyn-White (coll. 103 *FGrHist* 62) **47** Λῖνον L **49** Ὄρτην: Δρῆν Goettling Nietzsche Rzach Evelyn-White (coll. 103 *FGrHist* 62) Ὄθρυν Barnes Ὄτρυν Welcker (1835: 149); τοῦ δὲ Εὐκλέα post Ὄρτην add. Goettling Nietzsche Rzach Evelyn-White West (coll. 103 *FGrHist* 62); Ἁρμονίδην: Ἰαδμονίδην Nietzsche Rzach Evelyn-White (coll. Hdt. 2.134, Plu. *De Sera Numinis Vindicta* 557a) id est Ἰδμονίδην (cf. 103 *FGrHist* 62, Procl. *Vit. Hom.* 4) **51** Ἀπέλλην Nietzsche Ἀπελλῆν Rzach Evelyn-White Wilamowitz **52** Πέρσου: Ἀπέλλου Nietzsche Ἀπελλοῦ Rzach Evelyn-White Wilamowitz Ἀπελλαίου West **53** θυγατρὸς καὶ: καὶ θυγατρός Nietzsche Rzach Evelyn-White **55** <γενομένους> Busse (1909: 112–3) Wilamowitz West; ἐν Χαλκίδι τῆς Εὐβοίας Nietzsche Evelyn-White ἐξ Αὐλίδος τῆς Βοιωτίας Gallavotti (1929: 40 n. 2) Avezzù (coll. Hes. *Op.* 651)

[4] So, some say that he was older than Hesiod, some younger and of the same kin. They describe their genealogy as follows: from Apollo and Thoosa, daughter of Poseidon, they say Linus was born, from Linus Pierus, from Pierus and the nymph Methone Oeagrus, from Oeagrus and Calliope Orpheus, from Orpheus Ortes, from him Harmonides, from him Philoterpes, from him Euphemus, from him Epiphrades, from him Melanopus, from this man Dius and Apellaius, from Dius and Pycimedes, daughter of Apollo, Hesiod and Perses; from Perses Maeon, from the daughter of Maeon and the river Meles Homer.

[5] Some say they flourished at the same time, so that they even competed after convening at Aulis in Boeotia. For after composing the *Margites*, Homer wandered from town to town and performed his poems; and when he went to Delphi, too, he enquired about his fatherland, and the Pythia said:

> There is an island, Ios, homeland of your mother, which will receive you after you die; but mind the riddle of the young boys.

As he heard this, he avoided any departure to Ios and spent time in the surrounding area.

χρόνον Γαννύκτωρ ἐπιτάφιον τοῦ πατρὸς Ἀμφιδάμαντος
βασιλέως Εὐβοίας ἐπιτελῶν πάντας τοὺς ἐπισήμους ἄνδρας
65 οὐ μόνον ῥώμῃ καὶ τάχει, ἀλλὰ καὶ σοφίᾳ ἐπὶ τὸν ἀγῶνα
μεγάλαις δωρεαῖς τιμῶν συνεκάλεσεν. καὶ οὗτοι οὖν ἐκ
τύχης, ὥς φασι, συμβαλόντες ἀλλήλοις ἦλθον εἰς τὴν
Χαλκίδα. τοῦ δὲ ἀγῶνος ἄλλοι τέ τινες τῶν ἐπισήμων
Χαλκιδέων ἐκαθέζοντο κριταὶ καὶ μετ᾽ αὐτῶν Πανοίδης,
70 ἀδελφὸς ὢν τοῦ τετελευτηκότος. ἀμφοτέρων δὲ τῶν ποιητῶν θαυμαστῶς ἀγωνισαμένων νικῆσαί φασι τὸν Ἡσίοδον
τὸν τρόπον τοῦτον· προελθόντα γὰρ εἰς τὸ μέσον πυνθάνεσθαι τοῦ Ὁμήρου καθ᾽ ἓν ἕκαστον, τὸν δὲ Ὅμηρον ἀποκρίνασθαι. [7] φησὶν οὖν Ἡσίοδος·
75 υἱὲ Μέλητος Ὅμηρε θεῶν ἄπο μήδεα εἰδὼς
εἴπ᾽ ἄγε μοι πάμπρωτα τί φέρτατόν ἐστι βροτοῖσιν;
Ὅμηρος·
ἀρχὴν μὲν μὴ φῦναι ἐπιχθονίοισιν ἄριστον,
φύντα δ᾽ ὅμως ὤκιστα πύλας Ἀίδαο περῆσαι.
80 Ἡσίοδος τὸ δεύτερον·
εἴπ᾽ ἄγε μοι καὶ τοῦτο θεοῖς ἐπιείκελ᾽ Ὅμηρε
τί θνητοῖς κάλλιστον οἴεαι ἐν φρεσὶν εἶναι;
ὁ δέ·
ὁππότ᾽ ἂν εὐφροσύνη μὲν ἔχῃ κατὰ δῆμον ἅπαντα,
85 δαιτυμόνες δ᾽ ἀνὰ δώματ᾽ ἀκουάζωνται ἀοιδοῦ
ἥμενοι ἑξείης, παρὰ δὲ πλήθωσι τράπεζαι
σίτου καὶ κρειῶν, μέθυ δ᾽ ἐκ κρητῆρος ἀφύσσων
οἰνοχόος φορέῃσι καὶ ἐγχείῃ δεπάεσσιν.
τοῦτό τί μοι κάλλιστον ἐνὶ φρεσὶν εἴδεται εἶναι.

69–102 cf. P.Petr. I 25 (1)   **78–9** Thgn. 425 et 427, Stob. 4.52.22   **78** ἀρχήν: πάντων Thgn.   **79** ὅπως Thgn. Stob. P.Petr. I 25 (1), l. 14   **84–89** Od. 9.6–11   **84** ὁππότ᾽ ἂν εὐφροσύνη: ἢ ὅτ᾽ εὐφροσύνη Od. 9.6   **89** εἴδεται: φαίνεται P.Petr. I 25 (1), l. 27–8

63 Γανύκτης edd.   **69** Πανείδης Hermann (1835: 151) Nietzsche Evelyn-White Πανήδης Rzach Allen Wilamowitz Colonna West Colbeau (coll. P.Petr. I 25 (1), l. 4)   **79** ὅπως Nietzsche Rzach Wilamowitz Evelyn-White West Colbeau (coll. Thgn. 425)   **82** θνητοῖσιν ἄριστον L corr. Rzach Evelyn-White Allen West (coll. P.Petr. I 25 (1), l. 18)

[6] At about the same time Gannyctor, who was organising the funeral of his father Amphidamas, king of Euboea, invited to the contest all the men distinguished not only for strength and speed, but also for wisdom, enticing them with great gifts. And so Homer and Hesiod, after meeting up by chance, as they say, went to Chalcis. Some of the distinguished Chalcideans were sitting as judges of the contest, and with them was Panoides, brother of the dead man. Although both poets competed admirably, they say that Hesiod won in this way: he took the centre of the stage and challenged Homer with one question after another, and Homer answered each one.

[7] So, Hesiod said:

> Son of Meles, Homer, you who know the counsel of the gods; come, tell me first of all, what is the best thing for mortals?

Homer:

> Not to be born at all is the best thing for people on earth, and once born, to pass through the doors of Hades as soon as possible.

Hesiod, for the second time:

> Come, tell me this, then, godlike Homer, what do you reckon in your heart to be the finest thing for mortals?

And he replied:

> When good cheer spreads over all the people, and the guests in the house listen to a bard, sitting in rows, and nearby there are tables full of bread and meat, and drawing wine from a large bowl, the cupbearer carries it around and pours it into the beakers. This, in my heart, seems to me to be the finest thing.

[8] ῥηθέντων δὲ τῶν ἐπῶν, οὕτω σφοδρῶς φασι θαυμασθῆναι ὑπὸ τῶν Ἑλλήνων τοὺς στίχους ὥστε χρυσοῦς
αὐτοὺς προσαγορευθῆναι, καὶ ἔτι καὶ νῦν ἐν ταῖς κοιναῖς
θυσίαις πρὸ τῶν δείπνων καὶ σπονδῶν προκατεύχεσθαι
πάντας. ὁ δὲ Ἡσίοδος ἀχθεσθεὶς ἐπὶ τῇ Ὁμήρου εὐημερίᾳ
ἐπὶ τὴν τῶν ἀπόρων ὥρμησεν ἐπερώτησιν καί φησι τούσδε
τοὺς στίχους·
    Μοῦσ' ἄγε μοι τά τ' ἐόντα τά τ' ἐσσόμενα πρό τ' ἐόντα
    τῶν μὲν μηδὲν ἄειδε, σὺ δ' ἄλλης μνῆσαι ἀοιδῆς.
ὁ δὲ Ὅμηρος βουλόμενος ἀκολούθως τὸ ἄπορον λῦσαι φησίν·
    οὐδέ ποτ' ἀμφὶ Διὸς τύμβῳ <καναχήποδες ἵπποι>
    ἅρματα συντρίψουσιν ἐρίζοντες περὶ νίκης.
[9] καλῶς δὲ καὶ ἐν τούτοις ἀπαντήσαντος ἐπὶ τὰς ἀμφιβόλους
γνώμας ὥρμησεν ὁ Ἡσίοδος, καὶ πλείονας στίχους λέγων
ἠξίου καθ' ἕνα ἕκαστον συμφώνως ἀποκρίνασθαι τὸν Ὅμηρον.
ἔστιν οὖν ὁ μὲν πρῶτος Ἡσιόδου, ὁ δὲ ἑξῆς Ὁμήρου, ἐνίοτε δὲ
καὶ διὰ δύο στίχων τὴν ἐπερώτησιν ποιουμένου τοῦ Ἡσιόδου·
Hes.   δεῖπνον ἔπειθ' εἵλοντο βοῶν κρέα καὐχένας ἵππων
Hom.   ἔκλυον ἱδρώοντας, ἐπεὶ πολέμοιο κορέσθην.
Hes.   καὶ Φρύγες, οἳ πάντων ἀνδρῶν ἐπὶ νηυσὶν ἄριστοι
Hom.   ἀνδράσι ληιστῆρσιν ἐπ' ἀκτῆς δόρπον ἑλέσθαι.
Hes.   χερσὶ βαλὼν ἰοῖσιν ὅλων κατὰ φῦλα γιγάντων
Hom.   Ἡρακλῆς ἀπέλυσεν ἀπ' ὤμων καμπύλα τόξα.
Hes.   οὗτος ἀνὴρ ἀνδρός τ' ἀγαθοῦ καὶ ἀνάλκιδός ἐστι
Hom.   μητρός, ἐπεὶ πόλεμος χαλεπὸς πάσῃσι γυναιξίν.

---

98 μηθέν P.Petr. I 25 (1), l. 40 **100–1** Plu. *Sept. Sap. Conv.* 154a **100** τύμβον P.Petr. I 25 (1), l. 45 **101** ἐρίζοντες: ἐπειγόμενοι Plu. **107–8** Ar. *Pax* 1282–3 **107** δεῖπνον ἔπειθ' εἵλοντο: ὣς οἱ μὲν δαίνυντο Ar. **108** ἐπεὶ πολέμου ἐκόρεσθεν Ar.

90 τούτων τῶν ἐπῶν Allen Rzach Evelyn-White Wilamowitz West (coll. P.Petr. I 25 (1), l. 28–9) **91** τοὺς στίχους: τὰ ἔπη L corr. Rzach Evelyn-White Wilamowitz (coll. P.Petr. I 25 (1), l. 31) τοὺς στίχους ὑπὸ τῶν Ἑλλήνων Allen West Colbeau **92** αὐτοὺς στίχους Nietzsche (στίχους in marg. S) **100** <καναχήποδες ἵπποι> Barnes (coll. Plu.; cf. et P.Petr. I 25 (1), l. 45–6) **108** πτολέμοιο L S corr. Stephanus; κόρεσθεν Nietzsche; πολέμου ἐκορέσθην Wilamowitz **110** δόρπα πένεσθαι Wilamowitz West δοῦλοι ἕπεσθαι in app. Nietzsche **111–112** hoc ordine Nietzsche pler. edd. 112–111 L Allen Colonna Colbeau **111** βαλέων Goettling Rzach Evelyn-White; ἰοῖσιν ὅλων L corr. Nietzsche: ἰοὺς ὠμῶν Nietzsche in app. ἰοὺς οὔλων Rzach Evelyn-White Avezzù ἰοὺς ἀνόμων Wilamowitz West **112** Ἡρακλέης edd. praeter Wilamowitz

[8] And after the verses were spoken, they say that the lines were so deeply admired by the Greeks that they were called 'golden', and even now all people perform them in the common sacrifices before meals and libations. Hesiod, annoyed by Homer's success, turned to posing insoluble challenges and spoke these lines:
> Come, Muse, the things that are, shall be and were – sing nothing to me of those: but remember another song.

And Homer, desiring to solve the challenge in a fitting manner, said:
> Never around the tomb of Zeus will loud-hoofed horses shatter chariots, striving for victory.

[9] As he replied well also on these occasions, Hesiod turned to ambiguous propositions and, uttering several lines, expected Homer to reply in a fitting manner to each. So the first [line in each exchange] is Hesiod's, the following Homer's, though occasionally Hesiod composed the question by using two lines:

Hes. Then they dined on beef and necks of horses
Hom. they cleansed, since they were sweaty, being sated with war.
Hes. And the Phrygians, who of all men on ships are the best
Hom. at having a meal on the shore with pirates.
Hes. Shooting arrows at the tribes of all the Giants with his hands
Hom. Heracles loosed from his shoulders a bent bow.
Hes. This man is the son of a good man and a coward
Hom. mother, since war is hard for all women.

115	*Hes.*	οὔτ' ἄρ σοί γε πατὴρ ἐμίγη καὶ πότνια μήτηρ
	Hom.	†σῶμα τό γ' ἐσπείραντο† διὰ χρυσῆν Ἀφροδίτην.
	Hes.	αὐτὰρ ἐπεὶ δμήθη γάμῳ Ἄρτεμις ἰοχέαιρα
	Hom.	Καλλιστὼ κατέπεφνεν ἀπ' ἀργυρέοιο βιο<ῖο>.
	Hes.	ὣς οἳ μὲν δαίνυντο πανήμεροι, οὐδὲν ἔχοντες
120	*Hom.*	οἴκοθεν, ἀλλὰ παρεῖχεν ἄναξ ἀνδρῶν Ἀγαμέμνων.
	Hes.	δεῖπνον δειπνήσαντες ἐνὶ σποδῷ αἰθαλοέσσῃ
	Hes.	σύλλεγον ὀστέα λευκὰ Διὸς κατατεθνειῶτος
	Hom.	παιδὸς ὑπερθύμου Σαρπηδόνος ἀντιθέοιο.
	Hes.	ἡμεῖς δ' ἂμ πεδίον Σιμοέντιον ἥμενοι οὕτως
125	*Hes.*	ἴομεν ἐκ νηῶν ὁδὸν ἀμφ' ὤμοισιν ἔχοντες
	Hom.	φάσγανα κωπήεντα καὶ αἰγανέας δολιχαύλους.
	Hes.	δὴ τότ' ἀριστῆ<ες> κοῦροι χείρεσσι θαλάσσης
	Hom.	ἄσμενοι ἐσσυμένως τε ἀπείρυσαν ὠκύαλον ναῦν.
	Hes.	κολχίδ' ἔπειτ' ἤγοντο καὶ Αἰήτην βασιλῆα
130	*Hom.*	φεῦγον, ἐπεὶ γίγνωσκον ἀνέστιον ἠδ' ἀθέμιστον.
	Hes.	αὐτὰρ ἐπεὶ σπεῖσάν τε καὶ ἔκπιον οἶδμα θαλάσσης
	Hom.	ποντοπορεῖν ἤμελλον ἐυσσέλμων ἐπὶ νηῶν.
	Hes.	τοῖσιν δ' Ἀτρείδης μεγάλ' εὔχετο πᾶσιν ὀλέσθαι
	Hom.	μηδέ ποτ' ἐν πόντῳ, καὶ φωνήσας ἔπος ηὔδα·
135	*Hes.*	ἐσθίετ' ὦ ξεῖνοι, καὶ πίνετε· μηδέ τις ὑμῶν
	Hes.	οἴκαδε νοστήσειε φίλην ἐς πατρίδα γαῖαν
	Hom.	πημανθείς, ἀλλ' αὖθις ἀπήμονες οἴκαδ' ἵκοισθε.

115 ἦ τ'ἄρα Hermann (1835: 284) Nietzsche αὐτάρ Rzach Evelyn-White οὔ τάρ Wilamowitz; ἔμιγεν Goettling Nietzsche ἐμίγην Wilamowitz **116** cruces West: τότε σπείραντε Hermann Nietzsche Wilamowitz τό γε σπείραντε Rzach Evelyn-White; χρυσέην Nietzsche Allen Rzach Evelyn-White Colonna Colbeau **122** κατατεθνηῶτος Goettling Allen Rzach Evelyn-White Colonna Avezzù Colbeau **124** ἀμπεδίον Nietzsche; σιμοούντιον L; αὕτως Barnes edd. praeter Wilamowitz; ἥμενοι οὕτως inter cruces West; post 124 lacunam stat. Barnes Goettling Westermann Avezzù **128** post 129 Nietzsche **129** ἔπειθ' ἵκοντο L corr. Wilamowitz Rzach Evelyn-White West; βασιλεῖα L **130** γίνωσκον L **132** ἐυσέλμων L **133–7** sic Goettling Evelyn-White Di Benedetto (1969: 163) Avezzù West: 133–134 Hesiodo 135–137 Homero tribuit Hermann, 133–136 Hesiodo 137 Homero Nietzsche, 134 καὶ φωνήσας ἔπος ηὔδα Hesiodo Busse (1909: 115 n. 1) Rzach Wilamowitz **135** ὑμέων Nietzsche Rzach Evelyn-White **137** αὖτις Nietzsche Allen Rzach Evelyn-White Colonna Avezzù Colbeau

Hes.	And not for [conceiving] you did your father and revered mother make love
Hom.	†the body that they sowed† by the action of golden Aphrodite.
Hes.	As she had yielded to marriage, Artemis shooter of arrows
Hom.	killed Callisto [with an arrow] from her silver bow.
Hes.	So they feasted all day, having nothing
Hom.	of their own, but Agamemnon lord of men arranged it.
Hes.	Having dined among the smoky ashes
Hes.	they gathered up the white bones of the deceased, Zeus'
Hom.	son, the proud and godly Sarpedon.
Hes.	Sitting thus over the plain of the Simois
Hes.	we make our way from the ships carrying upon our shoulders
Hom.	hilted swords and long-socketed javelins.
Hes.	Then the best young men with their hands from the sea
Hom.	pleased and eager dragged off the swift ship.
Hes.	Then they took away the Colchian girl and king Aietes
Hom.	they fled, as they recognised him as inhospitable and unlawful.
Hes.	After they had made libations and drunk up the sea's swell
Hom.	they made themselves ready to sail on well-benched ships.
Hes.	For them all the son of Atreus prayed very much, that they might perish
Hom.	never in the sea, and he uttered this verse:
Hes.	Eat, o foreigners, and drink; may none of you
Hes.	return home to your dear fatherland
Hom.	harmed, but may you reach home unharmed.

[10] πρὸς πάντα δὲ τοῦ Ὁμήρου καλῶς ἀπαντήσαντος πάλιν
φησὶν ὁ Ἡσίοδος·
   τοῦτό τι δή μοι μοῦνον ἐειρομένῳ κατάλεξον,
   πόσσοι ἅμ' Ἀτρείδῃσιν ἐς Ἴλιον ἦλθον Ἀχαιοί;
ὁ δὲ διὰ λογιστικοῦ προβλήματος ἀποκρίνεται οὕτως·
   πεντήκοντ' ἦσαν πυρὸς ἐσχάραι, ἐν δὲ ἑκάστῃ
   πεντήκοντ' ὀβελοί, περὶ δὲ κρέα πεντήκοντα·
   τρὶς δὲ τριηκόσιοι περὶ ἓν κρέας ἦσαν Ἀχαιοί.
τοῦτο δὲ εὑρίσκεται πλῆθος ἄπιστον· τῶν γὰρ ἐσχαρῶν
οὐσῶν πεντήκοντα ὀβελίσκοι γίνονται πεντακόσιοι καὶ
χιλιάδες β´, κρεῶν δὲ δεκαδύο μυριάδες ͵ε†ῡ̄† . . . [11] κατὰ
πάντα δὴ τοῦ Ὁμήρου ὑπερτεροῦντος φθονῶν ὁ Ἡσίοδος
ἄρχεται πάλιν·
   υἱὲ Μέλητος Ὁμηρ' εἴ περ τιμῶσί σε Μοῦσαι,
   ὡς λόγος, ὑψίστοι<ο> Διὸς μεγάλοιο θύγατρες,
   λέξον μέτρῳ ἐναρμόζων ὅ τι δὴ θνητοῖσι
   κάλλιστόν <τε> καὶ ἔχθιστον· <πο>θέω γὰρ ἀκοῦσαι.
ὁ δέ φησι·
   Ἡσίοδ' ἔκγονε Δίου ἑκόντα με ταῦτα κελεύεις
   εἰπεῖν· αὐτὰρ ἐγὼ μάλα τοι πρόφρων ἀγορεύσω.
   κάλλιστον μὲν τῶν ἀγαθῶν ἔσται μέτρον εἶναι
   αὐτὸν ἑαυτῷ, τῶν δὲ κακῶν ἔχθιστον ἁπάντων.
   ἄλλο δὲ πᾶν ὅ τι σῷ θυμῷ φίλον ἐστὶν ἐρώτα.
Hes.   πῶς ἂν ἄριστ' οἰκοῖντο πόλεις καὶ ἐν ἤθεσι ποίοις;
Hom.   εἰ μὴ κερδαίνειν ἀπὸ τῶν αἰσχρῶν ἐθέλοιεν,
       οἱ δ' ἀγαθοὶ τιμῷντο, δίκη δ' ἀδίκοισιν ἐπείη.
Hes.   εὔχεσθαι δὲ θεοῖς ὅ τι πάντων ἐστὶν ἄμεινον;
Hom.   εὔνουν εἶναι ἑαυτῷ <ἀεὶ> χρόνον ἐς τὸν ἅπαντα.

146–8 interpolationem stat. West 148 μυριάδες ͵ε*** Westermann Nietzsche Rzach Allen Colonna Avezzù Colbeau μυριάδες <χιλιάδες> ͵ε Wilamowitz μυριάδες ... Evelyn-White μυριάδες <καὶ χιλιάδες> ε´,†ῡ̄† West   152 ὑψίστοι<ο> S in marg.   153 μέτρον L corr. Barnes Wilamowitz West; ἐναρμόζον L corr. Boissonade   154 <τε> S; <πο>θέω S in marg.; post 159 versum 165 pos. S lacunam stat. Nietzsche Rzach   163 τιμοῖντο L S Stephanus; post 163 lacunam stat. Hermann   164 θεοῖσι τί Rohde Nietzsche Rzach Evelyn-White Wilamowitz West   165 <ἀεὶ> S Nietzsche Allen Evelyn-White Colonna: εὔνομον εἶναι ἑῷ θυμῷ Rzach εὔνουν εἶναι ἑοῖ αὐτῷ Wilamowitz εὔνουν †εἶναι ἑαυτῷ† West

[10] As Homer replied well to all [the challenges], Hesiod said, again:
> Tell me only this, as I ask you: how many Achaeans went to Ilion with the Atreides?

And he answered with a numerical problem, as follows:
> Fifty were the fire-hearths, and in each one fifty spits, around each of which were fifty pieces of meat; and three times three hundred Achaeans were around one piece of meat.

But this results in an incredible number: for if there are 50 hearths, then there are 2,500 spits, and 125,000 pieces of meat †...

[11] Since Homer was constantly holding the lead, the envious Hesiod starts again:
> Son of Meles, Homer, if the Muses honour you as they say, the daughters of great Zeus the highest, then tell me, fitting it to metre, what is the finest and worst thing for mortals – I long to hear.

And he said:
> Hesiod, progeny of Dius, I willingly say what you ask – indeed I shall speak most readily. To be the measure of good for oneself is the finest thing, and the worst of all is to be the same with regard to evil. Ask me whatever else is dear to your heart.

Hes. In what way would cities best be governed, and by what customs?
Hom. If they did not wish to profit from immoral acts,
and the good were honoured, and justice pursued wrongdoers.
Hes. What is the best thing of all to pray for to the gods?
Hom. That one may always be well-disposed to oneself at all times.

Hes.	ἐν δ' ἐλαχίστῳ ἄριστον ἔχεις ὅ τι φύεται εἰπεῖν;
Hom.	ὡς μὲν ἐμῇ γνώμῃ, φρένες ἐσθλαὶ σώμασιν ἀνδρῶν.
Hes.	ἡ δὲ δικαιοσύνη τε καὶ ἀνδρείη δύναται τί;
Hom.	κοινὰς ὠφελίας ἰδίοις μόχθοισι πορίζειν.
170	Hes.	τῆς σοφίης δὲ τί τέκμαρ ἐπ' ἀνθρώποισι πέφυκεν;
Hom.	γινώσκειν τὰ παρόντ' ὀρθῶς, καιρῷ δ' ἅμ' ἕπεσθαι.
Hes.	πιστεῦσαι δὲ βροτοῖς ποῖον χρέος ἄξιόν ἐστιν;
Hom.	οἷς αὐτὸς κίνδυνος ἐπὶ πραχθεῖσιν ἔπηται.
Hes.	ἡ δ' εὐδαιμονίη τί ποτ' ἀνθρώποισι καλεῖται;
175 | Hom. | λυπηθέντ' ἐλάχιστα θανεῖν ἡσθέντα <τε> πλεῖστα. |

[12] ῥηθέντων δὲ καὶ τούτων οἱ μὲν Ἕλληνες πάντες τὸν Ὅμηρον ἐκέλευον στεφανοῦν, ὁ δὲ βασιλεὺς Πανοίδης ἐκέλευσεν ἕκαστον τὸ κάλλιστον ἐκ τῶν ἰδίων ποιημάτων εἰπεῖν. Ἡσίοδος οὖν ἔφη πρῶτος·

180   Πληιάδων Ἀτλαγενέων ἐπιτελλομενάων
      ἄρχεσθ' ἀμήτου, ἀρότοιό τε δυσομενάων·
      αἵ δή τοι νύκτας τε καὶ ἤματα τεσσαράκοντα
      κεκρύφαται, αὖθις δὲ περιπλομένου ἐνιαυτοῦ
      φαίνονται, τὰ πρῶτα χαρασσομένοιο σιδήρου.
185   οὗτός τοι πεδίων πέλεται νόμος, οἵ τε θαλάσσης
      ἐγγύθι ναιετάουσ', οἵ τ' ἄγκεα βησσήεντα
      πόντου κυμαίνοντος ἀπόπροθι πίονα χῶρον
      ναίουσιν· γυμνὸν σπείρειν, γυμνὸν δὲ βοωτεῖν,
      γυμνόν τ' ἀμάειν, ὅταν ὥρια πάντα πέλωνται.

180–9 Hes. *Op.* 383–92   **181** ἀρότοιο δὲ Hes.   **183** αὖτις Hes.   **189** εἴ χ' ὥρια πάντ' ἐθέλῃσθα Hes.

166 ἔχειν σ' L corr. edd.   **167** ἐμῇ γνώμῃ Nietzsche Rzach Allen Evelyn-White Colonna West Colbeau; σώμασιν: στήθεσιν West   **168** ἀνδρία L; δύναταί τι L   **169** ὠφελείας L corr. S   **171** γιγνώσκειν Nietzsche Rzach Evelyn-White Allen Colonna Avezzù Colbeau   **172** βροτοῖσι L S Stephanus corr. Barnes   **173** οἷς αὐτοῖς Wilamowitz; ἔτι L corr. S in marg.   **175** <τε> S   **177** Πανοίδης cf. 69   **181** ἀμητοῖο L corr. edd. (coll. *Op.* 384)   **183** αὖτις Nietzsche Allen Rzach Evelyn-White Colonna Avezzù (coll. *Op.* 386)   **186** ἄγγεα L   **188** ναίουσι L   **189** γυμνούς θ' L; ὅτ' ἂν Allen Rzach Colonna Avezzù West Colbeau

Hes.	Can you say what is the best thing that comes into being in the smallest space?
Hom.	In my opinion, noble minds in the bodies of men.
Hes.	What can justice and manly spirit achieve?
Hom.	Offering common profit from private labours.
Hes.	What is the mark of wisdom among human beings?
Hom.	Assessing the circumstances correctly, and seizing the moment.
Hes.	On which matters is it worth putting trust in mortals?
Hom.	When the same risk accompanies their actions.
Hes.	What can ever be called happiness by human beings?
Hom.	To die having experienced the least pain and the greatest pleasure.

[12] After these verses too were spoken, all the Greeks asked for Homer to be crowned the winner, but king Panoides asked each of them to perform the finest passage from their own poems. So Hesiod said first:

When the Atlas-born Pleiades rise, start the harvest, and the ploughing when they set. For forty nights and days they lie hidden, and after the year has gone round again they appear, for the first time, when the iron is sharpened. This is the law of the land for those who dwell close to the sea as well as for those who inhabit the winding valleys, fertile terrain distant from the swelling sea. Sow naked and plough naked, and harvest naked, when everything is in due season.

μεθ' ὃν Ὅμηρος·
  ἀμφὶ δ' ἄρ' Αἴαντας δοιοὺς ἵσταντο φάλαγγες
  καρτεραί, ἃς οὔτ' ἄν κεν Ἄρης ὀνόσαιτο μετελθών,
  οὔτε κ' Ἀθηναίη λαοσσόος. οἱ γὰρ ἄριστοι
  κρινθέντες Τρῶάς τε καὶ Ἕκτορα δῖον ἔμιμνον
  φράξαντες δόρυ δουρί, σάκος σάκει προθελύμνῳ·
  ἀσπὶς ἄρ' ἀσπίδ' ἔρειδε, κόρυς κόρυν, ἀνέρα δ' ἀνήρ,
  ψαῦον δ' ἱππόκομοι κόρυθες λαμπροῖσι φάλοισι
  νευόντων· ὡς πυκνοὶ ἐφέστασαν ἀλλήλοισιν.
  ἔφριξεν δὲ μάχη φθισίμβροτος ἐγχείῃσι
  μακραῖς, ἃς εἶχον ταμεσίχροας. ὄσσε δ' ἄμερδεν
  αὐγὴ χαλκείη κορύθων ἄπο λαμπομενάων
  θωρήκων τε νεοσμήκτων σακέων τε φαεινῶν
  ἐρχομένων ἄμυδις. μάλα κεν θρασυκάρδιος εἴη
  ὅς τότε γηθήσειεν ἰδὼν πόνον οὐδ' ἀκάχοιτο.
[13] θαυμάσαντες δὲ καὶ ἐν τούτῳ τὸν Ὅμηρον οἱ Ἕλληνες
ἐπῄνουν, ὡς παρὰ τὸ προσῆκον γεγονότων τῶν ἐπῶν, καὶ
ἐκέλευον διδόναι τὴν νίκην. ὁ δὲ βασιλεὺς τὸν Ἡσίοδον
ἐστεφάνωσεν εἰπὼν δίκαιον εἶναι τὸν ἐπὶ γεωργίαν καὶ
εἰρήνην προκαλούμενον νικᾶν, οὐ τὸν πολέμους καὶ σφαγὰς
διεξιόντα. τῆς μὲν οὖν νίκης οὕτω φασὶ τυχεῖν τὸν
Ἡσίοδον καὶ λαβόντα τρίποδα χαλκοῦν ἀναθεῖναι ταῖς
Μούσαις ἐπιγράψαντα·
  Ἡσίοδος Μούσαις Ἑλικωνίσι τόνδ' ἀνέθηκεν
  ὕμνῳ νικήσας ἐν Χαλκίδι θεῖον Ὅμηρον.
τοῦ δὲ ἀγῶνος διαλυθέντος διέπλευσεν ὁ Ἡσίοδος εἰς
Δελφοὺς χρησόμενος καὶ τῆς νίκης ἀπαρχὰς τῷ θεῷ ἀναθή-
σων. προσερχομένου δὲ αὐτοῦ τῷ ναῷ ἔνθεον γενομένην
τὴν προφῆτίν φασιν εἰπεῖν·
  ὄλβιος οὗτος ἀνὴρ ὃς ἐμὸν δόμον ἀμφιπολεύει,
  Ἡσίοδος Μούσῃσι τετιμένος ἀθανάτῃσιν·
  τοῦ δ' ἤτοι κλέος ἔσται ὅσην τ' ἐπικίδναται ἠώς.
  ἀλλὰ Διὸς πεφύλαξο Νεμείου κάλλιμον ἄλσος·
  κεῖθι δέ τοι θανάτοιο τέλος πεπρωμένον ἐστίν.

191–204 Hom. *Il.* 13.126–33 et 13.339–44   **200** μακρῆς Hom.   **213–14** *AP* 7.53, Procl. *Vit. Hom.* 6, D. Chr. *Or.* 2.11, P.Freib. 1.1b   **213** ἀνέθηκα *AP*   **219–23** Tz. *Vita Hesiodi* 166–70 Colonna   **221** τοῦ δή τοι Tz.; ὅσον Tz.   **223** καὶ γάρ τοι Tz.

194 κριθέντες L   **196** ἀσπὶς δ' ἄρ' L corr. edd. (coll. *Il.* 13.131): ἀσπὶς δ' Allen Colonna Avezzù Colbeau   **199** φθεισίμβροτος Allen Rzach Colonna Avezzù West Colbeau   **210** οὕτως West   **221** τοῦ δή τοι L S Stephanus corr. Nietzsche West: τοῦ δ' ἦ τοι Allen Rzach Wilamowitz Colonna Avezzù Colbeau; ὅσον Nietzsche Rzach Evelyn-White Wilamowitz

After which, Homer:
> Around the two Ajaxes the battle lines stood strong, and neither Ares would have found fault, had he joined them, nor Athena who rouses the people. For the best chosen men were awaiting the Trojans and godly Hector, joining spear close to spear, shield to overlapping shield; shield pushed on shield, helmet on helmet, man on man, and the horsehair crests on the bright helmet-ridges touched as they were bending forward; so compact they stood against each other. The deadly battle bristled with the long skin-cutting spears they were holding. The gleam of the bronze from the bright helmets, the newly polished corslets, and the shining shields dazzled the eyes as they came close against each other. The man who enjoyed watching this struggle and did not feel consternation would have been most bold of heart.

[13] On this occasion too, the Greeks in admiration praised Homer, as his verses were extraordinary beyond expectation, and they asked [Panoides] to award him the victory. But the king crowned Hesiod, saying that it was just for the one who promoted agriculture and peace to win, and not the one who expounded wars and slaughters. So they say that Hesiod gained victory in this way and, receiving a bronze tripod, he dedicated it to the Muses with this inscription:
> Hesiod dedicated this to the Heliconian Muses when he defeated divine Homer with a hymn at Chalcis.

After the contest was dissolved, Hesiod sailed to Delphi to consult the oracle and dedicate a tribute of his victory to the god. As he entered the temple, they say that the prophetess became divinely inspired and said:
> Blessed is this man who attends my house, Hesiod, honoured by the immortal Muses. Certainly his fame will spread as far as the light of day. But beware the beautiful grove of Nemean Zeus: for there the fulfilment of your death has been fated.

[14] ὁ δὲ Ἡσίοδος ἀκούσας τοῦ χρησμοῦ τῆς Πελοποννήσου
μὲν ἀνεχώρει νομίσας τὴν ἐκεῖ Νεμέαν τὸν θεὸν λέγειν,
εἰς δὲ Οἰνόην τῆς Λοκρίδος ἐλθὼν καταλύει παρὰ Ἀμφιφάνει καὶ Γανύκτορι, τοῖς Φηγέως παισίν, ἀγνοήσας τὸ
μαντεῖον. ὁ γὰρ τόπος οὗτος ἅπας ἐκαλεῖτο Διὸς Νεμείου
ἱερόν. διατριβῆς δ' αὐτῷ πλείονος γενομένης ἐν τοῖς
†Οἰνῶσιν† ὑπονοήσαντες οἱ νεανίσκοι τὴν ἀδελφὴν αὐτῶν
μοιχεύειν τὸν Ἡσίοδον, ἀποκτείναντες εἰς τὸ μεταξὺ τῆς
Εὐβοίας καὶ τῆς Λοκρίδος πέλαγος κατεπόντισαν. τοῦ δὲ
νεκροῦ τριταίου πρὸς τὴν γῆν ὑπὸ δελφίνων προσενεχ-
θέντος, ἑορτῆς τινος ἐπιχωρίου παρ' αὐτοῖς οὔσης Ἀριαδνείας,
πάντες ἐπὶ τὸν αἰγιαλὸν ἔδραμον καὶ τὸ σῶμα γνωρίσαντες
ἐκεῖνο μὲν πενθήσαντες ἔθαψαν, τοὺς δὲ φονεῖς ἀνεζήτουν.
οἱ δὲ φοβηθέντες τὴν τῶν πολιτῶν ὀργὴν κατασπάσαντες
ἁλιευτικὸν σκάφος διέπλευσαν εἰς Κρήτην. οὓς κατὰ
μέσον τὸν πλοῦν ὁ Ζεὺς κεραυνώσας κατεπόντωσεν, ὥς
φησιν Ἀλκιδάμας ἐν Μουσείῳ. Ἐρατοσθένης δέ φησιν
ἐν †ἐνηπόδῳ† Κτίμενον καὶ Ἄντιφον τοὺς Γαννύκτορος ἐπὶ τῇ
προειρημένῃ αἰτίᾳ ἀνελόντας σφαγιασθῆναι θεοῖς
ξενίοις ὑπὸ Εὐρυκλέους τοῦ μάντεως. τὴν μέντοι παρθένον
τὴν ἀδελφὴν τῶν προειρημένων μετὰ τὴν φθορὰν ἑαυτὴν
ἀναρτῆσαι, φθαρῆναι δὲ ὑπό τινος ξένου συνόδου τοῦ
Ἡσιόδου Δημώδους ὄνομα· ὃν καὶ αὐτὸν ἀναιρεθῆναι ὑπὸ
τῶν αὐτῶν φησιν. ὕστερον δὲ Ὀρχομένιοι κατὰ χρησμὸν
μετενέγκαντες αὐτὸν παρ' αὐτοῖς ἔθαψαν καὶ ἐπέγραψαν
ἐπὶ τῷ τάφῳ·

226–35 cf. P.Ath.Soc.Pap. inv. M2

226 Οἰνεῶνα Westermann Avezzù **230** Οἰνιῶσιν Barnes Οἰνοεῦσιν Friedel (1878–9: 236) Allen Rzach Evelyn-White Colonna West Colbeau Οἰνεωνεῖσιν Sauppe (1850: 155) Nietzsche Avezzù Οἰνεῶσιν Goettling ἐν τῷ Οἰνεῶνι in app. Westermann 'certo emendari nequit' Wilamowitz **231–2** τῆς Βολίνας (vel τῆς Εὐπαλίας) καὶ τῆς Μολυκρίας in app. Nietzsche τῆς Μολυκρίας καὶ τῆς Λοκρίδος Goettling τῆς Ἀχαίας καὶ τῆς Λοκρίδος Westermann Evelyn-White **234** Ῥίου ἁγνείας Nietzsche West (coll. Plu. *Sept. Sap. Conv.* 162e) **241** ἐν †ἐνηπόδῳ† Allen Colonna Colbeau: ἐν Ἡσιόδῳ Goettling Nietzsche Rzach Wilamowitz Evelyn-White West ἐν Ἀνδραπόδῳ Barnes Westermann ἐν ἐνάτῃ Ὀλυμπιάδι Bernhardy (1822: 241); Γανύκτορος edd. **242** ἀνελθόντας S Stephanus ἐνελόντας Friedel Rzach ἀνελόντας <τὴν ποιητήν> West; θεοῖς <τοῖς> Bernhardy (1822: 241) Nietzsche Rzach Allen Evelyn-White Colonna **246** δημώδους <Τρωίλου> Nietzsche Rzach

[14] Hesiod, after hearing the oracle, kept far away from the Peloponnese, as he thought that the god was referring to the Nemea there, and upon arriving at Oenoe in Locris he stayed with Amphiphanes and Ganyctor, the sons of Phegeus, having misunderstood the oracle. For that entire area is called sacred to Nemean Zeus. After he had spent some considerable time among the inhabitants of Oenoe, the young men, suspecting that Hesiod was having intercourse with their sister, killed him and threw him in the sea between Euboea and Locris. When on the third day his corpse was brought back to land by dolphins, during a certain local festival in honour of Ariadne, everyone ran to the shore and, recognising the body, buried him in mourning and looked for the murderers. Fearing the anger of their fellow citizens, they set sail for Crete after hauling down a fishing boat. But in the middle of the sea journey Zeus struck them with a thunderbolt and drowned them, as Alcidamas says in his *Museum*. But Eratosthenes says in the †*Enepodos*† that Ctimenus and Antiphus, the sons of Gannyctor, after committing the murder for the reason mentioned above, were sacrificed to the gods of hospitality by the seer Eurycles; as for the girl, their sister, she hanged herself after her dishonour – she had in fact been dishonoured by a certain foreigner who was travelling with Hesiod, called Demodes; and he says that this man was also killed by them. Later on, the Orchomenians moved him and buried him on their land in accordance with an oracle, and inscribed on his tomb:

Ἄσκρη μὲν πατρὶς πολυλήιος, ἀλλὰ θανόντος
   ὀστέα πληξίππων γῇ Μινυῶν κατέχει
Ἡσιόδου, τοῦ πλεῖστον ἐν ἀνθρώποις κλέος ἐστὶν
   ἀνδρῶν κρινομένων ἐν βασάνῳ σοφίης.
[15] καὶ περὶ μὲν Ἡσιόδου τοσαῦτα· ὁ δὲ Ὅμηρος ἀποτυχὼν
τῆς νίκης περιερχόμενος ἔλεγε τὰ ποιήματα, πρῶτον μὲν
τὴν Θηβαίδα ἔπη ͵ζ ἧς ἡ ἀρχή·
   Ἄργος ἄειδε θεὰ πολυδίψιον ἔνθεν ἄνακτες·
εἶτα Ἐπιγόνους ἔπη ͵ζ ὧν ἡ ἀρχή·
   νῦν αὖθ' ὁπλοτέρων ἀνδρῶν ἀρχώμεθα Μοῦσαι.
φασὶ γάρ τινες καὶ ταῦτα Ὁμήρου εἶναι. ἀκούσαντες
δὲ τῶν ἐπῶν οἱ Μίδου τοῦ βασιλέως παῖδες Ξάνθος καὶ
Γόργος παρακαλοῦσιν αὐτὸν ἐπίγραμμα ποιῆσαι ἐπὶ τοῦ
τάφου τοῦ πατρὸς αὐτῶν, ἐφ' οὗ ἦν παρθένος χαλκῆ τὸν
Μίδου θάνατον οἰκτιζομένη. καὶ ποιεῖ οὕτως·
   χαλκῆ παρθένος εἰμί, Μίδου δ' ἐπὶ σήματος ἧμαι.
   ἔστ' ἂν ὕδωρ τε νάῃ καὶ δένδρεα μακρὰ τεθήλῃ
   καὶ ποταμοὶ πλήθωσι, περικλύζῃ δὲ θάλασσα,
   ἠέλιος δ' ἀνιὼν φαίνῃ λαμπρά τε σελήνη,
   αὐτοῦ τῇδε μένουσα πολυκλαύτῳ ἐπὶ τύμβῳ
   σημανέω παριοῦσι Μίδης ὅτι τῇδε τέθαπται.
λαβὼν δὲ παρ' αὐτῶν φιάλην ἀργυρᾶν ἀνατίθησιν ἐν
Δελφοῖς τῷ Ἀπόλλωνι, ἐπιγράψας·
   Φοῖβε ἄναξ δῶρόν τοι Ὅμηρος καλὸν ἔδωκα
   σῇσιν ἐπιφροσύναις· σὺ δέ μοι κλέος αἰὲν ὀπάζοις.

250–3 *AP* 7.54, Paus. 9.38.4, Tz. *Vita Hesiodi* 179–82 Colonna   **251** πληξίππου γῇ Μινύης Tz.   **252** ἀνθρώποις κλέος ἐστὶν: Ἑλλάδι κῦδος ὀρεῖται Paus.   **253** βασάνοις Tz.   **265–70** Ps.-Hdt. *Vit. Hom.* 11, Pl. *Phdr.* 264d, D. Chr. 37.38, D. L. 1.89, Phlp. *In APo.* 156, *AP* 7.153   **265** Μίδα Pl., *AP*, Dio; ἐπὶ σήματος ἧμαι: ἐπὶ σήματι κεῖμαι test. cett.   **266** cf. et Ps.-Longin. 36.2, S.E. *M.* 1.28 et 8.184, id. *P.* 2.37, Lib. 17.34. ὄφρ' Pl. Lib.; ῥέῃ Ps.-Hdt., D. Chr., Ps.-Longin.   **267** om. Pl., D. Chr., Phlp., *AP*; post 268 Ps.-Hdt., D. L.; γε ῥέωσιν Ps.-Hdt., D. L.; ἀνακλύζῃ Ps.-Hdt., D. L.   **268** om. Pl., D. Chr., *AP*; post 266 Ps.-Hdt., D. L.; φαίνῃ: λάμπῃ test. cett.   **269** cf. et Suda s.v. αὐτοῦ. ἐνὶ Phlp.; πολυκλαύτου ἐπὶ τύμβου Ps.-Hdt., Pl.   **270** cf. et Suda s.v. αὐτοῦ. σημανέω: ἀγγελέω test. cett.; Μίδας Pl., D. L., *AP*, Suda   **273–4** cf. et Tz. ad Lyc. 21–3 Scheer   **273** ἑλὼν ὁ Ὅμηρος ἔδωκα Tz.   **274** ἧσιν ἐπ' εὐφροσύναις Tz.

251 πληξίππων γῇ Μινυὰς **L** Allen Colonna Colbeau corr. Barnes Nietzsche Wilamowitz West (coll. *AP*, Paus.) : πληξίππος γῇ Μινυὰς Rzach Evelyn-White Avezzù   **256** ξ **L** corr. Hermann (1835: 286)   **258** ἐπειγομένου **L** corr. Barnes; ξ **L** corr. Hermann   **265** χαλκέη … Μιδέῳ Rzach Evelyn-White   **266** ἔσ τ' ἂν Allen Rzach Colonna Colbeau

Ascra, rich in cornfields, is his fatherland, but in death the land of the horse-driving Minyans holds the bones of Hesiod, whose fame is greatest among men, when men are judged by the touchstone of wisdom.

[15] And this is it for Hesiod. Homer, after losing the contest, wandered around and recited his poems, first the *Thebaid*, of 7,000 verses, which begins:

Sing of thirsty Argos, goddess, whence the lords;

and then the *Epigoni*, of 7,000 verses, which begins:

But now let us begin singing of younger men, Muses.

For some say that these are also by Homer. Having heard these verses, the sons of king Midas, Xanthus and Gorgus, invited him to compose an epigram for their father's tomb, upon which there stood a bronze statue of a virgin lamenting Midas' death. And he composed the following:

I am a virgin of bronze, and I sit upon Midas' grave. As long as water flows, and trees grow high, and rivers swell, and the sea washes all around, and the sun rises and shines, and the bright moon, I, staying here on this much lamented tomb, shall signal to passers-by that Midas is buried here.

And receiving from them a silver cup, he dedicated it to Apollo in Delphi, with the following inscription:

Lord Phoebus, I, Homer, offer you this beautiful gift for your thoughtfulness. May you always grant me fame.

[16] μετὰ δὲ ταῦτα ποιεῖ τὴν Ὀδύσσειαν ἔπη μ̣β ́, πεποιηκὼς
ἤδη τὴν Ἰλιάδα ἐπῶν μ̣εφ ́. παραγενόμενον δὲ ἐκεῖθεν
εἰς Ἀθήνας αὐτὸν ξενισθῆναί φασι παρὰ Μέδοντι τῷ
βασιλεῖ τῶν Ἀθηναίων. ἐν δὲ τῷ βουλευτηρίῳ ψύχους
ὄντος καὶ πυρὸς καιομένου σχεδιάσαι λέγεται τούσδε τοὺς
στίχους·
  ἀνδρὸς μὲν στέφανοι παῖδες, πύργοι δὲ πόληος,
  ἵπποι δ' αὖ πεδίου κόσμος, νῆες δὲ θαλάσσης,
  λαὸς δ' εἰν ἀγορῇσι καθήμενος εἰσοράασθαι.
  αἰθομένου δὲ πυρὸς γεραρώτερος οἶκος ἰδέσθαι
  ἤματι χειμερίῳ ὁπότ' ἂν νίφῃσι Κρονίων.
[17] ἐκεῖθεν δὲ παραγενόμενος εἰς Κόρινθον ἐρραψῴδει τὰ
ποιήματα. τιμηθεὶς δὲ μεγάλως παραγίνεται εἰς Ἄργος
καὶ λέγει ἐκ τῆς Ἰλιάδος τὰ ἔπη τάδε·
  οἳ δ' Ἄργος τ' εἶχον Τίρυνθά τε τειχιόεσσαν
  Ἑρμιόνην τ' Ἀσίνην τε, βαθὺν κατὰ κόλπον ἐχούσας,
  Τροιζῆν' Ἠιόνας τε καὶ ἀμπελόεντ' Ἐπίδαυρον
  νῆσόν τ' Αἴγιναν Μάσητά τε κοῦροι Ἀχαιῶν,
  τῶν αὖθ' ἡγεμόνευε βοὴν ἀγαθὸς Διομήδης
  Τυδείδης οὗ πατρὸς ἔχων μένος Οἰνείδαο,
  καὶ Σθένελος Καπανῆος ἀγακλειτοῦ φίλος υἱός·
  τοῖσι δ' ἅμ' Εὐρύπυλος τρίτατος κίεν ἰσόθεος φώς,
  Μηκιστέως υἱὸς Ταλαιονίδαο ἄνακτος.
  ἐκ πάντων δ' ἡγεῖτο βοὴν ἀγαθὸς Διομήδης.
  τοῖσι δ' ἅμ' ὀγδώκοντα μέλαιναι νῆες ἕποντο·
  ἐν δ' ἄνδρες πολέμοιο δαήμονες ἐστιχόωντο
  Ἀργεῖοι λινοθώρηκες, κέντρα πτολέμοιο.

281–5 Ps.-Hdt. *Vit. Hom.* 31, Suda s.v. Ὅμηρος 88–92 Adler **281** στέφανος παῖδες Ps.-Hdt. παῖδες στέφανος Suda **282** ἐν πεδίῳ Ps.-Hdt., Suda; ἐν θαλάσσαις Suda; χρήματα δ' αὔξει οἶκον· ἀτὰρ γεραροὶ βασιλῆες / ἥμενοι εἰν ἀγορῇ κόσμος τ' ἄλλοισιν ὁρᾶσθαι post 282 add. Ps.-Hdt., Suda **283** om. Ps.-Hdt., Suda **285** om. Ps.-Hdt., Suda **289–93 et 295–9** cf. Hom. *Il.* 2.559–68 **292** οἵ τ' ἔχον Αἴγιναν *Il.* 2.562 (cf. et Hes fr. 204.47 MW) **294** om. Hom. **296** Εὐρύαλος *Il.* 2.565 **298** συμπάντων *Il.* 2.567 **300–1** om. Hom.

275 μβφ L corr. Nietzsche **276** με L corr. Nietzsche; παραγενόμενος L S Stephanus corr. Westermann **281** στέφανος Wilamowitz West (coll. Ps.-Hdt. Suda); lacunam post **282** stat. Nietzsche Rzach: χρήματα δ' οἶκον ἀέξει, ἀτὰρ κοσμὸς βασιλῆες in app. Nietzsche χρήματα δ' οἶκον ἀέξει, ἀτὰρ γεραροὶ βασιλῆες suppl. Rzach **283** λαοῖς εἰν ἀγορῇσι καθήμενοι Nietzsche Rzach **292** οἵ τ' ἔχον Αἴγιναν S in marg. (cf. *Il.* 2.562); Αἴγιναν τε Μάσητά τε L **296** Εὐρύαλος Barnes Wilamowitz (coll. *Il.* 2.565) **297** Μηκιστέος Rzach

[16] Afterwards he composed the *Odyssey*, of 12,000 verses, having already composed the *Iliad*, of 15,500 verses. As he went from there to Athens, they say that he was hosted by Medon, king of the Athenians. And in the council chamber, since the weather was cold and a fire was burning, it is said that he improvised these lines:

> Sons are the crowns of a man, walls of a city; horses, then, are the ornament of a plain; ships, of the sea; and the people sitting in the assembly is a beautiful sight. And when a fire is burning the house looks more honourable on a winter's day, when the son of Cronus brings snow.

[17] As he went from there to Corinth, he performed his poems. Having received great honours, he went to Argos and spoke these verses from the *Iliad*:

> And those who inhabited Argos and high-walled Tiryns, and Hermione and Asine, which lie over a deep gulf, and Troezen and Eiones and Epidaurus rich in vines, and the island of Aegina, and Mases – Achaean youths – were commanded by Diomedes good at the war cry, the son of Tydaeus, who had the strength of his father, the son of Oeneus, and Sthenelus, the dear son of renowned Capaneus; with them third went Eurypylus, godlike man, son of Mecisteus, son of lord Talaus; but among them all Diomedes good at the war cry was the leader. With them, eighty black ships followed; and inside these, men skilled in war were lined up, Argives with linen cuirasses, goads of war.

τῶν δὲ Ἀργείων οἱ προεστηκότες ὑπερβολῇ χαρέντες
ἐπὶ τῷ ἐγκωμιάζεσθαι τὸ γένος αὐτῶν ὑπὸ τοῦ ἐνδο-
ξοτάτου τῶν ποιητῶν, αὐτὸν μὲν πολυτελέσι δωρεαῖς
305 ἐτίμησαν, εἰκόνα δὲ χαλκῆν ἀναστήσαντες ἐψηφίσαντο
θυσίαν ἐπιτελεῖν Ὁμήρῳ καθ' ἡμέραν καὶ κατὰ μῆνα καὶ
κατ' ἐνιαυτὸν <καὶ> ἄλλην θυσίαν πενταετηρίδα ἐς Χίον
ἀποστέλλειν. ἐπιγράφουσι δὲ ἐπὶ τῆς εἰκόνος αὐτοῦ·
θεῖος Ὅμηρος ὅδ' ἐστὶν ὃς Ἑλλάδα τὴν μεγάλαυχον
310 πᾶσαν ἐκόσμησεν καλλιεπεῖ σοφίῃ,
ἔξοχα δ' Ἀργείους, οἳ τὴν θεοτειχέα Τροίην
ἤρειψαν ποινὴν ἠυκόμου Ἑλένης.
οὗ χάριν ἔστησεν δῆμος μεγαλόπ<τ>ολις αὐτὸν
ἐνθάδε καὶ τιμαῖς ἀμφέπει ἀθανάτων.

---

301 *AP* 14.73.6 **309–12** P.Duk. inv. 665 **311** θεοτειχέα: .ριαυχεα P.Duk. inv. 665 (ἐριαυχέα Menci 2012)

307 <καὶ> θυσίαν Westermann : ἀλλὰ καὶ θυσίαν Wilamowitz **309** μεγαλαύχην **L** corr. Barnes **310** καλλιεπίηι σοφίη τε **L** corr. S in marg. **312** ποινῆς **L** corr. Barnes **313** ἔστησε **L**; μεγαλόπ<τ>ολις **S** supra lineam

The notables among the Argives were exceedingly pleased to have their people praised by the most famous of poets, and they honoured him with expensive gifts, and, setting up a bronze statue of him, decreed to make a sacrifice to Homer every day and every month and every year, and to send another to Chios every fifth year as well. They inscribed on his statue:

> This is divine Homer, who adorned all proud Hellas with his beautifully expressed wisdom, and in particular the Argives, they who destroyed Troy with its wall built by gods as satisfaction for the conduct of fair-haired Helen. For this reason, the people of this great city have set him up here and venerate him with the honours of the immortals.

315 [18] ἐνδιατρίψας δὲ τῇ πόλει χρόνον τινὰ διέπλευσεν εἰς Δῆλον
εἰς τὴν πανήγυριν, καὶ σταθεὶς ἐπὶ τὸν κεράτινον βωμὸν
λέγει ὕμνον εἰς Ἀπόλλωνα οὗ ἡ ἀρχή·
    μνήσομαι οὐδὲ λάθωμαι Ἀπόλλωνος ἑκάτοιο.
ῥηθέντος δὲ τοῦ ὕμνου οἱ μὲν Ἴωνες πολίτην αὐτὸν κοινὸν
320 ἐποιήσαντο, Δήλιοι δὲ γράψαντες τὰ ἔπη εἰς λεύκωμα ἀνέ-
θηκαν ἐν τῷ τῆς Ἀρτέμιδος ἱερῷ. τῆς δὲ πανηγύρεως
λυθείσης ὁ ποιητὴς εἰς Ἴον ἔπλευσε πρὸς Κρεόφυλον κἀκεῖ
χρόνον διέτριβε πρεσβύτης ὢν ἤδη. ἐπὶ δὲ τῆς θαλάσσης
καθήμενος παίδων τινῶν ἀφ' ἁλείας ἐρχομένων ὥς φασι
325 πυθόμενος·
    ἄνδρες ἀπ' Ἀρκαδίης θηρήτορες ἦ ῥ' ἔχομέν τι;
εἰπόντων δὲ ἐκείνων·
    ὅσσ' ἕλομεν λιπόμεσθα, ὅσ' οὐχ ἕλομεν φερόμεσθα,
οὐ νοήσας τὸ λεχθὲν ἤρετο αὐτοὺς ὅ τι λέγοιεν. οἱ δέ φασιν
330 ἐν ἁλείᾳ μὲν ἀγρεῦσαι μηδέν, ἐφθειρίσθαι δέ, καὶ τῶν
φθειρῶν οὓς ἔλαβον καταλιπεῖν, οὓς δὲ οὐκ ἔλαβον ἐν τοῖς
ἱματίοις φέρειν. ἀναμνησθεὶς δὲ τοῦ μαντείου ὅτι τὸ τέλος
αὐτοῦ ἥκοι τοῦ βίου, ποιεῖ τὸ τοῦ τάφου αὐτοῦ ἐπίγραμμα.
ἀναχωρῶν δὲ ἐκεῖθεν, ὄντος πηλοῦ ὀλισθὼν καὶ πεσὼν ἐπὶ
335 τὴν πλευράν, τριταῖος ὥς φασι τελευτᾷ· καὶ ἐτάφη ἐν Ἴῳ.
ἔστι δὲ τὸ ἐπίγραμμα τόδε·
    ἐνθάδε τὴν ἱερὴν κεφαλὴν κατὰ γαῖα καλύπτει,
    ἀνδρῶν ἡρώων κοσμήτορα θεῖον Ὅμηρον.

---

318 h.Ap. 1 **326** Procl. Vit. Hom. 5, Anon. Vit. Hom. 2.3, Anon. Vit. Hom. 3.5, Tz. Exeg. in Il. 37; ἀλιήτορες Anon. Vit. Hom. 2, Anon. Vit. Hom. 3, Tz. **327–38** cf. P.Mich. inv. 2754 ll. 1–14 **328** P.Mich. inv. 2754 ll. 2–3, Ps.-Hdt. Vit. Hom. 35, Procl. Vit. Hom. 5, Anon. Vit. Hom. 1.6, Anon. Vit. Hom. 2.3, Anon. Vit. Hom. 3.5, Ps.-Plu. Vit. Hom. 1.4, Suda s.v. Ὅμηρος 206 Adler; ἄσσ' ἕλομεν … ἃ δ' οὐχ ἕλομεν Ps.-Hdt., Suda οὓς ἕλομεν … οὓς δ' οὐχ ἕλομεν Procl. ἄσσ' ἕλομεν … ἄσσ' οὐχ ἕλομεν Anon. Vit. Hom. 1 ὅσσ' ἕλομεν … ὅσσ' οὐχ ἕλομεν Anon. Vit. Hom. 2, Anon. Vit. Hom. 3, Ps.-Plu. **337–8**. P. Mich. inv. 2754 ll. 11–12, AP 7.3, Ps.-Hdt. Vit. Hom. 36, Ps.-Plu. Vit. Hom. 1.4, Anon. Vit. Hom. 1.6, Anon. Vit. Hom. 2.3, Anon. Vit. Hom. 3.5, Suda s.v. Ὅμηρος 54–5 et 220–221 Adler, Tz. Exeg. in Il. 37 **338** κάλυψεν Ps.-Hdt. κάλυψε P.Mich. inv. 2754

322 Κρεώφυλον edd. praeter Wilamowitz **326** ἀπ' Ἀρκαδίης: ἄγρης ἁλίης Koechly (1857: 222) Evelyn-White **328** λιπόμεσθ', ὅσα δ' οὐχ Nietzsche Evelyn-White **333** αὐτῷ Wilamowitz

[18] After passing some time in the city, he set sail to Delos for the general assembly, and standing at the Altar of Horns he recited the *Hymn to Apollo*, which begins:

May I remember and not forget Apollo, the far-shooter.

After the hymn was spoken, the Ionians jointly made him their fellow citizen, and the Delians wrote down the verses on a tablet and dedicated it in Artemis' temple. When the general assembly was dissolved, the poet set sail for Ios to Creophylus and there he spent time, being already an old man. As he was sitting by the sea, so they say, he asked some boys who were coming back from fishing:

Huntsmen from Arcadia, have we caught anything?

And as they said in reply:

All that we caught we left behind, all that we did not catch we carry with us,

since he did not understand what had been said, he asked them what they meant. They said that during the fishing they had not caught anything, but deloused themselves, and they had left behind the lice that they had caught, while those that they had not caught they were carrying with them in their clothes. And remembering the oracle, that the end of his life had come, he composed an epigram for his tomb. Having departed that place, since it was muddy, after having slipped and fallen on his side, he died, they say, on the third day; and he was buried in Ios. This is the epigram:

Here the earth covers the sacred head, adorner of warrior heroes, divine Homer.

Part 4: Commentary

Introductory remarks

Sources

<u>The extant text</u>. The *Certamen* has been transmitted anonymously and with no date of composition. Mention of the emperor Hadrian, the only clue for dating the text, provides a *terminus post quem*, and may have been inserted in the narrative when the memory of Hadrian's actual visit to Delphi, in 125 AD, was still fresh (32–43n.).

<u>Alcidamas</u>. The fourth-century BC sophist Alcidamas is the main source for the core of the narrative: two verses uttered by Homer in the *Certamen* are attributed by Stobaeus to Alcidamas, and P.Petr. I 25 (1) proves that these verses were connected to the story of the contest of Homer and Hesiod at the latest by the third century BC (78–9n.; on P.Petr. I 25 (1) see Part 2). Furthermore, mention of Alcidamas at 240 and P.Mich. inv. 2754 (see Part 2) show the sophist's interest in the traditions concerning the deaths of both poets. Alcidamas may well be the source of the elaborate narrative structure that presents the two poets according to parallel patterns (56–62n.).

<u>Earlier sources</u>. Some of the materials included in the *Certamen*, however, was already in circulation by Alcidamas' time. Two hexameters transmitted in our text are found in Aristophanes' *Peace*, performed for the first time in 421 BC (107–8n.). Other older traditions that are reflected in the *Certamen* are those concerning Hesiod's and Homer's death, known already to Thucydides (215–23n.) and Heraclitus (321–38n.) respectively. More generally, some of the 'ambiguous propositions' (107–37) represent fifth-century BC concerns about Homeric language that can be associated with sophistic circles, as does the syntax of this section (102–37n.). The verses at 151–75 also deal with topics that stem from fifth- and fourth-century philosophical and political discourse (148–75n.). The narrative framework surrounding the contest also seems to foster the image of Homer as a democratic poet, which would be appropriate to the same era (see esp. 276–85n.).

Interpretation

The work opens by mentioning Homer and Hesiod as seemingly equal (1–2n.), but the two poets are soon set in contrast to each other. The first difference underlined by the text concerns their place of origin: while Hesiod has mentioned his own birthplace in his works (2–6n.), Homer's silence on the matter inspired a big debate and a wide range of local claims (7–17n.). Similarly, there is no certainty with respect to Homer's parents and even to his original name. The text thus gives a list of seven alleged fathers and mothers (18–27n.), and discusses how the poet acquired the name Homer (27–32n.). In both cases, well-known biographical traditions are mixed with otherwise unknown pieces of information. Afterwards, the text offers a genealogy of the two poets which resembles one found in other biographical texts, but is purposefully adapted to the new context (44–53n.). To the discussion of the poets' chronology, the text links the episode of the contest: Homer avoids going to Ios, since an oracle had suggested that he should do so (56–62n.), and ends up meeting Hesiod at Aulis and then competing at Chalcis (62–74n.).

Throughout the contest, Homer appears as the champion of traditional Greek values, and shows expertise on typically Hesiodic topics. Homer starts the contest by defining the 'best' and the 'finest' thing for mortals in terms conforming to dominant Greek views (74–89n.), and then solves a theological impropriety put in the form of an 'insoluble challenge' (94–101n.). Perhaps the most impressive poetic enterprise on which Homer embarks during the contest is in reply to Hesiod's 'ambiguous propositions', a series of verses proposing unacceptable views on issues such as the life and behaviour of heroes and gods, which he turns into expressions of standard Greek morality (102–37n.). He then answers a seemingly impossible 'numerical problem', thereby revealing his closeness to the Muses (138–48n.), and when, in the next stage of the competition, he demonstrates his expertise on topics that were traditionally considered Hesiodic (148–75n.), he appears to be the inevitable winner of the competition. However, king Panoides unexpectedly asks the two poets to perform what they consider the finest passage from their poetry. Homer's performance makes him appear to be a truly divinely inspired poet, enabling humans to share, through poetry, the gaze of the gods, while viewing something that they could not bear in reality – war and death; Hesiod, with his description of the cycle of nature and agriculture, does not offer anything that a man cannot experience in his everyday life (180–204n.). Panoides awards the victory to Hesiod on the basis of the supposedly greater ethical value of his verses. However, the text does not endorse explicitly Hesiod's victory (205–14n.), and the events that follow compensate Homer for his loss.

After the contest, Hesiod is never said to compose or perform poetry; he only visits Delphi to dedicate a tribute of his victory, and Locris, where he dies a violent death following his misunderstanding of an oracle (224–53n.). By contrast, Homer composes two cyclic poems (254–60n.), then the *Iliad* and the *Odyssey* (275–6n.), and finally the *Hymn to Apollo* (315–21n.). This list selects significant examples for each kind of poem linked to him and builds to a climax: the works that were considered of lower status in antiquity are located in the initial phases of his career, and through the *Hymn to Apollo* the poet is finally consecrated as a Panhellenic poet. Homer also composes the funeral epigram for the Phrygian king Midas, a dedication to Apollo engraved on a silver cup (260–74n.), and the verses he recites at Athens before king Medon (276–85n.). The composition of the individual works is not always connected to a specific city, and Homer is consistently depicted as a travelling poet from the beginning of his career (56n.). As he goes around Greece performing his poems, the honours he receives increase. At Argos, for example, he is made the object of a cult (287–314n.), and on Delos he performs for the first time in a Panionian context (315–21n.). Even the fulfillment of the prophecy concerning the poet's death in Ios, and his inability to solve a riddle proposed by some boys, do not lead the reader of the *Certamen* to question the greatness of the divine Homer.

1. Introduction (1–2); Hesiod's birthplace (2–6)

Title: the title given in the manuscript, *On Homer and Hesiod, Their Life, and Their Contest*, offers a precise description of the contents of the work. The title *Certamen Homeri et Hesiodi*, by which the work is commonly known, derives from a Latin translation of a shortened form of the title (Ὁμήρου καὶ Ἡσιόδου ἀγών) which goes back to Stephanus' *editio princeps*.

1–2. Ὅμηρον ... λέγεσθαι: the opening sentence elevates Homer and Hesiod above all other poets (for the possibility that other versions of the story of the contest may have included other participants, see Part 1, 'Plutarch'). However, although Homer and Hesiod are formally presented as equal poets, in fact the description given in these introductory lines fits Homer and subordinates Hesiod as his companion. To start with, 'most divine' (θειότατος) and 'divine' (θεῖος) are standard epithets of Homer but not of Hesiod: θειότατος is used of Homer and Hesiod together only here in extant Greek literature, and is rarely given to Homer (only a few occurrences: e.g., Pl. *Ion* 530b) but never to Hesiod alone; furthermore, θεῖος is a standard epithet of Homer (and 'divine Homer', θεῖος Ὅμηρος, is a hexametric formula: Skiadas 1965: 63–75; Burkert 1987: 44; Graziosi 2002: 67), but is applied to Hesiod only once (Plu. *The Obsolescence of Oracles* 431e). Thus, the *Certamen* draws on, and endorses, the traditional image of Homer as the divine poet *par excellence* in Greek literature (see esp. 180–204n.), and indeed in the text Homer is repeatedly called θεῖος (214, 309 and 338). Hesiod, on the other hand, will never again be associated with divine nature or wisdom. The opening is geared towards Homer to such an extent that West 1967: 444 suggests that the author may have simply adapted the opening of a lost Life of Homer for his own work. However, the author of the *Certamen* may, just as easily, have thought of Homer as generally depicted in many ancient Lives, and adapted the description to include Hesiod.

2. λέγεσθαι: the popular emendation γενέσθαι does not account for the fact that the biographical material was arguably perceived as fictional already in antiquity. In order for a city to make its local tradition successful, the poet should persuasively 'be called' – not necessarily 'be born' – a fellow citizen.

2–6. ἀλλ' Ἡσίοδος ... ἐσθλῇ: by quoting *Op.* 639–40 as a biographical source, the *Certamen* exploits the practice, common in the ancient Lives, of drawing information about the life of a poet from his own work. For other biographical anecdotes on Hesiod derived from his *Theogony* or *Works and Days* see most recently Kivilo 2010a: 7–61; Koning 2010: 31–2, 38–9; Lefkowitz 2012: 6–13. Although these lines are not quoted in other Hesiodic biographies, they had undisputed influence on the matter of Hesiod's birthplace. They are echoed in Tzetzes' *Life of Hesiod* (80–1 Colonna) and feature in many other works (see West 1978: 126, apparatus on *Op.* 639–40) – they are in fact memorable, partly because it is an unusual rhetorical move to disparage one's own place of origin.

5. εἴσατο: the Hesiodic manuscripts and the other *testimonia* read νάσσατο ('dwelled'); the *Certamen* clearly preserves an otherwise unattested variant reading of *Op.* 639, despite a minor slip in the manuscript (**L** reads εἴσατο, from εἶμι, 'to go', emended by Stephanus to εἴσατο, from ἵζω – a near-synonym of the Hesiodic reading).

2. Homer's birthplace (7–17)

7–17. The initial lines of the paragraph clearly engage with the standard claim in Homeric biographies that Homer's silence about himself occasioned a big debate about his life, and ultimately made him the possession of every city (see, e.g., Ps.-Plu. *Vit. Hom.* 1.1; Procl. *Vit. Hom.* 2; Heraclit. *All.* 76.8–9). This view of Homer as a Panhellenic poet is prominent in the *Certamen*, and is endorsed more explicitly in other passages: see esp. 90–1n., 176 and 205 (where Homer is said to appeal to 'the Greeks' or indeed 'all the Greeks'), and the episodes told at 286–338. Of 'virtually all the cities' (πᾶσαι ὡς εἰπεῖν αἱ πόλεις), the text discusses only three. The number is small but the list includes the cities that were generally recognised as having the strongest and most ancient claims for Homer's origins: Smyrna, Chios and Colophon. These are mentioned at the beginning of the list of Homer's alleged birthplaces in most of the ancient biographies and in other literary works (Ps.-Plu. *Vit. Hom.* 1.4 (= *AP* 16.296) and 2.2; Procl. *Vit. Hom.* 2; Suda s.v. 'Homer' 2; Anon. *Vit. Hom.* 2.2; Anon. *Vit. Hom.* 3.1; Lucian *VH* 2.20; *AP* 16.298). Because of the wide circulation of this triad, the author of the *Certamen* may have made this selection without the help of any specific source (*contra* West 1967: 445 who suggests a fourth-century source because other birthplaces, which are attested in later times, are missing in this list). Connections between Homer and these three cities are very old and in fact seem to go back to three passages in the Homeric corpus itself, analysed in Graziosi 2002: 62–79: the *Hymn to Apollo* (172–3) introduces the figure of the Chian blind man, whom already Thucydides (3.104) identified with Homer; in the *Margites* (fr. 1 West 2003a) the old divine singer who came to Colophon is characterised in a way that fits the traditional descriptions of Homer; finally, in the *Hymn to Artemis* 9 there is a possible reference to the legend of Homer's birth by the river Meles near Smyrna. Nagy 2004 suggests that Athens, as the Ionian metropolis, had an interest in stressing the importance of Chios, Smyrna and Colophon. Smyrna appears again at 75 and 151 (Homer is called 'son of Meles') and Chios at 307–8 (the Argives send periodical sacrifices to Chios in Homer's honour), but the text shows awareness of other local traditions too: Ithaca at 23, 25 and 37–40 (some of the alleged parents and the Pythia's response to Hadrian); Ios at 59–60 (the Pythia to Homer).

8–12. καὶ πρῶτοί ... προσηγορίαν: the Smyrneans are πρῶτοι ('first') because their claim as Homer's birthplace is both one of the most prominent and one of the most ancient. The Smyrnean tradition about Homer was very well known already in the classical period (see Pi. fr. 264 SM, who claims that Homer is both from Chios and from Smyrna, and the other sources listed at 9–10n.), and it seems likely that legends about Homer circulated in Smyrna before Alyattes' destruction of the city in 600 BC (Jacoby 1933: 31; Graziosi 2002: 75). The *Hymn to Artemis* 9, which seems to connect Homer with Smyrna via the river Meles, may also be dated to the same period (West 2003a: 17; 7–17n.). Some of the most common features of Homer's persona, accepted even in other local claims, belong to the Smyrnean tradition: Homer's original name Melesigenes (10n.); the epithet 'son of Meles' (75–6n.), used for Homer also in an epigram aiming to prove that Homer was a Colophonian (Ps.-Plu. *Vit. Hom.* 1.4 = *AP* 16.292); the very birth of Homer in Smyrna, accepted in the traditions of Ios and Cyme (Ps.-Plu. *Vit. Hom.* 1.2–3).

9–10. Μέλητος ὄντα ... Κρηϊθίδος νύμφης: the parental couple Cretheis-Meles is one of the most widely attested for Homer. In the ancient sources, Meles is paired only with Cretheis, but Cretheis was also paired with Maeon (Ps.-Plu. *Vit. Hom.* 2.2; Anon. *Vit. Hom.* 1.3). The presence in the *Odyssey* of a similar story (Poseidon rapes Tyro disguised as the river Enipeus, *Od.* 11.235–52) may have contributed to the success of this anecdote; it seems also relevant that Tyro is said to marry Cretheus, a son of Aeolus, whose name is very similar to Cretheis'. The similarity between the two stories was certainly seen by Philostratus (*Im.* 2.8). The river Meles is said to be the father of Homer also in Ps.-Plu. *Vit. Hom.* 2.2; Castricius of Nicaea in Suda s.v. 'Homer'1; Anon. *Vit. Hom.* 1.3; Anon. *Vit. Hom.* 2.1; Anon. *Vit. Hom* 3.1. In other sources, it is the place where Cretheis gave birth to the poet (Ps.-Hdt. *Vit. Hom.* 2–3; Procl. *Vit. Hom.* 3). Both versions are attested already in the fifth century BC (Meles as Homer's father: Critias fr. 50 DK; Eugaion 535 *FGrHist* 2 = *Cert.* 20–1; Homer born by the river Meles: Stesimbr. 107 *FGrHist* 22). The author of the *Certamen* perhaps uses the former version of the legend because it was the one that best illustrated the Smyrneans' claim about Homer, since the mere fact that Homer was born in Smyrna is not sufficient to prove his Smyrnean origins: Ephorus and Aristotle (Ps.-Plu. *Vit. Hom.* 1.2–3) claim that Homer was born by the river Meles in Smyrna only because Cretheis, who was from either Cyme or Ios, had to leave her city after becoming pregnant – therefore, according to them, the poet is a native of Cyme or Ios. Furthermore, by accepting this version of the story, the *Certamen* can later report a genealogy of Homer according to which the poet is the son of Meles (53), and have Hesiod address Homer as 'son of Meles' during the contest section (75 and 151): all these details strengthen the image of Homer as a divine poet. Both Meles and Cretheis are mentioned later in the text in the list of Homer's alleged fathers and mothers respectively (21 and 24) and although they are mentioned separately, there too we are probably meant to see them as a couple (see 18–27n.). Meles is also given as one of Homer's alleged original names at 27–8.

10. Κρηΐθίδος: the manuscript reading Κρηΐθίδος has been unanimously emended based on the form Κρηθηίδος at 24. The form Κρηθηίδος is one of the best attested in the manuscripts of other Homeric biographies, as S indicates in margin ('confirmatur ab aliis'). However, other different spellings of the name are transmitted elsewhere: an emendation here is not necessary, and only evokes a unified tradition that never existed, especially in the case of proper names.

κεκλῆσθαί φασι πρότερον Μελησιγενῆ: that the original name of Homer was Melesigenes, explained either as 'Born by the river Meles' or 'Born of the river Meles', is a common feature of all Homeric biographies. The etymology has no linguistic basis (see, e.g., Wilamowitz 1916: 370; Marx 1925: 406–8). Marx suggests that the real meaning of Melesigenes is 'he who takes care of his people' (since 'born of/by the Meles' would be Μελητογένη), a name that suited the rhapsodes who sometimes claimed to be Homer's descendants (Graziosi 2002: 75 n. 72). The connection with

1. Introduction (1–2); Hesiod's birthplace (2–6)

Meles must have come later in order to support the Smyrneans' claim, and the popular etymology presumably spread together with the Smyrnean traditions about Homer. However, the manuscripts of other Homeric biographies also testify to forms of the name that show its versatility, and this versatility may have played a role in its wide diffusion: the variants Μελισσογενής, Μελισσογενῆ and Μελιτογενής (cf., e.g., Allen's apparatus on Ps.-Hdt. *Vit. Hom.* lines 54 and 64, and more significantly that on Anon. *Vit. Hom.* 2 line 4) seem to connect this name with the words μέλι ('honey') or μέλισσα ('bee'), common symbols for poetry and poets, rather than to a specific place (cf. also Eust. *Od.* 1713.21, where honey is said to flow from Homer's mouth). Fluctuation between -ησ- and -ισσ- is also attested for two other 'original' names of Homer, Μελησιάναξ (Anon. *Vit. Hom.* 2.1) and Μελησαγόρας (Anon. *Vit. Hom.* 1.5). Of these, only Melesigenes features in the list of alleged original names at 28.

11–12. Melesigenes changes his name into Homer after becoming blind, because ὅμηρος is a common term for blind people in the Aeolian dialect: this is another very well-known and widespread piece of information on the poet (see also Ps.-Hdt. *Vit. Hom.* 13; Anon. *Vit. Hom.* 1.5; Anon. *Vit. Hom.* 2.1). It is again based on folk etymology (cf. 10n.), since the word ὅμηρος is not attested with the meaning 'blind' in extant Greek literature. The etymologising explanation connects the poet with a paradigmatic feature of his work: on Homer's blindness as a sign of his closeness to the gods see esp. Graziosi 2002: 138–63. Other ancient sources dismiss the link between the name Homer and blindness (perhaps because they did not believe the folk etymology, or because they denied the very fact that Homer was blind) and on the basis of an independently attested meaning of the word ὅμηρος claim that Melesigenes was called Homer because he was taken hostage (Procl. *Vit. Hom.* 3; Suda s.v. 'Homer' 3; Anon. *Vit. Hom.* 1.5). The *Certamen* knows and mentions this alternative view (see 29–32n.) but does not express any preference. However, Beecroft 2011: 9 notes that Homer in the *Certamen* is never said to write, which may suggest that according to this text he was indeed blind.

13–15. Χῖοι δὲ ... Ὁμηρίδας καλουμένους: Chian traditions about Homer are well attested in Greek literature and from ancient times (Simon. fr. 19 West; Anaximen. 72 *FGrHist* 30; Damastes fr. 11 Fowler; Pi. fr. 264 SM; Theoc. *Id.* 7.47 and 22.218). The link between the Homeridae and Chios is attested already in the classical period: see Acus. 2 *FGrHist* 2 and Hellanic. 4 *FGrHist* 20 (in Harp. O 19 Keaney). *Pace* Fehling 1979: 198, who claims that there was no connection between Chios and the Homeridae, this and the following passage clearly link the two. A scholium to Pindar draws a connection between the Homeridae and Chios and also refers to their kinship with Homer (Schol. Pi. *Nem.* 2.1 Drachmann: Ὁμηρίδας ἔλεγον τὸ μὲν ἀρχαῖον τοὺς ἀπὸ τοῦ Ὁμήρου γένους οἳ καὶ τὴν ποίησιν αὐτοῦ ἐκ διαδοχῆς ᾖδον· μετὰ δὲ ταῦτα καὶ οἱ ῥαψῳδοὶ οὐκέτι τὸ γένος εἰς Ὅμηρον ἀνάγοντες, 'in ancient times they called Homeridae those descended from Homer's lineage, and who sang his poetry by right of succession; in later times, this name was also given to the rhapsodes who no longer traced their lineage back to Homer'). The expression ἐκ διαδοχῆς, intended as 'by right of succession' (Burkert 1979: 54; Graziosi 2002: 214), refers to a genealogical connection with Homer, though, as pointed out most recently by Collins 2004: 183, it can also be interpreted as 'by relay', with reference to a continuous performance of the Homeric verses. Some ancient scholars questioned the descent of the Homeridae from Homer (see Seleucus in Harp. *loc. cit.*). Nevertheless, it is clear that our text drew on a very well attested tradition, which is also found in one of the ancient Homeric biographies: in Ps.-Hdt. *Vit. Hom.* 25 Homer married a woman in Chios and had two daughters, one of whom died unmarried while the other married a Chian man. It must have been easy for ancient readers acquainted with this material to see in these lines a reference to the Homeridae (*contra* West 1999: 372); for the use of the Homeridae as evidence for Homer's Chian origins see e.g. Str. 14.1.35. The Homeridae seem to have been personally involved in the making of Homer's biographical legends: Isoc. *Hel.* 65 testifies to their activity in this respect, while according to Eustathius, the Homeridae hesitated even to mention that Homer was defeated by Hesiod in a poetic contest (see Part 1, 'Eustathius'). The idea that Homer was from Chios probably became predominant in fifth- and fourth-century Athens precisely thanks to the Homeridae and their connection with the Peisistratids (see also 302–8n. and 315–21n.).

15–17. Κολοφώνιοι δὲ ... Μαργίτην: Homer's Colophonian origins are attested also by Nicander (fr. 14 Schneider) and Antimachus (fr. 130 Wyss = 166 Matthews). Colophon has ancient claims to Homer, probably connected to *Margites* fr. 1 West 2003a (for a useful discussion of the problems related to this fragment see Gostoli 2007: 20–3 and 71–4). This section of the text confirms that the *Margites* was fundamental to the Colophonian claims on Homer, although the poet is not here associated with the old singer of *Margites* fr. 1 West 2003a. Rather, the *Certamen* is aligning itself with the tendency, common in the imperial period, to consider the *Margites* a juvenile work of Homer. The attribution of the *Margites* to Homer seems to have been accepted from the time of Archilochus (Eustr. in *EN* 6.7; see Gostoli 2007: 11–13 on this difficult testimony) to at least the fourth century BC (Arist. *Po.* 1448b24–1449a1). But in later times, when Homer was coming to be strictly and solely associated with the *Iliad* and the *Odyssey*, the *Margites* was considered the work of a young (and immature) Homer (D. Chr. 53.4) and was gradually excluded from the Homeric corpus, together with other works (Ps.-Plu. *Vit. Hom.* 1.5; Procl. *Vit. Hom.* 9; Anon. *Vit. Hom.* 3.3). The

Certamen claims explicitly that the *Margites* was Homer's first poetic work; in addition to this, the text makes clear that Homer had not yet composed any other poem before competing against Hesiod (55n.): according to the text, Homer composed the *Margites* as his first work (17: ποιῆσαι πρῶτον τὸν Μαργίτην, 'first composed the *Margites*'); after that (55: ποιήσαντα γὰρ τὸν Μαργίτην, 'for after composing the *Margites*...'), he went round from town to town reciting poetry; 'at about the same time' (62–3: κατὰ δὲ τὸν αὐτὸν χρόνον) Gannyctor organised the contest. Homer's young age emphasises his poetic achievements in the contest, where, despite the unexpected outcome (205–14n.), he constantly provides successful answers to Hesiod's challenges and gains the support of the audience. It also allows Homer the time to travel extensively around Greece and increase his fame after the contest, thus getting a compensation for his defeat (see 254–338).

3. Homer's parents (18–27); Homer's name (27–32); Hadrian (32–43)

18–27. περὶ δὲ ... τὴν Νέστορος: the text lists seven alleged fathers and seven mothers for Homer, many of whom would be otherwise unknown to us. In other texts, the number seven is also used to control the sprawling tradition about Homer's birthplaces (e.g., *AP* 16.297–8). Sources are indicated only in some cases, and only in relation to the list of fathers. Some mothers seem to match names in the list of fathers so as to form couples attested by external evidence (Maeon-Metis; Meles-Cretheis; Masagoras-Themiste; Telemachus-Polycaste), which may help to explain the lack of authorities for the mothers. Some of these characters are explicitly paired up in Suda s.v. 'Homer' 1, which reports a similar list. But it is not possible to prove that the two separate lists derive in fact from one single list in which the names were paired up (as suggested by West 1967: 445): we do not know enough about the remaining characters to speculate about the legends circulating on the topic of their life and relationship to Homer. As far as we can tell, the lists offer a fairly comprehensive overview of the tradition by alluding to several of its main branches (it is possible to recognise Smyrnean, Cypriot, and Ithacan claims). The lists seem to be carefully structured: they start off by referring to the best-known traditions and their characters (Smyrna: Maeon, Meles, Metis, Cretheis; Cyprus: Masagoras, Themiste) and conclude with less common and at the same time more striking names (Telemachus, Calliope, Polycaste). Tzetzes (*Alleg.* Prol. 59–66 Boissonade) and Suda s.v. 'Homer' 1 transmit similar lists: Tzetzes reports the same list of fathers as in the *Certamen*, sometimes with different spellings and sporadically incorporating additional information; the Suda, after reporting a shorter but very similar list, goes on to give the same genealogy as that found at 45–53. Either the *Certamen* was the source for these later texts, or a list circulating in antiquity was a common source for all.

19–20. Ἑλλάνικος ... Μαίονα: 4 *FGrHist* 5c = fr. 5c Fowler; Fowler 2013: 608–10. Hellanicus (mythographer and ethnographer, fifth-fourth century BC) is mentioned to confirm the Smyrnean tradition, which heads the list as in the case of Homer's birthplaces (8–12n.). Maeon is indeed often connected to Smyrna (e.g., Procl. *Vit. Hom.* 3; on Maeon see also 20n.). We know that Hellanicus took an interest in Homer's and Hesiod's genealogy from 4 *FGrHist* 20, on the Homeridae, and 4 *FGrHist* 5a-b-c, according to which Maeon was Homer's father, and Homer and Hesiod were both descended from Orpheus. The *Certamen* too reports this genealogy (45–53) but with the important difference that Homer is here the son of Meles. From Charax (103 *FGrHist* 62), we can infer that according to Hellanicus Maeon was paired with Metis (West 1967: 445; Fowler 2000 *ad loc.*).

19. Κλεάνθης: fr. 592 Arnim; see also 84 *FGrHist* 40. This claim may come from Cleanthes' *On the Poet* (Περὶ τοῦ ποιητοῦ. See Wachsmuth *apud* Pearson 1891: 51; Pearson 1891 fr. 67; the title is known from D. L. 7.174–5), to which most of Cleanthes' fragments on Homer are attributed (frr. 55, 65, 66, 67 Wachsmuth *apud* Pearson 1891; 54, 55, 63, 65, 66, 67 Pearson; 526, 535, 549, 592 Arnim). Arnim 1905: 133 (on fr. 592) suggested that Κλεάνθης in **L** is a mistake for Νεάνθης (see also fr. 593 Arnim). The suggestion is attractive, because while Cleanthes' fragments on Homer mainly deal with allegorical interpretation of the Homeric poems, Neanthes certainly did have biographical interests. He wrote a work titled *On Illustrious Men* (Περὶ ἐνδόξων ἀνδρῶν, see 84 *FGrHist* 13) and dealt with lives of philosophers and poets (84 *FGrHist* 18 on Sophocles' death; 84 *FGrHist* 20 on Plato's death; 84 *FGrHist* 25 on Epicurus' death; 84 *FGrHist* 27 on the young Empedocles' poetic activity). However, the emendation here seems unsafe because it is not impossible that Cleanthes, too, included some biographical information about the poet in his work.

20. Μαίονα: Maeon is the most prominent paternal figure in Homer's biographies together with Meles, which explains the fact that these two names start off the list. Maeon is also mentioned in the genealogy at 52–3, but as Homer's grandfather (his daughter generated Homer with the river Meles). The name of Maeon as Homer's father may have originated in connection with the Homeric poems, where Maeon is the name of a minor character from Thebes who led an attack on Tydeus (*Il.* 4.391–400). Furthermore, in some biographical texts Maeon is connected with Lydia (Aristotle in Ps.-Plu. *Vit. Hom.* 1.3; Lucian *Dem. Enc.* 9), and we know that Maeones (Μαίονες) was an alternative name for the Lydians, which allegedly derived from the name of the eponymous hero or that of a local river (Hdn. *De Pros. Cath.* 3.1.296).

Homer himself used the ethnic Μήονες, whence the later form Μαίονες (see Eust. *Il.* I 575, 26). In the Lives, Maeon is paired with Eumetis, Cretheis and Hyrnetho (Suda s.v. 'Homer' 1; Ps.-Plu. *Vit. Hom.* 2.2; Anon. *Vita Hom.* 2.1; Stesimbr. in Anon. *Vit. Hom.* 1.3).

20–1. Εὐγαίων δὲ Μέλητα: 535 *FGrHist* 2 = 2 Fowler; Fowler 2013: 608–10. The source is a historian from Samos who lived in the fifth century BC. The sources report different forms of his name: **L** gives Εὐγαίων, but an inscription from Priene (535 *FGrHist* 3), the oldest attestation of the name (180 BC), suggests that he was in fact called Εὐάγων. He may have been singled out here because he seems to be one of the most ancient sources for Meles as the father of Homer. The scarcity of information about his work (only four fragments and two *testimonia*) leaves us without a context for this biographical claim. However, we know that Euagon had a strong interest in biographies: in 535 *FGrHist* 4 he deals with the life of Aesop and claims that he was a Thracian slave. Euagon's choice of Meles as the father of Homer may reflect his interest in *mirabilia*: cf. 535 *FGrHist* 1 (on the Neia, mythological wild beasts living in Samos). Like later sources, Euagon may already have paired the river Meles with Cretheis (thus Fowler).

21. Καλλικλῆς δὲ †Μασαγόραν: 758 *FGrHist* 13c. Callicles was a historian or grammarian from the Hellenistic era. In this context, he is likely mentioned to introduce the Cypriot tradition about Homer: we know from Anon. *Vit. Hom.* 1.2 (= 758 *FGrHist* 13a) that Callicles thought that Homer was from Salamis in Cyprus. At 29–30 (= 758 *FGrHist* 13c) the *Certamen* claims that Homer's father was offered as a hostage by the Cypriots to the Persians: Callicles may be the source for that claim too. As we learn from Paus. 10.24.3 (= 758 *FGrHist* 13d) the Cypriots reckoned Themisto to be Homer's mother. The name Themiste at 25 may refer to the same character, so that we would have another parental couple implicitly paired up in the text. In the Homeric biographies, a Cypriot origin for Homer is referred to also at Suda s.v. 'Homer' 2; Ps.-Plu. *Vit. Hom.* 2.2. Connections between Homer and Cyprus were also established by interpreting the Homeric poems: for the *Iliad* see Schol. T *Il.* 21.12 (= 758 *FGrHist* 13b); for the *Cypria*, a poem given by Homer to Stasinus of Cyprus as the dowry of his daughter, see Pi. fr. 265 SM; Tz. *H.* 13.637–40; Phot. *Bibl.* 319a 24.

†Μασαγόραν: the name is not clearly legible in **L**. Tzetzes (*Alleg*. Prol. 62) gives it in the form Μασσαγόραν, while *AP* 7.5 gives it, in the genitive, in the form Δμησαγόρου. According to the Byzantine scholar, Mas(s)agoras was a merchant: this may be due to the fact that he confused this character with Daemon (cf. 21–2n.) or because he had access to now lost information. The form Δμασαγόραν, restored by Barnes on the basis of the name of Homer's father as transmitted by Eustathius (*Od.* 1713.20) and accepted by most editors, goes back to a tradition according to which Homer was from Egypt, rather than Cyprus, and therefore does not seem to have any connection with the source and the story referred to here.

21–2. Δημόκριτος δὲ <ὁ> Τροιζήνιος Δαήμονα ἔμπορον: *Suppl. Hell.* 378. Democritus of Troezen was a writer who lived in the first century AD. His extant fragments deal with poets (e.g., Aristophanes: *Suppl. Hell.* 377) and philosophers (e.g., Empedocles: *Suppl. Hell.* 375). It is difficult to contextualise the claim attributed to him in the present passage of the *Certamen*: the view that Homer's father was a merchant is unique (except for Tzetzes' claim about Massagoras, on which see 21n.). The name Daemon is attested only here and in Tzetzes. It may be seen as a speaking name designed to explain Homer's special talents (δαήμων means 'skilled', 'experienced'). Democritus is not mentioned anywhere else as a source in relation to Homer's biography. The spelling of his name varies in the manuscript tradition: while Athenaeus gives Δημήτριος (*Suppl. Hell.* 376–7), the form Δημόκριτος in **L** is transmitted also by the manuscripts of Diogenes Laertius (*Suppl. Hell.* 374). Allen's suggestion to reduce this claim of the *Certamen* and that of Anon. *Vit. Hom.* 1.3 (κατὰ δὲ Δημοκρίνην Ἀλήμονος, 'according to Democrines, [his father was] Alemon') to the same tradition is interesting, but needs more evidence. First, it would presuppose yet another different form of the name of Democritus of Troezen. Secondly, if Allen was right, then Alemon and Daemon would be two different names given to the same person, but they may in fact represent two different traditions about Homer's origins. Even if it is possible that these two names were confused in the manuscript tradition of Democritus' work, or of the two Lives, Democritus may be presenting Homer's father as a 'skilled, experienced' (δαήμων) merchant, while Democrines suggests a poor beggar (ἀλήμων is the Homeric word for beggars: cf. *Od.* 17.376 and 19.74). Finally, a person called Democrines is mentioned in Schol. A *Il.* 2.744 in relation to a textual problem, but we do not have evidence for the philological activity of Democritus: Democritus and Democrines may in fact be two different people.

22. ἔνιοι δὲ Θαμύραν: this character must be identified with Thamyris (see also Tz. *Alleg.* Prol. 64, who writes Θάμυριν), the bard who according to the Homeric poems challenged the Muses in song and was punished by them (*Il.* 2.591–600). Thamyris is nowhere else mentioned as the father of Homer, and the *Certamen* does not indicate his source. However, it is a common habit in the ancient biographies to manufacture genealogical links between poets, and the character Thamyris in particular seems to present some features that make him suitable for such a role. First, he is a Homeric character. Secondly, some sources say specifically that Thamyris was punished by the Muses by becoming blind (e.g., Hes. fr. 65 MW; Paus. 4.33.7; D. Chr.

13.21). On Thamyris see Wilson 2009. Nothing else is known about the biographical legend linking Thamyris and Homer. The corresponding character in the list of mothers is another unknown character, a girl from Ithaca who was sold by the Phoenicians. West 1967: 445 pairs Thamyris with the Muse Calliope (found at 26–7), but he is on no safe ground: according to tradition, Thamyris asked to marry one of the Muses if he won the contest against them (Schol. b *Il.* 2.595), but he was defeated and punished, and there is no trace of an actual union of Thamyris with any of the Muses.

22–3. Αἰγύπτιοι δὲ Μενέμαχον ἱερογραμματέα: there is no other known source for Menemachus besides Tzetzes (*Alleg.* Prol. 60) who, as usual in that passage, does not mention his own source. The reading ἱερογραμματέα is taken from Tzetzes, but is not completely clear in **L**. In the *Certamen* there is no explicit mention of Menemachus' origins, but Tzetzes claims he was an Egyptian. The *Certamen* therefore seems to connect Homer's Egyptian origins with an Egyptian source, and it is alone in doing so. Suda s.v. 'Homer' 2 does not give any source; Anon. *Vit. Hom.* 1.2 (ἄλλοι δὲ Αἰγύπτιον αὐτὸν εἶπον διὰ τὸ [ἢ] παράγειν τοὺς ἥρωας ἐκ στόματος ἀλλήλους φιλοῦντας, ὅπερ ἐστὶν ἔθος τοῖς Αἰγυπτίοις ποιεῖν, 'others have asserted that he was an Egyptian because he represents the heroes kissing one another on the mouth, as is customary among the Egyptians') may point to the ancient habit of inferring Homer's birthplace from his poetry, not always with a view to making him a fellow citizen (Zenodotus of Mallos made him a Chaldaean: see Schol. AT *Il.* 23.79b; Aristarchus an Athenian: see Schol. A *Il.* 13.197). Homer was considered an Egyptian also by a Cypriot, Alexander of Paphos (known from Eust. *Od.* 1713.19). See also Heliodorus' parodic allusion to the Aegyptian tradition (*Aeth.* 3.12–15). In his list of Homer's seven birthplaces, Tzetzes lists Egyptian Thebes, which is the only Egyptian city that seems to have had claims on Homer (perhaps because of its mention in *Il.* 9.381–4; see also Anon. *Vit. Hom.* 3.1). There is no evidence of a connection between Menemachus and any of the women in the list of mothers, so that pairing him with Calliope (the corresponding name in the list of mothers) or the girl from Ithaca (West 1967: 445) is mere speculation.

23–4. εἰσὶ δ' οἳ Τηλέμαχον τὸν Ὀδυσσέως: another case of a genealogical connection between the poet and his characters: see also Thamyris, 22n. The reference to Telemachus and consequently to the Ithacan claims on Homer is repeated at 37–43. In Suda s.v. 'Homer' 1, Telemachus and Polycaste are mentioned as parents of Homer, and in the *Certamen* too Polycaste is mentioned in the list of mothers (27): this is another couple that seems to be implicitly matched up in our text. The legend derives from the meeting between Polycaste and Telemachus described in *Od.* 3.464, where Polycaste bathed Telemachus upon his arrival at Pylos. Despite the concerns of the ancient scholiasts (see Schol. *Od.* 3.464–9), legends about the offspring of the couple were current already in archaic times (cf. Hes. fr. 221 MW, where they have a child called Persepolis). In the oracle uttered by the Pythia to Hadrian, however, Telemachus is matched with Epicaste (37–40).

24. οἱ μὲν Μῆτιν: this character is mentioned as the mother of Homer only here; Suda s.v. 'Homer' 1 gives the name Εὔμητις. Fowler 2013: 609 even suggests that 'perhaps we should emend the *Certamen* to "Eumetis"'. Her name, which means 'cleverness', is appropriate for the mother of Homer. The Suda confirms that Maeon is connected to Metis in one strand of the tradition (on Maeon see 20n.): the *Certamen* too seems to pair them up as both names are in the first position in their respective lists. The Suda also adds that Eumetis was the daughter of Euepes son of Mnesigenes and married Maeon who went to Smyrna at the same time as the Amazons. The names Euepes and Mnesigenes are otherwise unknown, but both are speaking names (built on the words ἔπος and μνήμη). The fact that Maeon went to Smyrna together with the Amazons, who are connected to foundation myths of Smyrna (see, e.g., Str. 12.3.21), may also connect Homer with these myths, and certainly makes him one of the first citizens of Smyrna. For the Smyrnean tradition on Homer see 8–12n.

οἱ δὲ Κρηθηίδα: on Cretheis, and the couple Cretheis-Meles, see 9–10n.

25. οἱ δὲ Θεμίστην: this seems to be another form for the name Themisto, Homer's mother in the Cypriot tradition according to Pausanias (10.24.3): see 21n.

οἱ δὲ Εὐγνηθώ: this name is not attested elsewhere. The merchant Daemon is the man in the corresponding position in the list of fathers, but there is no safe ground to connect him to Eugnetho. Emending Εὐγνηθώ to Ὑρνηθώ (see apparatus) in order to connect this character to Maeon (Hyrnetho's partner in the Homeric Lives: Anon. *Vit. Hom.* 1.3; Anon. *Vit. Hom.* 2.1) is not safe either, as the *Certamen* suggests no explicit connection between this character and Maeon. The appearance of Eugnetho here may perhaps have been inspired by Hyrnetho (because of the similar sound of the two names), but it is no mere slip: somebody created a speaking name, and it should stand.

25–6. ἔνιοι δὲ Ἰθακησίαν τινὰ ὑπὸ Φοινίκων ἀπεμποληθεῖσαν: this character is nowhere attested in the Homeric biographies, but displays some features that are common in this type of literature: the fact that she is said to be from Ithaca is clearly an attempt to connect Homer with the *Odyssey* (see also the case of Telemachus, 23–4n.); stories about forced movements of the mother of the poet, and more generally his modest origins, were common: see, e.g., Cretheis, who had to escape from her home town after becoming pregnant (Ps.-Plu. *Vit. Hom.* 1.2–3). The role of the Phoenicians as traders and their connection with abduction stories in the *Odyssey* (esp. *Od.* 15.415–84) seem also relevant here. It is unclear why Rzach proposed the emendation Ἰδακησίαν.

26–7. οἱ δὲ Καλλιόπην τὴν Μοῦσαν: a transparent attempt to make Homer the inspired poet *par excellence*. Ancient readers were attuned to the symbolic force of this claim: compare *AP* 16.296; *AP* 16.295; Ps.-Plu. *Vit. Hom.* 1.4; Isaac Porphyrogenitus *Praefatio in Homerum* 8 Kindstrand. Calliope is Homer's mother also in Anon. *Vit. Hom.* 2.1. In Suda s.v. 'Homer' 1 her partner is Apollo, who does not appear in the *Certamen*'s list of fathers. Apollo and Calliope are mentioned in the genealogy at 46 and 48 respectively, but with different roles.

27. τινὲς δὲ Πολυκάστην τὴν Νέστορος: see 23–4n.

27–32. ἐκαλεῖτο δὲ ... πηροὶ καλοῦνται: the issue of the poet's original name, already mentioned earlier in the text (see 10–12n. for a discussion of the connection between Smyrna and the name Melesigenes), now becomes the focus of attention. The *Certamen* offers three alleged original names (thus echoing the list of birthplaces at 8–17) and suggests two explanations as to why they were dropped. As in the other lists (18–27n.), the text combines well known traditions with less widely attested ones: this is the only text giving Meles and Auletes as Homer's original names, while Melesigenes is very common. The change of name is motivated with reference to the most widely circulating etymologies for the name Homer ('blind' and 'hostage') but unlike what we are told in all the extant *Lives*, here it is Homer's father, rather than Homer himself, who has been taken hostage.

27–8. ἐκαλεῖτο δὲ Μέλης: elsewhere the name of Homer's father, not of the poet himself (21 and 53). As a proper name, Meles is attested for a singer mentioned by Plato (*Grg.* 502a4).

28. ὡς δέ τινές φασι Μελησιγενής: see 10n.

28–9. ὡς δὲ ἔνιοι Αὐλητής: an otherwise unknown name for Homer, clearly referring to his poetic activity; for other speaking names in Homer's family see the genealogy at 45–53. Welcker 1835: 149 proposed the emendation Ἄλτης, unanimously accepted by later editors, on the basis of Schol. T *Il.* 22.51 (ὀνομάκλυτος Ἄλτης· Ἀθηνοκλῆς φησι τὸν Ὅμηρον πρώην Ἄλτην καλεῖσθαι διὰ τὸ ἐπαινεῖν αὐτὸν ὀνομάκλυτος, '"Altes of glorious name": Athenocles says that Homer was originally called Altes because the poet praises him for his "glorious name"'). Altes is a minor Homeric character, the father of Priam's first wife Laotoe, and is mentioned in the *Iliad* only twice (*Il.* 21.85–6 and *Il.* 22.51). The fact that Homer called Altes' name 'glorious', despite his minor role, led Athenocles to think that Altes was Homer's original name. But although it is possible that Αὐλητής results from a corruption of Ἄλτης, it also testifies to the continued creative energy of the biographical tradition and may respond to a shift in pedagogical emphasis: the name Altes responds to the habit of drawing biographical information on Homer from his works; Auletes would be a speaking name, like many others transmitted in the poets' genealogies and in the *Certamen* too. There is no need therefore to emend the name given by the manuscript, except for its ending: the accusative in the manuscript (see apparatus) is due to a misunderstanding of the copyist, who probably thought that this name was connected to the following infinitive ὀνομασθῆναι (as the absence of the necessary punctuation seems to point out).

29–32. ὀνομασθῆναι … καλοῦνται: the text lists the two most common etymologies for the name Homer, 'blind' and 'hostage': for discussion of this alternative etymology see 11–12n. The *Certamen* does not express a preference for either of the etymologies listed. For the possibility that Homer's Cypriot father Masagoras was taken hostage by the Persians, and more generally for the Cypriot tradition on Homer, see 21n. The fact that it is Homer's father who was taken hostage, and that he was given to the Persians, are details unique to the *Certamen*. For modern discussion of Homer's name see Durante 1957; Bonfante 1968; Deroy 1972; Nagy 1979: 296–300 and 2006; West 1999; Debiasi 2001 and 2012: 463–70.

32–43. ὅπερ δὲ ἀκηκόαμεν … δεδοξακότος: the mention of the emperor Hadrian (reign 117–38 AD) is our only clue for dating the *Certamen*, and it is not easy to interpret. The Greek seems to imply that Hadrian was still alive (Nietzsche 1870: 536; Uden 2010), but does not exclude the possibility that the compilation was made a little after the emperor's death: see Wilamowitz 1916: 397 ('der Verfasser wird nicht viele Dezennien nach Hadrian gelebt haben'); Vogt 1959: 196 n. 9 ('Freilich darf man nicht an eine Entstehung noch in hadrianischer Zeit denken, sondern lediglich an die Regierungszeit Hadrians als *terminus post quem*'); West 1967: 433 ('Hadrian is dead but of fresh memory'). Furthermore, the epithet 'most divine' (cf. 33, θειοτάτου) was used of Hadrian both during his life and after his death (cf. Mason 1974: 53 and 125; Uden 2010: 122 n. 6). However, the claim that we must trust the oracle 'because of the enquirer and the respondent' (41–2) and the very presence of the episode in this work seem to indicate that it was inserted in the narrative while the emperor was still alive, perhaps not long after his visit to Delphi (125 AD). Uden 2010 (esp. 123–9) argues that this claim is to be seen in the context of Hadrian's role in contemporary debates about Greek literature and culture, which did not always meet with approval. The presence of a different response by the Pythia to the same question later on in the text (56–60) suggests that the author of the *Certamen* did not really believe that the answer given to Hadrian was the most trustworthy, and probably inserted that claim only as a formal sign of respect for the emperor. But the content of Pythia's response does not necessarily need to be read as ironic: Uden 2010: 127 claims that the notion of an Ithacan Homer would have appeared absurd to anyone in antiquity, but there is nothing to prove this claim. In fact, within the *Certamen* the Ithacan tradition is presented as equal to any other (see 23–4 on Telemachus and 25–6 on the Ithacan girl). The episode and the epigram transmitted in these lines caught the attention of the Renaissance scholar Marcus Musurus (see Part 2).

37–40. ἄγνωστόν ... ἄνδρα: H65 Fontenrose. This epigram is found only in this passage (and in Musurus' notes taken from it, see Part 2), and in *AP* 14.102. There are some textual variations, among which the name Epicaste instead of Polycaste (see also *Od.* 3.464 and *Cert.* 27). In *AP* 14 it is transmitted among riddles, mathematical problems and other oracular texts. For other stories of people interrogating the oracle about Homer, and other oracular responses, see *AP* 16.292–299, and Lucian *Alex.* 53.

4. Homer's and Hesiod's chronology and genealogy (44–53)

44–53. The *Certamen* now discusses another much debated issue of Homer's biography, namely his chronology. The discussion is based on a comparison between Homer and Hesiod, which was one of the most common ways of approaching the matter in antiquity. Graziosi 2002: 90–124 identifies three distinct ways of dating Homer: by connecting him to a particular place or event, to a specific individual (usually another poet), or to his subject matter. Focusing on Homer's connection with Hesiod is a meaningful choice in the present context, in that it allows the text to introduce their contest. In antiquity, moreover, such discussion of Homer's and Hesiod's relative chronology was also seen as a means to assess the relationship between heroic and didactic poetry: as explained most recently by Beecroft 2010: 79, genealogical claims function as claims about genre theory, and therefore the variations in the relationships between two poets are a means of assigning priorities to the different genres and configuring their relationships in different ways. The *Certamen* introduces three options, apparently without taking sides. But only the second option, which portrays Homer as younger than Hesiod, is supported by a genealogy, while the first (Homer is older than Hesiod) and the third (Homer and Hesiod are contemporaries and competed with each other) are presented without any further support. This agrees with the view, expressed early on in the text, that at the time of the contest Homer was only at the beginning of his artistic career (see 15–17n.). Even more than that, the genealogy in the *Certamen* seems to present the contest as potentially implausible: according to the final part of the genealogy found in **L**, which suggests a gap of three generations between Homer and Hesiod (unlike other sources of the genealogy, see esp. 51–3n.), the two poets' lifetime may well not have overlapped at all.

44–5. ἔνιοι μὲν οὖν αὐτὸν προγενέστερον Ἡσιόδου φασὶν εἶναι: Homer's chronological priority over Hesiod, mentioned here without any support, was often used to assert his greater authority (Hes. T5–T9 Most) – a view which is clearly incompatible with Homer's defeat in the contest.

45–53. τινὲς δὲ νεώτερον ... Ὅμηρον: the presence of an extended genealogy makes this option look like the most trustworthy among the three proposed. The genealogy must have been in circulation as early as the fifth century BC: Proclus (*Vit. Hom.* 4) attributes it to the historians Hellanicus (4 *FGrHist* 5b = fr. 5 Fowler), Damastes (5 *FGrHist* 11b = fr. 11 Fowler), and Pherecydes (3 *FGrHist* 167 = fr. 167 Fowler); another version is transmitted in Suda s.v. 'Homer' 1, with reference to the historian Charax (103 *FGrHist* 62). For an overview see also Kivilo 2010a: 12–17; Fowler 2013: 608–10. For graphic representations of the genealogies, see Figures 2, 3, and 4. This traditional material, however, is deliberately adapted in the *Certamen* to suit specific views on Homer and Hesiod. Thus, the *Certamen* provides the two poets with divine origins, in accordance with the opening claim that Homer and Hesiod are the most divine poets (see 1–2.). Examples include Apollo, Poseidon, Methone, Calliope, Meles, and the nymph Thoosa, whose counterpart in Charax was a Thracian mortal woman, Aethousa. For the same purpose the genealogy includes some divine mothers: we find them together with those male figures who are neither gods nor poets, thus ensuring that each level of the genealogy features either a divine or a divinely inspired figure (Methone is mentioned with Pierus, Calliope with Oeagrus). Divine mothers are also mentioned at the beginning and end of the genealogy: Thoosa, daughter of Poseidon, appears at the beginning, while Hesiod's mother Pycimede, daughter of Apollo, appears at the end. (Homer's own mother does not need to be a goddess as his divine origins are secured by his father, the river god Meles.) As well as poets (Linus, Orpheus, and Melanopus), the genealogy also features names that would suit poets (Harmonides, Philoterpes, Euphemus, Epiphrades). Some of the names are attested elsewhere too, but with different roles (Melanopus, Dius, Apellaius, Maeon) and the precise relations among some of the characters also vary; for example, while Homer and Hesiod are first cousins in Proclus and the Suda, the genealogy in the *Certamen* supports the claim that Homer was younger than Hesiod: accordingly, the positions of some of the characters are changed and additional characters inserted (Perses, Maeon's daughter, and Meles) in order to increase the chronological gap between the two poets.

46. Ἀπόλλωνός φασι καὶ Θοώσης τῆς Ποσειδῶνος: Thoosa is a character known also from other sources, but with different roles than the one attributed to her in this context: Poseidon's wife rather than his daughter, and never Apollo's partner (*Od.* 1.71–3: she is a nymph, daughter of Phorcys, mother of Polyphemus by Poseidon; Schol. *Od.* 1.71; Schol. Theoc. 11.67–8; Apollod. 7.4.6; Emp. fr. 122.9; Nonn. *D.* 39.293; Hsch. s.v.). In Charax' version Aethousa, described as a woman from Thrace, takes Thoosa's place: unlike the *Certamen*, Charax does not emphasise the divine origins of the poets. In other sources, Aethousa is the name of a nymph, who is also said to be Poseidon's daughter and to have had a son by Apollo (Apollod. 3.10.1; Paus. 9.20.1; Schol. Hes. *Th.* 54b1; the son is named Eleuther, not Linus). Some early editors followed Charax and emended Θοώσης to Αἰθούσης, but there is no reason to believe that that was the name used in a hypothetical original version of this genealogy.

47. Λίνον: on this character see West 1983: 56–67 and Ford 2002: 151. Linus and the Linus song, a funeral dirge to which he is connected, are known to both Homer and Hesiod (*Il.* 18.569–70; Hes. frr. 305–306 MW); his presence is thus suitable for the genealogy of these two poets. Several myths circulated about Linus in antiquity; cf. Paus. 9.29.9, who reports the view that at least two poets of this name existed. Linus is also connected to poetic competitions: he is said to have competed with the god Apollo, and after losing the contest was killed by the god (Paus. 9.29.6).

Λίνου δὲ Πίερον: Pierus is a mythical figure known for having brought the cult of the Muses to Thespiae and as the father of the nine maidens called Pierides. As was the case with Linus (see above), his family too is connected to a contest story: the Pierides are said to have challenged the Muses in a poetic contest and to have been turned into birds after their defeat. Sources on Pierus include Paus. 9.29.3–4. In the *Certamen* he is the son of Linus and father of Oeagrus. In the genealogy of Charax he occupies the same position. Other sources suggest a different lineage: according to Melisseus (402 *FGrHist* 1) Pierus is Linus' father and Methone his sister.

47–8. Πιέρου δὲ καὶ νύμφης Μεθώνης Οἴαγρον: of the extant versions of this genealogy, this is the only one that mentions Methone: Proclus starts with the next generation (Orpheus) and Charax gives only the names of the male characters. Methone is a nymph, one of the Alcyonids, who threw themselves into the sea after Heracles killed their father, and subsequently turned into halcyons: see Suda s.v. 'Alcyonids'. There seems to be no other trace of Oeagrus' being the son of Pierus and Methone. In D. S. 3.65.6 he is the son of the Thracian king Charops and king of Thrace himself. The claim that he fathered Orpheus is found in all versions of this genealogy (see 48n.).

48. Οἰάγρου δὲ καὶ Καλλιόπης Ὀρφέα: several witnesses agree that Orpheus' parents were Calliope and Oeagrus (A. R. 1.23; Tz. *Ad Lyc.* 831); though others give no name for the mother (e.g., Pl. *Smp.* 179d). Oeagrus has a different son according to Proclus (Dorion) and Charax (Dres). According to Apollod. 1.3.2, Calliope and Oeagrus also had Linus, who in this genealogy is in another position (47n.). On Orpheus see Burges-Watson 2013 with bibliography. On Calliope see 26–7n., where she is mentioned in the list of Homer's mothers. Here she guarantees the presence of a divinity in earlier levels of Homer's genealogy. This genealogy is the only extant witness of the tradition according to which Homer and Hesiod are descendants of Orpheus. Orpheus is arguably the most important poet in this genealogy, and indeed Proclus reports the genealogy only from Orpheus onwards, claiming that 'Hellanicus, Damastes, and Pherecydes trace his descent back to Orpheus'. According to Kivilo 2010a: 16–17 and 54–6, his presence in the genealogy may point to the role of the Orphic poets in creating it, and more generally in shaping biographical traditions (see esp. pp. 54–6, where she also spots Orphic influences in the traditions about Hesiod). The connection between Homer, Hesiod and Orpheus was not only genealogical: frequent references to the group 'Orpheus, Musaeus, Hesiod, and Homer' (usually in this order, cf. Hes. T17, T18, T116a, T119bi, bii Most) suggest that together they were seen as the most ancient and authoritative poets. For the possibility that this series of names is to be interpreted chronologically, see Graziosi 2002: 107 n. 51; most recently Koning 2010: 52–5.

49. Ὀρφέως δὲ Ὄρτην: this seems to be the only attestation of a character named Ortes. His counterpart in the genealogy of Charax is called Dres (Δρῆς): some editors emend the text of **L** on that basis, but Dres too is otherwise unknown. Proclus gives yet another name, Dorion. Both Proclus and Charax add Eucles, a name that is integrated into the *Certamen*'s genealogy by many editors (see apparatus) but on no safe ground.

Ἁρμονίδην: like many other names in this context, Harmonides is nowhere else attested in relation to the genealogy of Homer and Hesiod. However, it is suitable for a poet (because of its obvious connection to the word ἁρμονία), and is also attested as a Homeric character: in *Il.* 5.60 he is the father of Phereclus, and, like his son, is described as a Trojan ship-builder. Proclus and Charax transmit the name Ἰδμονίδης, another unknown character. The emendation Ἰαδμονίδην, proposed by Nietzsche, is unconvincing: it must have been meant to achieve consistency with the name given by Charax and Proclus, and create a connection with Aesop's biographical tradition (which features the character Ἰάδμων, or Ἴδμων: see Hdt. 2.134; Suda s.v. 'Aesop'; Plu. *On the Delays of the Divine Vengeance* 557a); however, it is not attested elsewhere, seems to be irrelevant in this context, and misses the importance of speaking names in the text.

Φιλοτέρπην: this name is attested only in this genealogy, in all of its versions. It is clearly another speaking name ('fond of pleasure') which may suit a poet. The compound is also attested as an adjective (e.g., Nonn. *D.* 40.366).

50. Εὔφημον: another speaking name suitable for a poet, or for a poet's ancestor. It is frequently found as the name of Stesichorus' father (e.g., Pl. *Phdr.* 244a; Suda s.v. 'Stesichorus' – see Kivilo 2010a: 65–7) and also appears in Museus' genealogy (Suda s.v. 'Museus'). As an ancestor of Homer and Hesiod, Euphemus is attested only here and in the genealogy of Charax. Proclus gives the form Chariphemus. For Chariphemus as the founder of Cyme see Ephorus, 70 *FGrHist* 99 (= Anon. *Vit. Hom.* 1.2). Euphemus is also a Homeric character: see *Il.* 2.846 (he is the son of Troezenus and the captain of the Ciconian spearmen).

Ἐπιφράδην: another little-known character with a name that may suit a poet; cf. the attested ἐπιφραδέως ('wisely', 'circumspectly'). The name is not attested outside this genealogy.

Μελάνωπον: a mythical poet from Cyme (Paus. 5.7.8) who features also in other biographies of Homer and Hesiod, though in different roles. In the *Certamen* Melanopus is the father of Apellaius and Dius; in Proclus he is the father of Apelles and grandfather of Dius and Maeon; in Charax, the grandfather of Maeon only – but cf. also Suda s.v. 'Hesiod' (father of Apelles, grandfather of Dius). The name of Melanopus is also attested elsewhere in connection with Homer: in Ps.-Hdt. *Vit. Hom.* 1 a character with the same name, although not safely identifiable with the poet mentioned by Pausanias, is a man of modest means who went from Magnesia to Aeolian Cyme when this city was founded, and there fathered Homer's mother Cretheis; in Lucian *Dem. Enc.* 9 he is again said to be the father of Homer's mother.

51–3: as this genealogy is used here as evidence for Homer's being younger than Hesiod and related to him, the final part differs substantially from Proclus' version, in which the poets are said to be contemporaries: Procl. *Vit. Hom.* 4: Μαίονα γάρ φασι τὸν Ὁμήρου πατέρα καὶ Δῖον τὸν Ἡσιόδου γενέσθαι Ἀπέλλιδος τοῦ Μελανώπου, 'they say that Maeon, Homer's father, and Dius, Hesiod's father, were sons of Apelles, the son of Melanopus'. (Charax reports only Homer's parentage, without inserting Dius and Hesiod.) Differences concern the roles given to Apelles, Maeon, and Dius, as well as other details. In the *Certamen* Maeon is presented as two generations younger than Dius, Hesiod's father, and Homer is not his son but his grandson by his daughter. The ultimate result is to present Homer as three generations younger than Hesiod. The reading Πέρσου makes Maeon the son of Hesiod's brother, and the kinship between the two poets is thus reinforced. There is no apparent need to emend it to Ἀπέλλου or a different form of this same name (see apparatus). This emendation is meant to balance the genealogy, otherwise brutally interrupted by Apelles' side, and makes it more similar to its counterparts in other sources; but complete consistency between the various versions cannot be achieved and should not be expected. Inserting another female character, the daughter of Maeon, allows the text to introduce the river god Meles and give Homer a divine parent (thus balancing the fact that Hesiod's mother Pycimede is the daughter of Apollo). Nietzsche's emendation (καὶ θυγατρός instead of θυγατρὸς καί) is not necessary.

51–2. Δίου δὲ καὶ Πυκιμήδης τῆς Ἀπόλλωνος θυγατρὸς Ἡσίοδον καὶ Πέρσην: while the name of Hesiod's brother comes from *Works and Days*, and perhaps that of his father too (cf. *Op.* 299: Πέρση, δῖον γένος, 'Perses, divine stock'), Hesiod makes no mention of his mother in his work. The tradition, however, unanimously transmits the name of Pycimede since at least the fourth century BC (Ephorus 70 *FGrHist* 1 = Ps.-Plu. *Vit. Hom.* 1.2). The name Pycimede is of unknown origins, but appropriate for the mother of a didactic poet: it means 'cautious minded', 'wise' (see also Kivilo 2010a: 9). Ephorus (*loc. cit.*) claims that Dius married Pycimede in Ascra, after leaving Cyme because of debts. In Tz. *Life of Hesiod* 1 Colonna, Dius and Pycimede leave Cyme together; in this context she is also explicitly said to be the mother of Perses. In P.Oxy. 3537 r. she is mentioned as 'most blessed mother' (ὀλβίστη μήτειρα); cf. also Suda s.v. 'Hesiod'. The fact that Pycimede is said to be Apollo's daughter (a suggestion not found anywhere else) reinforces the claim of kinship between the god of poetry, mentioned at the very beginning of the genealogy, and the two poets who at the beginning of the work were introduced as 'most divine' (1: θειότατοι).

5. Homer's oracle (54–62)

54–5. τινὲς δὲ συνακμάσαι ... ἐν Αὐλίδι τῆς Βοιωτίας: in a work that devotes much space to the contest of Homer and Hesiod, the contest itself is introduced in a surprising way. The phrasing implies that Homer and Hesiod had to be contemporaries in order to be able to compete, but this option is introduced in the same way as the others (44–53n.) and, unlike the second one (Homer is younger than Hesiod), is supported by no evidence. Some authors in antiquity refused to believe that the contest happened on the basis that the two poets did not live at the same time (see Part 1, esp. 'Proclus' and 'John Tzetzes'). The connection between the story of the contest and the view that the two poets lived at the same time is found elsewhere too (see Part 1,

'Philostratus'; and Aul. Gell. *NA* 3.11.3–4) and the two traditions may well have developed to support each other (see also Kivilo 2010a: 22); but note Hdt. 2.53.2; Clem. Al. *Strom.* 1.21.117.4; Sync. *Chron.* 202.21–2 and 206.9 (Hes. T 10, 12, 14 Most), where no such connection seems to be implied.

55. ὁμόσε <γενομένους> ἐν Αὐλίδι τῆς Βοιωτίας: by saying that Homer and Hesiod met up in Aulis before the contest, the *Certamen* draws yet another detail of the story from Hesiod's *Works and Days* 648–62: the two poets are said to make the trip from Aulis to Chalcis mentioned in that passage, through which Hesiod sets his poetry against that of Homer – see Part 1, 'Hesiod'. It is unlikely that Aulis is mentioned here as the location of the contest itself, *pace* Nagy 2010: 43 among others. First, there is a linguistic problem in the transmitted text of the manuscript: the expression ἀγωνίσασθαι ὁμόσε ('compete with each other'?) is never attested in Greek literature, and it is therefore unlikely that ὁμόσε should be taken together with ἀγωνίσασθαι. Moreover, at 67–8 the contest is explicitly said to have taken place at Chalcis. Because the location of the contest was fixed at Chalcis by Hesiod himself, Chalcis must be the correct location of the contest in the *Certamen* too. Nietzsche's emendation ἐν Χαλκίδι τῆς Εὐβοίας may thus seem tempting (see Nietzsche's apparatus *ad loc.*: 'Εὔβοια et Βοιωτία nomina saepius confunduntur, veluti in schol. ad Hesiod. Theog. v. 54'), but it too founders on the difficulty of construing ἀγωνίσασθαι with ὁμόσε. Busse's supplement <γενομένους> elegantly restores the gist of the text before corruption occurred: the two poets met at Aulis before the contest, and together sailed to Chalcis to compete. Importantly, this sequence of events is also implied in the following lines: 66–8: καὶ οὗτοι οὖν ἐκ τύχης, ὥς φασι, συμβαλόντες ἀλλήλοις ἦλθον εἰς τὴν Χαλκίδα, 'and so Homer and Hesiod, after meeting up by chance, as they say, went to Chalcis'. The particles γάρ at 55 (ποιήσαντα γὰρ τὸν Μαργίτην) and οὖν at 66 (καὶ οὗτοι οὖν), that brings the narrative back to the contest, indicate the presence of a digression that explains how the poets ended up competing in Chalcis after their initial meeting in Aulis.

ποιήσαντα γὰρ τὸν Μαργίτην: the idea, current in imperial times, that the *Margites* is a juvenile work, and more specifically that it was Homer's first, was already introduced during the discussion of the Colophonian tradition (15–17n.). This passage makes clear that the *Margites* is the only work that Homer composed before the contest; all other works are attributed to the period after it (*Thebaid* and *Epigoni* at 256 and 258; *Iliad* and *Odyssey* at 275–6; *Hymn to Apollo* at 317; some epigrams).

56. περιέρχεσθαι κατὰ πόλιν ῥαψῳδοῦντα: from the beginning of his artistic career Homer is presented as a travelling poet and performer. The verb ῥαψῳδέω appears twice in the *Certamen*, and in both instances it refers to

Homer with the meaning 'to perform'; see also 286–7. By contrast, compounds of ποιέω are used in the text to indicate acts of poetic creation. Homer is thus depicted here both as a poet and as a proto-rhapsode, that is, the first performer of his own poetry. The latter idea may have been promoted by Homeric rhapsodes keen to give their profession a respectable ancestry: on the rhapsodes see Graziosi 2002: 21–40; on 'wandering poets' more generally see Hunter/Rutherford 2009. Some Greek texts present Hesiod too as a rhapsode, and indeed as a proto-rhapsode, sometimes along with Homer: [Hes.] fr. 357 MW (on which see Part 1) and 4 *FGrHist* 464, both transmitted in Schol. Pi. *N.* 2.1; Pl. *R.* 10.600d. Rhapsodes must have performed Hesiod's works too: cf. Pl. *Lg.* 2.658d; Pl. *Ion* 531a–535a, on which see Yamagata 2010: 76–7. For the hypothesis that Hesiod depicts himself as a rhapsode in *Th.* 30, see Patzer 1993. In the *Certamen*, however, the fact that the verb ῥαψῳδέω is only used of Homer represents one of several points of contrast between the two poets. While Homer travels extensively and his travels are always connected to his poetic performances, Hesiod travels far less: he goes to Chalcis to participate in the contest; after that, he goes to Delphi to dedicate a tribute of his victory and consult the oracle, and then to Oenoe in an unsuccessful attempt to escape his fate. The text thus reinforces the image of Hesiod as a poet who was always, and from the beginning, connected to a particular place. Homer, by contrast, emerges as a poet who travelled around the cities of Greece during his lifetime and could therefore be claimed by every Greek community after his death.

56–62. ἐλθόντα δὲ καὶ εἰς Δελφοὺς ... περὶ τὴν ἐκεῖ χώραν: Homer himself goes to interrogate the Pythia about his own birthplace: this fits well in a text that opens by emphasising the debate existing over the poet's origins. The Pythia establishes a genealogical connection between Homer and Ios: an apparent contradiction with 37–40, according to which the Pythia told Hadrian that Homer was from Ithaca. This gives the impression that the author of the *Certamen* does not consider this utterance truthful, despite the claim at 41–3. On the Pythia's response to Homer see 59–60n. The oracle also contains a prophecy on Homer's death, and thus creates a parallel for the oracle given to Hesiod later in the text (215–23). The fact that Homer's oracle is mentioned at such an early stage, while Hesiod visits Delphi only after the contest, is meaningful. The oracles (and the fate of the two poets) and the contest seem to have strong causal relations with each other. The meeting between Homer and Hesiod, hence their contest, takes place ultimately because of the oracle Homer received, since the poet ended up in Aulis in an attempt to stay away from the established place of his death as revealed by the Pythia; Hesiod, in turn, consults the oracle precisely because of the contest (he goes to Delphi to dedicate a tribute of his victory). As

Vogt 1959 and West 1967 argue, it is possible that the episode of Homer's oracle was present already in Alcidamas' account: Alcidamas was the source for the the episode of Hesiod's oracle and death (240), and the source for Homer's death too (P.Mich. inv. 2754, see Part 2): the episode of Homer's oracle thus completes an elaborate narrative structure and depicts a clear nexus oracle-contest-death, which may well have been present already in one of the *Certamen*'s literary sources.

59–60: L80 Fontenrose. The epigram is transmitted with several variations in other sources (see apparatus), some of which mix it with verses from another oracle given by the Pythia to Homer, i.e. *AP* 14.66. On this epigram, see Skiadas 1965: 49–52. Pausanias (10.24.2) and Stephanus of Byzantium (s.v. 'Ios') report a version of the oracle that starts with the first two verses of *AP* 14.66 and then continues with our *AP* 14.65. Pseudo-Plutarch reports both the epigrams in succession, as they are in the *Greek Anthology*.

61–2. τὸν δὲ ἀκούσαντα ... περὶ τὴν ἐκεῖ χώραν: at this stage in the narrative Homer keeps far from Ios, as the oracle suggests, and this allows him to meet Hesiod (see 56–62n.); but later on, as an old man, he does go to the island, and the prophecy is fulfilled (321–38).

6. Introduction to the contest (62–74)

62–74. κατὰ δὲ τὸν αὐτὸν χρόνον ... ἀποκρίνασθαι: these lines are part of the short digression that explains how Homer and Hesiod ended up in Chalcis (55n.) and introduce the episode of the poetic contest between them. Many of the details concerning the setting of the poetic contest are taken from Hes. *Op.* 649–62: Hesiod's sea trip from Aulis; Amphidamas' funeral games as the occasion for the contest; Amphidamas' sons as the organisers of the games; the remarkable prizes offered; Hesiod's victory. The figure of the king Panoides is not present in the Hesiodic account (69n.).

63. Γαννύκτωρ: this name occurs in two circumstances in the account of the life of Hesiod. In the present passage and in Tzetzes' *Life of Hesiod* (126 Colonna), he is the son of Amphidamas, organiser and judge of his father's funeral games. But according to other traditions, of which the *Certamen*, among others, is also aware, this character is connected to Hesiod's death: he is either a man from Locris, son of Phegeus and Hesiod's murderer with his brother Amphiphanes (226–7n.), or a man from Naupactus who fathered Hesiod's murderers (241n.).

63–4. Ἀμφιδάμαντος βασιλέως Εὐβοίας: this character is mentioned only by Hesiod (*Op.* 654) and in passages related to the story of his contest against Homer. Plutarch (fr. 84 Sandbach and *Dinner* 153f, see Part 1, 'Plutarch') says that Amphidamas died during the Lelantine War, which was fought between Chalcis and Eretria approximately between the end of the eighth and the beginning of the seventh century BC. Hesiod's mention of Amphidamas and Plutarch's claims have been taken as a chronological clue for Hesiod. However, given the scarcity of precise information on Amphidamas and the Lelantine war, some scholars have doubted the credibility of Plutarch's claim (for discussion see Evelyn-White 1914: XVI; Sinclair 1932: 68; West 1966: 43–4 and 1978: 321; Edwards 1971: 203–4; Fehling 1979; Janko 1982: 94–8; Kivilo 2010a: 46; Ercolani 2010: 16; Kõiv 2011; Baier 2013: 147–8; Gainsford 2016: 4–6). However, regardless of the historical reliability of Plutarch's claim, ancient comments on the Lelantine War suggest that the event had the features of an appropriate historical background for the contest of the two greatest poets: Thucydides (1.15.3) shows that this war was perceived as a big event that took place in a remote and undefined past, and in which for the first time the rest of the Greek world was divided in alliance with one side or the other.

64–6. πάντας τοὺς ἐπισήμους ἄνδρας ... συνεκάλεσεν: this claim highlights the importance of the event. The fact that other competitions besides the poetic one were included in Amphidamas' funeral games is not explicitly claimed in Hesiod's *Works and Days* but could easily have been inferred from the fact that the poet specifies that he won 'with a hymn' (657: ὕμνῳ), thus not ruling out the possibility of other kind of games. For the centrality of wisdom (σοφία) to contests in song see Griffith 1990: esp. 188. The idea of an opposition between wisdom and physical strength (65) appears already in Xenophanes (fr. 2 West) and was a common contrast for Alcidamas: Richardson 1981: 5; O'Sullivan 1992: 80.

66–8. καὶ οὗτοι ... Χαλκίδα: see 55n.

68–70. τοῦ δὲ ἀγῶνος ... τοῦ τετελευτηκότος: the way in which the judges are introduced creates expectations about how the competition will be judged, but these expectations will be soon left unfulfilled: no one would expect that Panoides, who appears here as equal to the other Chalcideans sitting as judges, and is apparently singled out only as brother of the deceased, will in fact have the final say at the end of the competition (205–10n.).

69. Πανοίδης: a character who is attested only in texts relating to the contest of Homer and Hesiod. In the form given by **L** (here and at 177) it is a speaking name meaning 'All-knowing'. However, it seems to be used ironically here: the *Certamen* does not seem to agree with the final verdict, and other texts too show that he became famous precisely because he gave an unwise judgement (205–10n.). P.Petr. I 25 (1) gives the form Πανήδης (4), which has been used by all the editors to emend the reading of **L**. But the two forms represent two different attempts at etymologising the name, and should both be kept in the text of their respective witnesses. Πανήδης has been interpreted as 'he who enjoys everything' (πᾶν + ἡδύς: see Kirchhoff 1892: 887) and again indicates the king's ineptitude as a judge. Another attested form is Πανίδης (Philostratus, Tzetzes – on which see Part 1 – and Michael Apostolius' *Collectio Paroemiarum* 15.88). Iotacism alone does not explain the existence of the different forms of the name.

70–2. ἀμφοτέρων δὲ τῶν ποιητῶν ... τὸν τρόπον τοῦτον: the outcome of the contest is well known, and not modifiable. Thus, the text reveals it already at the beginning of the account of the competition, and focuses thereafter on the 'way' (τρόπον) Hesiod came to win.

72–4. προελθόντα ... Ὅμηρον ἀποκρίνασθαι: the words that describe Hesiod taking centre stage, εἰς τὸ μέσον, are common in the description of perfomative contexts in antiquity: see Ford 2002: 32 (esp. n. 25 for references). The text then briefly explains that, throughout the competition, Hesiod will ask questions and Homer will reply to each of them. This general summary is a substitute for more precise indications given in earlier versions before each exchange of verses: cf. Part 2, 'P.Petr. I 25 (1)'. The roles of Homer and Hesiod were different in other accounts of the contest: see Plu. *Dinner of the Seven Sages* 153f–154a, where Hesiod answers a riddle, and Tzetzes (*Life of Hesiod* 127 Colonna) who claims that the two poets exchanged improvised verses 'with each other' (πρὸς ἀλλήλους). See Part 1, 'Plutarch' and 'John Tzetzes'.

7. The 'riddles of the superlative' (74–89)

74–89. The first two exchanges of verses aim to define the 'best' and the 'finest' thing for mortals. These are examples of the so-called 'riddles of the superlative', that is 'questions which ask what thing or what person possesses a quality to the highest degree' (Konstantakos 2005: 20) and were especially connected to the Seven Sages (see, e.g., Plu. *Dinner of the Seven Sages* 153a for Thales replying to similar questions; Konstantakos 2004: 126–8 and 2005: 20–2). These themes are very common in lyric and symposiastic poetry (see, e.g., Sappho fr. 16 Voigt; Ford 1997: 92–3). Taken together, the first two sequences of challenge and response are expressions of common Greek thoughts and therefore put Homer in a privileged position from the start: Homer claims that the 'best' thing for mortals is not to be born, or to die as soon as possible; the 'finest' thing for men, the activity that gives most pleasure to mortals once they are born, is the symposium. It should be noted that the first answer is not Homeric in form or sentiment, while the second is taken from a Homeric poem that however Homer has not yet composed at this stage in the text: ancient biographies, including the *Certamen*, are more concerned with giving a particular image of Homer (in this case, the image of a wise, popular poet) than with issues of attribution and internal consistency. At a formal level, the hexameters of the *Certamen* fully draw on the epic tradition. They are created by using a large number of epic formulae and metrical patterns (e.g., the caesura after the third trochee, on which see, e.g., West 1982: 35–6 and Kirk 1985: 18–24), or else are quotations of pre-existing poetic material (see below for details). An earlier version of the text shows that these two exchanges of challenge and response were connected to the poetic competition between Homer and Hesiod already by the third century BC, although the changes of speaker (74, 77, 80, 83) were circulating in a longer and more elaborate form: see Part 2, 'P. Petr. I 25 (1)'.

75–6. υἱὲ Μέλητος ... βροτοῖσιν: the first couplet uttered by Hesiod concerns the 'best' thing for mortals, with the actual question being effectively contained in the last part of the second verse (76: τί φέρτατόν ἐστι βροτοῖσιν;). The rest of the couplet is made up of expressions found in (or inspired by) the epic tradition. At 75 υἱὲ Μέλητος Ὅμηρε ('son of Meles, Homer', see 9–10n.) is created on the model of similar invocations of epic heroes: Ἀτρέος υἱέ (Agamemnon: e.g., *Il.* 2.23); Τυδέος υἱέ (Diomedes: e.g., *Il.* 4.370); υἱὲ Πριάμοιο (Hector: e.g., *Il.* 7.47); Μενοιτίου υἱέ (Patroclus: e.g., *Il.* 9.202); Πηλῆος υἱέ (Achilles: e.g., *Il.* 16.21). In the *Certamen* it is also found at 151 where it parallels and contrasts with the epithet 'progeny of Dius' (ἔκγονε Δίου) used by Homer for Hesiod at 156 (see 151–60n.). In the second half of the hexameter, θεῶν ἄπο μήδεα εἰδώς is formulaic too (*Od.* 6.12; Hes. fr. 136.12 MW). Both parts of the verse highlight Homer's divine nature. The first part of the hexameter at 76 is again created by using formulaic expressions: εἴπ' ἄγε μοι is used at the beginning of the hexameter in, e.g., *Il.* 3.192. Πάμπρωτα connects with καὶ τοῦτο (81) that follows the second instance of εἴπ' ἄγε μοι ('come, tell me first of all' ... 'come, tell me this, then'). The expression φέρτατόν ... βροτοῖσιν provides a metrically suitable substitute for the corresponding words in the verses that Homer uses to answer, ἐπιχθονίοισιν ἄριστον (78).

78–9. ἀρχὴν μὲν μὴ φῦναι ... Ἀίδαο περῆσαι: Homer replies with traditional verses, attested for the first time in Theognis (425–8, with added pentameters) – although Campbell 1983: 233 suggests that Theognis may have taken these hexameter lines from an earlier source. These verses are widely attested in Greek literature (for a list of occurences see West 1971: 194) and, more generally, the concept they express was very common (see, e.g., S. *OC* 1225–7 and B. 5.160–2). Their wide circulation certainly explains Homer's success in this stage of the competition, although the verses, or the sentiment they express, are not Homeric (74–89n.). The presence of this couplet in P.Petr. I 25 (1), 12–15, proves that it was connected to the story of the contest between Homer and Hesiod at least by the third century BC, but the association may well be even older: the couplet is quoted by Stobaeus (4.52.22) under the lemma 'Encomium of death' (ἔπαινος θανάτου) as coming 'from Alcidamas' *Museum*' (ἐκ Ἀλκιδάμαντος Μουσείου), and on the basis of this quotation Nietzsche (1870 and 1873) found in Alcidamas' *Museum* the source for the agonistic section of the *Certamen* (for a more sceptical view see Muir 2001: xix). Theognis' version has πάντων at the beginning of the couplet, while all the passages that connect these verses to the contest story (implicitly, i.e. Stobaeus, or explicitly, i.e. *Certamen* and P.Petr. I 25) transmit the reading ἀρχήν (78). For detailed discussion see Nietzsche 1870: 536; Busse 1909: 113 n. 1; Wilamowitz 1916: 401 n. 2; Vogt 1959: 220. At 79, ὅμως is found only in the *Certamen*, but the emendation to ὅπως (see apparatus) is unnecessary. For πύλας Ἀίδαο περῆσαι cf. *Il.* 5.646: πύλας Ἀίδαο περήσειν; *Il.* 23.71: πύλας Ἀίδαο περήσω.

81–2. εἴπ' ἄγε μοι ... εἶναι; Hesiod's new question centres on the theme of the 'finest thing' for mortals and the core of the question is again placed in the second verse (82). For εἴπ' ἄγε μοι καὶ τοῦτο at 81 see 75–6n. The second part of the verse is used to address Homer with a formulaic epithet, 'godlike' (θεοῖς ἐπιείκελος). This epithet appears in Homeric poetry, always in the same metrical position, in connection to Achilles (θεοῖς ἐπιείκελ' Ἀχιλλεῦ: e.g. *Il.* 9.485) and is found in Hesiod's *Theogony* in the forms θεοῖς ἐπιείκελα τέκνα and θεοῖς ἐπιείκελον ἄνδρα (*Th.* 968, 987 and 1020). Homer's divine nature is again emphasised by Hesiod's use of epithets (see also 75–6n.). The emendation θνητοῖς κάλλιστον (first proposed by Rzach on the basis of the corresponding papyrus reading), in place of θνητοῖσιν ἄριστον of the manuscript, is here accepted. Homer has already defined the 'best thing' (ἄριστον) for mortals in the first session (75–9): it would make no sense for Hesiod to ask again the same question and for Homer to give a different answer; moreover, Homer in this answer explicitly defines the 'finest' thing (89: κάλλιστον). The manuscript reading ἄριστον may be due to the influence of the same word a few lines above, at 78.

84–9. ὁππότ' ἂν εὐφροσύνη ... εἴδεται εἶναι: the verses used for Homer's response to Hesiod's challenge are a description of feasting taken from the *Odyssey* (9.6–11), although Homer has not yet composed this work at this point in the narrative (see 275–6n.). These verses in their original context start Odysseus' speech, when Alcinous invites him to reveal his identity and tell his story. In the *Certamen*, Homer's choice of performing these verses guarantees his success (see 90–4n. for the audience's reaction), for they express another common Greek view (Heldmann 1982: 77: 'typisch griechische Lebensfreude und Diesseitigkeit'). In antiquity, these hedonistic Homeric lines were often seen as problematic and criticised (e.g. by Plato, see *R.* 3.390a–b), and were very famous and widely quoted and discussed (see Hillgruber 1999: 335–6; Russell/Konstan 2005: 128–31; F. Pontani 2005b: 236 n. 232). Heubeck/Hoekstra 1989: 12 also remark that the joyful banqueting scene depicted by Odysseus 'is an outward and visible sign of a stable and peacefully ordered community as exemplified by the Phaeacian utopia': Homer, by choosing to perform these verses in reply to Hesiod's question, appears therefore as a supporter of the social order that they signify. This image of Homer will be central in the exchanges at 151–75. Like the verses of the previous answer, these verses too were certainly connected to the contest story by the third century BC (P.Petr. I 25 (1), 21–8), and also in this case the connection may go as far as back as Alcidamas' *Museum*. The beginning of this passage has been adapted in the *Certamen* to the new context: while in the *Odyssey* the first verse starts with ἦ ὅτ' ἐϋφροσύνη (connected to the comparative in the previous verse: οὐ γὰρ ἐγώ γέ τί φημι τέλος χαριέστερον εἶναι / ἢ ὅτ' ἐϋφροσύνη..., 'For I say that nothing is more delightful than when good cheer...') the quotation here begins with ὁππότ' ἂν εὐφροσύνη to connect properly to Hesiod's question. In the last verse, the papyrus reads φαίνεται while both the *Certamen* and the vulgata of the *Odyssey* read εἴδεται.

8. The reaction to Homer's performance (90–4); the 'insoluble challenge' (94–101)

90–4. ῥηθέντων δὲ ... προκατεύχεσθαι πάντας: the first round asserts the position of prominence that Homer will hold throughout the competition. The reaction of the public highlights some of the most important features of Homer as depicted in the *Certamen*: the ability to provoke admiration and amazement in the public, the appeal to a Panhellenic audience, and the fact that his performance works as aetiology for festivals and performances in antiquity. The public's reaction is described in very similar terms in P.Petr. I 25 (1), 28–34 (see Part 2 and below).

90–1. ῥηθέντων ... τοὺς στίχους: after Homer's very first performance 'admiration' (θαῦμα) appears as a prominent feature of his poetry: it is a reaction that Homer will inspire throughout the contest and will lead the public to ask for him to be awarded the victory (205–6; see commentary on Homer's 'finest passage' at 180–204n.). Reactions to poetic performances are described in similar terms already in the *Odyssey* (see, e.g., *Od.* 1.325–6 and 1.339–40), and in other Homeric biographies (Ps.-Hdt. *Vit. Hom.* 5, 12,

22, 36). θαῦμα is an important idea in Alcidamas' stylistic theory too (O'Sullivan 1992: 74), and he attributes it explicitly to Homer: cf. P.Mich. inv. 2754, 15–18 (on which see Part 2). Homeric poetry is also characterised here by its Panhellenic appeal: by calling the public that is attending the contest 'the Greeks' (cf. also 176 and 205), the *Certamen* parallels the claims made about Homer's Panhellenism on biographical grounds at the opening of the text (dispute over his birthplace: see 7–17n.). P.Mich. inv. 2754 offers a similar assessment (17–19 and 22) thus showing that this idea was supported by Alcidamas too.

90. ῥηθέντων δὲ τῶν ἐπῶν: most editors add τούτων after δέ on the basis of the papyrus reading, but this seems unnecessary.

91. τοὺς στίχους: the manuscript reading τὰ ἔπη causes a grammatical problem with the following χρυσοῦς αὐτούς (91–2). Rzach's emendation τοὺς στίχους (based on the papyrus) is the most convincing solution (and more economical than Nietzsche's αὐτοὺς <στίχους>). The manuscript reading may be simply due to the influence of the previous τῶν ἐπῶν at 90.

91–2. ὥστε χρυσοῦς αὐτοὺς προσαγορευθῆναι: the definition of *Od.* 9.6–11 as 'golden verses' is attested only here and in P.Petr. I 25 (1), 31–2, and it is not possible to know whether it goes back to Alcidamas, or to an earlier source (discussion in Kaiser 1964: 213–14, with references at p. 214 n. 3). It is nevertheless clear in meaning and based on traditional elements. It recalls the definition of χρυσέα ἔπη for Pythagoras' words, or Epicurus' *aurea dicta* (Lucretius, *De rerum natura* 3.12–13). The metaphorical use of the adjective χρύσεος is already attested in epic poetry (referred to Aphrodite in, e.g., *Il.* 3.64) and, perhaps more pertinently, Homer himself is called 'golden' (Tz. *Life of Hesiod* 141 Colonna; *AP* 11.442 in Anon. *Vit. Hom* 2.2 and Anon. *Vit. Hom.* 3.4).

92–4. καὶ ἔτι καὶ νῦν ... προκατεύχεσθαι πάντας: Homeric poetry was recited on public occasions (see e.g. Pl. *Ion* 535d: ἐν θυσίαις καὶ ἑορταῖς, 'during sacrifices and festivals') but there is no evidence for such performances of this specific passage. It is therefore impossible to know whether this claim was inspired by actual performative experience or not, but it surely fits the habit of the *Certamen* to use (or perhaps create) myths of performances by Homer as aetiology for other (actual?) festivals and sacrifices: cf. Homer at Argos, at 302–8. Such claims emphasise the persistence of Homer's legacy. There is no space in P.Petr. I 25 (1) for καὶ ἔτι καὶ νῦν ('even now') and those words may have been added by the author of the *Certamen* in an attempt to make his sources seem relevant to his own time (discussion in Wilamowitz 1916: 401 n. 1 and Vogt 1959: 216 n. 65).

94–101. ὁ δὲ Ἡσίοδος ... περὶ νίκης: the contest moves on to a more difficult level: Hesiod proposes an ἄπορον, i.e., an 'insoluble challenge' (on which see 95n.). He asks Homer not to talk about anything that is, was, or shall be (97–8n.), and Homer replies by giving a negative prophecy: there will never be funeral games for Zeus, since he is an immortal god (100–1n.). Plutarch mentions this part of the contest with several variations (*Dinner of the Seven Sages* 153f–154a, see Part 1).

94. ὁ δὲ Ἡσίοδος ἀχθεσθεὶς ἐπὶ τῇ Ὁμήρου εὐημερίᾳ: this description of Hesiod's reaction to Homer's success depicts a great contrast between the two poets. From this point onwards, Hesiod will appear keener than Homer on quarrels and competition (see also 148–50n.), in striking contrast to the grounds on which Panoides will issue his judgement (205–10n.).

95. ἐπὶ τὴν τῶν ἀπόρων ὥρμησεν ἐπερώτησιν: the next question is an ἄπορον ('insoluble challenge'), that is a question to which there seems to be no possible answer. Like the 'riddles of the superlatives' (74–89n.), this type of riddle was common in ancient Greece: for example, in the *Dinner of the Seven Sages* 151a–e Plutarch tells the famous story of the king of the Ethiopians asking the Pharaoh Amasis to drink up the ocean (see also Plu. *Alex.* 64 for the Gymnosophists answering questions of this kind posed by Alexander). See Konstantakos 2004: esp. 120–6. The concept of ἀπορία is also relevant to a source of the *Certamen*, Alcidamas: in his *On Sophists* he uses that word to describe the condition of 'helplessness' in which those who are used to written speeches find themselves when it comes to speak on the spot (*Soph.* 8, 15, 16, 21; in contrast to εὐπορία, 'resourcefulness': see *Soph.* 3, 6, 13, 19, 24, 34): for him, therefore, the fact that Homer does not find himself in an 'aporetic' situation, but is able to solve challenges immediately, may be a relevant illustration of good rhetorical performance.

97–8. Μοῦσ' ἄγε μοι ... σὺ δ' ἄλλης μνῆσαι ἀοιδῆς: Hesiod asks Homer not to sing of anything that is, was or shall be. The impossibility of such a task is highlighted by the use of enjambment: the words τῶν μὲν μηδὲν ἄειδε at 98 ('sing nothing of those') reverse the standard epic formula τά τ' ἐόντα τά τ' ἐσσόμενα πρό τ' ἐόντα in the previous verse ('the things that are, shall be and were'; for this use of the enjambment in the *Certamen* see the exchanges in the next paragraph). The presence of the formula τά τ' ἐόντα τά τ' ἐσσόμενα πρό τ' ἐόντα, together with Homer's successful answer to Hesiod's question, outlines once again Homer's divine inspiration: knowledge of present, past, and future is usually connected to the Muses and to their ability to sing everything (Hes. *Th.* 38; cf. also *Th.* 32 where the formula appears in a shortened version) and to the seer Calchas as well (*Il.* 1.70). See also Baier 2013: 151 for discussion and further bibliography. For Alcidamas, this section of the contest may have been particularly significant as an expression of another key point of his literary theory: the freedom to choose any subject for a declamation (in response, e.g., to the attack put forth by Isocrates, *Hel.*

11; see O'Sullivan 1992: 83). Μοῦσ' ἄγε μοι is not formulaic but it may have been constructed on the model of εἴπ' ἄγε μοι (76) with the addition of an invocation to the Muses since the formula that follows, as mentioned above, is often connected to them. The second verse too is reminiscent of the epic formulaic vocabulary. Collins 2004: 104 sees in μηδὲν ἄειδε a parodic reference to the Homeric μῆνιν ἄειδε (*Il.* 1.1); σὺ δ' ἄλλης μνῆσαι ἀοιδῆς is an adaptation of the verse that closes many Homeric *Hymns*: αὐτὰρ ἐγὼ καὶ σεῖο καὶ ἄλλης μνήσομ' ἀοιδῆς, see e.g. *h.Hom.* 2.495, 3.546.

100–1. οὐδέ ποτ' ἀμφὶ Διὸς ... ἐρίζοντες περὶ νίκης: the funeral games for an immortal god cannot happen at any present, past or future time, and prove therefore to be an appropriate solution to Hesiod's challenge. It is appropriate also because it allows Homer to support the traditional image of the gods presented in his work, against a long tradition of attacks, and alternative versions. Callimachus (*Jov.* 6–9) and Euhemerus (T 69 A Winiarczyk) testify to the existence of a well-developed debate about the existence of a tomb of Zeus in Crete in the Hellenistic period, and this debate can be probably traced further back in time (Kokolakis 1995; discussion and references in Cook 1914: 157–63 and 1925: 940–3). Homer in the *Certamen* goes back to the topic of Zeus' immortality at 121–3n. (there, Hesiod provokingly mentions 'the white bones of the deceased, Zeus') and defends another orthodox view of the gods when he denies the possibility of Artemis' marriage at 117–18. The tomb of Zeus seems to have been a topic for declamations, even if there is only one late witness for this: Philostr. *VS* 2.569. O'Sullivan's suggestion about the significance of this exchange of verses for Alcidamas (see 97–8n.) finds some confirmation in Philostratus.

9. The 'ambiguous propositions' (102–37)

102–37. Because of Homer's success in solving the 'insoluble challenge' (94–101), Hesiod turns to a more difficult test and puts forward 'ambiguous propositions'. Hesiod's challenges are ambiguous in that they present, more or less explicitly, improper views on issues that mattered to the Greeks, such as the life and behaviour of heroes (e.g., 107), the enemies of the Greeks (e.g., 109), and the nature and behaviour of the gods (e.g., 117); sometimes the exchanges of verses also reflect points of disagreement between Homeric and Hesiodic poetry (e.g., 113–14). Homer solves the impropriety of Hesiod's claims by adding a new line that enjambs an element of Hesiod's and changes its meaning. Thematic connections marking the transition between groups of exchanges may have helped memorise the sequence (one series of verses is on banquets, one on men and women, another on water and navigation). Some of the hexameter material contained in this section was circulating by Alcidamas' time and may have been known to him: the verses at 107–8 are transmitted in Aristophanes' *Peace*, performed in 421 BC; furthermore, as has been noted, in terms of content the challenges in this section are often sophistic in flavour (see, e.g., 113–14n.). For sophistic approaches to archaic epic see: Richardson 1975; Ford 2002: 80–5; Morgan 2000: ch. 4; Koning 2010: 111–15 and 217–23; Boys-Stones 2010: 40–5. Sophistic influences are apparent in terms of syntax too: in order to present an acceptable thought, Homer is forced to introduce into hexameter poetry complicated syntactical structures reminiscent of sophistic prose. Like most epic hexameters, Hesiod's verses in the *Certamen* stand on their own in terms of both syntax and meaning, and express ideas that can be conceived in principle (see, e.g., 100–1n.). Enjambment is also a common feature in epic poems. However, in most cases it is used to expand or elaborate the thought expressed in the previous line ('progressive' enjambment), while in the *Certamen* it is used to change the syntactical structure of Hesiod's lines and consequently its meaning. In other words, Homer gives Hesiod's line a new syntactical structure by reinterpreting it as requiring 'necessary enjambment'. The final result is that each 'proper' unit of thought is now contained in two lines, rather than in one, as is generally the case in the Homeric poems. Possibilities inherent in the Homeric tradition ('necessary' and corrective enjambments) are in these lines set in dialogue with new intellectual developments. For studies on the Homeric enjambments see, e.g., Parry 1971; Kirk 1966; Higbie 1990; Bakker 1990; Clark 1997. For an analysis of the practice of capping verses in performance and in different literary genres see Collins 2004.

103–6. καὶ πλείονας ... Ἡσιόδου: in the manuscript the verses are reported in succession, two on each line, with no indication of the speaker and no separation between the different exchanges. The statement made in the present passage is the only guideline for the attribution of verses to either speaker and will turn out to be not detailed enough (see esp. 133–7n). It is a sign of the text's tendency towards conciseness (contrast P.Petr. I 25 (1), on which see Part 2).

107–8. δεῖπνον ... κορέσθην: in Hesiod's verse the heroes are said to be dining on beef and necks of horses. But eating necks of horses is reminiscent of barbarian, rather than Greek, food habits (Collins 2004: 187), and Homer corrects Hesiod's improper suggestion by enjambing καὐχένας ἵππων ('and necks of horses') with another verb, ἔκλυον ('they cleansed'): now the heroes dine on beef, and cleanse the horses' necks of sweat. The couplet is transmitted, with variants, in Aristophanes' *Peace* 1282–3. There, it is not used as an example of ambiguous proposition (the two verses are recited by the same character and the first verse is not seen as problematic), but offers the opportunity for a comic response by Trygaeus, who asks the son of Lamachus to sing of how the heroes kept on eating even though they were 'sated'. On this Aristophanic passage see Sommerstein 1985: 194 and Olson 1998: 308–9. The mention of these verses in *Peace*, performed for the first time in 421 BC, confirms that at least some of the hexameters contained in the *Certamen* pre-date Alcidamas (see also 74–89). It is also possible that Aristophanes was aware of the couplet's connection to the story of the contest of Homer and Hesiod. On a general level, both Aristophanes and the *Certamen* present the couplet in contexts where the opposition between poetry of war and poetry of peace is a core issue; many of the verses mentioned in the passage from *Peace* come from Homeric poetry (cf. also Richardson 1981: 2); the first words of Aristophanes' quotation, ὡς οἱ μὲν δαίνυντο, are also transmitted in the *Certamen* in another passage connected to a feasting scene (119); hence Aristophanes may have been aware of a collection of verses similar to that in the *Certamen*. The whole scene in *Peace*, then, starts by quoting at 1270 another verse transmitted in the *Certamen* as well, namely the incipit of the *Epigoni* (259; the scholium to Aristophanes attributes the *Epigoni* to Antimachus, while the *Certamen* attributes it to Homer; see also Di Benedetto 1969). Even more interestingly, Aristophanes seems to echo, in his re-enactment of a contest between a poet of peace and a poet of war, the same poetic strategies Homer and Hesiod use in this section of the *Certamen*: at *Peace* 1270, the boy begins the verse, but Trygaeus completes it and adds a new one, which reverses the words of the previous speaker. The description of a cruel battle at 1273–8, 'a slight misquotation from *Il.* 4.446–9' (Sommerstein 1985: 194), echoes Homer's finest passage in the *Certamen* (191–204). For discussion see also Meyer 1892: 377–80; Busse 1909; Kirk 1950: 150; Compton-Engle 1999. Alcidamas therefore was perhaps not responsible for the insertion of these hexameters within the story of the contest, nor for the invention of the story itself. The hexameter at 108 as it stands in the manuscript does not scan. Emending πτολέμου to πολέμοιο seems the most convenient solution: πολέμοιο is a very common epic form (e.g., *Il*. 1.165), while πτολέμου is rarer and never found in this metrical position. Aristophanes' πολέμου ἐκόρεσθεν is fifth-century language and may be Aristophanes' own adaptation of the epic forms πολέμοιο and κορέσθην (e.g., *Od.* 4.541); βοῶν κρέα in this metrical position and καὐχένας ἵππων are not Homeric.

109–10. καὶ Φρύγες ... δόρπον ἑλέσθαι: Hesiod's verse claims that the Phrygians are the best men on ships. Homer's answer is difficult and different interpretations have been proposed, where the dative ἀνδράσι ληιστῆρσιν is given a variety of meanings and functions: Evelyn-White translates 'to filch their dinner from pirates on the beach' and Collins 2004: 187 translates 'among thieves to take their dinner on the shore'. Wilamowitz suggests the emendation δόρπα πένεσθαι and he is followed by West who translates 'at preparing supper on shore for a pirate crew'. In any case, unclear though it may be, by giving this answer Homer achieves two goals. First, he denies the Phrygians' maritime supremacy: in the *Iliad* (e.g. 2.862–3) they were not a maritime force, so Homer's ἐπ' ἀκτῆς ('on the shore') provides a more appropriate location for them than ἐπὶ νηυσίν ('on ships') in the previous verse. Second, by associating them with pirates, he presents them in an overall negative light, and in this respect Homer expresses a typically Greek attitude toward these people. The Phrygians were allies of the Trojans, and in the Athens of the fifth century BC these two names were interchangeable. The Phrygians were also associated with cruelty, luxury and cowardice (see Hall 1988 and 1989 *passim*; Erskine 2001: 73–4; West 2003a: 329; Collins 2004: 187; Bryce 2006: 140–2). καὶ Φρύγες at the beginning of verse is also at *Il.* 10.431; ληιστῆρσιν is in the same position at *Od.* 16.424; δόρπον ἑλέσθαι recalls δόρπον ἕλοντο at *Od.* 14.347.

111–12. χερσὶ ... τόξα: in Hesiod's verse, someone (as yet unspecified) is said to shoot arrows at the Giants 'with his hands', χερσί. Homer solves the problem by linking χερσί to ἀπέλυσεν (ἀπ' ὤμων καμπύλα τόξα) and introducing a subject: with his hands Heracles 'loosed from his shoulders a bent bow', and then used it to shoot arrows. Hesiod describes the Giants as 'holding long spears in their hands' (*Th.* 186: δολίχ' ἔγχεα χερσὶν ἔχοντας) and this may explain why the difficulty of Hesiod's verse is based precisely on the word χερσί. This exchange seems to refer to the Gigantomachy, the battle between gods and Giants in which Heracles helped the gods; in extant epic poetry, the episode is mentioned, or alluded to, at *Th.* 954 and Hes. fr. 43a.65 MW (see West 1966: 419; Clay 2003: 113–15). In the manuscript, the verses are presented in the opposite sequence to this edition: it seems necessary to reverse the order, as proposed first by Nietzsche, because at 112 there is no apparent difficulty that could be solved by an element in the previous line. Line 111 as transmitted in **L** does not scan, but it seems sufficient to emend ὅλλων to ὅλων. The manuscript reading Ἡρακλῆς (unattested in epic) has been often emended to the form Ἡρακλέης attested in Hes. *Th.* 318 and 527 in the same metrical position, but this is superfluous. καμπύλα τόξα is formulaic and often occurs in the same metrical position as at 112 (e.g., *Il.* 3.17).

113–14. οὗτος ... γυναιξίν: these two verses start off a series of three couplets on the theme of the union between man and woman. Hesiod is applying two opposite adjectives to the same person: a man is said to be the son of someone who is at the same time a 'good man and a coward'. Homer enjambs the second adjective, ἀνάλκιδος, with a new, feminine noun, μητρός. As a result, the man is now said to be the son of 'a good man and a coward mother': war, as Homer explains, is 'hard for all women'. The play on the double value of the adjective ἄναλκις may reflect early fifth-century concerns about Homeric language (see the discussion of Protagoras 80 A 28 DK in Graziosi 2001: 67). Perhaps engaging with such concerns, in this exchange Homer shows his ability to use language properly: ἄναλκις is an adjective for women, not for the Homeric 'good man' (ἀγαθὸς ἀνήρ). For such a man, ἀλκή is an important martial quality (Kirk 1990: 97), while ἄναλκις is strongly connected to inability in war (together with ἀπτόλεμος: *Il.* 2.201; 9.35; 9.41), and it is usually applied to warriors as a rebuke (see also the formulaic κακὸν καὶ ἀνάλκιδα 'bad and coward', on which see below); or indeed to women, as in the present couplet after Homer's contribution: ἄναλκις is used in connection with Aphrodite when Diomedes recognises her in *Il.* 5.330–2 and is used of women more generally at *Il.* 5.349. The verse as proposed by Hesiod and the way Homer corrects it also seem to reflect two different views, one more Hesiodic and the other more Homeric, on what an ἀγαθὸς ἀνήρ is: unlike Homeric poetry, Hesiod does not emphasise ability in war as a necessary requirement for good men. In this respect, it is interesting that in order to create his verse Hesiod reverses a Homeric formula, found always in the same metrical position: ἀγαθοῦ καὶ ἀνάλκιδος replaces the Homeric κακὸν καὶ ἀνάλκιδα (*Il.* 8.153; 14.126) and κακὸν καὶ ἄναλκιν (*Od.* 3.375).

115–16. οὔτ' ἄρ ... Ἀφροδίτην: according to Hesiod's verse, in order to conceive a child (σοί, 'for you', i.e., 'for conceiving you') a father and a mother did not have a physical union (οὔτ' ἄρ ... ἐμίγη). It is not precisely clear how the syntactic connection between this and the following verse works, and the text of Homer's answer seems corrupt. But it seems that the key element for Homer's solution is διὰ χρυσῆν Ἀφροδίτην: that is, the body was sowed 'by the action of golden Aphrodite', presented here as a substitute for physical union. That phrase is generally used in epic in the opposite sense to Homer's answer: that is, it indicates sexual union. The fact that the formula occurs only in Hesiod, sometimes in 'suspect' verses (for discussion see West 1966: 78 and 398; the phrase occurs at *Th.* 822, 962, 1005, 1014; fr. 23a.35 MW; fr. 221.3 MW; cf. also *LfrgE* s.v.), and is here pronounced by Homer may suggest that the couplet is centred on a parodic use of that formula, and may point to ancient and now lost discussions about it. πατὴρ ἐμίγη καὶ πότνια μήτηρ is built on the Homeric πατὴρ καὶ πότνια μήτηρ which occurs both in the *Iliad* (e.g., 9.561) and in the *Odyssey* (e.g., 6.30). The emendation αὐτάρ by Rzach and Evelyn-White, which eliminates the negation οὔτε at the beginning of the verse, does not clarify the meaning of the couplet, nor does the translation proposed by Evelyn-White: 'But for you, your father and lady mother lay in love – / when they begot you by the aid of golden Aphrodite'. West gives yet a different meaning to the first verse, but by putting σῶμα τό γ' ἐσπείραντο between *cruces* does not offer a definitive solution: 'Nor with you your father and lady mother make love – / †the body which† they sowed through golden Aphrodite'.

117–18. αὐτὰρ ... βιο<ῖο>: this couplet closes the series of verses about men and women. The concept of marriage (δμήθη γάμῳ) cannot be allowed to refer to the virgin goddess Artemis, as Hesiod's verse implies. Homer's contribution clarifies that it was Callisto who got married, and for this reason Artemis killed her with an arrow. Homer is referring here to the story of Callisto, friend and hunting companion of Artemis, of which several versions were known in antiquity (see *LfrgE* s.v. Καλλιστώ). Callisto had sworn to preserve her virginity in honour of Artemis but was seduced by Zeus, and as a punishment she was either transformed into a bear or, as in this couplet, killed by Artemis. Like 113–14, this exchange too may be seen to reflect fifth-century sophistic concerns about the possibility of alternative word division in the Homeric poems (Graziosi 2001: 66–7). Ἄρτεμις ἰοχέαιρα (or its accusative form) is formulaic (e.g., *Il.* 5.53; Hes. *Th.* 14) and generally occurs at the end of the hexameter. ἀπ' ἀργυρέοιο βιοῖο occurs only once in epic, at *Il.* 24.605 (but cf. *Il.* 1.49: ἀργυρέοιο βιοῖο) and refers to Apollo rather than Artemis. Nevertheless, in *Il.* 24.605 it is closely connected to the formula Ἄρτεμις ἰοχέαιρα (found in the next verse) and introduced by the same verb (πέφνεν) as in this couplet: *Il.* 24.605–6: τοὺς μὲν Ἀπόλλων πέφνεν ἀπ' ἀργυρέοιο βιοῖο / χωόμενος Νιόβῃ, τὰς δ' Ἄρτεμις ἰοχέαιρα.

119–20. ὣς οἳ μὲν ... Ἀγαμέμνων: the poets deal again with the topic of feasting (see also 107–8 and 109–10). Homer corrects the absurd suggestion that the heroes feasted 'all day, having nothing' by saying that they had nothing 'of their own' (οἴκοθεν), but food was provided by Agamemnon. Through this exchange of verses Homer and Hesiod seem to be presenting and defending their respective conceptions of feasting, food, and society. Hesiod's verse may be an exaggeration of the frugality advocated in the *Works and Days* (see, e.g., 40–1), while Homer transforms this couplet into a typically Homeric scene of feasting. The visible difference is Agamemnon's generous behaviour: the only banquet offered by Agamemnon in the Homeric poems is in *Il.* 9.89–91, where he is said to invite the Achaean leaders (for feasting in Homer see Foley 1999: 169–200; list of Homeric feasting episodes in Foley 1999: 272–3). Perhaps not surprisingly, the *Certamen* uses here the highly formulaic epithet 'lord of men' (ἄναξ ἀνδρῶν) for Agamemnon, which is also found later in the abovementioned Iliadic passage (*Il.* 9.96). The exchange also looks like a comment on the question of how the heroes support themselves, as they are never seen to work, while according to the Hesiodic ideal of self-sufficiency, one cannot eat without working, and it is a bad idea to rely on gift-eating kings, or even on neighbours. Homer transforms this couplet into a typically Homeric scene of royal patronage, as the food was provided by Agamemnon.

121–3. δεῖπνον ... ἀντιθέοιο: according to Hesiod's ambiguous proposition, after dining the heroes gathered up the bones of the deceased Zeus. But Homer, who cannot accept the idea of Zeus' mortality (see also 115–16n. on another theological impropriety, and 100–1n. more pertinently on the tomb of Zeus), connects the genitive Διός at 122 ('Zeus'') with παιδός in the next verse ('Zeus' son') and thereby specifies that the bones are those of Sarpedon, the mortal son of Zeus, and not those of the god himself. Sarpedon's death causes much grief to Zeus in the *Iliad* (16.419–683), and the episode was also popular on vases (*LIMC* s.v. 'Sarpedon'). On Sarpedon and his death see Nagy 1983. On this occasion, Hesiod's question takes up two lines (cf. 105–6). Hesiod's first verse (121) also contains a difficulty, which is solved by Hesiod's own second verse (122): according to 121 the heroes are improperly said to be dining 'among the smoky ashes': the second verse connects more suitably the ashes with another action, the gathering of bones. The fact that the bones are said to be those of Zeus, then, brings about a second difficulty, which the next verse solves as explained above. In this context, according to the statement of the text at 105–6, we have to see in 121–2 Hesiod's question, and in 123 Homer's answer (so Evelyn-White leaves out the difficulty and solution at 121–2 and focuses on 122–3: 'When they had feasted, they gathered among the glowing ashes the bones of the dead Zeus – / born Sarpedon, that bold and godlike man'). In other contexts, though, we may imagine that the verses were distributed in a different way, as a back and forth, or even between a number of speakers, as follows: Speaker A: 121; Speaker B: 122; Speaker A or C: 123 – see also West 1967: 441. The phrase ἐνὶ σποδῷ αἰθαλοέσσῃ is not epic (but cf. *Il.* 18.23 and *Od.* 24.316 where αἰθαλόεσσαν is at the end of the verse); ὀστέα λευκά is in the same metrical position in Hes. *Th.* 540, 555 and 557 (cf. also *Il.* 16.347 and 23.252 at the end of the verse; *Il.* 24.793 at the beginning of the verse); ἀντίθεος is a common epithet for Sarpedon (e.g., *Il.* 5.629) although never used in the same case and metrical position, while ὑπέρθυμος is never connected to him; κατατεθνειῶτος is not attested in epic (the epic form is κατατεθνηῶτος: see, e.g., *Il.* 7.89, also in the same metrical position), but this is not a sufficient ground for an emendation (see apparatus).

124–6. ἡμεῖς ... δολιχαύλους: a new theme links, from now onwards, the last group of verses: water and navigation. As in the previous exchange (121–3), Hesiod asks his question in two verses and Homer replies with one. This too may be a double riddle (that is, the first verse presents a difficulty that the second verse of the question itself seems to solve) but the text is quite unclear. At 124, ἂμ πεδίον ('over the plain') is improperly accompanied by ἥμενοι ('sitting') instead of a verb of motion as would normally be required (cf. the instances of ἂμ πεδίον in the *Iliad*: 5.87; 5.96; 23.464). This is provided at 125 (ἴομεν), but in this new line there is nothing that attaches to ἥμενοι (cf. also West 1967: 441 n. 1). For this reason, it has been proposed that after 124 a line attributed to Homer has fallen out. In any case, Homer's skills are put to test on the basis of the difficulty at 125. The paradox contained in the new line is that ὁδόν seems to be the object of ἀμφ' ὤμοισιν ἔχοντες (carrying the road on their shoulders?). Hence, Homer in his line gives a new object to the verb ἔχοντες, and leaves ὁδόν in connection with ἴομεν ('we make our way'; cf. also Hdt. 6.34: ἰόντες τὴν ἰρὴν ὁδόν). 'Hilted swords and long-socketed javelins' seems an obvious continuation for Homer, as in Homeric poetry ἀμφ' ὤμοισιν is often connected to weapons (cf. *Il.* 2.45; 3.328; 11.527). φάσγανα occurs only three times in Homer (*Il.* 15.713; *Od.* 16.295; *Od.* 22.74) and only once with κωπήεντα (this adjective is more often connected to ξίφος). αἰγανέας δολιχαύλους is Homeric and occurs in the same metrical position at *Od.* 9.156.

127–8. δὴ τότ' ἀριστῆ<ες> ... ὠκύαλον ναῦν: the problem posed by Hesiod's verse lies in the expression χείρεσσι θαλάσσης ('with their hands from the sea'). Homer enjambs it with elements that change its function within the sentence: with their hands the boys 'dragged off' (ἀπείρυσαν) from the sea a 'swift ship' (ὠκύαλον ναῦν). In this exchange of verses there may be a reference to the problem of personification of rivers, such as the Scamander at *Il.* 21.136–60. In that passage the river Scamander is angry at Achilles because the hero has thrown many bodies of Trojan warriors into his water. The river is repeatedly said to talk to Achilles, and to chase him with its water, but in one particular verse its human appearance is explicitly mentioned (21.213: ἀνέρι εἰσάμενος, 'resembling a man'). Interestingly, this verse is omitted in some of the manuscripts of the *Iliad*, which may point to the fact that an anthropomorphic appearance of the river god may have been seen as problematic. This verse, certainly known to Aristarchus (cf. scholia on that passage) was either included in later times because 'it was thought that the river god could not address Akhilleus unless he took human form', as Richardson 1993: 71 observes, or omitted precisely because the river god was thought not to be human in form. The expression ἀριστῆες κοῦροι is not attested in Homeric or Hesiodic poetry (but cf. Hes. fr. 1.2–3 MW: Μοῦσαι Ὀλυμπιάδες, κοῦραι Διὸς αἰγιόχοιο / αἳ τότ' ἄρισται ἔσαν), while ἄσμενοι is found at the beginning of verse, in the formulaic ἄσμενοι ἐκ θανάτοιο, at *Od.* 9.63, 9.566, 10.134; ἐσσυμένως is suitable in several metrical positions: it is found in the same position as in this couplet at *Od.* 9.73 and 16.51; ὠκύαλον ναῦν at the end of verse is found, in the metrically equivalent nominative form, at *Od.* 12.182 and 15.473.

129–30. κολχίδ' ... ἀθέμιστον: the Colchian girl, i.e. Medea, was taken away from King Aietes, but there is no mention of King Aietes himself being taken away, as Hesiod's verse suggests. Through Homer's reply Αἰήτην βασιλῆα becomes the object of φεῦγον: they took away the Colchian girl, and fled King Aietes, recognised as 'inhospitable and unlawful'. The episode of Medea being carried away by Jason is told by Hesiod (*Th.* 992–5) but does not feature in Homer. See also *Th.* 956–62 for another mention of both Aietes and Medea in Hesiod. This exchange between Homer and Hesiod also reflects the different attributes of King Aietes in their respective poetry: against the Hesiodic 'god-nurtured king' (*Th.* 992: διοτρεφέος βασιλῆος), Homer defines Aietes as 'baleful' (*Od.* 10.137: ὀλοόφρονος Αἰήταο), in line with the negative epithets used in the answer: ἀνέστιον ἠδ' ἀθέμιστον, 'inhospitable and unlawful'. L reads Κολχίδ' ἔπειθ' ἵκοντο ('when they reached Colchis'), a reading that does not allow the verse to be an 'ambiguous proposition' since there is no apparent difficulty. It was Wilamowitz who interpreted κολχίδα as the 'Colchian girl', rather than as 'Colchis', and then emended the text that follows to ἔπειτ' ἤγοντο, arguably inspired by the Hesiodic κούρην δ' Αἰήταο... ἦγε παρ' Αἰήτεω (*Th.* 992–5, '...took away...the daughter of Aietes'). The manuscript reading can easily be due to the double meaning of the form κολχίδα and the similar sound of ἵκοντο and ἤγοντο, each of which suits one of the meanings of κολχίδα. Also Αἰήτην βασιλῆα in the same metrical position is found in the Hesiodic passage (*Th.* 957). For ἀνέστιον ἠδ' ἀθέμιστον cf. *Il.* 9.63–4: ἀφρήτωρ ἀθέμιστος ἀνέστιός ἐστιν ἐκεῖνος / ὃς πολέμου ἔραται ἐπιδημίου ὀκρυόεντος ('clanless, inhospitable, and unlawful is this man, who loves horrible war among his people'), a single but very famous instance, as the many quotations of it show (e.g., Ar. *Pax* 1097).

131–2. αὐτὰρ ... ἐπὶ νηῶν: the 'sea's swell', οἶδμα θαλάσσης, cannot be the object of ἔκπιον ('they drunk up'). Homer connects it to another verb and makes it the object of ποντοπορεῖν ἤμελλον ('they made themselves ready to sail the sea's swell'). Drinking up the sea is used in the context of an 'insoluble challenge' (ἀπορία) in another relevant text, where the Egyptian king Amasis, during an exchange of riddles in a competition in wisdom with the king of the Ethiopians, was asked to do so (Plu. *Dinner of the Seven Sages* 153f, on which see Part 1, 'Plutarch', and Konstantakos 2004). The first part of the first verse is clearly and extensively based on a Homeric formulaic verse: αὐτὰρ ἐπεὶ σπεῖσάν τε πίον θ' ὅσον ἤθελε θυμός (e.g., *Il.* 9.177; *Od.* 3.342; cf. also *Od.* 21.273), conveniently modified on the basis of the new context (inclusion of the difficulty at the end and slight variations in the central feet of the hexameter). οἶδμα θαλάσσης is in the *Hymn to Demeter* 14 in the same metrical position; ἐυσσέλμων ἐπὶ νηῶν too is based on Homeric practice: ἐύσσελμος is a common epithet for ships and the phrase ἐυσσέλμων ἐπὶ νηῶν is found in *Od.* 8.500 and 24.117. Similar forms (in different cases or with different prepositions, but always in the same metrical position) are also common: cf., e.g., *Il.* 7.419; *Od.* 12.358.

133–7. τοῖσιν ... ἵκοισθε: these verses contain two distinct but connected sequences of challenges and responses. At 133 Hesiod claims that Agamemnon prayed that the heroes 'might perish'. Homer corrects this statement in his line (134) by making Agamemnon pray that the heroes might 'never' perish 'in the sea' (μηδέ ποτ' ἐν πόντῳ); and with the second part of his verse seems to invite Hesiod to go on with another challenge on the same topic, and more specifically to create an utterance by Agamemnon (καὶ φωνήσας ἔπος ηὔδα, 'and he uttered this verse'). Hesiod then creates the new challenge in two verses (this time only the second one seems to contain a difficulty, cf. 121–23 and 124–26): Agamemnon is again said to pray that the Achaeans may never return home to their fatherland. In the last verse, thanks to Homer's intervention, Agamemnon is said to pray that that Achaeans may never return home 'harmed' (πημανθείς), but rather 'unharmed' (ἀπήμονες). The text here seems to reflect Agamemnon's problematic standing as a leader in the *Iliad*. The issue of returning home is dramatised with particular force at the beginning of the poem, through Agamemnon's false dream, and its demoralising consequences; on Agamemnon's leadership see Haubold 2000: 52–68. The suggested division of the verses among the speakers seems to be the one that best suits the structure of the competition as described in this section of the *Certamen*: the verses which contain the challenges (133 and 135–6) are attributed to Hesiod, while the solutions belong to Homer (134 and 137). Moreover, the number of verses attributed to both speakers is in agreement with the general guidelines given at the beginning of the section: Homer always replies with one verse, while Hesiod sometimes asks the question in two verses. Other solutions have been proposed. Nietzsche suggests attributing to Homer only the last verse. Hermann's proposal (133–4 to Hesiod, 135–7 to Homer) would not involve any solution of difficulty by Homer. Busse's suggestion of dividing line 134 between the two speakers would again go against the set rules. The expression καὶ φωνήσας ἔπος ηὔδα is inspired by the Homeric formulaic verse καί μιν (or σφεας) φωνήσας ἔπεα πτερόεντα προσηύδα (e.g., *Il.* 1.201; *Od.* 1.122; *Hymn to Apollo* 451). Line 136 is inspired by *Od.* 19.258: οἴκαδε νοστήσαντα φίλην ἐς πατρίδα γαῖαν (but see also other similar forms such as οἴκαδε νοστήσειε at *Od.* 2.343).

10. The 'numerical problem' (138–48)

138–48. πρὸς πάντα ... ‚ε†ῢ̈†: Homer's success continues, and seems to be increasing after each stage of the competition (cf. also the previous descriptions at 90–4 and 102, and the praise he received from 'all the Greeks', 176). Hence, Hesiod turns to proposing to Homer a 'numerical problem', a type of riddle in hexameter that was common in antiquity: see, e.g., the contest between Calchas and Mopsus (Hes. fr. 278 MW; Pherecyd. 3 *FGrHist* 142; see Fowler 2013: 546–8), and the collection of arithmetical riddles in Book 14 of the *Palatine Anthology*. Hesiod's question centres on the number of Achaeans who went to Ilium with the Atreides: this challenge allows Homer to explore further an issue addressed in his poems, as well as establishing his privileged relationship with the Muses. It also touches on a topic that interested various audiences and readers of Homeric poetry at different times (140–1n.).

140–1. τοῦτό ... Ἀχαιοί: in the *Iliad*, during the invocation to the Muses that opens the Catalogue of Ships (*Il*. 2.484–93), Homer claims that it would not be possible for him to describe or name the entire crowd of soldiers who went to Troy without the help of the Muses. By answering Hesiod's riddle, Homer here proves that he has the Muses on his side. On the value of this invocation to the Muses for Homeric poetics see most recently Ford 1992: 57–90; Graziosi/Haubold 2010: 1–8; Clay 2011 (esp. ch. 1). Whether or not Homer knew the actual number of Achaeans who participated in the war was also an object of debate in antiquity, and was naturally related to the interpretation of the poet's claim (see the scholia on the Iliadic passage). Such exchange may have been of interest to a fifth-century audience: the size of the Achaean expedition was calculated and discussed by Thucydides (1.10.3–5), according to whom the Trojan War was not as large as those fought in his own time. See also Graziosi 2001: 68. The first verse contains a request to speak that draws on the formulaic vocabulary of epic poetry. ἐειρομένῳ is found in the expression εἰπέ μοι εἰρομένῳ at *Od*. 15.263 and 24.114. The imperative κατάλεξον is in the same metrical position in a highly formulaic verse with the same introductory function (ἀλλ' ἄγε μοι τόδε εἰπὲ καὶ ἀτρεκέως κατάλεξον, e.g. *Il*. 10.384). It also occurs in *Od*. 16.235–6, in an analogous context, as Odysseus asks Telemachus to count the number of suitors; ἅμ' Ἀτρείδῃσιν occurs only three times in epic poetry and always in relation to the Achaean expedition: at *Il*. 2.761–2 the poet asks the Muses to tell him who were the best among the Achaeans who followed the Atreides to Troy; at *Od*. 17.103–4 Penelope says that her bed is always wet with her tears since Odysseus went to Troy with the Atreides; at *Od*. 19.182–3 Idomeneus is said to have gone to Troy with the Atreides.

142. ὁ δὲ ... οὕτως: the expression ἀποκρίνομαι διὰ λογιστικοῦ προβλήματος does not have parallels in extant Greek literature. Nevertheless, its meaning is clear: 'to answer with a numerical problem' (cf. also West's translation: 'to answer by means of an arithmetical problem').

143–5. πεντήκοντ' ... Ἀχαιοί: Homer calculates that the Achaeans who took part in the expedition to Troy numbered 112,500,000 (50 fire-hearths x 50 spits x 50 pieces of meat x 900 Achaeans; on the recurrence of the number fifty in Homer's reply see Unanua Garmendia 2003). The number Homer proposes is striking, and lines 146–8 present an interesting comment in this respect (see 146–8n.). But the fact that Homer gives an answer to this question is in itself sufficient to prove that he is a divinely inspired poet (see 140–1n.). The way in which Homer makes his calculation seems to be inspired by a few Iliadic passages, some of which have strong thematic connections with this exchange: see *Il.* 8.562–3, where the Trojans are gathered in groups of fifty around a thousand fire-hearths, and turn out to be considerably fewer than the Achaeans. For other examples of the epic practice of counting people by dividing them into groups, see *Il.* 2.123–8 (another passage on the numerical superiority of the Achaeans over the Trojans); *Il.* 2.509–10 (on the contingents of the Boeotians); *Il.* 2.719–20 (on the contingent of Philoctetes in the Catalogue of Ships).

146–8. τοῦτο δὲ εὑρίσκεται ... μυριάδες ͵ε†ῠν̄†: the claim that 'this results in an incredible number' seems incompatible with 149, where it is said that Homer has replied successfully to all the challenges. Hence West 1967: 442 n. 2 suggests that it is a marginal gloss that was interpolated in the text in later times (see also West 2003a: 335 n. 13). The suggestion is fascinating, because it suggests that the topic of the exchange – the number of Achaeans who went to Troy – generated debate from antiquity (see 140–1n. on Thucydides) through to the Byzantine age. However, only the discovery of new manuscript witnesses could prove it with certainty. The manuscript text is incomplete and unclear towards the end. The sentence may have been incomplete already in the source, perhaps because of physical damage (West 1967: 442 n. 2); alternatively, the copyist may have stopped transcribing the sentence after the letters ͵ευν̄ because he found them difficult to interpret – ͵ε may well be the symbol for 5,000 (which, with δεκαδύο μυριάδες, would make 125,000 – the expected quantity of pieces of meat) but ῠ and ν̄ are more problematic: if they, too, are numerals (400 and 50 respectively), they result in the wrong total.

11. The 'philosophical questions' (148–75)

148–75. κατὰ πάντα ... πλεῖστα: Hesiod now moves to asking a series of questions that deal with issues of morality, religion, good government, and citizenship. Some of the questions touch on topics that were already presented in the previous sections, but there are remarkable differences. As West 1967: 442 notes, the verses 'reek of the late fifth or early fourth century'.

11. The 'philosophical questions' (148–75)

In terms of language, the epic formulaic vocabulary is less frequently exploited, and some words are rarely or never used in early epic (see, e.g., δικαιοσύνη at 168). The topics discussed in this section widely informed fifth- and fourth-century philosophical and political discourse, and sophistic influences are identifiable throughout the section. More specifically, there are several and clear connections with Alcidamas' *On Sophists*, which explain why these verses might have been relevant to him, or why he might have created them. Furthermore, more explicitly than in the previous sections, Homer masterfully discusses and covers topics that were traditionally considered Hesiod's fields of expertise and sometimes even recall specific passages from *Works and Days* (e.g., justice and the city at 161–3; warning against corruption at 162; wisdom at 170–1; interactions between men at 172–3; see Koning 2010: 161–86). By this stage of the competition, Homer has demonstrated all-encompassing wisdom.

148–50. κατὰ ... πάλιν: once again Homer is able to reply well to every question and Hesiod's disappointment continues. Hesiod this time reacts with φθόνος, 'envy'. The presence of this word recalls *Works and Days* 24–6 (and may indeed be a pointed reference to that passage), where Hesiod says that the Good Strife regulates, among other things, the competition between bards: φθόνος is an important component of it (Hes. *Op.* 25: καὶ πτωχὸς πτωχῷ *φθονέει* καὶ ἀοιδὸς ἀοιδῷ, 'and beggar envies beggar, and poet poet'). On this passage see West 1978: 147; Verdenius 1985: 27. Hesiod therefore seems to be acting in accordance with his own teaching, and is stimulated by the success of his opponent (Koning 2010: 257–8). However, this mention of φθόνος occurs in a context where the Hesiodic idea of it can easily be misinterpreted: the contrast with Homer's peaceful and nevertheless successful attitude is very clear and can put the Hesiodic φθόνος in a negative light (see also Clay 2003: 179 on Hesiod being a 'bad sport' here). The *Certamen* seems to be putting in action a perceptive reading of a Hesiodic passage and inviting readers to do the same.

151–60. υἱὲ Μέλητος ... ἐρῶτα: this exchange recalls the first section of the contest, when Hesiod asked Homer about the best and finest things for mortals (75–9 and 81–9), but here the issue is presented in different terms: the practice of making opposite speeches on the same topic is sophistic, and the contents of both answer and question seem to refer to specific philosophical doctrines. The word μέτρον (see also below) may be a reference to the Protagorean doctrine according to which 'man is the measure of all things' (80 B 1 DK: πάντων χρημάτων μέτρον ἐστὶν ἄνθρωπος, τῶν μὲν ὄντων ὡς ἔστιν, τῶν δὲ οὐκ ὄντων ὡς οὐκ ἔστιν), to which sometimes Homer was connected in antiquity (Pl. *Tht.* 160d); but by claiming that being 'the measure for oneself' can also be the worst thing, Homer seems to be firmly distancing himself from that doctrine. For another possible reaction by Homer to Protagorean attacks see 113–14n. Another sophistic influence on this exchange can be found in the last verse of Homer's answer (160: ἄλλο δὲ πᾶν ὅ τι σῷ θυμῷ φίλον ἐστὶν ἐρώτα, 'ask me whatever else is dear to your heart'): Homer here is inviting Hesiod to ask another question in the same way in which rhetoricians and sophists like Alcidamas and Gorgias invited the public to put forth a topic on which they would test their improvisation skills (Vogt 1959: 198 for references). The way Hesiod addresses Homer seems to respond to the previous exchange, where Homer answered Hesiod's question about the number of the Achaeans who went to Troy and thereby showed that the Muses are on his side (see 140–1n. and 143–5n.), and this may be the reason why Hesiod uses the epithet 'son of Meles' (151: υἱὲ Μέλητος), which refers to Homer's divine origins (for the river god Meles as Homer's father see 9–10n.), and asks for yet another piece of evidence for the fact that Homer is honoured by the Muses (151: εἴ περ τιμῶσί σε Μοῦσαι, 'if the Muses honour you'). Hesiod's insistence on this matter may also be due to the fact that he had famously claimed in his works a connection with the Muses himself, and indeed this was a constant feature in the reception of his *persona* (Heldmann 1982: 83): for the first time in this section, Homer is taking upon himself some Hesiodic features. The expression 'progeny of Dius' (156: Ἡσίοδ' ἔκγονε Δίου), used by Homer to address Hesiod, parallels and at the same time contrasts the epithet υἱὲ Μέλητος: while Homer's father is a river god, Hesiod's father Dius is never said to be more than a common mortal in the extant sources (Koning 2010: 133; Kivilo 2010a: 8). The next words of Homer's answer make the contrast between the two poets even sharper: to Hesiod's φθόνος (148–50), Homer responds willingly and most readily (156–7). For πρόφρων in epic cf., e.g., *Hymn. Merc.* 561. The epithet ὑψίστοιο Διὸς μεγάλοιο θύγατρες (152) is never attested for the Muses in this form; Διὸς μεγάλοιο θύγατρες is used also, in the same metrical position, in Antim. fr. 1 Wyss; Διὸς μεγάλοιο is in the same metrical position at *Od.* 11.268 (Διὸς μεγάλοιο μιγεῖσα). Zeus in early hexameter poetry is never called ὕψιστος, but he is in later sources: Pi. *N.* 1.60; A. *Eum.* 28. For ὅ τι σῷ θυμῷ φίλον ἐστίν (160) cf. the formulaic φίλον ἔπλετο θυμῷ (e.g., *Il.* 7.31).

153. μέτρῳ: the manuscript reads μέτρον but the emendation μέτρῳ, first proposed by Barnes and followed by Wilamowitz and West, seems necessary. Editors and translators have given two different meanings to this word, depending on whether they accepted the transmitted accusative or the emendation to the dative: 'standard' for those who have kept the accusative (Evelyn-White translates 'tell me a standard that is both best and worst'; Avezzù: 'dimmi una misura che sia la migliore e la peggiore insieme'); 'metre' (i.e. hexameter) for those who have emended to the dative (West: 'say – fitting into metre – what it is for mortals that is finest and what worst'; De Martino

1984: 'dimmi, nel metro adatto, qual è per i mortali la cosa più bella e più odiosa'). The form μέτρῳ solves grammatical inconsistencies in the text and gives the most appropriate meaning for the word μέτρον in this context. The accusative of the manuscript reading does not suit the verb ἐναρμόζων (which is itself a necessary and unanimously accepted emendation of the transmitted ἐναρμόζον): 'to adapt a standard', or even 'to adapt a metre', would not make sense in this context. Those who keep the accusative and give to μέτρον the meaning of 'standard' in fact do not translate ἐναρμόζων. With the emendation to the dative and the meaning 'metre', the sentence would mean 'fitting it to metre': ἐναρμόζων is given a role in the sentence, and the question assumes an additional nuance, since this request to fit the contents of the answer into metre may be seen as an allusion to the fact that the issues touched on in it are typical also of some sophistic literary production in prose (cf. also Gorgias, *Hel.* 9: τὴν ποίησιν ἅπασαν καὶ νομίζω καὶ ὀνομάζω λόγον ἔχοντα μέτρον, 'I consider and call all the poetry as speech in metre'). Homer in his answer uses μέτρον as 'standard' but this does not mean that the word must have the same meaning in the question as well: there may be an intentional play on these several meanings of the word of the same type as in Critias fr. 4 West (ll. 3–4), on which see Ford 2002: 43.

161–3. πῶς ἂν ... ἐπείη: how to run a *polis* in the best way is another central issue in Hesiodic poetry (see Clay 2003: esp. ch. 2; Koning 2010: 172–7), and a topic of great interest to the sophists too. Homer replies in a very Hesiodic fashion. The warning against profits from immoral acts (162) is typical of Hesiod and informs his addresses to Perses and the kings: e.g., *Op.* 352: μὴ κακὰ κερδαίνειν· κακὰ κέρδεα ἶσ' ἀάτῃσιν ('avoid dishonest profit – dishonest profit is as bad as ruin'). The role of justice (163) in the government of a city is prominent in *Works and Days*: in the Iron Age, the fact that men are χειροδίκαι (*Op.* 189), that is, that 'justice is decided by main force' (West 1978: 202), results in a lack of mutual help and assistance, and in the ruin of cities; conversely, the just cities and their people will blossom (*Op.* 225–7). For the necessity of punishing unjust behaviour (163) see Hes. fr. 286, according to which Justice is done (δίκη κ' ἰθεῖα γένοιτο) if a wrongdoer suffers the same injustice he brought about. Once again, we can see a contrast to certain sophistic doctrines according to which 'justice is nothing other than the advantage of the stronger' (Thrasymachus, 85 B 6a DK). As Colbeau 2005: 218 notes, the formulation of Hesiod's question recalls the title of Theophrastus' treatise Πῶς ἂν ἄριστα πόλεις οἰκοῖντο (D. L. 5.49). The topic was widely discussed in antiquity, from Hesiod's times to the Hellenistic age and beyond, and in addressing it the *Certamen* reflects various stages of this discussion.

164–5. εὔχεσθαι ... ἅπαντα: although the text of the answer is metrically incomplete and possibly corrupt, the general meaning of this exchange seems clear: humans should pray that one may always 'be well-disposed to oneself at all times' (cf. Evelyn-White's translation: 'That he [a man] may be always at peace with himself continually'). Homer therefore agrees with the traditional Greek views on religion, according to which the gods should be objects of prayers and honours, and in saying so, he appears to be distancing himself from sophistic opinions on divine intervention in human affairs. Protagoras claimed that he 'could not know anything about the gods' (80 B 4 DK: περὶ μὲν θεῶν οὐκ ἔχω εἰδέναι) and therefore interaction is impossible. Thrasymachus claims that the gods do not care about human affairs, which makes prayers ineffective (85 B 8 DK: οἱ θεοὶ οὐχ ὁρῶσι τὰ ἀνθρώπινα, 'the gods do not see human affairs').

<ἀεί>: Stephanus' supplement allows the hexameter to scan correctly and does not involve substantial modifications of the manuscript text.

166–7. ἐν δ' ἐλαχίστῳ ... ἀνδρῶν: the contents of both question and answer recall a *dictum* attributed to Periander by Stobaeus (3.3.45: Περίανδρος ἐρωτηθείς, τί μέγιστον ἐν ἐλαχίστῳ, εἶπε 'φρένες ἀγαθαὶ ἐν σώματι ἀνθρώπου', 'Periander, being asked what is the greatest thing in the smallest one, said "good minds in the human body"'; see also Baier 2013: 160). Homer seems therefore connected to traditional Greek morality. The identification of the 'smallest place' with human bodies evokes other sections of the contest: cf. 75–9, 81–9, and 174–5, where Homer discusses the brevity of human life, the suffering it involves, and the consequent exhortation to enjoy life. By contrast to the human body, the 'noble minds' (φρένες ἐσθλαί) are here presented as the typically and exclusively human compensation for the unpleasant mortal condition. As O'Sullivan 1992: 87–8 notes, the phrase ἐν δ' ἐλαχίστῳ may also refer directly to εἰπεῖν, rather than to φύεται: the question would thus mean 'what is the best thing you can say *in the shortest time?*'. This interpretation discloses a reference to the issue of the length of speeches, relevant to Gorgias and to his pupil Alcidamas: already Nietzsche 1873: 540 related this verse to Pl. *Grg.* 449c–d as evidence for Alcidamas' influence on the *Certamen*; O'Sullivan goes so far as to see in these verses a hint at the polemic between Alcidamas and Isocrates on this point, which they both inherit from Gorgias as a concern. Alcidamas proclaimed the importance of regulating the length of a speech depending on the audience's needs and level of attention, and claimed that this could be achieved only by those who perform improvised – rather than written – speeches: see *On Sophists* 22–3.

168–9. ἡ δὲ δικαιοσύνη ... πορίζειν: the topic of this exchange, namely justice and manly spirit, is relevant to both Homer's and Hesiod's works, although to different extents and in different ways. However, this answer in particular seems to fit Hesiod better: for Hesiod and justice, see 161–3n. The word δικαιοσύνη is never used by Homer or Hesiod: it is first attested in Theognis 1.147 (145–8: βούλεο δ' εὐσεβέων ὀλίγοις σὺν χρήμασιν οἰκεῖν / ἢ πλουτεῖν ἀδίκως χρήματα πασάμενος. ἐν δὲ δικαιοσύνῃ συλλήβδην πᾶσ' ἀρετή 'στιν, / πᾶς δέ τ' ἀνὴρ ἀγαθός, Κύρνε, δίκαιος ἐών, 'Be willing to live with little wealth as a pious man, rather than being rich by acquiring wealth unjustly. All virtue is contained in Justice, and each just man, o Cyrnus, is a good man'). However, from its first appearance it seems to be strongly linked with a very Hesiodic concept, exemplified at *Op.* 40–1: νήπιοι, οὐδὲ ἴσασιν ὅσῳ πλέον ἥμισυ παντός, / οὐδ' ὅσον ἐν μαλάχῃ τε καὶ ἀσφοδέλῳ μέγ' ὄνειαρ, 'fools, they do not know how much greater the half is than the whole, nor how great a profit there is in mallow and asphodel'; on this parallel see also Jellamo 2005: 79.

170–1. τῆς σοφίης ... ἕπεσθαι: in this answer, just like in the previous ones, Homer deals with two concepts that were in antiquity closely associated with Hesiod: σοφία (wisdom) and καιρός (the right moment). For Hesiod as the wise poet see Koning 2010: 161–5: 'wise' (σοφός) seems to be Hesiod's *epitheton ornans* as much as 'divine' (θεῖος) is Homer's, and even though Homer is often said to be wise, this epithet seems to be more closely connected to Hesiod – so much so that σοφία is mentioned in both his funeral epigrams (250–3n.). As for the καιρός, O'Sullivan 1992: 91–2 notes that Homer does not use this word in his poems (although he uses the adjective καίριος). Hesiod, by contrast, uses it in a verse that is widely quoted: μέτρα φυλάσσεσθαι· καιρὸς δ' ἐπὶ πᾶσιν ἄριστος, 'consider measures – the right moment is best in all affairs' (*Op.* 694; quoted, e.g., by Thgn. 401). It is noteworthy that in this section of the contest Homer becomes the poet of σοφία and καιρός. The notion of καιρός is also important to Alcidamas, and these verses have often been taken as evidence for his influence on the *Certamen* (Vogt 1959: 215; O'Sullivan *loc. cit.*). In Alcidamas' *On Sophists*, καιρός is connected to the ability of improvising speeches; importantly, the occurrences of this word in *On Sophists* show that the concept as expressed by Alcidamas fits the image of Homer built throughout the contest, as well as in this specific section: seizing the right moment is not for everyone but only for gifted people, who are therefore admired as if they were divine (e.g., *Soph.* 9). On the contrary, according to Alcidamas, performers of written speeches are not able to seize the moment (e.g., *Soph.* 10).

172–3. πιστεῦσαι ... ἔπηται: Hesiod's question deals with πίστις, 'trust'. This concept is not Homeric, and indeed it is first attested in Hes. *Op.* 370–2, where Hesiod warns that both trust and distrust have destroyed men. The way in which Homer formulates his answer, therefore, suggests that he is championing another Hesiodic idea. Koning 2010: 148 also points out that the abovementioned Hesiodic passage is one of those that 'seem to invite treatment by successors' (cf., e.g., Thgn. 1.831–2) because of what he calls the catch-word factor: it is therefore possible that the *Certamen*, in its attempt to show how 'Hesiodic' Homer could be, refers precisely to this passage from *Works and Days*.

174–5. ἡ δ' εὐδαιμονίη ... πλεῖστα: happiness (εὐδαιμονίη) is another concept dealt with in Hesiodic, rather than Homeric, poetry. While in the latter the word εὐδαιμονίη is attested only once in the *Hymn to Athena* (11.5: Χαῖρε θεά, δὸς δ' ἄμμι τύχην εὐδαιμονίην τε, 'Hail, goddess, and grant good fortune and happiness to us') and never in the *Iliad* or *Odyssey*, the definition of the εὐδαίμων man closes Hesiod's *Works and Days* and sums up Hesiod's teaching: happy is he who works without offending the gods, understands the omens of birds and avoids transgression (*Op.* 826–8). Although the answer that Homer gives does not find parallels in Homeric poetry, it fits the image of Homer given in the *Certamen*: it is in line with what he had said in the first two exchanges of verses, namely that in spite of the inevitability of pain and death, which are intrinsic to the mortal condition, human beings should enjoy life as they can. See especially 84–9n. for the association of Homer with hedonistic thoughts. The reaction of the public is, in both cases, positive.

12. The 'finest passages' (176–204)

176–9. ῥηθέντων δὲ καὶ τούτων ... εἰπεῖν: up to this point in the narrative, King Panoides has been mentioned only once at the beginning of the contest (see 68–70n. and 69n.). But now he makes a new and unexpected appearance. Although the public confirm their preference for Homer, he imposes a new test on the two poets: a performance of what they consider the finest passage from their own poems. It is only now that the competition explicitly assesses and contrasts Homer's and Hesiod's poems against each other. For Panoides' verdict see 205–10n.

180–204. (For more details on the arguments proposed here see Bassino 2017). Hesiod chooses as his finest piece *Works and Days* 383–92, the opening of the farmer's calendar; Homer, on the other hand, describes a battle scene by stitching together two passages from *Iliad* 13 (126–33 and 339–44). This selection associates Homer with poetry of war and Hesiod with poetry of peace, and invites us to compare Homeric and Hesiodic poetry on several levels, especially those of contents and style. As is explained below, this selection ultimately shows that Homer's poetry allows humans to share the gaze of the gods on the world, thus allowing them to transcend their mortal nature, while Hesiod's poetry, with its description of the cycle of nature and agricultural activities, does not offer anything that a man cannot experience in his everyday life.

At a general level, the passages are taken from the two works that, already by the time of Aristophanes (*R.* 1033–6), were traditionally considered representative of the opposition between Homer and Hesiod on the basis of their subject matters. On this traditional opposition see esp. Graziosi 2002: 168–80; Koning 2010: 269–84. This effect is heightened when the two passages are read together, since they respond to each other in a number of details which are presented in one context as symbols of peace, and in the other as symbols of war (see also Hunter 2009: 264 and 2014: 304–5; Koning 2010: 253): both passages start by presenting an image of non-human entities and then focus on humans – Hesiod mentions the constellation of the Pleiades that regulates the productive cycle of agriculture (180), Homer mentions Ares and Athena rejoicing in the spectacle of the battle (191–3); the Hesiodic man works in order to ensure a means of life for himself, while the Homeric fighters strive in the 'deadly battle' (199: μάχη φθισίμβροτος); iron is sharpened in the Hesiodic passage to reap (184), and interestingly a scholium to this line of *Works and Days* specifies that the iron in question is indeed used for reaping – not as an instrument of death, as the Homeric ταμεσίχροας (200) suggests; the Hesiodic man is emphatically and repeatedly said to be naked, while the Homeric heroes are covered by their armour; the metaphor in the Homeric passage, 'the deadly battle bristled' (199), responds to the literal reaping in Hesiod. *Works and Days* 383–92 'underlines like no other Hesiod's image of the peace-loving farmer poet' (Koning 2010: 252), thus proving an appropriate selection to represent poetry of peace. Furthermore, these verses must have been considered especially compatible with Panoides' verdict because of their acknowledged ethical value: according to the scholium to *Works and Days* 381–2, they encourage agricultural work and the just (the scholium uses the word δίκαιον) income that comes from it; according to Panoides, it was just (208: δίκαιον) for Hesiod to win because he sang of peace and agriculture.

Homer proposes a joint performance of two passages from *Iliad* 13. The verses may have been selected and stitched together to suit a fifth-century Athenian audience interested in seeing in Homer the poet of communal fighting (Graziosi 2002: 180), but they also provide a means of exploring the relationship between the Muses, the poet and audience: Homer turns out to be an inspired intermediary between the Muses and the audience, and therefore shares and allows the audience to share the divine gaze on something that their human nature would and could not bear in reality, namely war and death. Divine and human perspectives on war are described next to each other: the gods enjoy it (192–3), but an internal spectator cannot do so (203–4). Homer's poetry, however, allows mortals to face the spectacle of war in safety (Hunter 2009: 265 and 2014: 305) – that is, from a divine perspective. The claim that the audience in the *Certamen*, as external spectators, find these verses 'extraordinary beyond expectation' (206: ὡς παρὰ τὸ προσῆκον γεγονότων τῶν ἐπῶν) may be read in this sense. By putting at the centre of Homeric poetry its ability to allow humans to share the divine perspective on the world, the *Certamen* gives a perceptive reading of the Homeric epics: cf. the gods' reaction to the sight of war at *Il*. 17.398–9; see also the internal human spectator at 4.539–44, led and protected by Athena, with Eustathius' remark that this man watching safely the battle scene can be identified with the public who listens to the poet (*Il*. IV 802, 5–26). The fact that the gleam of the armour 'dazzled the eyes' (200–3) underlines once again that human beings cannot see the spectacle of war, since the sight of it for a man means becoming blind; one of the Homeric biographies (Anon. *Vit. Hom.* 1.5) shows that the same was true for Homer as well, for he was blinded by the dazzle of Achilles' armour. However, he was enabled to 'see' it (and to make us 'see' it, through his description of it in *Il*. 18) by Thetis and the Muses, who felt pity for him and honoured him with the gift of poetry. The parallel with the story of Demodocus' blindness in *Od*. 8.63–4 is obvious: it seems therefore, that the *Certamen* offers a perceptive reading of the epics that is in tune with biographical representations of Homer.

These two passages are also representative of the Homeric 'grand' style and of the Hesiodic 'middle' style as interpreted in antiquity – see Hunter 2009: 262–9 and 2014: 302–15: Homer's style is characterised by *dysphonia* ('clash', or 'heaviness' of sounds, e.g., at 191–2), use of metaphors (199: ἔφριξεν δὲ μάχη, 'the battle bristled') and use of compounds nouns and adjectives (e.g., 193: λαοσσόος, 'who rouses the people'); Hesiod's style, on the other hand, is characterised by memorability, musicality, anaphora, and repetition.

181. ἀμήτου is the necessary emendation for the unmetrical ἀμητοῖο transmitted by **L**. The form ἀμητοῖο is also present in some Hesiodic manuscripts.

183. αὖθις is the reading of **L**, emended by some scholars to αὖτις on the basis of the passage in Hesiod. But the manuscript reading seems unproblematic.

189. ὅτ' ἂν ὥρια πάντα πέλωνται: these words in the second part of 189 differ substantially from the corresponding section of the verse in Hesiod's work (*Op*. 392): εἴ χ' ὥρια πάντ' ἐθέλῃσθα ('if in good season you want all –'). The sentence in the Hesiodic text stops only at 395. The variant in the *Certamen* is nowhere else attested, and it seems to be an *ad hoc* re-elaboration of this Hesiodic verse in order to make the passage shorter and therefore suitable for the *Certamen*; at the same time, importantly, the verse as it is in the *Certamen* ensures that the references to begging and to the poet's quarrel with his 'foolish' brother Perses, that follow these lines in their original context in *Works and Days*, do not disrupt the peacefulness of the passage. (On the absence of Hesiod's quarrel with Perses from the *Certamen*, and from the Hesiodic biographical tradition more generally, see Stamatopoulou 2016.) Therefore, against West 1967: 442 n. 3, there is no need to suggest on the basis of Philostratus' passage that Hesiod's selection, in an 'original' version of the contest, may have been longer and included *Op.* 393ff. (see Part 1, 'Philostratus').

196. The reading of **L** ἀσπὶς δ' ἄρ', which does not work metrically, can be emended to ἀσπὶς ἄρ' on the basis of the reading of the Homeric manuscripts.

13. The verdict (205–14); Hesiod's oracle (215–23)

205–14. 'So much for the will of the people!' (Rosen 2004: 301). The *Certamen* does not express any explicit opinion on this verdict, but many clues suggest a disagreement with it (205–10n.). With this judgement, the *Certamen* seems to suggest that while the aim of true art is to create peace and consensus, as embodied by Homer's performance and the public's unanimously positive reaction to it, favouring peace as the object of art disrupts aesthetic appreciation. On the poetics of conflict and consensus in early Greek hexameter poetry, see Bassino/Canevaro/Graziosi 2017.

205–10. θαυμάσαντες … διεξιόντα: once again, the public reacts to Homer's performance with 'admiration' (θαῦμα, see also 90–1n.), because the verses 'were extraordinary beyond expectation' (see above, 180–204n.). Panoides, however, prefers Hesiod because of the greater ethical value of his poetry. The king bases his judgement not on the aesthetic value of the two passages, but merely on their contents: 'agriculture and peace', as opposed to 'wars and slaughters' (note also the opposition between two epic genres expressed by the two verbs: προκαλούμενον, 'to promote', for the didactic epic embodied by Hesiod, and διεξιόντα, 'to expound', for Homer's narrative, heroic epic). The two finest passages themselves, however, have established the superiority of Homer's poetry over Hesiod's (see 180–204n.), and although the *Certamen* does not explicitly argue against the verdict, it seems to present it, at least implicitly, in an unfavourable light.

First of all, as Elmer 2013: 220 has pointed out, the whole episode recalls the opening assembly of the *Iliad*, an 'example of injustice but also a violation of social norms' where the king, Agamemnon, 'defies collective will in favor of his own inclination'. Furthermore, Panoides' judgement is partial:

it takes into account only the last stage of the competition, and is issued by one single person, even though other judges were said to be present (68–70) and the public constantly expressed their opinion. Moreover, the very introduction of the figure of Panoides casts doubt on the verdict. In the entirety of the extant tradition, Panoides is never presented as a competent judge, and all the sources who mention him disagree with his decision; on the other hand, Themistius – the only ancient author pleased with Hesiod's victory – attributes the verdict to the audience and leaves out Panoides (see Part 1). Furthermore, the *Certamen* does not portray the victory of Hesiod as the central point of the story. Indeed, it reveals the outcome already in the introduction to the competition, and rather keeps the focus on the fact that both poets competed admirably, and on the way the competition developed until Hesiod eventually won (70–2). Likewise, the final verdict and the celebration of Hesiod's victory occupy relatively little space, and φασί ('they say') at 210 seems to indicate some distance on the part of the author of our text.

Consequently, the arguments of those scholars who see Panoides' judgement as fair seem problematic. Koning 2010: 255–6 claims that 'there is no explicit indication that Panedes' judgement is a bad one: neither the author, nor Homer or the public comments on it. *Sophia* is in the end defined as knowing what is beneficial to the *polis*, a type of wisdom with which Hesiod was traditionally associated, and his victory thus remain unchallenged'. This interpretation does not acknowledge that Homer too has been able to show what is beneficial to the *polis* in the exchanges at 149–75. Koning also adds that it is not surprising that the king, whose brother has just been killed in war, should make such a decision. However, Plutarch is the only source to mention that Amphidamas died in a battle, and it seems unwise to integrate so straightforwardly one text with the other, especially since they differ in the presentation of so many aspects of the story. Koning also advances the hypothesis that the newly appointed king uses the contest to announce a change of politics; but, again, this concedes that his judgement is concerned not with poetics, but merely with the contents of the poetry performed: it still appears as partial. West 1967: 443 claims that 'there is not a word to suggest that the decision was unjust', and that 'the story belongs to a type much favoured by the Greeks, in which a man does the opposite of what is expected, and justifies himself with an original and by no means contemptible analysis of the situation'. West adds that Alcidamas, who according to him was the inventor of the contest story, agreed with the fact that Hesiod, as the poet of peace, deserved to win. But every attempt to interpret the final verdict in the *Certamen* on the basis of its alleged presentation in Alcidamas is speculation, as it is impossible to know how faithful the author of the *Certamen* was to his source, and how and to what extent he modified his source's words. Moreover, the scholars who have attempted to interpret the verdict on the basis of what it may have meant for Alcidamas have reached quite opposite conclusions: Vogt 1959, for example, sees Homer in the *Certamen* as the champion of improvised speech, who certainly deserved the victory in the contest. Therefore, he claims that Alcidamas could not have agreed with Panoides, and that the king's judgement in the *Certamen* is presented as biased. O'Sullivan 1992: 98, on the other hand, concludes that Alcidamas did not attach any importance to the mere fact of Hesiod's victory, but rather to the manner of it.

210–14. τῆς μὲν οὖν νίκης ... Ὅμηρον: a tripod was the usual prize at games in Homeric poetry (e.g., *Il*. 11.700, 22.164, 23.259) and in historical times. A famous extant tripod, a prize at a musical contest, is *SGDI* 5786 (fifth c. BC, from Dodona). For the relationship between this epigram and the Hesiodic passage from which the tradition of the contest stems, see Part 1, 'Hesiod'. The text itself of the epigram is transmitted in several accounts of the contest, but it also had independent circulation in anthologies of epigrams and schoolbooks (see apparatus; see also Part 2, 'P.Freib. 1.1b').

It is worth noting with Stamatopoulou 2016: 14 n. 23 that the allusion to the initiation scene in *Th*. 22–34 contained in *Op*. 659 is omitted in the epigram and 'replaced by details about the poetic competition, namely where it took place (ἐν Χαλκίδι) and who Hesiod's opponent was (θεῖον Ὅμηρον)'. Not only does this 'level the playing field for the two poetic contestants', but also fits with the image of Hesiod given throughout the *Certamen* as a 'human' poet, as opposed to the 'divine' Homer.

215–23. τοῦ δὲ ... ἐστίν: after winning the contest, Hesiod consults the Delphic oracle, which predicts to him the place of his death. Homer, too, consulted the oracle and was warned against going to Ios; this suggests that the *Certamen* is building an elaborate narrative structure which connects the oracles, the contest and the deaths of the poets: see 56–62n. The legend of the death of Hesiod following the misinterpretation of an oracle was circulating already in the fifth century BC. The oldest attested witness of it is Thucydides (3.96.1), who however does not report the verses given by the oracle (see Fontenrose 1978: 371). The misunderstanding of an oracle predicting the place of one's death is a common pattern of many ancient biographies: for a list of occurrences see Fontenrose 1978: 59–60.

219–23. ὄλβιος ... ἐστίν: L41 Fontenrose. The text of this oracle is transmitted only by the *Certamen* and Tzetzes (*Life of Hesiod* 166–70 Colonna). The greeting with which the oracle starts is common in oracular epigrams: see, e.g., the oracle received by Cypselus in Hdt. 5.92, and in D. Chr. 37.5; and see also *AP* 14.77. The third verse of the oracle is Homeric: see *Il*. 7.451, and also, a few verses later, *Il*. 7.458, with a slight variation at the beginning.

221. ὅσην: this is the reading of the manuscript **L**, emended by some editors to ὅσον on the basis of the Iliadic verse (7.451, see above). But the emendation is unnecessary, and the scholia show that ὅσην was the reading preferred by one of the major ancient editors of Homer, namely Aristarchus.

14. Hesiod's death (224–53)

224–53. ὁ δὲ Ἡσίοδος ... ἐν βασάνῳ σοφίης: the text devotes relatively little space to the events of Hesiod's life after the contest. There is no mention of the works the poet might have composed afterwards, or of his travels – with the only exception of his movement to Locris, following the oracle (contrast the long and detailed description of Homer's life, 254–338). The *Certamen* offers two different accounts of the story of Hesiod's death, one by Alcidamas and one by Eratosthenes. In both cases the title of the work used as a source is cited along with the name of the author, although in the case of Eratosthenes the manuscript gives a problematic reading (see 241n.). The two versions share the same basic narrative structure, which is found in other accounts too: Hesiod was accused of having violated a girl, and as a consequence was killed by her brothers. Some of the elements in this section suggest that Hesiod became in antiquity the object of a hero cult: e.g., his violent death, the rescue of his corpse by dolphins during a religious festival, the participation of the community at his burial, and the divine punishment for the murderers. For recent collections of testimonia on Hesiod's death see Most 2006: T30–T34 and Kimmel-Clauzet 2013: 319–31; most recent discussions in Kivilo 2010a: 25–36; Koning 2010: 134–8; Kimmel-Clauzet 2013: 48–54, 135–41, 218–23, with earlier bibliography. More specifically on the cult of Hesiod see Brelich 1958: 320–2; Nagy 1979: 296 and 2009: 306; Calame 1996; Beaulieu 2004; Clay 2004: 74–6; Koning 2010: 134–8. The two versions given in the *Certamen* also present important differences, which concern the location of the murder (Eastern Locris according to Alcidamas, 226n.; not specified in Eratosthenes), the identity of Hesiod's murderers and their destiny (see 226–7n., 237–40n., 241n., 242–3n.), and whether or not Hesiod was actually guilty of the crime (229–32n.). In general, Eratosthenes' version appears more positive than Alcidamas' in its depiction of Hesiod, since the innocence of the poet is clearly stated. This may point again to Alcidamas' dissatisfaction with the verdict of the contest. Furthermore, the exclusion of Zeus' intervention and of the miraculous rescue of Hesiod's body by dolphins make Eratosthenes' account more rationalising than Alcidamas'.

224–9. ὁ δὲ Ἡσίοδος ... ἱερόν: the oracle (219–23n.) warned Hesiod not to go to 'the beautiful grove of Nemean Zeus', because it was his destiny to die there, but Hesiod did not understand the prophecy – in contrast with Homer, who will be never said to misunderstand the god's utterance (see 329–33n.). While trying to escape his fate, Hesiod is in fact fulfilling it by going to the place the oracle actually meant, namely Oenoe in Locris.

226. εἰς δὲ Οἰνόην τῆς Λοκρίδος: the city where the death of Hesiod was located by most of the ancient sources was in Ozolean (Western) Locris and close to Naupactus. Thucydides (3.96.1) locates the episode in the Ozolean Locris too. Pausanias (9.31.6) connects it to Ozolean Locris as well: he says that the murderers fled from Naupactus (in the Ozolean Locris) to Molycria, on the opposite coast. Plutarch mentions that Hesiod's corpse was brought to Rhium in Molycria (*Dinner of the Seven Sages* 162d; *The Cleverness of Animals* 984d), and that the murderers were the sons of Ganyctor of Naupactus (*The Cleverness of Animals* 969e). However, the mention of 'the sea between Euboea and Locris' (231–2) shows that Alcidamas locates the episode of Hesiod's death in the Opuntian (Eastern) Locris, rather than in the Ozolean (Western) Locris; and so does Tzetzes in his *Life of Hesiod* (175 Colonna). Although the majority of scholars seem to think that Alcidamas may have just confused the two locations (West 2003a: 343 n. 15; Lefkowitz 2012: 10–11; Kimmel-Clauzet 2013: 49–50), Nagy 2009: 306 fascinatingly suggests that different locations may respond to different claims about the poet: this detail in particular may originate from the version of the myth promoted by the people of Orchomenus. Furthermore, to solve this seeming inconsistency it is necessary to emend two readings of the manuscript that are, however, not problematic: τῆς Εὐβοίας καὶ τῆς Λοκρίδος (231–2), and Ἀριαδνείας (234): see apparatus. The fragmentary text transmitted in P.Ath. Soc.Pap. inv. M2 also shows that the story could be located in Eastern Locris, and that there is no need for an emendation: the word Εὐβοίας visible at line 9 proves it (Mandilaras 1990: 61; see Part 2).

226–7. παρ' Ἀμφιφάνει καὶ Γανύκτορι, τοῖς Φηγέως παισίν: according to Alcidamas, Hesiod's murderers are Amphiphanes and Ganyctor the sons of Phegeus. This is only one of the couples to whom the tradition attributes the crime, and it is found also in Tzetzes (*Life of Hesiod* 171–2 Colonna, as well as 155–6 Colonna quoting Aristotle, fr. 565 Rose); for the other couple see 241n. It is difficult to see the reasons for these differences in the names of the killers, but it is certainly striking that Alcidamas chooses the option according to which one of the murderers has the same name as the son of Amphidamas who organised the funeral games where the contest took place (63). In fact, Alcidamas is the oldest testimony to this identity of the murderers and he may have even created this particular detail as a sort of reversal of Hesiod's undeserved victory at the contest. Debiasi 2012: 476 notes that the onomastics of the killers point to Euboea, the site of the controversial contest: this confirms, first of all, that the location of the episode for Alcidamas was Eastern Locris, and secondly suggests again a connection of the poet's death with the episode of the contest. Phegeus is mentioned, as the father of Amphiphanes and Ganyctor, only in the context of Hesiod's death.

229–32. διατριβῆς δὲ ... κατεπόντισαν: the manner in which Hesiod dies, killed after violating his hosts' sister, seems 'sordid' to many readers (Scodel 1980: 304; O'Sullivan 1992: 98; Rosen 2004: 303), and indeed the image of the poet that emerges from this account is far from positive, especially when compared to Eratosthenes' version in which Hesiod's innocence is pointedly asserted. The ultimate impression is that Hesiod's 'dreary end is vengeance for his unfair victory' (Debiasi 2012: 490). Further details on the identity of the girl seduced by Hesiod and her offspring are given by Tzetzes (*Life of Hesiod* 154–5 Colonna), who informs us that the son of Hesiod and the girl, called Ctimene, was Stesichorus. Other sources give different details about the girl and the child, but do not connect them explicitly to the episode of the rape (sources listed in Kivilo 2010a: 10–11). There is also mention of a son in Hesiod's own *Works and Days* (270–1), and this may have been connected to this story in antiquity and fostered its development.

230. †Οἰνῶσιν†: the reading of the manuscript is not attested anywhere else. Stephanus of Byzantium (s.v. Οἰνεών) gives for Oenoe the ethnic adjective Οἰνεωνεύς, which however looks incompatible with the manuscript reading. Other attested forms are Οἰνοαῖος (St. Byz. s.v. Οἰνόη) and Οἰναῖος (*IG* 22.99, 1623.5, 1926.130), but it is uncertain whether they refer to our city or not. A locative Οἰνόησι is attested (*IG* 12.845.5) and the reading of the manuscript looks like a contracted form of it. But there seems to be no definitive solution to this textual problem. P.Ath.Soc.Pap. inv. M2 (line 5) cannot help here because of its poor condition.

231–2. τῆς Εὐβοίας καὶ τῆς Λοκρίδος: this reading locates the story in Eastern Locris, against the emendations proposed to relocate the episode to Western Locris. See also 226n. and apparatus.

232–6. τοῦ δὲ ... ἀνεζήτουν: according to Alcidamas, the body was brought back to land by a group of dolphins on the third day, during a festival in honour of Ariadne. The claim that the people 'buried him in mourning' (236: πενθήσαντες ἔθαψαν) is the only mention of Hesiod's funeral ceremony and underlines Hesiod's importance to the community (Kimmel-Clauzet 2013: 135). This description also connects the episode of Hesiod's death and burial with the divine, by situating it during a religious festival. The rescue of Hesiod's corpse by dolphins closely parallels an episode told in myths about the lives of other cult heroes (Nagy 2009: 306) and in fact it is the 'most strongly heroic trait of Hesiod's vita' (Koning 2010: 135). Similar episodes are present in the biographies of many characters who enjoyed heroic status in antiquity: among the singers, most famously Arion (first attested in

Hdt. 1.23–4). The choice of the dolphins for this role must be due to the particular consideration they enjoyed in antiquity and to widespread beliefs concerning their enjoyment of music. Furthermore, these animals were sacred to different gods: Poseidon, Aphrodite, Apollo, and Dionysus (Apollo and Dionysus being especially relevant in the case of singers and poets). The intervention of the dolphins may be seen therefore as a sign of divine support: after they miraculously rescue Hesiod's body, Zeus punishes the murders and throws them into the sea. This episode may also be related to the legend of the second birth and youth of Hesiod (247–53n.), and may be a 'mythical expression of the poet's death and rebirth' (Koning 2010: 135–6). The episode of the dolphins rescuing Hesiod's body is also told by Plutarch (*Dinner of the Seven Sages* 162c–e; *The Cleverness of Animals* 984d) and Tzetzes (*Life of Hesiod* 174–5 Colonna). Other animal helpers are involved in the legend of Hesiod's death are a crow sent by the Pythia to guide the Orchomenians to the poet's grave (Paus. 9.38.3–4), and Hesiod's dog who helps find the murderers by barking (Plu. *The Cleverness of Animals* 984d, 969e; Poll. 5.42).

234. Ἀριαδνείας: the emendation Ῥίου ἁγνείας in place of Ἀριαδνείας, proposed by Nietzsche on the basis of the account of Hesiod's death by Plutarch (*Dinner of the Seven Sages* 162e), connects again the episode to Western Locris, where Rhion is located. A further reason for the emendation is that a cult of Ariadne in Locris is testified only in this passage of the *Certamen*. But the fact that the murderers try to escape to Crete (238), and are punished during this trip, may suggest a connection between this story and Ariadne. It has also been suggested that the story of Hesiod's death is an aetiological myth for this festival, which may have been performed similarly to that in Crete (Nilsson 1906: 383–4; Lefkowitz 2012: 161 n. 19). Colbeau 2005: 243–4 notes that Ariadne is often connected with Dionysus and wine, in Greek οἶνος, which evokes the root of the name Oenoe.

237–40. οἱ δὲ φοβηθέντες ... ἐν Μουσείῳ: the fate of the murderers according to Alcidamas: the two brothers try to escape the anger of their fellow citizens, and set sail for Crete, but 'Zeus struck them with a thunderbolt and drowned them'. Zeus' intervention may have been inspired by Hesiodic poetry, where Zeus oversees Justice: see esp. the discussion of δίκη at *Op.* 213–85. For the fact that the murderers go to Crete (238: εἰς Κρήτην) and its possible connection with Ariadne (234: ἑορτῆς ... Ἀριαδνείας), see 234n. The mention of Alcidamas was one of the reasons why Nietzsche first postulated that Alcidamas' work was used as a source by the author of the *Certamen* (see Introductory remarks, 'Sources'). Furthermore, the way Alcidamas is mentioned may suggest that he was the main source: it seems that he is named explicitly only because an alternative version, that by Eratosthenes, was about to be quoted.

240–3. Ἐρατοσθένης ... τοῦ μάντεως: Eratosthenes follows the mainstream tradition on Hesiod's death, but presents different details concerning the names of the murderers (241n.) and their punishment (242–3n.).

241. ἐν †ἐνηπόδω†: this is a particularly difficult reading. It has been variously emended (see apparatus and below) because it does not make sense, and there is no attested work by Eratosthenes with a title similar to the manuscript reading. One of the earliest and most widely accepted emendations is Goettling's ἐν Ἡσιόδῳ, based on Hiller's suggestion that Ἡσίοδος could be a second title of Eratosthenes' Ἀντερινύς, a poem which may have contained the story of Hesiod's death and his murderers' punishment (see Eratosth. fr. 17 Powell = Schol. Nicand. *Ther.* 472). However, there is no evidence that the *Anterinus* had such a second title and, as pointed out by Fraser 1972: 902 n. 200, there is no sufficient ground to justify the suggestion that the poem dealt with the legend of Hesiod. Another fragment by Eratosthenes (fr. 21 Powell = Choerob. *In Theod.* Gaisf. i, p. 81.27) mentions Ganyctor, a character who is always linked to this legend, and therefore confirms Eratosthenes' interest in it, but again this fragment does not offer a solution for this textual problem. Eratost. fr. 19 Powell (= schol. Nic. *Ther.* 400) gives another interesting but doubtful clue: in this fragment, Eratosthenes mentions Erigone's dog, which played an important role after its owner's death – like Hesiod's (232–6n.). This fragment is attributed by the ancient source to the *Anterinus*, but as far as we know that story is told in Eratosthenes' *Erigone*. From Eratosthenes' poetic fragments, therefore, an interest in the legend of Hesiod's death emerges quite clearly, but they do not reveal the title of the work in which he discussed it. On the other hand, there is no trace of an account of the episode of the poetic contest of Homer and Hesiod in Eratosthenes, and therefore we cannot know whether his account of Hesiod's death was attached to the contest, as it is in the *Certamen*. A passage in Strabo (7.3.6) seems to suggest that, according to Eratosthenes, Hesiod was younger than Homer, and if this is the case then he could hardly have spoken of their contest, which presupposes the two poets being contemporaries: see Pfeiffer 1968: 164, who however does not mention Strabo's passage, and Koning 2010: 123 n. 67 and 124 n. 71. Eratosthenes' broad interests in the biographies of the poets are testified by two other fragments that attribute to him two (discordant) claims concerning Homer's chronology: see 241 *FGrHist* 9a (= Tat. *Ad Graec.* 31) and 241 *FGrHist* 9b (= Anon. *Vit. Hom.* 1.4).

Κτίμενον καὶ Ἄντιφον τοὺς Γανύκτορος: other sources for these names for Hesiod's murderers are Plutarch (*The Cleverness of Animals* 969e), Pausanias (9.31.4) and Suda s.v. 'Hesiod'. For the other couple see 226–7n. Antiphus is a Homeric name (*Il.* 2.864, 2.678). The name Ctimenus is not attested in archaic literature, while Ctimene (who is also the sister of Amphiphanes and Ganyctor according to Tzetzes, *Life of Hesiod* 155 Colonna) is Odysseus' sister (*Od.* 15.363). These Homeric names suggest once again that the *Certamen* draws on an intimate knowledge of the poems.

242–3. σφαγιασθῆναι θεοῖς ξενίοις ὑπὸ Εὐρυκλέους τοῦ μάντεως: Eratosthenes is the only witness to this version of the story, according to which the murderers 'were sacrificed to the gods of hospitality by the seer Eurycles'. The very fact that the murderers are punished and the modality of the punishment testify to the divine protection granted to Hesiod. As in Alcidamas' version, it is specifically Zeus who grants justice (as noted by Lefkowitz 2012: 161 n. 25, 'there is only one *theos xenios*, Zeus' – therefore the phrase θεοῖς ξενίοις, 242–3, must refer to Zeus), but this time through the seer Eurycles. The name Eurycles is mentioned in several ancient sources, possibly with reference to different characters (see, e.g., Ar. *V.* 1019–20; Pl. *Sph.* 252c; sources and discussion in MacDowell 1971: 264 and Ogden 2002: 30–2). Hence it is not possible to establish certain connections between this passage of the *Certamen* and other traditions on the seer.

243–7. τὴν μέντοι παρθένον ... τῶν αὐτῶν φησιν: unlike Alcidamas, Eratosthenes gives details on the fate of the girl after Hesiod's death, and claims that she 'hanged herself after her dishonour' (243–5) – a detail that contributes to increase the pathos that surrounds the episode of Hesiod's unjust death in this version. On the girl see also 229–32n. Hesiod's innocence is made clear by the presence of Demodes, 'a certain foreigner who was travelling with Hesiod' (245–6), to whom Eratosthenes attributes the crime. Protestations of the poet's innocence are found in most of the sources on the poet's death. Particularly apologetic is the version by Plutarch in *Dinner of the Seven Sages* 162d. According to Plutarch's account, Hesiod was suspected not of having committed the crime against his hosts' sister, but only of having helped Troilus, his friend and the actual perpetrator of the crime, to conceal it. The same version features in the Suda, s.v. 'Hesiod'.

246. Δημώδους ὄνομα: the only other name given to Hesiod's friend in the tradition is Troilus (Plu. *Dinner of the Seven Sages* 162c). The name Demodes given by Eratosthenes does not seem to be attested anywhere else as a personal name. It is found as an adjective and means 'of the people, popular' (LSJ). It was used as such by Nietzsche and Rzach who proposed to add the name Troilus in the text (<Τρωίλου>, see apparatus): this character would therefore be 'a certain man of the people, a foreigner travelling with Hesiod, Troilus by name'.

247–53. ὕστερον δὲ Ὀρχομένιοι ... ἐν βασάνῳ σοφίης: the story of Hesiod's second burial follows in the text the account by Eratosthenes, and there is no sufficient ground to speculate on whether or not it was told by Alcidamas as well. The story however was very widespread, and is mentioned in several other sources (Plu. fr. 82 Sandbach and Arist. fr. 524 Rose = Schol. *Op.* 631; Plu. *Dinner of the Seven Sages* 162; Paus. 9.38.3–4; Tz. *Life of Hesiod* 177–85 Colonna). The story goes as follows: after the Thespians destroyed Ascra, the Ascreans who survived went to Orchomenus. A plague broke out in the city and the Pythia (in Aristotle's, Pausanias' and Eratosthenes' versions) suggested taking Hesiod's bones to Orchomenus. According to Pausanias, a crow helped the Orchomenians to find Hesiod's first grave. The story of the transportation of Hesiod's bones and second burial in Orchomenus has been taken as evidence for a cult of Hesiod in that city (in particular, the beneficial power that the poet's bones were thought to have, and the fact that according to Pausanias a crow guided the Orchomenians to Hesiod's first grave). Another tomb epigram that presupposes the story of Hesiod's second burial in Orchomenus is transmitted by Arist. fr. 565 Rose, Suda s.v. τὸ Ἡσιόδειον γῆρας, Tz. *Life of Hesiod* 184–5 Colonna, and is attributed to Pindar: χαῖρε δὶς ἡβήσας καὶ δὶς τάφου ἀντιβολήσας / Ἡσίοδ', ἀνθρώποις μέτρον ἔχων σοφίης, 'hail, you who were young twice and twice met your grave – Hesiod, who have the measure of wisdom for men'. The anecdotes and the epigrams are discussed at length in Scodel 1980, Bershadsky 2011, and Kimmel-Clauzet 2013: 136–41.

250–3. ἐπέγραψαν μὲν πατρὶς ... ἐν βασάνῳ σοφίης: unlike Homer (333), Hesiod did not compose his own tomb inscription. The whole text of the epigram is transmitted also in *AP* 7.54, Paus. 9.38.4 and Tz. *Life of Hesiod* 179–82 Colonna. The *Greek Anthology* attributes it to Mnasalces, Pausanias to Chersias. For a detailed discussion of attribution and chronology of this epigram see Debiasi 2010. Like the other epigrams in the *Certamen*, this too presents many variant readings compared to other attestations of it. The most remarkable is at 252, where Pausanias gives Ἑλλάδι κῦδος ὀρεῖται (see discussion in Debiasi 2010: 263).

15. Homer's *Thebaid* and *Epigoni* (254–60); the Midas epigram and the silver cup (260–74)

254–60. καὶ περὶ ... Ὁμήρου εἶναι: the text now starts to describe Homer's artistic production and travels after the contest. For Homer's activity as a travelling poet, as opposed to Hesiod's more sedentary career, see 56n. The first poems that Homer is said to compose after the contest are the *Thebaid* and the *Epigoni*. Their position in the sequence of Homer's works, after the *Margites* (55) and before his two major poetic works (*Iliad* and *Odyssey*, 275–6), reflects the status of the cyclic epics in antiquity: see, e.g., Aristotle's view that *Iliad* and *Odyssey* 'exceed all other [poems] in respect to their diction and thought' (*Po.* 1459b16: λέξει καὶ διανοίᾳ πάντα ὑπερβέβληκεν). Although they were considered minor works, the insertion of *Thebaid* and *Epigoni* here serves to highlight the extent of Homer's knowledge of the epic past and the range of his artistic production. Both poems belong to the Theban saga, and the choice of these two works among all those belonging to the Epic Cycle allows the text to present Homer as an expert on the Theban expedition as well as the Trojan one, dealt with in the later stages of his career. It also shows how consistent Homer's knowledge was, because, as the ancient public may have known, acquaintance with some of the events of the Theban saga is presupposed in the *Iliad* (see Davies 1989a: 22–3). The *Thebaid*, in comparison with other poems of the Cycle, enjoyed a good reputation, and this too may have encouraged its inclusion in this selective list of poems by Homer. Pausanias claims that it was his favourite Homeric poem after the *Iliad* and the *Odyssey* (Paus. 9.9.5: ἐγὼ δὲ τὴν ποίησιν ταύτην μετά γε Ἰλιάδα καὶ τὰ ἔπη τὰ ἐς Ὀδυσσέα ἐπαινῶ μάλιστα, 'I reckon that, after the *Iliad* and *Odyssey*, that poem is the best'). The attribution of the *Thebaid* to Homer may be very ancient: according to Pausanias it goes back to Callinus in the seventh century BC, and seems to have been usually accepted in antiquity (Paus. 9.9.5: τὰ δὲ ἔπη ταῦτα Καλλῖνος ἀφικόμενος αὐτῶν ἐς μνήμην ἔφησεν Ὅμηρον τὸν ποιήσαντα εἶναι, Καλλίνῳ δὲ πολλοί τε καὶ ἄξιοι λόγου κατὰ ταὐτὰ ἔγνωσαν, 'Callinus, who mentioned these verses, said that Homer is the author, and many and trustworthy people are of the same opinion as Callinus'). On this testimony see Bowie 2010: 152). Ps.-Hdt. *Vit. Hom.* 9 too depicts Homer as the author of a poem concerning the Theban cycle, although the work that in the *Life* is called *Amphiaraus' expedition against Thebes* may contain 'not the whole *Thebaid*, but a partial narrative covering perhaps Eriphyle's machinations and the seer's instruction of his sons' (West 2003b: 9; on this issue see also Torres-Guerra 2015: 240). It is uncertain whether Herodotus was referring to the *Thebaid* when he mentions the 'Homeric poems in which the Argives and Argos are the main subject of the songs' (Hdt. 5.67.1: τῶν Ὁμηρείων ἐπέων εἵνεκα, ὅτι Ἀργεῖοί τε καὶ Ἄργος τὰ πολλὰ πάντα ὑμνέαται): see Cingano 1985 and West 2003b: 8. If he does, this confirms that Herodotus too accepts the attribution of that poem to Homer, although at 4.32 Herodotus denies the attribution to Homer of the other Theban poem mentioned here, the *Epigoni* (see below). In other passages the authorship of the *Thebaid* is dealt with more vaguely using expressions such as 'the person who composed/wrote the *Thebaid*' (e.g. Ath. 465e: ὁ τὴν κυκλικὴν Θηβαΐδα πεποιηκώς; Schol. S. *O.C.* 1375: ὁ τὴν κυκλικὴν Θηβαΐδα ποιήσας; Apollod. 1.8.4: ὁ γράψας τὴν Θηβαΐδα), but its attribution to Homer is never challenged explicitly, and – importantly – no other author's name is associated with the *Thebaid* in extant testimonia. By contrast, the *Epigoni* was less widely accepted as Homeric: Herodotus, for example, expresses his doubts (4.32: ἔστι δὲ καὶ Ὁμήρῳ ἐν Ἐπιγόνοισι, εἰ δὴ τῷ ἐόντι γε Ὅμηρος ταῦτα τὰ ἔπεα ἐποίησε, 'and Homer too [speaks about the Hyperboreans] in the *Epigoni* – if it was actually Homer who composed that poem'), and our text seems to share them: the claim that 'some say that these are also by Homer' (260: φασὶ γάρ τινες καὶ ταῦτα Ὁμήρου εἶναι) may perhaps refer only to the *Epigoni*, rather than to both epics, and tallies with wide-spread doubts about Homer's authorship of the *Epigoni*. This may be a way for the text to defend its own scholarly authority, and, if this is right, there is no need to think that these words are 'evidently interpolated' and that 'they cannot have been written by a man who has just stated as a fact that Homer did recite these among his poems' (West 1967: 447 n. 1). On the authorship of the *Epigoni* see also Cingano 2015: 244–6. The scarcity of fragments and testimonia makes it difficult to understand why Homeric authorship was doubted or denied. Aristophanes in his *Peace* quotes the verse transmitted here as the incipit of this poem (see 107–8n.) and the scholium to that Aristophanic verse attributes the poem to Antimachus of Teos.

256, 258. ἔπη ͺζ: in the case of the two Cyclic poems and of the *Iliad* and *Odyssey* the text gives the number of lines for each work – a detail that would suit a school environment. The manuscript reads ἔπη ξ (60 verses) for both works. The number is implausible and the emendation ͺζ (7,000) proposed by Hermann is unanimously accepted in both cases. See also discussion in West 1967: 447. The only other known source that may have contained information about the length of the two poems is the *Tabula Borgiana*, a marble fragment that preserves a list of titles of epic poems, their authors and lengths; however, the length of the *Thebaid* is not visible on the fragment and the presence of the *Epigoni* is only reconstructed (on the *Tabula Borgiana* see McLeod 1985).

257, 259: the *Certamen* is an important source for the first verses of the two poems, especially since the incipit of the *Thebaid* is attested nowhere else (for the *Epigoni*, see 107–8n.). On the two verses, see Torres-Guerra 2015: 229 and Cingano 2015: 254–5. Another Homeric biography transmitting an incipit of a poem of the Epic Cycle, the *Little Iliad*, is Ps.-Hdt. *Vit. Hom.* 16, and also in this case there is no reason to doubt the reliability of this piece of information (see Part 1, 'Plutarch').

258. Ἐπιγόνους: the manuscript reading ἐπειγομένου does not make sense here, and the emendation proposed by Barnes is necessarily to be accepted both because the *Epigoni* is the sequel of the previously mentioned *Thebaid*, and because the verse that follows is attributed to the same work (although the work itself is attributed to a different author) in Schol. Ar. *Pax* 1270.

260–74. ἀκούσαντες ... ὀπάζοις: following the success of his performances, Homer is asked to compose a funeral epigram to be engraved on king Midas' tomb; after that, he receives a silver cup and dedicates it to Apollo, to whom the poet prays for fame. The insertion of these episodes at this point is functional to the development of the narrative. As West 1967: 447–8 remarks, this story parallels the episode of Hesiod's victory of the tripod at the contest (both include an invitation by sons of a dead king, a prize, a dedication, and an inscription). These similarities between the two episodes may well be more than coincidental. The episode indeed seems to be meant to re-establish Homer's credentials as a poet after the contest and is used as a means of securing future fame for him: see below 271–4n. West also suggests that the inclusion of this episode in the contest narrative may stem from Alcidamas, as he tended to fit Homer and Hesiod into a similar story-pattern (oracle, death, epitaph). It is impossible to establish with certainty whether Alcidamas included this episode in his narrative or not (cf. Avezzù 1982: xxx: 'se [...] la coppa [...] è indubbiamente un parallelo, seppur inadeguato, del tripode [...], non per questo si dimostra che l'esigenza di contrappesare la sconfitta col dono sia alcidamantea'), but West's suggestion seems attractive.

260–4. ἀκούσαντες ... οὕτως: Midas was a king of Phrygia who ruled, according to Eusebius, between 738 and 696 BC. For discussion of his funeral monument see Munn 2006: 70–3. Although this episode, which involves Homer's synchronisation with a historical figure, could have been used as a clue for Homer's chronology, there seems to be no trace of such connection in other extant sources. Homer and Midas are mentioned together in a discussion concerning chronology only once, and the source (Diogenes Laertius, 1.89) strongly denies the possibility that they could be contemporary; on this ground, he then rejects the Homeric authorship of the Midas epigram. Synchronisation with Midas was instead proposed for Terpander (by Hellanicus, 4 *FGrHist* 85b; discussion in Kivilo 2010a: 159–60).

265–70. χαλκῆ ... τέθαπται: the epigram for Midas' tomb is one of the two so-called Homeric epigrams reported in *Certamen* (the other one is at 281–5). These are short poems that Homer is said to have composed for specific occasions, usually on the spot. Many of them are transmitted in the Ps.-Herodotean *Life of Homer*. Markwald 1986 remains the most thorough study of these texts. This epigram is transmitted by several other sources (see apparatus), including the *Vita Herodotea*, which offers the only other biographical framework for the quotation. As usual in the transmission of the epigrams reported in the *Certamen*, the text is presented in each of its extant sources with variant readings, but the case of this epigram is particularly interesting: some of the sources present it in a shorter form, and some invert the order of the verses. Variants probably reflect oral circulation of the epigram (Gutzwiller 2010: 243). Some of these variations are significant: Livingstone/Nisbet 2010: 43 argue that the reason why Plato omits two lines (267–8) is that the omission is necessary for Socrates to make his point about the structure of this text (see below). Similarly, it can be argued that a fuller version of the text, including two lines that strongly emphasise the concept expressed in the preceding line, contributes to making the point of the *Certamen*: the epigram will perpetuate Midas' fame, but at the same time is a means by which Homer's own fame becomes everlasting as well (see 271–4n.). Variants attested only in the *Certamen* are: ἐπὶ σήματος ἧμαι at 265; πλήθωσι and περικλύζῃ at 267; φαίνῃ at 268; σημανέω at 270. Omissions and reversal of the order of the verses concern mainly lines 267 and 268: Plato, Dio Chrysostom and the *Anthologia Palatina* transmit only four verses and omit both lines; Philoponus omits only 267. The *Vita Herodotea* and Diogenes Laertius invert the order of the two verses. Indeed the possibility of reversing the order of the verses was considered in antiquity as a peculiar characteristic of this epigram and is the reason why Plato mentions it. In *Phdr.* 264e he criticises this epigram on the ground that 'whether any verse of it is mentioned first or last is indifferent' (οὐδὲν διαφέρει αὐτοῦ πρῶτον ἢ ὕστατόν τι λέγεσθαι), because the speech lacks organisation and a fixed structure. The Neoplatonist Hermias, commenting on this Platonic passage, claims that 'some call these epigrams "triangular", because it is possible to start from whatever verse one wishes' (*In Phdr.* 231 Couvreur: τινὲς τὰ τοιαῦτα ἐπιγράμματα τρίγωνα καλοῦσιν, ἐπειδὴ ὅθεν ἂν ἐθέλῃς δύνασαι ἄρξασθαι). Ancient readers therefore were aware that fluidity was the main peculiarity of this epigram, which makes it futile to try to identify a possible original version of the text. The attribution of the Midas epigram to Homer was not unanimously accepted in antiquity. Only Ps.-Hdt. *Vit. Hom.* attributes it to him. Plato is not explicit: he either does not know or rejects the Homeric attribution of the epigram (Beecroft 2010: 71 n. 18). The poet who shared the attribution of this epigram with Homer was Cleobulus of Lindus, one of the Seven Sages. The *Anthologia Palatina* testifies to this double attribution with the lemma ΟΜΗΡΟΥ οἱ δὲ ΚΛΕΟΒΥΛΟΥ ΤΟΛ ΛΙΝΔΙΟΥ, 'by Homer, but according to some, by Cleobulus of Lindus'. Diogenes Laertius attributes it to Cleobulus on the basis of a passage from Simonides, in which the poet criticises a passage by Cleobulus that compares some natural elements to a stone, and because of the difficulties of making Homer and Midas contemporaries. For modern discussion of the relationship between the quotation from Simonides and the Midas epigram, and of the epigram more generally, see Weber 1917; Kegel 1962: 60; De Vries 1969: 212–13; Ford 2002: 105–9.

271–4. λαβὼν δὲ ... ὀπάζοις: Homer's request for fame, object of this couplet, seems to be fulfilled when, at the end of his career (315–21), he composes the *Hymn to Apollo*, which guarantees eternal fame to the 'blind bard from Chios' (172). This episode has thus been inserted in the narrative as part of the overall reversal of the final verdict of the contest in favour of Homer and to reinforce his relationship with Apollo. This particular episode follows naturally after the epigram for Midas, since both episodes are concerned with fame, and Midas too is connected to Apollo and Delphi (Hdt. 1.14.2).

16. *Iliad* and *Odyssey* (275–6); Homer in Athens (276–85)

275–6. μετὰ δὲ ταῦτα ... ἐπῶν μ̣.εφ: Homer composes his major works at a late stage in his career, and his poetic production is pesented in an ascending sequence: this reflects the status that each of his poems had in antiquity, and emphasises Homer's young age at the time of the contest (see also 15–17n. and 254–60n.). The text specifies that Homer composes the *Odyssey* 'having already composed the *Iliad*' (πεποιηκὼς ἤδη τὴν Ἰλιάδα), and thus takes part in the lively ancient debate concerning which of the two poems was composed first (see, e.g., Lucian *VH* 2.20, discussed in Part 1; Seneca, *De Brevitate Vitae* 13.2; Anon. *On Sublime* 9.12–13). The claim of the priority of the *Iliad* also allows for a correspondence between the order of the composition of the poems and that of the events they narrate: Homer first sings the Theban saga (255–9), then the Trojan war and finishes with Odysseus' return home. The composition of *Iliad* and *Odyssey* is not linked to any specific place, but is rather mentioned in between Homer's visits to Delphi and Athens: the text may be remaining purposefully vague on the matter, thus hinting at Homer's Panhellenic appeal, but at the same time it makes the poems gravitate towards Athens where Homer next stops. In the agonistic section, Homer already recited verses from the *Odyssey* (*Od.* 9.6–11 at 84–9) and the *Iliad* (*Il.* 13.126–33 and 13.339–44 at 191–204), but their provenance was not stated. This seeming inconsistency suits narrative needs: each sequence of Homeric verses was an appropriate response to a specific challenge, while the composition of *Iliad* and *Odyssey* fits this particular point of the narrative. West 1967: 447 notes that the mention of the composition of *Iliad* and *Odyssey* is odd, and if Alcidamas had included it in his narrative 'he would surely have done it less awkwardly'. He concludes that this section of our text cannot derive from Alcidamas' narrative. It is hard to believe that Alcidamas did not mention the composition of Homer's two major poems in the *Museum*, but admittedly it is not possible to know whether he did so at the same point of the narrative as in our *Certamen*, and how concerned he was with the internal consistency of the narrative framework. The problem, in any case, hardly seems pronounced: Homer may have composed some extemporaneous verses which he later included in his major poems. The text gives the length of the two poems in line numbers, as it did for the *Thebaid* and the *Epigoni* (256, 258). In this case, too, the manuscript readings seem problematic, as is often the case with the transmission of numbers (see apparatus; cf. 146–8 n.).

276–85. παραγενόμενον ... Κρονίων: Homer goes from Delphi to Athens. There, he is hosted by King Medon, and in the council chamber performs an epigram. The fact that Homer is hosted and honoured by a king works as a reversal of (and a compensation for) the unfavourable judgement on Homer's poetry by King Panoides, already suggested by the Midas episode (260–74). Although Athens is here said to be ruled by a monarch, there are also hints in the text that prefigure the democratic constitution of the city: Medon (who was himself a debated character – see 277–8n.) is in the βουλευτήριον ('council chamber'), a building that in Athens was built at the end of the sixth c. BC to host the meetings of the βουλή (see 278n.); the epigram praises the people sitting in an assembly as a beautiful sight and, especially when compared to other versions, the text appears democratically oriented (see 281–5n.). The epigram seems to foster the image of Homer as a democratic poet, which would fit a fifth- or fourth-century BC source.

276–7. παραγενόμενον ... εἰς Ἀθήνας: the scarcity of verses in praise of Athens in the Homeric poems may explain why Homer performs an epigram there – and a piece from the *Iliad* at Argos (288–301). That Homer in his works praised those two cities to different degrees was acknowledged already in antiquity: at Ps.-Hdt. *Vit. Hom.* 28, Homer composes verses for Athens and adds them to the *Iliad* 'realising that he had composed many great eulogies for Argos, but none for Athens' (κατανοήσας δὲ ὅτι ἐς μὲν Ἄργος πολλαὶ καὶ μεγάλαι εἶεν εὐλογίαι πεποιημέναι, ἐς δὲ τὰς Ἀθήνας οὔ). Late sources testify that Homer was sometimes thought to be Athenian by birth (cf., e.g., Ps.-Plu. *Vit. Hom.* 2.2; Suda s.v. 'Homer' 2; Anon. *Vit. Hom.* 2.2; Anon. *Vit. Hom.* 3.1), the most important supporters of this view being Aristarchus and Dionysius Thrax. For Aristarchus, who seems to have based his claim on Homer's use of the dual, see Schol. *Il.* 13.197 (on which Janko 1992: 71). For studies on the successful Athenian strategy for the appropriation of the Homeric texts, which may have involved a connection between the Peisistratids and the Homeridae to different degrees, see West 1999; Graziosi 2002: 220–8; Nagy 2010.

277–8. παρὰ Μέδοντι τῷ βασιλεῖ τῶν Ἀθηναίων: ancient sources disagree as to whether Medon was a king or rather the first of the archons elected for life. Aristotle in his *Constitution of the Athenians* expresses the existing uncertainties about this issue (Arist. *Ath.* 3, on which see Fritz/Kapp 1950:

150–2; Rhodes 1981: 66 and 100). Hellanicus (4 *FGrHist* 125) does not specify whether the young Medon would become king or archon. According to Pausanias (4.5.10), with Medon's dynasty the political role of the members of the royal family changed. By presenting him as a king, the *Certamen* reverses the outcome of the contest due to another king's verdict (see also the episode of the silver cup dedicated by Homer to the Muses, which responds to Hesiod's victory and dedication of the tripod after the contest: 271–4n.).

278. ἐν δὲ τῷ βουλευτηρίῳ: buildings known as βουλευτήρια are testified to in Greece from the late sixth century BC onwards, and the old βουλευτήριον in Athens dates back to the same period (Rhodes 1972: 18 and 30). This anachronism helps to create the democratic orientation of the episode of Homer's stay in Athens (see esp. 281–5n.).

281–5. ἀνδρὸς ... Κρονίων: for Homer reciting an epigram rather than a piece from the *Iliad* or the *Odyssey* see 276–7n. This epigram is transmitted by two other sources, the *Vita Herodotea* and the Suda (s.v. 'Homer'). The Suda transmits it in the section derived from the *Vita Herodotea*, and therefore the two versions do not differ substantially. The differences compared to the version of the *Certamen* are much greater: the epigram is recited in different contexts, and there are substantial variations in the text and form of the epigram itself. In the *Certamen* Homer recites it at Athens before King Medon, in order to praise the fire burning in the council chamber; in the *Vita Herodotea* Homer recites it at Samos on his way to Athens, because a fire was burning in the room or in order to encourage the clansmen to light one. The version of the epigram performed here has been seen as fitting the Athenian democratic regime: line 283, which reads λαὸς δ' εἰν ἀγορῇσι καθήμενος εἰσοράασθαι ('and the people sitting in the assembly is a beautiful sight') seems a democratic adaptation of the two lines transmitted in the version of Ps.-Herodotus and Suda: χρήματα δ' αὔξει οἶκον· ἀτὰρ γεραροὶ βασιλῆες / ἥμενοι εἰν ἀγορῇ κόσμος τ' ἄλλοισιν ὁρᾶσθαι ('and wealth enhances the house; and honourable kings sitting in the assembly are a beautiful sight to others') (see West 2003a: 347 n. 16 and, more recently, Beecroft 2010: 70 n. 16 and 88). The verse at 285 ('on a winter's day, when the son of Cronus brings snow'), which closes the epigram in this version, is attested only in the *Certamen*, where the epigram is said to be recited when 'the weather was cold' (278–9: ψύχους ὄντος). The *Vita Herodotea* does not emphasise this point.

17. Homer in Corinth (286–7); Homer in Argos (287–314)

286–7. ἐκεῖθεν δὲ ... μεγάλως: Homer goes from Athens to Corinth, but his visit to the city is 'uneventful' (West 1967: 447 n. 3). There is no mention of the piece of poetry Homer performs on that occasion (for ἐρραψῴδει see 56n.) or of the people he meets there, but we are told that he is greatly honoured after his performance (287). Thus, despite the lack of details, this visit contributes further to the construction of a Panhellenic Homer, who travels extensively and is honoured across different cities. Nagy 2010: 53 suggests, based on the use of the verb τιμάω here (287), that this anecdote shows that Homer was honoured as a local cult hero in Corinth and that anecdotes such as these were an aetiology that explained the reality of seasonally recurring Homeric performances at a given festival. There is no corroborating evidence for a cult of Homer or for such festivals in Corinth, but the presence of Corinth among the cities Homer visits indicates that it too may have claimed some connection with the poet. Corinth features in some passages of the *Iliad*, and this may have facilitated or inspired its mention here: the first mention of Corinth is in the Catalogue of Ships, where it is favourably defined as 'prosperous Corinth' (*Il*. 2.570: ἀφνειόν τε Κόρινθον). That passage may be suitable for a performance by Homer in Corinth: the passage he performs in Argos is from the Catalogue of Ships too, and in general that section of the *Iliad* offers suitable material for local performances: see further 287–301n. The second mention of Corinth in the *Iliad* is at 13.664, where the poet tells the story of the Corinthian Euchenor (defined, like the city itself, as ἀφνειός). West 1967: 447 n. 3 connects Homer's visit to Corinth to the mention of Ἐφύρη at *Il*. 6.152 and 6.210 (Glaucus' speech): on the basis of a claim by Aristarchus, according to whom Homer refers to Corinth by the name Ἐφύρη in the character speeches, but by the more recent name Κόρινθος when he speaks in his own voice (Sch. *Il*. 6.152), West concludes that Homer 'is made to visit Corinth, in this account, simply to make sure that he is acquainted with the place'. But the actual identification of Ephyre with Corinth in this Iliadic passage is still debated: see for discussion Kirk 1990: 177–9; Graziosi/Haubold 2010: 119.

287–314. παραγίνεται ... ἀθανάτων: Homer's performance of a passage from the *Iliad* at Argos may have been inspired by the major role the city plays in the poem, which was acknowledged already in antiquity (276–7n. and 287–301n.). This episode plays a crucial role in Homer's life and career: the poet will effectively become the object of cult worship while still alive (302–8n.).

287–301. παραγίνεται ... πτολέμοιο: at Argos Homer performs a passage from the Catalogue of Ships (*Il*. 2.559–68) – an appropriate set-piece for his travels, because each community represented in the Catalogue will cherish 'its' own lines. The efficacy of the verses from the Catalogue is shown in the *Vita Herodotea* too (27–8), where Homer inserts in the Catalogue verses for Athens before going there (on Athens in the *Certamen*, see 276–7n.). Moreover, sections from the Catalogue may be easily detached from their original context and recited on their own; they also lend themselves to the omission or insertion of verses. For the suggestion that Homer may have recited a passage from this Catalogue at Corinth too, see 286–7n. As usual, the quotation in the *Certamen* presents some variant readings compared to the text as we have it in the *Iliad* (see below for discussion). The *Certamen* also transmits three verses that are not present in the Iliadic manuscripts (294, 300, 301). Even though we do not know their provenance, they are recognisably constructed from elements well attested in the hexameter tradition. One of them (301) is also known from another source (*AP* 14.73.6).

292. νῆσόν τ' Αἴγιναν Μάσητά τε κοῦροι Ἀχαιῶν: the Homeric text (*Il.* 2.562) begins οἵ τ' ἔχον Αἴγιναν and S records this reading in the margin of the line. The verse as transmitted in the *Certamen* is also in Hes. fr. 204.47 MW. The manuscript reading Αἴγιναν τε Μάσητά needs to be emended by deleting τε, for metrical reasons.

294. Τυδείδης οὗ πατρὸς ἔχων μένος Οἰνείδαο: this verse is not transmitted in the Iliadic manuscripts but draws fully on Homeric hexameters. Τυδείδης appears at the beginning of the line at, e.g., *Il.* 5.18; οὗ πατρός in the same metrical position at *Od.* 7.3, and ἔχων μένος at *Il.* 22.96; Οἰνείδαο closes the verse at *Il.* 5.813. As has been suggested (Colbeau 2005: 265), this hexameter may have been inserted here to give a piece of information about Diomedes (the fact that he is the son of Tydeus) which is very common in the *Iliad*, but not present in this specific passage. More generally, the fact that this verse did not make it into the vulgate of the *Iliad* may be due to the difficult position of Tydeus as a role model for his son Diomedes in the *Iliad* (on which see Graziosi/Haubold 2010: 38 and 140).

296. Εὐρύπυλος: in the *Iliad* the character mentioned in this passage is Euryalus (2.565: Εὐρύαλος), an Argive hero mentioned in two other episodes: his *aristeia* at 6.20–8, and his competition on the occasion of the funerary games for Patroclus at 23.677–99. Eurypylus is an Iliadic character too (e.g., 2.734–7: he was the leader of forty ships), but his presence here is slightly problematic. Kirk 1985: 234–5 discusses the realm of Eurypylus as presented in the Catalogue of Ships, and remarks that its borders are quite vague. Furthermore, he is not explicitly said to be Argive. Moreover, it is in fact Euryalus who is the son of Mecisteus (see 297), while Eurypylus is the son of Euemon. Furthermore, as Kirk notes, Eurypylus appears at several points in the poem and seems to be a well-known figure in the epic tradition: this would justify the confusion between these two names. Wilamowitz consequently emends the name given in the *Certamen* to the one transmitted in the Iliadic manuscripts, but he is alone in doing so.

297. Μηκιστέως: in the Iliadic manuscripts several variant readings are attested for the genitive form of this name, and Μηκιστέως, which is what **L**

transmits, is one of those. It does not seem problematic and it is the reading that Van Thiel accepts in his edition of the *Iliad* in this verse. There is no reason to emend it to Μηκιστέος (Rzach, see apparatus). West publishes Μηκιστῆος in his text of the *Iliad* and keeps Μηκιστέως in the text of the *Certamen*. For discussion of the genitive forms listed above, see Kirk 1985: 211 and Janko 1992: 264.

298. ἐκ πάντων: this verse, as transmitted at *Il.* 2.567, begins with the word συμπάντων. This word is found in the same metrical position also at *Il.* 1.90. But ἐκ πάντων too is used at the beginning of Homeric hexameters: cf. *Il.* 4.96.

300–1. Like 294, these two verses are not present in our version of the *Iliad*, but they fit well this encomiastic context for Argos. While 300 is attested nowhere else, 301 is transmitted also in *AP* 14.73.6. In that epigram the Pythia, responding to a Megarian enquiry, claims that the Argives are the best warriors and uses this very same verse to characterise them; ἐν δ' ἄνδρες is at the beginning of the hexameter in the verse ἐν δ' ἄνδρες ναίουσι πολύρρηνες πολυβοῦται which occurs at *Il.* 9.154 and 9.296; ἄνδρες is in the same metrical position at *Il.* 10.525 (ὅσσ' ἄνδρες); 21.405 (τόν ῥ' ἄνδρες); *Od.* 9.126 (οὐδ' ἄνδρες); πολέμοιο is in the same metrical position at, e.g., *Il.* 3.150: γήραϊ δὴ πολέμοιο; δαήμονες at *Od.* 8.263; ἐστιχόωντο occurs nine times in the *Iliad*, eight of which at verse end, as here (e.g., *Il.* 2.92); λινοθώρηκες: only the singular form λινοθώρηξ occurs in Homer, at *Il.* 2.529 (Ajax the lesser) and 2.830 (Amphius), both times at verse end. At least in the case of Ajax, the linen corslet is not characterised positively (see Kirk 1985: 202). The phrase κέντρα πτολέμοιο is found only in the occurrences of this verse (*Certamen*, *AP* and quotations from *AP*).

302–8. τῶν δὲ Ἀργείων ... εἰς Χίον ἀποστέλλειν: as a result of a performance of the *Iliad*, his highest poetic accomplishment yet, Homer becomes the object of an actual cult, while he is still alive. This episode seems to mark another turning point for Homer, for some elements in the text point to his achievement of lasting fame. The text lists the honours paid to Homer in an emphatically climactic order and with an effect of accumulation. First, the Argives honour him 'with expensive gifts' (304: πολυτελέσι δωρεαῖς), then they set up 'a bronze statue of him' (305: εἰκόνα δὲ χαλκῆν), and then they decree to make the establishment of periodic sacrifices in his honour (305–8). The 'expensive gifts' parallel the gifts offered by the organisers of the poetic contest that Homer lost (66), and thus complete the compensation for the outcome of the competition. The statue gives material and lasting support to Homer's fame. For another mention of a statue of the poet in his biographies see Ps.-Plu. *Vit. Hom.* 1.4: that statue is in Colophon and an epigram was inscribed on it too (see West 2003a: 411 n. 34). For the dedication of statues of poets, and especially those of Homer, see Clay

2004: 89–92. For surveys and discussion of ancient portrayals of Homer see Boehringer/Boehringer 1939; Mansuelli 1963: 686–9; Richter 1965: 45–56; Wallis 2014. Another interesting mention of a cult of Homer at Argos is a passage from Aelian that seems to confirm that the honours the Argives paid to Homer were in fact divine, as the poet is invoked together with Apollo (Ael. *VH* 9.15). Archaeological and literary evidence shows that Homer was an object of cult, which may have included offerings of sacrifices too, in several other cities: for surveys of available testimonia see Pinkwart 1965: 169–73; Brink 1972; Clay 2004: 74–6 and 136–43; Kimmel-Clauzet 2013: 201–18 and 299–318.The number of sacrifices offered to Homer (every day, month, year, and four years) seems hyperbolic, but this surely mirrors the fact that the Argives 'were exceedingly pleased' (302: ὑπερβολῇ χαρέντες) with Homer's verses in praise of their city. It is not possible to know whether Argos (or indeed any other city) ever sent sacrifices to Chios to honour Homer; Nagy 2010: 81 assumes on the basis of Pl. *Ti.* 26e that θυσία means not only 'sacrifice', but also, metonymically, 'festival', and more specifically a Panhellenic festival; he therefore suggests that this passage hints at a quadrennial festival in Chios during which Homeric poetry was performed, and sees it as a prototype of the Great Panathenaea in Athens – but it is also possible, of course, that this passage is itself modelled on the Great Panathenaea. The fact that the Argives send sacrifices to Chios seems to suggest that they saw Chios as the poet's birthplace: in fact this connection seems to have been made already in the sixth-fifth c. BC by another Argive, Acusilaus, who reports that the descendants of Homer, the Homeridae, are from Chios (2 *FGrHist* 2). Nevertheless, there was also a tradition according to which Homer was born in Argos (Ps.-Plu. *Vit. Hom.* 2.2; Anon. *Vit. Hom.* 3.1; Anon. *Vit. Hom* 1.2, which mentions Philochorus as a source, see 328 *FGrHist* 209), but the *Certamen* does not acknowledge it.

309–14. θεῖος Ὅμηρος ... ἀμφέπει ἀθανάτων: the formula 'divine Homer' (309: θεῖος Ὅμηρος), emphatically placed at the beginning of the epigram, underlines the poet's divine nature, which is also stressed at the very end of the epigram by the claim that the people of Argos 'venerate him with the honours of the immortals' (314: τιμαῖς ἀμφέπει ἀθανάτων). The claim that he 'adorned all proud Hellas' (309–10: Ἑλλάδα [...] πᾶσαν ἐκόσμησεν) underlines Homer's appeal as a Panhellenic poet which emerged after the contest. Some features of this epigram are found in other epigrams on Homer too. For θεῖος Ὅμηρος see 1–2n.; ἐκόσμησεν recalls the epithet κοσμήτωρ given to him in his funerary epigram at 348; for Ἑλλάδα [...] πᾶσαν cf. *AP* 7.7.1 (ἐνθάδε θεῖος Ὅμηρος, ὅς Ἑλλάδα πᾶσαν ἄεισε) and Ps.-Plu. *Vit. Hom.* 1.4 (... σὺ γὰρ κλέος Ἑλλάδι πάσῃ ... θῆκας ἐς ἀίδιον). Lines 309–12 are preserved in P.Duk. inv. 665, seventh century AD (see Part 2). Note especially the variants θεοτειχέα in the manuscript and ἐριαυχέα in the papyrus, line 4.

310. καλλιεπεῖ σοφίῃ: despite losing the contest on the ground that his verses, according to Panoides, did not have ethical value (205–10n.), Homer confirms here his reputation for wisdom, as well as for verbal art. The manuscript reading καλλιεπίηι σοφίη τε ('with beautiful expression and wisdom', where καλλιεπίηι is a form for καλλιεπείᾳ) does not allow the pentameter to scan. The correction καλλιεπεῖ σοφίη ('with his beautifully expressed wisdom') was proposed by **S** in the margin and has been unanimously accepted. P.Duk. inv. 665 l. 2 reads καλλιεπι[and Lapini (in Menci 2012: 46) suggests that this confirms the circulation of the manuscript's mistaken reading; Menci thinks it more likely to be a iotacism.

313. μεγαλόπτολις: the reading of **L** μεγαλόπολις needs a correction for metrical reasons and μεγαλόπτολις (**S** above the line) is a satisfying emendation. But, interestingly, this form is attested nowhere else; furthermore, μεγαλόπολις is never attested for Argos; it is attested for Athens (Pi. *P.* 7.1) and Troy (Eur. *Tr.* 1291): see Colbeau 2005: 268.

18. Homer in Delos (315–21); Homer's death (321–38)

315–21. ἐνδιατρίψας δὲ τῇ πόλει ... ἐν τῷ τῆς Ἀρτέμιδος ἱερῷ: this is the only account of Homer's visit to Delos in his biographies. The tradition of Homer reciting the *Hymn to Apollo* at that location is nevertheless old and was known to Thucydides (3.104.3; see Part 1, 'Hesiod'). Famously, a scholium to Pindar's *Nemean* 2 attributes it to Cynaethus, who may have performed the *Hymn* during the festival organised by Polycrates in Delos in 524–3 BC (on Cynaethus see Burkert 1979; Janko 1982: 112–15 and 233–4; West 1975 and 2003a: 9–12; Aloni 1989). But the Homeric authorship of this text was mostly accepted and the *Certamen* does not need to mitigate this claim (contrast the case of the *Epigoni*, at 254–60n.) or to support it with evidence (cf. the case of the *Margites*, at 15–17n.). As in the case of *Thebaid* and *Epigoni* (255–8), the *Certamen* quotes the first verse of the work, perhaps for didactic purposes. The quotation fits the context because of its emphasis on the theme of memory. In the *Certamen*, this is the last poetic performance by Homer, and represents the peak of his career as well as the fulfilment of his request for future and everlasting fame expressed at Delphi on the occasion of the dedication of a silver cup to Apollo (271–4n.). This episode also seals the image of Homer as the Panhellenic poet *par excellence*: in other sections of the text Homer was praised and celebrated by each community he visited, but the celebration remained mostly on a local level. Here, however, Homer performs for the first time in a Panionian context (316n.), and his success on this occasion results in the attribution to him of the title of 'fellow citizen' by all the Ionians (319–20n.). The *Hymn to Apollo* is an appropriate choice in this context also because the process of Panhellenisation of Homer is historically connected to the image of the blind bard from Chios presented in that work (172) – the image accepted and promoted by the Athenians. Although an explicit claim for Homer's Chian origin is always avoided in the *Certamen*, as it would contradict the very opening of the work (esp. 7–8), the text seems to gravitate towards the Chian tradition as Homer assumes the role of the Panhellenic poet: see also 302–8n., where the Argives are said to send sacrifices to Chios to honour the poet. An inscription from 178 BC (*ID* 443, Bb l. 146–7) testifies to the existence on the island of a *Homereion*, which shows that Homer enjoyed special honours on the island; for discussion of the possible functions of the building Dürrbach 1929: 190; Bruneau 1970: 455; Farnoux 2002: 101; Kimmel-Clauzet 2013: 191–2.

316. εἰς τὴν πανήγυριν: this word never appears to be used to describe a Delian general meeting in archaic and classical times; it was instead used from the Hellenistic age onwards for other festivals (Bruneau 1970: 532). This word, together with the expression κοινὸς πολίτης (see 319–20n.) may therefore be a trace of the times of composition of our text.

καὶ σταθεὶς ἐπὶ τὸν κεράτινον βωμόν: this is the altar of horns, one of the major cult objects in Delos. For archaeological studies and collection of literary and epigraphic evidence, see Bruneau 1970 and Bruneau/Fraisse 2002. This altar was the setting of sacrifices to Apollo and it was said to have been built by the god himself by fastening together horns of several goats (Call. *Ap.* 60–4; the Delian altar mentioned in Call. *Del.* 312 too is to be identified with the altar of horns: see Mineur 1984: 242). Plutarch informs us that the altar was reckoned to be one of the seven wonders of the ancient world (*The Cleverness of Animals* 983e) and that Theseus performed a dance called Crane around it (*Thes.* 21). No other source claims that the altar of horns was the setting of a performance of the *Hymn to Apollo*, but there is no reason to exclude that the text or its sources knew that the *Hymn* was actually performed there. In any case, because of its function, this monument works well as the site of the performance through which Homer seals his relationship with Apollo: the poet offers his hymn to the god on the altar, and Apollo will grant fame in exchange.

319–20. ῥηθέντος ... ἐποιήσαντο: the Ionians jointly made Homer their 'fellow citizen': the text had somehow anticipated this outcome already during the contest, when Homer repeatedly got the approval of 'all the Greeks' (90–1n.). This title is not attested in confederations in the archaic and classical ages; it may derive from Hellenistic and Roman imperial institutions (Farnoux 2002: 102, with nn. 28–30 for further bibliography). The author of the *Certamen* has either inserted this anecdote in a narrative that originally did not contain it, or updated its language.

320–1. Δήλιοι δὲ ... ἐν τῷ τῆς Ἀρτέμιδος ἱερῷ: writing is used in the text of the *Certamen* in connection to the inscriptions on funeral monuments, statues, tripods and cups (213–14; 250–3; 265–70; 273–4; 309–14; 337–8). This use of writing emphasises its importance as a means to perpetuate fame. While in other biographical narratives the act of transcription is not depicted positively, in the *Certamen* it legitimates the text and the Homeric authorship of it (see also Beecroft 2010: 94). It is remarkable that the only literary work said to be inscribed is by Homer; transcription of Hesiod's *Works and Days,* which other sources do mention (Paus. 9.31.4), does not feature here. It is unclear whether this transcription (but also the performance) involved only the so-called Delian part of the *Hymn* or the whole of it (cf. West 2003a: 9) and there is no evidence that such transcription and dedication in Delos ever took place. However, as remarked already by Allen 1936: lxxv, the story may have some historical basis. It is relevant that the text uses the word λεύκωμα (a wooden tablet covered with gypsum), which was indeed used in the island to release information to the public and to make offerings (Farnoux 2002: 102). Richardson 2010: 13 also suggests that the inscription of the *Hymn* might date from a relatively early period, as the sources used by the *Certamen* may date as far back as the sixth century (as he himself had already suggested in Richardson 1981). Artemis' temple was older than Apollo's and this may explain the claim that the λεύκωμα was dedicated to her temple, rather than to Apollo's; see Janko 1982: 257. Farnoux 2002: 102 remarks that the exchanges of offerings between divinities were frequent at Delos: what is described here may also be one such case.

321–38. The *Certamen* engages with a well-developed biographical tradition on the death of Homer (overview in Kimmel-Clauzet 2013: 38–48 and 285–97) and gives an account which defends the poet's reputation for wisdom and divine nature: the inability to solve the riddle is not the cause of his death, but only works as a *terminus post quem* for the fulfillment of the oracle; furthermore, unlike Hesiod, Homer does not die a violent death, nor does he misunderstand the oracle – rather, he accepts his destiny and even composes his own epitaph (329–33n. and 334–5n.); the claim that Homer has become old by that time (323) may be seen as mitigating his failure in solving the riddle. The source for this part of the text must be Alcidamas: the most compelling evidence is P.Mich. inv. 2754 (in which an identical account of Homer's death is followed by Alcidamas' name, see Part 2); furthermore, the image of Creophylus given here is compatible with the one circulating in fifth-century Athens (321–3n.). Alcidamas, in turn, uses material that predates him: the episode of the riddle of the lice was known already to Heraclitus (22 B 56 DK) who seems to refer to it as to a traditional anecdote. Even though Heraclitus does not make an explicit connection between this episode and the poet's death, it is likely that such a connection was established early: see also Kirk 1950: 160 n. 1; Janko 2011: 529.

321–3. τῆς δὲ πανηγύρεως λυθείσης ... πρεσβύτης ὢν ἤδη: other sources too mention this episode, and add that Homer gave to Creophylus the poem *Oechaliae Halosis* in exchange for his hospitality (see, e.g., Strab. 14.1.18). In the *Certamen* no detail is given about Homer's visit to Creophylus, and Creophylus himself remains rather faceless. However, the fact that he is the last person Homer meets and that the poet dies while being his guest (cf. also Procl. *Vit. Hom.* 5, Tz. *H.* 13.658) leave open the possibility that the *Certamen* draws on a source where Creophylus was not depicted positively. This source may be Alcidamas, for he is the source for the account of Homer's death that follows (321–38n.); moreover, it seems that a meeting between Homer and Creophylus right before Homer's death would suit Alcidamas' time, when Creophylus was known as someone who did not take good care of Homer in his lifetime: Pl. *R.* 10.600b–c. This may also explain why, unlike in other sources, in the *Certamen* Creophylus is said to be from Ios, the predestined place of Homer's death (in Schol. Pl. *R.* 10.600b, Creophylus is from Chios; according to Call. *Epigr.* 7 from Samos; according to Tzetzes from Arcadia). Claims such as Plato's and Alcidamas' may be seen as an Athenian response to the tradition according to which Sparta was the first Greek city to receive the Homeric poems precisely through Creophylus or his descendants, the Creophylei (on which see Burkert 1972), which was in conflict with the Peisistratides' claims (on Creophylus and the Spartan tradition, and its relationship with the Athenian one, see Graziosi 2002: 189–93 and 217–22).

322. Κρεόφυλον: athough many sources give the name in the form Κρεώφυλος, the reading of **L** Κρεόφυλον does not need emendation (see apparatus), since Κρεόφυλος is testified in ancient sources (see, e.g., Plu. *Lyc.* 4.4), and this gives some authority to the reading of **L**.

323–8. ἐπὶ δὲ τῆς θαλάσσης ... φερόμεσθα: other sources too tell how Homer approaches the fishermen and asks if they have caught anything: Procl. *Vit. Hom.* 5; Ps.-Plu. *Vit. Hom.* 1.4; Anon. *Vita Hom.* 2.3; Anon. *Vita Hom.* 3.5; Tz. *H.* 13.660; id. *Exeg. in Il.* 37.22. In Ps.-Hdt. *Vit. Hom.* 36 Homer is instead approached by the boys and challenged by them. The fact that Homer's opponents are 'boys' (παῖδες) has been seen as a response to the assumed mental inferiority of the young men to their elders in the Homeric poems (Levine 2002: 147–50) and, more generally, the 'learned man surpassed by the ignorant' is a traditional feature of several folk-stories (Thompson 1957, 5: 13–14; Levine 2002: 144 n. 12). A death following a riddle is also a traditional motif: the most famous examples are the stories of Calchas and Mopsus and of Oedipus and the Sphinx. Scholars have tried to unfold possible hidden meanings in the boys' riddle. A key word is ἕλομεν (328: 'caught'), which can be interpreted as 'grasped', 'understood': Bergmann 2007: 75–6 suggests that the real solution of the riddle is the riddle itself, which brings about the fulfilment of the oracle. What the boys could not grasp is the riddle, which they are carrying with themselves and taking to Homer, whose destiny is thereby accomplished; Kahane 2005: 20–2 suggests that what has not been grasped, the unknown, is death, which is also signified by the very solution of the riddle, the lice ('*phtheires* bring about the disintegration of the flesh') – but for Homer death represents the start of the tradition, his 'immortality'.

326. The verse uttered by Homer is transmitted in several sources (see apparatus). Pseudo-Plutarch reports the question in prose and Tzetzes (*H.* 13.660) in a different metre. The reason why Homer addresses the boys as 'huntsmen from Arcadia' seems to remain obscure (see also Kivilo 2010b: 93 n. 65). Other sources (see apparatus) give the variant ἀλιήτορες ('fishermen') in place of θηρήτορες. Generally, it must be relevant that Arcadia is land-locked, and people from there cannot be fishermen, but hunters. This was surely felt as problematic already in late antiquity, for Tzetzes in both of his accounts of the episode seems to try to harmonise the tradition by making Ios a place in Arcadia.

328. The text of the riddle is transmitted in all the Homeric biographies, with some very minor variations (see apparatus). It is also partly visible on the wall of the *Casa degli Epigrammi* in Pompeii, as a caption for a fresco that represents two boys proposing the riddle to Homer: see Gigante 1979: 50–3, and most recently Bergmann 2007: 71–6.

329–33. οὐ νοήσας τὸ λεχθὲν ... αὐτοῦ ἐπίγραμμα: without hesitation, Homer asks for the solution of the riddle: he does not feel his reputation for wisdom to be in danger, and in fact this is the version of the episode where Homer seems to be least concerned with solving the riddle. The solution is given by the boys also in Ps.-Hdt. *Vit. Hom.* 35; other texts offer an explanation of the riddle without attributing it to the boys (Ps.-Plu. *Vit. Hom.* 1.4; Procl. *Vit. Hom.* 5; Anon. *Vit. Hom.* 3.5) or do not give it at all, which probably means that it was very widely known (Anon. *Vit. Hom.* 1.6; Anon. *Vit. Hom.* 2.3). Unlike Hesiod (see 227–8), Homer never misunderstood the oracle predicting his death. When he received it, at a young age before the contest, he carefully avoided Ios (61–2); when, as an old man, he eventually goes there and realises that the prophecy has been fulfilled, he accepts his destiny and writes his funeral epigram – which is, as Kahane 2005: 5 puts it, 'a symbolic form of suicide'. The view that the epigram was composed by Homer himself is shared also by Anon. *Vit. Hom.* 3.5. Ps.-Hdt. *Vit. Hom.*

18. Homer in Delos (315–21); Homer's death (321–38)

36 seems to respond to this tradition when the text specifies that the epigram was composed by the Ietans, and not, as some say, by Homer (καὶ τὸ ἐλεγεῖον τόδε ἐπέγραψαν Ἰῆται ὕστερον χρόνωι πολλῶι ... οὐδὲ Ὁμήρου ἐστίν, 'and long afterwards, the people of Ios inscribed the following elegy ... it is not by Homer'). Other sources too attribute it to the Ietans (Ps.-Plu. *Vit. Hom.* 1.4), others report it anonymously (Anon. *Vit. Hom.* 1.6; Anon. *Vit. Hom.* 2.3).

334–5. ἀναχωρῶν δὲ ἐκεῖθεν ... καὶ ἐτάφη ἐν Ἴῳ: according to most sources, Homer's death is a direct consequence of his inability to solve the riddle. In Ps.-Plu. *Vit. Hom.* 1.4, 'unable to make sense of this [i.e. the riddle], Homer died as a result of his despondency' (ὅπερ οὐ δυνηθεὶς συμβαλεῖν Ὅμηρος διὰ τὴν ἀθυμίαν ἐτελεύτησε); in Anon. *Vit. Hom.* 1.6 the poet died 'after finding himself at a loss, since he was not able to solve the riddle of the young fishermen' (...ἀμηχανίαι περιπεσόντα, ἐπειδήπερ τῶν παίδων τῶν ἁλιέων οὐχ οἷός τε ἐγένετο αἴνιγμα λῦσαι); in Anon. *Vit. Hom.* 2.3 he 'starved himself to death in grief because he was unable to solve a conundrum put to him by fishermen' (...διὰ λύπην ἀποκαρτερήσαντα τελευτῆσαι διὰ τὸ μὴ λῦσαι τὸ ζήτημα τὸ ὑπὸ τῶν ἁλιέων αὐτῶι προτεθέν); in Anon. *Vit. Hom.* 3.5 'having failed to understand their words, he died from despair' (οὐ νοήσας δὲ τὸ λεγόμενον, ἀπὸ θλίψεως ἐτελεύτησεν). In the *Certamen*, detaching Homer's failure in solving the riddle from his death is a way to save Homer's reputation; this is also confirmed by Ps.-Hdt. *Vit. Hom.* 36: 'As a result of this illness it happened that Homer died in Ios, not from his failure to understand what the boys had said, as some think, but because of his weakness' (ἐκ δὲ τῆς ἀσθενείας ταύτης συνέβη τὸν Ὅμηρον τελευτῆσαι ἐν Ἴωι, οὐ παρὰ τὸ μὴ γνῶναι τὸ παρὰ τῶν παίδων ῥηθέν, ὡς οἴονταί τινες, ἀλλὰ τῆι μαλακίηι). An account similar to that of the *Certamen* is told by Procl. *Vit. Hom.* 5, but Proclus was also influenced by the more widespread tradition according to which the poet dies because he cannot solve the riddle (οὕτω δ' ἐκεῖνον ἀθυμήσαντα σύννουν ἀπιέναι, τοῦ χρησμοῦ ἔννοιαν λαμβάνοντα, καὶ οὕτως ὀλισθέντα περιπταῖσαι λίθωι, καὶ τριταῖον τελευτῆσαι, 'and so he became despondent and went away deep in thought, having grasped the meaning of the oracle, and in this state he slipped and fell on a stone, and he died on the third day'). See also Tz. *H.* 13.663–5. Homer is then buried on the island of Ios, as in the rest of the tradition (Kimmel-Clauzet 2013: 129–35 and 297–99). Homer's tomb was displayed by the Ietans in Pausanias' day (Paus. 10.24.2) and the alleged site of Homer's tomb is a tourist attraction even today.

336–8. ἔστι δὲ τὸ ἐπίγραμμα τόδε ... θεῖον Ὅμηρον: the text of Homer's funeral epigram is transmitted by virtually all the biographies of Homer, and also in anthologies of epigrams with minimal textual variations (see apparatus). Two gravestones with Homer's epitaph have been found in Ios: *IG* 12.5.1.1[1] and 1[3]; they may have been displayed in front of the alleged tomb of Homer (see most recently Kimmel-Clauzet 2013: 446 n. 24 with earlier bibliography). A similar text has also been found in funeral inscriptions for other people: see, e.g., *IG* 12.5.1.678. There were other funeral epigrams for Homer: see *AP* 7.1–7. In the *Certamen* the fact that the epigram is situated at the end of the narration of Homer's death creates a structural parallel with the episode of Hesiod's death, closed by the epitaph of the poet (250–3). The overall effect is a final emphasis on the 'divine Homer'.

Figures

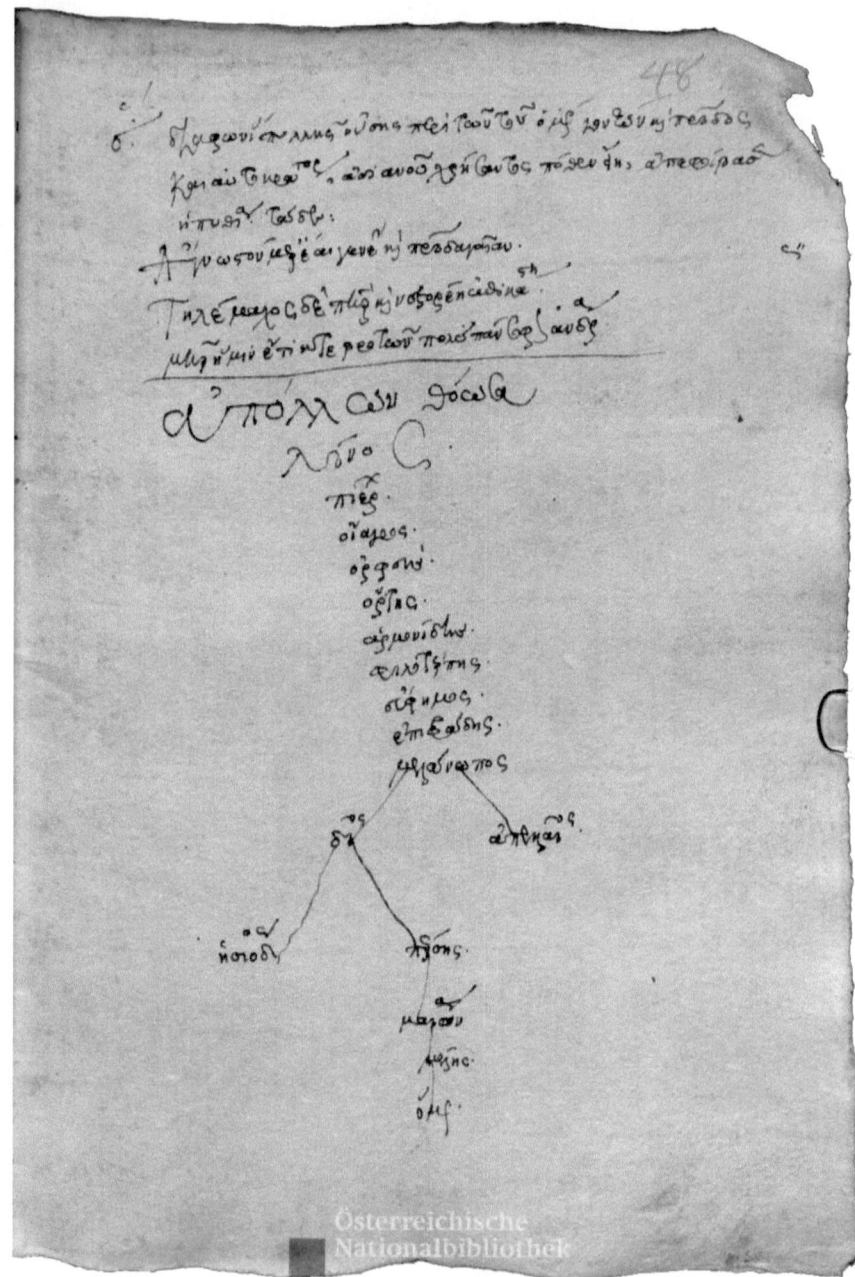

Figure 1: MS Vienna, Österreichische Nationalbibliothek, Phil. gr. 187 (48r)

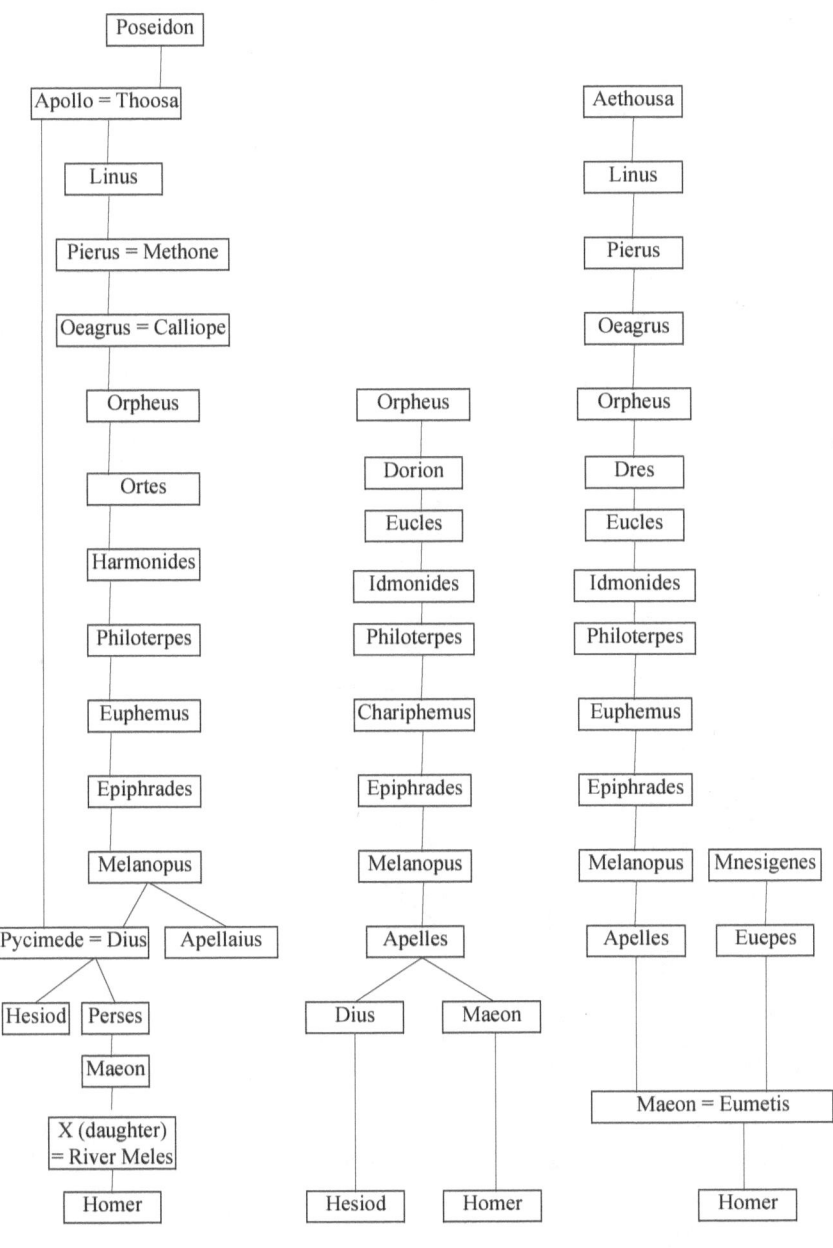

Figure 2:
Certamen 44–55

Figure 3
Proclus, *Life of Homer* 4

Figure 4
Suda s.v. 'Homer' 1

Bibliography

Allen, J. (2006), *Hostages and Hostage-Taking in the Roman Empire*. Cambridge.

Allen, T. W. (ed.) (1912), *Homeri Opera*, vol. 5. Oxford.

Allen, T. W. (1924), *Homer. The Origins and the Transmission*. Oxford.

Allen. T. W., et al. (eds) (1936), *The Homeric Hymns*. Oxford.

Aloni, A. (1989), *L'aedo e i tiranni: ricerche sull'inno omerico a Apollo*. Rome.

Aly, W. (1914), '1. Inv. N. 12. Aus einem Schulbuche'. *Mitteilungen aus der Freiburger Papyrussammlung, I. Literarische Stücke*. Heidelberg: 7–22.

Anderson, G. (1986), *Philostratus: Biography and Belles Lettres in the Third Century A.D.* London.

Arnim, I. von (ed.) (1905), *Stoicorum veterum fragmenta*, vol. 1. Stuttgart.

Arnott, W. G. (1999), 'Notes on some comic papyri'. *ZPE* 126: 77–80.

Arnott, W. G. (ed.) (2000), *Menander*, vol. 3. Cambridge (MA).

Avalle, S. (ed.) (1960), *Peire Vidal, Poesie*, 2 vols. Milan.

Avezzù, G. (ed.) (1982), *Alcidamante. Orazioni e frammenti*. Rome.

Babbit, F. C. (ed.) (1928), *Plutarch's Moralia*, vol. 2. Cambridge (MA).

Baier, M. (2013), *Neun Leben des Homer: eine Übersetzung und Erläuterung der antiken Biographien*. Hamburg.

Bakker, E. J. (1990), 'Homeric discourse and enjambement: a cognitive approach'. *TAPhA* 120: 1–21.

Bandini, A. M. (1768), *Catalogus codicum Graecorum Bibliothecae Laurentianae*, vol. 2. Florence.

Bassino, P. (2012), '*Certamen Homeri et Hesiodi*: nuovi spunti per una riconsiderazione delle testimonianze papiracee'. *ZPE* 180: 38–42.

Bassino, P. (2013a), 'Homer: A Guide to Selected Sources'. *Living Poets* (Durham, 2013): https://livingpoets.dur.ac.uk/w/Homer:_A_Guide_to_Selected_Sources

Bassino, P. (2013b), 'Lesches and the contest between Homer and Hesiod'. *Kyklos@Classics@* 1. Efimia D. Karakantza (ed.), The Center for Hellenic Studies of Harvard University: http://chs.harvard.edu/wa/pageR?tn=ArticleWrapper&bdc=12&mn=5189

Bassino, P. (2017), 'On constructive conflict and disruptive peace: the *Certamen Homeri et Hesiodi*', in *Conflict and Consensus in Early Greek Hexameter Poetry*. Bassino, P., Canevaro, L. G. and Graziosi, B. (eds). Cambridge: 190–207.

Bassino, P., Canevaro, L. G. and Graziosi, B. (eds) (2017), *Conflict and Consensus in Early Greek Hexameter Poetry*. Cambridge.

Bausi, F. (1996), *Silvae. Angelo Poliziano; a cura di Francesco Bausi*. Firenze.

Beaulieu, M.-C. (2004), 'L'héroïsation du poète Hésiode en Grèce ancienne'. *Kernos* 17: 103–17.

Beecroft, A. (2010), *Authorship and Cultural Identity in Early Greece and China: Patterns of Literary Circulation*. Cambridge.

Beecroft, A. (2011), 'Blindness and literacy in the Lives of Homer'. *CQ* 61: 1–18.

Berenson Maclean, J. K. and Bradshaw Aitken, E. (2001), *Flavius Philostratus: Heroikos*. Atlanta.

Bergmann, B. (2007), 'A painted garland: weaving words and images in the House of the Epigrams in Pompeii', in *Art and Inscriptions in the Ancient World*. Newby, Z., and Leader-Newby, R. E. (eds). Cambridge: 60–101.

Bernabé, A. (1984), '¿Mas de una Ilias Parva?'. *EClás* 87: 141–50.

Bernabé, A. (ed.) (1987), *Poetae Epici Graeci: testimonia et fragmenta*, vol. 1. Leipzig.

Bernhardy, G. (1822), *Eratosthenica*. Berlin.

Bershadsky, N. (2011), 'A picnic, a tomb, and a crow: Hesiod's cult in the *Works and Days*'. *HSPh* 106: 1–45.

Bietenholz, P. and Deutscher, T. B. (1986), *Contemporaries of Erasmus*, vol. 2. Toronto.

Boehringer, R. and Boehringer, E. (1939), *Homer: Bildnisse und Nachweise*. Breslau.

Bompaire, J. (ed.) (1998), *Lucien. Oeuvres, tome II: Opuscules 11–20*. Paris.

Bonfante, G. (1968), 'Il nome di Omero'. *PP* 23: 360–1.

Boutière, J. and Schutz, A. H. (eds) (1964 (1950)), *Biographies des Troubadours*. Paris.

Bowie, E. L. (2010), 'Historical narrative in archaic and classical Greek elegy', in *Epic and History*. Konstan, D. and Raaflaub, K. A. (eds). Malden (MA) and Oxford: 145–66.

Boys-Stones, G. (2010), 'Hesiod and Plato's history of philosophy', in *Plato and Hesiod*. Haubold, J. and Boys-Stones, G. (eds). Oxford: 31–51.

Brelich, A. (1958), *Gli eroi greci. Un problema storico-religioso*. Rome.

Brink, C. O. (1972), 'Ennius and the Hellenistic worship of Homer'. *AJPh* 93: 547–67.

Brodersen, K. (2010), 'Mannhafte Frauen bei Polyainos und beim Anonymus *de mulieribus*', in *Polyainos. Neue Studien. Polyaenus. New Studies*. Brodersen, K. (ed.). Berlin: 149–59.

Broggiato, M. (ed.) (2001), *Cratete di Mallo: i frammenti. Edizione, introduzione e note*. La Spezia.

Bruneau, P. (1970), *Recherches sur les cultes de Délos à l'époque hellénistique et à l'époque impériale*. Paris.

Bruneau, P. and Fraisse, P. (2002), *Le Monument à abside et la question de l'autel de cornes*. Athens.

Bryce, T. R. (2006), *The Trojans and their Neighbours*. London.

Burges-Watson, S. (2013), 'Orpheus: A Guide to Selected Sources'. *Living Poets* (Durham, 2013): https://livingpoets.dur.ac.uk/w/Orpheus:_A_Guide_to_Selected_Sources

Burgess, J. (2001), *The Tradition of the Trojan War in Homer and the Epic Cycle*. Baltimore.

Burkert, W. (1972), 'Die Leistung eines Kreophylos. Kreophyler, Homeriden und die archaische Heraklesepik'. *MH* 29(2): 74–85.

Burkert, W. (1979), 'Kynaithos, Polycrates, and the Homeric Hymn to Apollo', in *Arktouros: Hellenic Studies Presented to B. M. W. Knox on the Occasion of his 65th Birthday*. Bowersock, G. W., Burkert, W. and Putnam, M. C. J. (eds). Berlin: 53–62.

Burkert, W. (1987), 'The making of Homer in the sixth century BC: rhapsodes versus Stesichorus', in *Papers on the Amasis Painter and his World*. Bothmer, D. (ed.). Malibu: 43–62.

Busse, A. (1909), 'Der Agon zwischen Homer und Hesiod'. *RhM* 64: 108–19.

Calame, C. (1996), 'Montagne des Muses et Mouseia: la consécration des Travaux et l'héroïsation d'Hésiode', in *La Montagne des Muses*. Hurst, A. and Schachter, A. (eds). Geneva: 43–56.

Cameron, A. (2004), *Greek Mythography in the Roman World*. Oxford.

Campbell, D. A. (1983), *The Golden Lyre: The Themes of the Greek Lyric Poets*. London.

Canart, P. (2002), 'Il Bandini e la catalogazione dei manoscritti greci. Osservazioni di un catalogatore', in *Un erudito del Settecento: Angelo Maria Bandini*. Pintaudi, R. (ed.). Messina: 37–42.

Canevaro, L. G. (2015), *Hesiod's Works and Days: How to Teach Self-Sufficiency*. Oxford.

Cavallo, G. (2000), 'Scritture informali, cambio grafico e pratiche librarie a Bisanzio tra i secoli XI e XII', in *I manoscritti greci tra riflessione e dibattito, Atti del V colloquio internazionale di paleografia greca (Cremona, 4–10 ottobre 1998)*. Prato, G. (ed.). Florence: 219–38.

Cavallo, G. and Maehler, H. (2008), *Hellenistic Bookhands*. Berlin.

Cavarzeran, J. (2014), 'Due codici poetici marciani di Marco Musuro'. *Prometheus* 40: 3–37.

Cesaretti, P. (1991), *Allegoristi di Omero a Bisanzio: ricerche ermeneutiche (XI–XII Secolo)*. Milan.

Cingano, E. (1985), 'Clistene di Sicione, Erodoto e i poemi del ciclo tebano'. *QUCC* 49: 31–40.

Cingano, E. (2015), 'Epigonoi', in *The Greek Epic Cycle and Its Ancient Reception*. Fantuzzi, M. and Tsagalis, C. (eds). Cambridge: 244–60.

Clark, M. (1997), *Out of Line. Homeric Composition Beyond the Hexameter*. Lanham.

Clay, D. (2004), *Archilochos Heros. The Cult of Poets in the Greek Polis*. Cambridge (MA).

Clay, J. S. (2003), *Hesiod's Cosmos*. Cambridge.

Clay, J. S. (2011), *Homer's Trojan Theater: Space, Vision, and Memory in the Iliad*. Cambridge.

Colbeau, A.-M. (2005) *Raconter la vie d'Homère dans l'Antiquité: Edition commentée du traité anonyme, Au sujet d'Homère et d'Hésiode, de leurs origines et de leur joute, et de la Vie d'Homère attribuée à Hérodote*. Thèse soutenue à l'Université de Lille 3, le 1er décembre 2005. PhD Dissertation.

Collins, D. (2004), *Master of the Game: Competition and Performance in Greek Poetry*. Cambridge (MA).

Colonna, A. (1953), 'I Prolegomeni ad Esiodo e la Vita esiodea di Giovanni Tzetzes', *BollClass* 2: 27–39.

Colonna, A. (ed.) (1959), *Hesiodi Opera et dies. Recensuit Aristides Colonna*. Milan.

Compton-Engle, G. L. (1999), 'Aristophanes *Peace* 1265–1304: food, poetry, and the comic genre'. *CPh* 94: 324–9.

Cook, A. B. (1914), *Zeus: A Study in Ancient Religion*, vol. 1. Cambridge.

Cook, A. B. (1925), *Zeus: A Study in Ancient Religion*, vol. 2.2. Cambridge.

Cribiore, R. (1996), *Writing, Teachers, and Students in Graeco-Roman Egypt*. Atlanta.

Dain, A. (1940), *La collection florentine des tacticiens grecs. Essai sur une entreprise philologique de la Renaissance*. Paris.

Dain, A. (1950), 'Un manuscrit de Polyen, le Scorialensis T.i.12'. *Emerita* 18: 425–39.

Daneloni, A. (2005), 'Due libri postillati dal giovane Poliziano'. *Studi medievali e umanistici* 3: 165–212.

Daneloni, A. and Martinelli, L. (1994), 'Angelus Politianus: manoscritti e edizioni', in *Pico, Poliziano e l'Umanesimo di fine Quattrocento: Biblioteca Medicea Laurenziana 4 novembre – 31 dicembre 1994*. Viti, P. (ed.). Florence: 305–43.

Davies, M. (ed.) (1988), *Epicorum Graecorum fragmenta*. Göttingen.

Davies, M. (1989a), *The Greek Epic Cycle*. Bristol.

Davies, M. (1989b), 'Kinkel redivivus (review of Bernabé 1987)'. *CR* 39: 4–9.

De Lannoy, L. (1997), 'Le problème des Philostrate (État de la question)'. *ANRW* 2.34.3: 2362–449.

De Martino, F. (1984), *Omero quotidiano. Vite di Omero*. Venosa.

De Vries, G. J. (1969), *A Commentary on the Phaedrus of Plato*. Amsterdam.

Debiasi, A. (2001), 'Variazioni sul nome di Omero'. *Hespería. Studi sulla grecità di occidente* 14: 10–35.

Debiasi, A. (2010), 'Orcomeno, Ascra e l'epopea regionale minore', in *Tra Panellenismo e tradizioni locali: generi poetici e storiografia*. Cingano, E. (ed.). Alessandria: 255–98.

Debiasi, A. (2012). 'Homer ἀγωνιστής in Chalcis', in *Homeric Contexts: Neoanalysis and the Interpretation of Oral Poetry*. Montanari, F., Rengakos, A. and Tsagalis, C. (eds). Berlin: 471–500.

Defradas, J., Hani, J. and Klaerr, R. (eds) (1985), *Plutarque. Oeuvres Morales*, vol. 2. Paris.

Deroy, L. (1972), 'Le nom d'Homère'. *AC* 41: 427–39.

Desmed, R. (1974), 'La découverte et la première édition de la seconde centurie des *Miscellanea* de Politien'. *Scriptorium* 28: 314–19.

Di Benedetto, V. (1969), 'Aristophanes *Pax* 1282–1283 e il certamen tra Omero e Esiodo'. *RAL* 24: 161–5.

Dickey, E. (2007), *Ancient Greek Scholarship: A Guide to Finding, Reading, and Understanding Scholia, Commentaries, Lexica, and Grammatical Treatises, from Their Beginnings to the Byzantine*. New York.

Dodds, E. R. (1952), 'The Alcidamas-Papyrus again'. *CQ* 2: 187–8.

Durante, M. (1957), 'Il nome di Omero'. *RAL* 12: 94–111.

Dürrbach, F. (1929), *Inscriptions de Délos: Comptes des Hiéropes (Nos. 372–498)*. Paris.

Edwards, G. (1971), *The Language of Hesiod in its Traditional Context*. Oxford.

Elmer, D. (2013), *The Poetics of Consent: Collective Decision Making and the Iliad*. Baltimore.

Erbse, H. (1996), 'Homer und Hesiod in Chalkis'. *RhM* 139: 308–15.

Ercolani, A. (ed.) (2010), *Esiodo, Opere e Giorni*. Rome.

Erskine, A. (2001), *Troy between Greece and Rome: Local Tradition and Imperial Power*. Oxford.

Esposito Vulgo Gigante, G. (1996), *Vite di Omero*. Naples.

Evelyn-White, H. G. (ed.) (1936 (1914)), *Hesiod, the Homeric Hymns, and Homerica*. Cambridge (MA).

Farnoux, A. (2002), 'Homère à Délos'. *Ktema* 27: 97–104.

Faraggiana di Sarzana, C. (1978), 'Il commentario procliano alle *Opere e i Giorni*'. *Aevum* 52: 17–40.

Faraggiana di Sarzana, C. (1987), 'Le commentaire à Hésiode et la paideia encyclopédique de Proclus', in *Proclus. Lecteur et interprète des anciens*. Pépin, J. and Saffrey, H. D. (eds). Paris: 21–41.

Fehling, D. (1979), 'Zwei Lehrstücke über Pseudo-Nachrichten (Homeriden, Lelantischer Krieg)'. *RhM* 122: 193–210.

Ferrante, D. (ed.) (1957), *Proclo, Crestomazia: introduzione, testo, traduzione e commento degli estratti relativi ai generi letterari. Luoghi paralleli: testo e traduzione. Ciclo e vita di Omero: testo e traduzione*. Naples.

Ferreri, L. (2014), *L'Italia degli Umanisti. Marco Musuro*. Turnhout.

Foley, J. M. (1999), *Homer's Traditional Art*. University Park: Pennsylvania State.

Fontenrose, J. E. (1978), *The Delphic Oracle: Its Responses and Operations, with a Catalogue of Responses*. Berkeley.

Ford, A. (1992), *Homer: The Poetry of the Past*. Ithaca.

Ford, A. (1997), 'The inland ship: problems in the performance and reception of early Greek epic', in *Written Voices, Spoken Signs: Tradition, Performance, and the Epic Text*. Bakker, E. and Kahane, A. (eds). Cambridge (MA).

Ford, A. (2002), *The Origins of Criticism: Literary Culture and Poetic Theory in Classical Greece*. Princeton.

Fowler, R. L. (ed.) (2000), *Early Greek Mythography*, vol. 1: *Text and Introduction*. Oxford.

Fowler, R. L. (ed.) (2013), *Early Greek Mythography*, vol. 2: *Commentary*. Oxford.

Fraser, P. M. (1972), *Ptolemaic Alexandria*, vol. 2. Oxford.

Fritz, K. von and Kapp, E. (1950), *Constitution of Athens and Related Texts. Translated with an Introduction and Notes by Kurt von Fritz and Ernst Kapp.* New York.

Fryde, E. B. (1983), *Humanism and Renaissance Historiography*. London.

Fryde, E. B. (1996), *Greek Manuscripts in the Private Library of the Medici: 1469–1510*, vol. 2. Aberystwyth.

Gaisford, Th. (ed.) (1823), *Poetae minores Graeci*, vol. 2. Leipzig.

Gallavotti, C. (1929), 'Genesi e tradizione letteraria dell'Agone tra Omero ed Esiodo'. *RFIC* 7: 31–59.

Gentile, S. (1997), 'Pico filologo', in *Giovanni Pico della Mirandola: convegno internazionale di studi nel cinquecentesimo anniversario della morte (1494–1994): Mirandola, 4–8 ottobre 1994*. Garfagnini, G. C. (ed.). Florence: 465–90.

Georgiadou, A. and Larmour, D. H. J. (1998), *Lucian's Science Fiction Novel True Histories: Interpretation and Commentary*. Leiden.

Gera, D. L. (1997), *Warrior Women: The Anonymous Tractatus De Mulieribus*. Leiden.

Giannini, A. (ed.) (1965), *Paradoxographicorum Graecorum fragmenta*. Milan.

Gigante, M. (1979), *Civiltà delle forme letterarie nell'antica Pompei*. Naples.

Gostoli, A. (ed.) (2007), *Margite*. Pisa-Rome.

Goulet-Cazé, M.-O. (2006), 'Cosmopolitanism'. *Brill's New Pauly*.

Graziosi, B. (2001), 'Competition in wisdom', in *Homer, Tragedy and Beyond. Essays in Honour of P.E. Easterling.* Budelmann, F. and Michelakis, P. (eds). London: 57–74.

Graziosi, B. (2002), *Inventing Homer: The Early Reception of Epic.* Cambridge.

Graziosi, B. and Haubold, J. (eds) (2010), *Homer: Iliad Book VI.* Cambridge.

Griffith, M. (1990), 'Contest and contradiction in early Greek poetry', in *Cabinet of the Muses: Essays on Classical and Comparative Literature in Honor of Thomas G. Rosenmeyer.* Griffith, M. and Mastronarde, D. (eds). Atlanta: 185–207.

Gutzwiller, K. (2010), 'Heroic epitaphs of the classical age: the Aristotelian *Peplos* and beyond', in *Archaic and Classical Greek Epigram.* Baumbach, M., Petrovic, A. and Petrovic, I. (eds). Cambridge: 219–49.

Hall, E. (1988), 'When did the Trojans turn into Phrygians? Alcaeus 42.15'. *ZPE* 73: 15–18.

Hall, E. (1989), *Inventing the Barbarian: Greek Self-Definition through Tragedy.* Oxford.

Hanink, J. (2008), 'Literary politics and the Euripidean Vita', *CCJ* 54: 115–35.

Harsting, P. (2001), 'More evidence of Menander Rhetor on the Wedding Speech: Angelo Poliziano's transcription'. *Cahiers de l'Institut du Moyen-Age grec et latin* 72: 11–34.

Haubold, J. H. (2000), *Homer's People. Epic Poetry and Social Formation.* Cambridge.

Heath, M. (1998), 'Was Homer a Roman?' *Papers of the Leeds International Latin Seminar* 10: 23–56.

Heeren, A. H. L. (1789), 'Tractatus anonymi de mulieribus quae bello claruerunt'. *Bibliothek der Alten Litteratur und Kunst* 6: 3–24.

Heldmann, K. (1982), *Die Niederlage Homers im Dichterwettstreit mit Hesiod.* Göttingen.

Hermann, G. (ed.) (1835), *Opuscula*, vol 6. Leipzig.

Heubeck, A. H. and Hoekstra, A. (1989), *A Commentary on Homer's Odyssey*, vol. 2: *Books IX–XVI.* Oxford.

Higbie, C. (1990), *Measure and Music: Enjambment and Sentence Structure in the Iliad.* Oxford.

Hiller, E. (ed.) (1872), *Eratosthenis carminum reliquiae.* Leipzig.

Hillgruber, M. (1990), 'Zur Zeitbestimmung der *Chrestomathie* des Proklos'. *RhM* 133: 397–404.

Hillgruber, M. (1999), *Die pseudoplutarchische Schrift De Homero. Teil 2. Kommentar zu den Kapiteln 74–218.* Stuttgart.

Hornblower, S. (1991), *A Commentary on Thucydides*, vol. 1: *Books 1–3.* Oxford.

Hunger, H. (1961), *Katalog der griechischen Handschriften der Österreichischen Nationalbibliothek*, vol. 1. Vienna.

Hunter, R. (2006), *The Shadow of Callimachus. Studies in the Reception of Hellenistic Poetry at Rome.* Cambridge.

Hunter, R. (2009), 'Hesiod's style: towards an ancient analysis', in *Brill's Companion to Hesiod.* Montanari, F., Rengakos, A. and Tsagalis, C. (eds). Leiden: 253–69.

Hunter, R. (2014), *Hesiodic Voices. Studies in the Ancient Reception of Hesiod's Works and Days.* Cambridge.

Hunter, R. and Rutherford, I. (eds) (2009), *Wandering Poets in Ancient Greek Culture: Travel, Locality and Pan-Hellenism.* Cambridge.

Huxley, G. (1969), 'Choirilos of Samos'. *GRBS* 10: 12–29.

Jacoby, F. (1933). 'Homerisches I: Der Bios und die Person'. *Hermes* 68: 1–50.

Janko, R. (1982), *Homer, Hesiod, and the Hymns: Diachronic Development in Epic Diction.* Cambridge.

Janko, R. (1992), *The Iliad: A Commentary*, vol. 4: *Books 13–16.* Cambridge.

Janko, R. (ed.) (2011), *Philodemus On Poems. Book 3–4 with the Fragments of Aristotle On Poets.* Oxford.

Jellamo, A. (2005), *Il cammino di Dike. L'idea di giustizia da Omero a Eschilo.* Rome.

Jones, C. P. (1986), *Culture and Society in Lucian.* Cambridge (MA).

Kahane, A. (2005), *Diachronic Dialogues. Authority and Continuity in Homer and the Homeric Tradition.* Lanham.

Kaiser, E. (1964), 'Odyssee-Szenen als Topoi'. *MH* 21: 197–224.

Kegel, W. J. H. F. (1962), *Simonides.* Groningen.

Kim, L. (2010), *Homer Between History and Fiction in Imperial Greek Literature.* Cambridge.

Kimmel-Clauzet, F. (2013), *Morts, tombeaux et cultes des poètes grecs. Étude de la survie des grands poètes des époques archaique et classique en Grèce ancienne.* Pessac.

Kimmel-Clauzet, F. (2015), 'Homère, le premier des sophistes?' , in À l'école d'Homère *La culture des orateurs et des sophistes.* Dubel, S., Favreau-Linder, A.-M. and Oudot, E. (eds). Paris: 19–30.

Kirchhoff, A. (1892), *Der Roman eines Sophisten.* Berlin.

Kirk, G. S. (1950), 'The Michigan Alcidamas-Papyrus; Heraclitus fr. 56d; the riddle of the lice'. *CQ* 44: 149–67.

Kirk, G. S. (1966), 'Studies in some technical aspects of Homeric style'. *YClS* 20: 75–152.

Kirk, G. S. (1985), *The Iliad: A Commentary*, vol. 1: *Books 1–4.* Cambridge.

Kirk, G. S. (1990), *The Iliad: A Commentary*, vol. 2: *Books 5–8.* Cambridge.

Kivilo, M. (2000), 'Certamen'. *Studia Humaniora Tartuensia* 1: 1–5.

Kivilo, M. (2010a), *Early Greek Poets' Lives: The Shaping of the Tradition*. Leiden.

Kivilo, M. (2010b), 'The early biographical tradition on Homer', in *Identities and Societies in the Ancient East-Mediterranean Regions: Comparative Approaches*. Kämmerer, T., et al. (eds). Münster: 85–104.

Koechly, H. (1857), *Opuscula academica*, vol. 1. Leipzig.

Kõiv, M. (2011), 'A note on the dating of Hesiod'. *CQ* 61: 355–77.

Kokolakis, M. (1995), 'Zeus' tomb. An object of pride and reproach'. *Kernos* 8: 123–38.

Koniaris, G. L. (1971), 'Michigan Papyrus 2754 and the *Certamen*'. *HSPh* 75: 107–29.

Koning, H. H. (2010), *Hesiod, the Other Poet: Ancient Reception of a Cultural Icon*. Leiden.

Konstantakos, I. (2004), 'Trial by riddle: the testing of the counsellor and the contest of kings in the legend of Amasis and Bias'. *C&M* 55: 85–137.

Konstantakos, I. (2005), 'Amasis, Bias and the Seven Sages as riddlers'. *WJA* n.F. 29: 11–46.

Körte, A. (1927), 'Alkidamas Περὶ Ὁμήρου'. *APF* 8: 261–5.

Kuisma, O. (1996), *Proclus' Defence of Homer*. Helsinki.

Lamberton, R. (1986), *Homer the Theologian: Neoplatonist Allegorical Reading and the Growth of the Epic Tradition*. Berkeley.

Lamberton, R. (1988), 'Plutarch, Hesiod, and the Mouseia of Thespiai'. *ICS* 13: 491–504.

Landi, C. (1895), 'Opuscula de fontibus mirabilibus, de Nilo etc. ex cod. Laur. 56,1 descripta'. *SIFC* 3: 531–48.

Latacz, J. (1996), *Homer, His Art and His World*. Ann Arbor.

Latacz, J. (2014), 'On Nietzsche's philological beginnings', in *Nietzsche as a Scholar of Antiquity*. Jensen, A. K. and Heit, H. (eds). London: 3–26.

Lefkowitz, M. (1981 (2012)). *The Lives of the Greek Poets*. London.

Levine, D. (2002), 'Poetic justice: Homer's death in the ancient biographical tradition'. *CJ* 98: 141–160.

Livingstone, N. and Nisbet, G. (2010), *Epigram*. Cambridge.

Longo, A. (1995), 'Sull'attribuzione della *Crestomazia* a Proclo neoplatonico'. *SIFC* 13: 109–24.

MacDowell, D. (1971), *Aristophanes: Wasps*. Oxford.

Mahaffy, J. P. (1891), *The Flinders Petrie Papyri with Transcriptions, Commentaries and Index*. Dublin.

Maisano, R. (1995), *Discorsi di Temistio*. Turin.

Mandilaras, B. (1990), 'A new papyrus fragment of the *Certamen Homeri et Hesiodi*', *Platon* 42: 45–51.

Mandilaras, B. (1992), 'A new papyrus fragment of the *Certamen Homeri et Hesiodi* (reprinted)', in *Papiri letterari greci e latini (Papyrologica Lupiensia 1)*. Capasso, M. (ed.). Lecce: 54–62.

Manieri, A. (2009), *Agoni poetico-musicali nella Grecia antica*, vol. 1: *Beozia*. Pisa-Rome.

Mansuelli, G. A. (1963), 'Omero', in *Enciclopedia dell'arte antica, classica e orientale*, vol. 5. Rome.

Markwald, G. (1986), *Die Homerischen Epigramme: sprachliche und inhaltliche Untersuchungen*. Meisenheim.

Marx, F. (1925), 'Die Überlieferung über die Persönlichkeit Homers'. *RhM* 74: 395–431.

Marzillo, P. (ed.) (2010), *Der Kommentar des Proklos zu Hesiods Werken und Tagen. Edition, Übersetzung und Erläuterung der Fragmente*. Tübingen.

Mason, H. (1974), *Greek Terms for Roman Institutions: A Lexicon and Analysis*. Toronto.

Matteuzzi, M. (2000–2002), 'A proposito di Omero "babilonese"' (Lucian. *V.H.* II 20)'. *Sandalion* 23–25: 49–51.

McLeod, W. (1985), 'The epic canon of the Borgia table: Hellenistic lore or Roman fraud?'. *TAPhA* 115: 153–65.

Meineke, A. (1843), *Analecta Alexandrina*. Berlin.

Menci, G. (2012), 'Un epigramma del *Certamen Homeri et Hesiodi* (309–312 Allen) in P.Duk. inv. 665'. *ZPE* 180: 43–7.

Meyer, E. (1892), 'Homerische Parerga: der Wettkampf Homers und Hesiods'. *Hermes* 27: 363–80.

Milne, H. J. M. (1927), *Catalogue of the Literary Papyri in the British Museum*. London.

Milne, M. J. (1924), *A Study in Alcidamas and his Relation to Contemporary Sophists*. Bryn Mawr.

Mineur, W. H. (ed.) (1984), *Callimachus. Hymn to Delos*. Leiden.

Moles, J. (1996), 'Cynic Cosmopolitanism', in *The Cynics. The Cynic Movement in Antiquity and Its Legacy*. Bracht Branham, R. and Goulet-Cazé, M.-O. (eds). Berkeley: 105–20.

Möllendorff, P. von (2000), *Auf der Suche nach der verlogenen Wahrheit. Lukians Wahre Geschichten*. Tübingen.

Momigliano, A. D. (1993), *Development of Greek Biography, Expanded Edition*. Harvard.

Montanari, F. (2009), 'Ancient scholarship on Hesiod', in *Brill's Companion to Hesiod*. Montanari, F., Rengakos, A. and Tsagalis, C. (eds). Leiden: 313–42.

Montiglio, S. (2005), *Wandering in Ancient Greek Culture*. Chicago.

Morgan, K. A. (2000), *Myth and Philosophy from the Presocratics to Plato.* Cambridge.

Most, G. (ed.) (2006), *Hesiod. Theogony. Works and Days. Testimonia.* Cambridge (MA).

Muir, J. V. (ed.) (2001), *Alcidamas. The Works and Fragments.* Bristol.

Munn, M. H. (2006), *The Mother of the Gods, Athens, and the Tyranny of Asia: A Study of Sovereignty in Ancient Religion.* Berkeley.

Nagy, G. (1979), *The Best of the Achaeans: Concepts of the Hero in Archaic Greek Poetry.* Baltimore.

Nagy, G. (1982), 'Hesiod', in *Ancient Writers.* Luce, T. J. (ed.). New York: 43–73.

Nagy, G. (1983), 'On the death of Sarpedon', in *Approaches to Homer.* Rubino, C. A. and Shelmerdine, C. W. (eds). Austin: 189–217.

Nagy, G. (1990), *Greek Mythology and Poetics.* Ithaca.

Nagy, G. (2004), 'L'aède épique en auteur: la tradition des Vies d'Homère', in *Identités d'auteur dans l'Antiquité et la tradition européenne.* Calame, C. and Chartier, R. (eds). Grenoble: 41–67.

Nagy, G. (2006), 'Homer's name revisited', in *La langue poétique indo-européenne; Actes du Colloque de travail de la Société des Études Indo-Européennes. Paris, 22–24 octobre 2003.* Pinault, G.-J., and Petit, D. (eds). Leuven and Paris: 317–30.

Nagy, G. (2009), 'Hesiod and the ancient biographical traditions', in *Brill's Companion to Hesiod.* Montanari, F., Rengakos, A. and Tsagalis, C. (eds). Leiden: 271–311.

Nagy, G. (2010), *Homer the Preclassic.* Berkeley.

Nesselrath, H.-G. (2002), 'Homerphilologie auf der Insel der Seligen: Lukian *VH* II 20'. *Epea Pteroenta* 75: 151–62.

Nietzsche, F. (1870), 'Der Florentinische Tractat über Homer und Hesiod, ihr Geschlecht und ihren Wettkampf, 1–2'. *RhM* 25: 528–40.

Nietzsche, F. (1871), 'Certamen quod dicitur Homeri et Hesiodi. E codice florentino post Henricum Stephanum denuo edidit Fridericus Nietzsche Numburgensis'. *Acta societatis philologae Lipsiensis* 1: 1–23.

Nietzsche, F. (1873), 'Der Florentinische Tractat über Homer und Hesiod, ihr Geschlecht und ihren Wettkampf, 3–5'. *RhM* 28: 211–49.

Nilsson, M. P. (1906), *Griechische Feste von religiöser Bedeutung.* Leipzig.

Ní-Mheallaigh, K. (2009), 'Monumental fallacy: the teleology of origins in Lucian's *Verae Historiae*', in *A Lucian for our Times.* Bartley, A. (ed.). Newcastle upon Tyne: 11–28.

Öhler, H. (1913), *Paradoxographi Florentini anonymi opusculum de aquis mirabilibus: ad fidem codicum manu scriptorum editum commentario instructum.* Tübingen.

Ogden, D. (2002), *Magic, Witchcraft, and Ghosts in the Greek and Roman Worlds: A Sourcebook*. Oxford.

Olson, S. D. (1998), *Aristophanes, Peace. Edited with Introduction and Commentary*. Oxford.

O'Sullivan, N. (1992), *Alcidamas, Aristophanes, and the Beginnings of Greek Stylistic Theory*. Stuttgart.

Pagliaroli, S. (2004), 'Giano Lascari e il ginnasio greco'. *SMU* 2: 215–93.

Parry, M. (1971), *The Making of Homeric Verse: The Collected Papers of Milman Parry. Edited by Adam Parry*. Oxford.

Patzer, A. (1993), 'Hesiod als Rhapsode', in *Ut Poiesis Pictura: Antike Texte in Bildern*. Holzberg, N. and Maier, F. (eds). Bamberg: 83–96.

Pearson, A. C. (ed.) (1891), *The Fragments of Zeno and Cleanthes, with Introduction and Explanatory Notes*. London.

Penella, R. J. (2000), *The Private Orations of Themistius*. Berkeley.

Pernigotti, C. (2015), 'Comparatio Menandri et Philistionis'. *Corpus dei papiri filosofici greci e latini* 2.2: 41–54.

Pertusi, A. (1951), 'Intorno alla tradizione manoscritta degli scolii di Proclo ad Esiodo IV: Proclo e non Proclo'. *Aevum* 25: 147–59.

Pertusi, A. (ed.) (1955), *Scholia vetera in Hesiodi Opera et Dies*. Milan.

Pfeiffer, R. (1968), *History of Classical Scholarship: From the Beginnings to the End of the Hellenistic Age*. Oxford.

Piccolomini, E. (1874), 'Due documenti relativi ad acquisti di codici greci, fatti da Giovanni Lascaris per contro di Lorenzo de' Medici'. *RFIC* 2: 401–23.

Pinkwart, D. (1965), *Das Relief des Archelaos von Priene und die 'Musen des Philiskos'*. Kallmünz.

Pontani (Meschini), A. (ed.) (1976), *Giano Laskaris, Epigrammi Greci*. Padua.

Pontani, A. (2002a), 'L'umanesimo greco a Venezia: Marco Musuro, Girolamo Aleandro e l'«Antologia Planudea»', in *I Greci a Venezia. Atti del Convegno Internazionale di studio (Venezia, 5–7 novembre 1998)*. Tiepolo, M. F. (ed.). Venice: 381–466.

Pontani, A. (2002b), 'Per l'esegesi umanistica dell'«Antologia Planudea»: i marginalia dell'edizione del 1494', in *Talking to the Text. Marginalia from Papyri to Print*. Fera, V., Ferraù, G. and Rizzo, S. (eds). Messina: 557–613.

Pontani, F. (2002–2003), 'Musurus' Creed'. *GRBS* 43: 175–213.

Pontani, F. (2005a), *Sguardi su Ulisse. La tradizione esegetica greca all'Odissea*. Rome.

Pontani, F. (2005b), *Eraclito, Questioni Omeriche sulle allegorie di Omero in merito agli dèi*. Pisa.

Pontani, F. (2014), 'Preghiere, parafrasi e grammatiche: il Credo e L'Ave Maria di Marco Musuro'. *Bibliothèque d'humanisme et renaissance* 76: 325–40.

Pontani, F. M. (1973–1974), 'Epigrammi inediti di Marco Musuro'. *ArchClass* 25–6: 575–84.

Pontani, F. M. (1978), 'Patroclo, Musuro e Capodivacca', in *Miscellanea dell'Istituto di studi bizantini e neogreci dell'Università di Padova*, vol. 1. Padua: 81–7.

Pordomingo, F. (2010), 'Antologías escolares de época helenística', in *Libri di scuola e pratiche didattiche. Dall'Antichità al Rinascimento. Atti del Convegno Internazionale di Studi, Cassino, 7–10 maggio 2008.* Del Corso, L. and Pecere, O. (eds). Cassino: 37–69.

Powell, J. U. (1925), *Collectanea Alexandrina: reliquiae minores poetarum Graecorum aetatis ptolemaicae, 323–146 a.C.: epicorum, elegiacorum, lyricorum, ethicorum*. Oxford.

Renehan, R. (1971), 'The Michigan Alcidamas-Papyrus: A problem in methodology'. *HSPh* 75: 85–105.

Renehan, R. (1976), *Studies in Greek Texts: Critical Observations to Homer, Plato, Euripides, Aristophanes and Other Authors*. Göttingen.

Rhodes, P. J. (1972), *The Athenian Boule*. Oxford.

Rhodes, P. J. (1981), *A Commentary on the Aristotelian Athenaion Politeia*. Oxford.

Richardson, N. (1975), 'Homeric professors in the age of the Sophists'. *PCPhS* 21: 65–81.

Richardson, N. (1981), 'The contest of Homer and Hesiod and Alcidamas' *Mouseion*'. *CQ* 31: 1–10.

Richardson, N. (1984), Review of Heldmann 1982. *CR* 34: 308–9.

Richardson, N. (1993), *The Iliad: A Commentary*, vol. 6: *Books 21–24*. Cambridge.

Richardson, N. (ed.) (2010), *Three Homeric Hymns: To Apollo, Hermes, and Aphrodite*. Cambridge.

Richter, D. S. (2011), *Cosmopolis: Imagining Community in Late Classical Athens and the Early Roman Empire*. Oxford.

Richter, G. (1965), *The Portraits of the Greeks*, vol. 1. London.

Rose, V. (1864), *Anecdota Graeca et Graecolatina: Mitteilungen aus Handschriften zur Geschichte der griechischen Wissenschaft*, vol. 1. Berlin.

Rosen, R. M. (1990), 'Poetry and sailing in Hesiod's *Works and Days*'. *ClAnt* 9: 99–113.

Rosen, R. M. (1997), 'Homer and Hesiod', in *A New Companion to Homer*. Morris, I., and Powell, B. (eds). Leiden: 463–88.

Rosen, R. M. (2004), 'Aristophanes' *Frogs* and the *Contest of Homer and Hesiod*'. *TAPhA* 134: 295–322.

Rubinstein, N. (1990), 'Il Bruni a Firenze: retorica e politica', in *Leonardo Bruni cancelliere della Repubblica di Firenze: Convegno di Studi (Firenze, 27–29 ottobre 1987)*. Viti, P. (ed.). Florence: 20–8.

Russell, D. A. (1996), *Libanius: Imaginary Speeches: a Selection of Declamations Translated with Notes*. London.

Russell, D. A., and Wilson, N. G. (eds) (1981), *Menander Rhetor. Edited with Translation and Commentary by D. A. Russell and N. G. Wilson*. Oxford.

Russell, D., and Konstan, D. (2005), *Heraclitus: Homeric Problems*. Atlanta.

Rzach, A. (ed.) (1913), *Hesiodi Carmina recensuit Aloisius Rzach. Editio tertia. Accedit Certamen quod dicitur Homeri et Hesiodi*. Leipzig.

Sandbach, F. H. (ed.) (1969), *Plutarch's Moralia XV. Fragments*. Cambridge (MA).

Sauppe, H. (1850), *Oratores Attici: Scholia, Fragmenta, Indices*, vol. 2. Zurich.

Scafoglio, M. (2006), 'Two fragments of the Epic Cycle'. *GRBS* 46: 5–11.

Schindler, F. (1973), *Die Überlieferung der Stratagemata des Polyainos*. Vienna.

Scodel, R. (1980), 'Hesiod redivivus'. *GRBS* 21: 301–20.

Severyns, A. (ed.) (1938–1963), *Recherches sur la Chrestomatie de Proclos*, 4 vols. Paris.

Sinclair, T. J. (1932), *Hesiod: Works and Days*. London.

Skiadas, A. D. (1965), *Homer im Griechischen Epigramm*. Athens.

Solmsen, F. (1932), 'Drei Rekonstruktionen zur antiken Rhetorik und Poetik. I: Alkidamas'. *Hermes* 67: 133–44.

Solmsen, F. (1940), 'Some works of Philostratus the Elder'. *TAPhA* 71: 556–72.

Sommerstein, A. H. (1985), *The Comedies of Aristophanes: Peace*. Warminster.

Speranzi, D. (2010a), 'Giano Lascari e i suoi copisti. Gli oratori attici minori fra l'Athos e Firenze'. *Medioevo e Rinascimento* 24: 337–77.

Speranzi, D. (2010b), 'Vicende umanistiche di un antico codice. Marco Musuro e il Florilegio di Stobeo'. *S&T* 8: 313–50.

Speranzi, D. (2013), *Marco Musuro: libri e scrittura*. Rome.

Stamatopoulou, Z. (2014), 'Hesiodic poetry and wisdom in Plutarch's *Symposium of the Seven Sages*'. *AJPh* 135: 533–58.

Stamatopoulou, Z. (2016), 'The quarrel with Perses and Hesiod's biographical tradition'. *GRBS* 56: 1–17.

Sturz, F. G. (ed.) (1787), *Hellanici Lesbii Fragmenta e variis scriptoribus collegit emendavit illustravit et praemissa commentatione de Hellanici aetate vita et scriptis in universum edidit Fridericus Guilielmus Sturz*. Leipzig.

Thiel, H. van (ed.) (1991), *Homeri Ilias*. Zürich.

Thompson, S. (1957), *Motif-Index of Folk-Literature*. Bloomington.

Torres-Guerra, J. B. (2015), 'Thebaid', in *The Greek Epic Cycle and Its Ancient Reception*. Fantuzzi, M., and Tsagalis, C. (eds). Cambridge: 226–43.

Uden, J. (2010), 'The *Contest of Homer and Hesiod* and the ambitions of Hadrian'. *JHS* 130: 121–35.

Unanua Garmendia, M. Á. (2003), 'El catálogo de las naves de la Ilíada: un problema de cálculo'. *Helmantica* 54: 219–46.

Verdenius, W. J. (1985), *A Commentary on Hesiod Works and Days vv. 1–382*. Leiden.

Vinogradov, J. G. (1969), 'Cyclic Poetry in Olbia'. *VDI* 3(109): 142–8.

Vinogradov, J. G., and Zolotarev, M. (1990), 'La Chersonèse de la fin de l'archaïsme', in *Le Pont-Euxin vu par les Grecs*. Khartchilava, T., and Geny, E. (eds). Paris: 85–120.

Vogt, E. (1959), 'Die Schrift vom Wettkampf Homers und Hesiods'. *RhM* 102: 193–221.

Vox, O. (1980), 'Esiodo fra Beozia e Pieria'. *Belfagor* 35: 321–5.

Wallis, W. (2014), 'Homer: A Guide to Sculptural Types'. *Living Poets* (Durham, 2014). https://livingpoets.dur.ac.uk/w/Homer:_A_Guide_to_Sculptural_Types

Weber, L. (1917), 'Steinepigramm und Buchepigramm'. *Hermes* 52(4): 536–57.

Welcker, F. G. (1835), *Der epische Cyclus, oder die Homerischen Dichter*, vol. 1. Bonn.

West, M. L. (1966), *Theogony: Edited with Prolegomena and Commentary by M. L. West*. Oxford.

West, M. L. (1967), 'The Contest of Homer and Hesiod', *CQ* 17(2): 433–50.

West, M. L. (ed.) (1971), *Iambi et elegi Graeci ante Alexandrum cantati*, vol. 1. Oxford.

West, M. L. (1973), *Textual Criticism and Editorial Technique Applicable to Greek and Latin Texts*. Stuttgart.

West, M. L. (1975), 'Cynaethus' Hymn to Apollo'. *CQ* 25(2): 161–70.

West, M. L. (ed.) (1978), *Works and Days: Edited with Prolegomena and Commentary by M. L. West*. Oxford.

West, M. L. (1982), *Greek Metre*. Oxford.

West, M. L. (1983), *The Orphic Poems*. Oxford.

West, M. L. (1998), *Homeri Ilias*, vol. 1. Stuttgart/Leipzig.

West, M. L. (1999), 'The invention of Homer'. *CQ* 49(2): 364–82.

West, M. L. (ed.) (2003a), *Homeric Hymns. Homeric Apocrypha. Lives of Homer*. Cambridge (MA).

West, M. L. (ed.) (2003b), *Greek Epic Fragments from the Seventh to the Fifth Centuries BC*. Cambridge (MA).

West, M. L. (2013), *The Epic Cycle. A Commentary on the Lost Troy Epics*. Oxford.

Westermann, A. (ed.) (1839), *Paradoxographoi: Scriptores rerum mirabilium Graeci*. Braunschweig.

Westermann, A. (ed.) (1843), *Mythographoi: Scriptores poeticae historiae Graeci*. Braunschweig.

Westermann, A. (ed.) (1845). *Biographoi: Vitarum scriptores Graeci minores*. Braunschweig.

Wilamowitz, U. von (1875), *Analecta Euripidea*. Berlin.

Wilamowitz, U. von (1879), 'Parerga'. *Hermes* 14: 161–86.

Wilamowitz, U. von (ed.) (1929 (1916)), *Vitae Homeri et Hesiodi in usum scholarum*. Bonn.

Wilamowitz, U. von (1916), *Die Ilias und Homer*. Berlin.

Wilson, N. G. (1992), *From Byzantium to Italy. Greek Studies in the Renaissance*. London.

Wilson, P. (2009), 'Thamyris the Thracian: the archetypal wandering poet?', in *Wandering Poets*. Hunter, R., and Rutherford, I. (eds). Cambridge: 46–79.

Winter, J. G. (1925), 'A new fragment on the Life of Homer'. *TAPhA* 56: 120–9.

Yamagata, N. (2010), 'Hesiod in Plato: Second fiddle to Homer?', in *Plato and Hesiod*. Haubold, J., and Boys-Stones, G. (eds). Oxford: 68–88.

Zeitlin, F. (2001), 'Visions and revisions of Homer in the Second Sophistic', in *Greek Identity in the Second Sophistic*. Goldhill, S. (ed.). Cambridge: 195–266.

General index

Agamemnon 152, 156
Aietes 155
Alcidamas as source 47, 115, 168–69, 173, 181–82
   account of Hesiod's death 170, 171–72, 172–73, 173
   account of Homer's death 190–91
   evidence of P.Mich. inv. 2754 69–74
   Homer's oracle 138–139
   improvised speech 162, 163
   literary theory 145, 146–47
   Museum quotation 61, 143
   omission of Delos 8
   presentation of Homer 145, 169
Allen, Thomas W. 15–16, 126
'ambiguous propositions' 147–56
Amphidamas 15, 41, 139–40
Apelles 135–36
Apollo 136, *See also* genealogies
   contest with Linus 133
   Homeric connection to 179, 181, 187, 189
Argos 184, 186
Athens
   and the *Delia* 9–10
   and Homer's image 10, 119, 122, 182, 191
   view of Phrygians 150
   visit of Homer 181, 182–83
audience reaction 65, 144–45, 156–57, 164, 165–66
   to Homer in Argos 186–87
Avezzù, Guido 73, 160, 179
Beecroft, Alexander 2, 121, 131
biographical practice and tradition 29, 45–46, 82, 126, 142
   authorship of texts 16, 40, 44
   as fiction 118
   Homeridae and 122
   Orphic poets and 134
   parodied by Lucian 32–34
   use of subject's works *See also*

Hesiod: as source of contest story
   birthplace of Homer 119, 127
   in genealogy 126–27, 127, 128–29, 130, 134, 135, 136
   for Hesiod 118, 136
   variation 2–3, 21–22, 24
Byzantine age 40–46
Callicles 125
Calliope 129, 134
Callisto 152
Chalcis 7–8, 137
Chios 118–19, 119, 121–22, 187, 189
Chrestomathy, attribution of 20, 22–23
Cleobulus of Lindus 180
Collins, Derek 122, 147, 149
Colophon 118–19, 119, 122, 186
contest tradition
   accompanying games 140
   belief in 136–37
   form of contest 141
   location 7–9, 137
   other contests 133
   outcome 6–7, 23–24, 27, 30, 31, 34, 35–36
   verses used 24, 61, 65–66, 143, 144, 149
Corinth 183–84
Creophylus 191
Cretheis 119–20, 128, 135
   spelling 120
Cynaethus 188
Cypria 125
Cyprus 125
Daemon 126, 128
dating 115, 130
   inscription of *Hymn to Apollo* 190
   language and 115, 149, 159, 183, 189–90
   of sources 60–61, 119, 132, 149, 182
De Martino, Francesco 160–61

216 General index

Delos 8–10, 188–90
Democritus of Troezen 126
Dius 135, 160
divine descent 132, 134, 136, *See also* Meles
Dodds, Eric Robertson 71–72, 73
dolphins 172–73
editio princeps 48, 117
education
  use of **L** 51–52, 178, 188
  use of P.Duk. inv. 665 81
  use of P.Freib. 1.1. b 77
  use of story 46, 47, 130
Egypt 127
Elmer, David F. 167
enjambment 146, 147, 148
Epigoni 176–77, 177–78
epigrams
  Argive statue of Homer 80–82, 187–88
  Athenian 182, 183
  contest victory 39, 77–79, 169
  Hesiod's tomb 176
  Homer's tomb 70, 192–93, 193–94
  Midas' tomb 179–80
  Pythian
    to Hadrian 56, 57, 58, 60, 131
    to Hesiod 169
    to Homer 139
    to Megarians 186
Eratosthenes
  account of Hesiod's death 170, 174–76
Estienne, Henri (Henricus Stephanus) 48
Eugnetho 128
Eumetis *See* Metis
Euphemus 135
Eurycles 175
Eurypylus 185
Eutychius Proclus 22
Evelyn-White, Hugh G. 149, 151, 153, 160, 162
feasting 152–53
'finest passages' 24, 116, 164–67

Fowler, Robert L. 128
Gan[n]yctor 139, 171, 174–75
genealogies 56, 58–59
Gigantomachy 150
gods 147, 162, 165–66, *See also* Apollo; divine descent; Zeus
Graziosi, Barbara 1–2, 131
Hadrian 115, 130–31
Hanink, Johanna 2
happiness 164
Harmonides 134–35
Helicon, Mount 7
Hesiod
  birthplace 118
  characterisation 4, 146, 159
  chronology 131–32, 134, 135–36, 136–37, 174
  death 77, 139, 170–75
  Delos meeting with Homer 8–10
  finest passage 26, 164–65, 166–67
  genealogy 58–59, 60
  offspring 172
  parents 135, 136, 160
  reburial 175–76
  role in contest 141
  as source of contest story 2, 5–7, 139
  themes 26–27, 35–37, 152–53, 161, 162–64, 165
  travels 138, 170
  as victor over Lesches 14–15
  visit to Delphi 138–39, 169
Homer
  and Apollo 179, 181, 187, 189, *See also* genealogies
  and Argos 184, 186–87
  and Athens 181, 182, 183
  attribution of works
    Epigoni 149
    Hymn to Apollo 188
    Margites 122–23, 137
    Thebaid 176–178
  birthplace 32–33, 118–20, 125, 182, 187, 189
  blindness 23, 33, 119, 121, 166
  characterisation 4, 159, 163, 164

'Hesiodic' expertise 26–27, 159, 161, 163–64
view of gods 147, 162
chronology 29
  relative to Hesiod 131–32, 134, 135–36, 136–37, 174
  relative to Midas 179
in Corinth 183–84
death 69, 73–74, 190–93
Delos visit 8–10, 188–90
favoured by Muses 157, 160, 165, 166
finest passage 164–65, 165–66
'godlike' 117, 142, 143, 164–65, 165–66
'golden' 145
as 'historian' 74
honours 179, 182, 186–87, 189–90
legacy 145
  descendants 121–22
name 33, 120–21, 129–30
oracle given to 138–39
Panhellenisation of 118, 138, 145, 184, 187
  and Delian performance 10, 188–89
parents 125, 123–29, 132, 135, *See also* genealogies
poetic career 116–17, 123, 137–38, 176–78, 181–82, 188
role in contest 116, 141
as source of wisdom and inspiration 45, 188
themes and subject matter 152–53, 165–66, 177
  suitable for kings 24–27
tomb 193–94
Homeric epigrams 179
Homeridae 45–46, 121–22
Hymn to Apollo 8, 9–10, 10, 188–89
  transcription of 190
'insoluble challenges' 145–47, 155
Ithaca 127–28, 128–29, 131
Janko, Richard 9

judgment *See* Panedes/Panoides; verdict
justice 161, 162–63, 173, 175
Kirk, Geoffrey S. 71, 73, 74, 185
Kivilo, Maarit 8, 134
Koniaris, George L. 72, 73
Koning, Hugo H. 164, 168
Körte, Alfred 71
Lamberton, Robert 13
Lascaris, Janus 48, 53, 59
Latacz, Joachim 1
Late Antiquity 34–39
Lefkowitz, Mary R. 1, 2
Lelantine War 140
Lesches 14–20
Life of Hesiod, authorship of 40, 44
Linus 133, 134
Little Iliad 16–17, 178
Lydia 124
Maeon 124–25, 128, 135–36
Mahaffy, John Pentland 60
Mandilaras, Basil 75–77
manuscripts
  L (Florence, Biblioteca Medicea Laurenziana Plut. 56.1) 48–52
  M (Vienna, Österreichische Nationalbibliothek, Phil. gr. 187) 52–60
Mas[s]agoras 125–26
Medea 155
Medon 182–83
Melanopus 135
Meles 119–20, 125, 136
  as original name of Homer 129
Menci, Giovanna 80
Menemachus 127
Methone 133
Metis 128
Midas 179, 181
Musurus, Marcus 52–53, 59, *See also* manuscripts: M
Nagy, Gregory 8, 119, 171, 184
Nietzsche, Friedrich 49, 61, 134–35, 137, 173
O'Sullivan, Neil 147, 162, 169
Oeagrus 133–34

Oenoe 171, 172
oracles *See* Pythian oracles
Orchomenus 175–76
Orpheus 134
Ortes 134
Panedes/Panoides 140–41, 164, 167–68
  form of name 140–41
  other contest accounts 27, 61, 64, 139
  papyri 47–48
    P.Ath.Soc.Pap. inv. M2 75–77
    P.Duk. inv. 665 80–82
    P.Freib. 1.1 b (inv. 12) 77–79
    P.Mich. inv. 2754 (Alcidamas-papyrus) 67–75
    P.Petr. I 25 (1) (P.Lond.Lit. 191) 60–67, 115, 140–41
Pergamum, school of 33
'philosophical questions' 158–64
Philoterpes 135
Phoenicians 128
Phrygians 149–50
Pierus 133
Poliziano, Angelo 48
Polycaste 127–28
Polycrates 10
Protagoras 159–60
Protesilaus 27–28, 30
Pycimede 136
Pythian oracles
  to Hadrian 56, 57, 58, 60, 131
  to Hesiod 169, 170–71
  to Homer 138–39
  to Megarians 186
Renehan, Robert 72
rhapsodes 137–38
Rheneia 10
riddle of the fishermen 69–70, 73, 190, 191–92
  and Homer's death 193
'riddles of the superlative' 141–44
rivers, personification of 154
Rohde, Erwin 49
Rose, Valentin 49
Sarpedon 153

Second Sophistic 23–34
Smyrna 118–19, 128, *See also* Meles
Socrates 37–38
sophistic influences 148, 159–60, 161, 162
sources 115, 119, 124, 139, 191, *See also* Alcidamas as source
speaker attribution 64, 148, 153, 156
speaking names 126, 128, 129–30, 134–35, 140–41
Stamatopoulou, Zoe 169
Stephanus, Henricus (Henri Estienne) 48
style 52, 142
  compared with papyri 61, 64–65, 70–71, 76
  of 'finest passages' 166
  sophistic influence 147–48, 159
summary of *Certamen* 115–17
Tabula Borgiana 178
Telemachus 127–28
textual transmission 2–3, 46, *See also* manuscripts; papyri
Thamyris 126–27
Thebaid 176–78
Theban saga 177–78, 181
Thebes (Egypt) 127
Themiste/Themisto 125, 128
Thoosa 132, 133
title of the *Certamen* 117
trust 163–64
Uden, James 131
verdict 79, 167–69, *See also* Panedes/Panoides
  compensatory reversal 171–72, 179, 181, 182, 186
  as non-negotiable element 6–7, 79
  treatment in other versions 23–24, 27, 30, 31, 34, 35–36
victory tripod 7, 13, 27, 42, 169
  epigram 39, 77–79, 169
Vogt, Ernst 130, 169
Welcker, Friedrich Gottlieb 129

West, Martin Litchfield
  on variants in the Hesiodic text 12–13
  on date of composition 130
  on Delian fragment 8
  on Ephyre as Corinth 184
  on genealogy 127
  on Homer's 'compensation' 179
  on Homer's Theban poem 177
  reading of P.Mich. inv. 2754 73
  on sources 118, 179, 181
  on textual transmission 2–3, 18, 158, 178
  translation 150, 151–52, 160
  on verdict 168
Westermann, Anton 48, 50
Wilamowitz, Ulrich von 1, 50, 130, 155, 185
Winter, John Garrett 71, 73
wisdom 140
  Hesiodic attribute 35, 163, 168, 176
  Homeric attribute 45, 73–74, 159, 188, 190
writing 190
Zeus
  justice of 173, 175
  tomb of 147

Index of Greek words

Ἀδ<ρ>ιανοῦ 58
ἀλήμων 126
ἅμ' Ἀτρείδησιν 157
ἄναλκις 151
ἀνδράσι ληιστῆρσιν 149–50
ἄπορον/ἀπορία 146
Αὐλητής 129–30
βουλευτήριον 183
διὰ χρυσῆν Ἀφροδίτην 151
δικαιοσύνη 163
εἰς τὸ μέσον 141
ἐκ διαδοχῆς 122
ἕλομεν 192
ἐριαυχέα 81–82
εὐδαιμονίη 164
θαῦμα 144–45, 167
θεῖος/θειότατος 117, 130, 143, 187
θεοτειχέα 81–82
θυσία 187
καιρός 163
κοινὸς πολίτης 189–90
κοσμοπολίτης 23
λεύκωμα 190
μεγαλόπτολις 188
μέτρον 159–61
Μηκιστέως 185–86
ὅμηρος 121
πανήγυριν 189
ποιέω 138
πολέμοιο 149
ῥαψῳδέω 137–8
σοφία/σοφός 163
τά τ' ἐόντα τά τ' ἐσσόμενα πρό τ' ἐόντα 19, 146
χρυσοῦς 145

Index of passages

Note: page numbers are in italics, for ease of distinction from passage identifiers.

Acusilaus 2 *FGrHist* 2 *121, 187*
Aelian *VH* 9.15 *187*
Aeschylus *Eum.* 28 *160*
Alcidamas *See also* P.Mich. inv. 2754
  Soph. 146, 163
    22-3 *162*
Anaximenes 72 *FGrHist* 30 *121*
Anonymous
  On Sublime 9.12-13 *181*
  Vit. Hom. 1
    2 *125, 127, 135, 187*
    3 *119, 120, 125, 126, 128*
    4 *174*
    5 *121, 166*
    6 *192, 193*
  Vit. Hom. 2
    1 *120, 121, 125, 128, 129*
    2 *119, 145, 182*
    3 *191, 192, 193*
  Vit. Hom. 3
    1 *119, 120, 127, 182, 187*
    3 *122*
    4 *145*
    5 *191, 192, 193*
Anthologia Palatina
  7. 1-7 *194*
  7. 5 *125*
  7. 7.1 *187*
  7. 54 *176*
  7.153 *180*
  11.442 *145*
  14 *157*
  14. 66 *139*
  14. 73.6 *185, 186*
  14. 77 *169*
  14.102 *131*
  16.292 *119*
  16.292-9 *131*
  16.295 *129*
  16.296 *119, 129*
  16.297-8 *123*
  16.298 *119*
Antimachus fr. 130 Wyss = 166 Matthews *122*
Apollodorus
  1.3.2 *134*
  1.8.4 *177*
  3.10.1 *133*
  7.4.6 *133*
Apollonius Rhodius 1.23 *134*
Apostolius, Michael *Collectio Paroemiarum* 15.88 *141*
Aristophanes
  Pax
    1097 *155*
    1270-1283 *148–49*
  R. 1033-6 *165*
  V. 1019-20 *175*
  Scholia *Pax* 1270 *178*
Aristotle
  Ath. 3 *182*
  Po.
    1448b24-1449a1 *122*
    1459b16 *176–77*
  fr. 524 Rose *176*
  fr. 565 Rose *176*
Athenaeus 465e *177*
Aulus Gellius *NA* 3.11.3-4 *137*
Bacchylides 5.160-2 *142*
Callimachus
  Ap. 60-4 *189*
  Del. 312 *189*
  Epigr. 7 *191*
  Jov. 6-9 *147*
Charax 103 *FGrHist* 62 *124, 132, 133*
Cleanthes *On the Poet* (frr.) *124*
Clemens Alexandrinus *Strom.* 1.21.117.4 *137*

Critias
    fr. 4 West *161*
    fr. 50 DK *120*
Damastes 5 *FGrHist* 11b (= fr. 11 Fowler) *121, 132*
Delphic oracle (Fontenrose)
    H65 *131*
    L41 *169*
    L80 *139*
Democritus (or Demetrius) of Troezen See *Supplementum Hellenisticum*
Dio Chrysostom
    2.7-12 *24–27, 30*
    13.21 *126*
    37.5 *169*
    53.4 *122*
Diodorus Siculus 3.65.6 *133*
Diogenes Laertius
    1.89 *179, 180*
    5.49 *161*
Empedocles fr. 122.9 *133*
Eratosthenes
    fr. 17 Powell *174*
    fr. 19 Powell *174*
    fr. 21 Powell *174*
Eugaion (Euagon) See *Fragmente der greichischen Historiker, Die*: 535
Euhemerus T 69 A Winiarczyk *147*
Euripides *Tr.* 1291 *188*
Eustathius
    ad Hom.*Il.*
        I 6, 28-7, 1 *45–46*
        I 575, 26 *125*
        IV 802, 5-26 *166*
    ad Hom.*Od.*
        1713.*19 127*
        1713.20 *125*
        1713.21 *121*
Eustratius *in EN* 6.7 *122*
Fragmente der griechischen Historiker, Die
    2 (Acusilaus) 2 *121, 187*
    3 (Pherecydes)
        142 *157*
        167 *132*
    4 (Hellanicus)
        5a-b-c *124*
        5b *132*
        5c *124*
        20 *121, 124*
        85b *179*
        125 *183*
        464 *138*
    5 (Damastes) 11b (=fr. 11 Fowler) *121, 132*
    70 (Ephorus)
        1 *136*
        99 *135*
    72 (Anaximenes) 30 *121*
    84 (Neanthes)
        13 *124*
        40 *124*
    103 (Charax) 62 *124, 132, 133*
    107 (Stesimbrotus) 22 *120*
    241
        9a *174*
        9b *174*
    328 (Philochorus) 209 *187*
    402 (Melisseus) 1 *133*
    535 (Euagon/Eugaion)
        1 *125*
        2 *120, 125*
        3 *125*
        4 *125*
    758 13 *125*
Gorgias *Hel.* 9 *161*
Harpocration O 19 Keaney *121, 122*
Heliodorus *Aeth.* 3.12-15 *127*
Hellanicus See *Fragmente der greichischen Historiker, Die*: 4
Heraclitus
    All. 76.8-9 *118*
Heraclitus fr. 22 B 56 DK *191*
Hermias *In Phdr.* (Couvreur) 231 *180*
Herodian *De pros. cath.* 3.1.296 *124*
Herodotus
    1.14.2 *181*
    1.23-4 *173*

2. 53.2 *137*
2.134 *134*
4.32 *177–78*
5.67.1 *177*
5.92 *169*
6.34 *154*
Pseudo-Herodotus, *Vit. Hom.*
1 *135*
2-3 *120*
5 *144–45*
9 *177*
12 *144–45*
13 *121*
16 *178*
22 *144–45*
25 *122*
28 *182*
31 *183*
35 *192*
36 *144–45, 191, 192–93, 193*
54 *121*
64 *121*
Hesiod
  Op.
    24-6 *159*
    40-1 *163*
    189 *161*
    213-85 *173*
    225-7 *161*
    270-1 *172*
    299 *136*
    352 *161*
    370-2 *163*
    383-4 *26*
    383-92 *165*
    392-5 *166–67*
    639-40 *118*
    648-62 *5–7, 139*
    654 *139*
    659 *169*
    694 *163*
    826-8 *164*
  Th.
    14 *152*
    30 *138*
    32 *146*

38 *146*
186 *150*
540 *153*
555 *153*
557 *153*
822 *151*
954 *150*
956-62 *155*
957 *155*
962 *151*
968 *143*
987 *143*
992-5 *155*
1005 *151*
1014 *151*
1020 *143*
fr. 1.2-3 MW *154*
fr. 23a.35 MW *151*
fr. 43a.65 MW *150*
fr. 65 MW *126*
fr. 136.12 MW *142*
fr. 204.47 MW *185*
fr. 221 MW *128*
fr. 221.3 MW *151*
fr. 278 MW *157*
fr. 286 *161*
frr. 305-306 MW *133*
Scholia
  Op. 381-2 *165*
  Op. 631 *176*
  Op. 650-62 *10–13, 41–42*
  Th. 54b1 *133*
Testimonia (ed. Most)
  5-9 *132*
  10 *137*
  12 *137*
  14 *137*
  17 *134*
  18 *134*
  116a *134*
  119bi *134*
  119bii *134*
[Hesiod] fr. 357 MW *7–10, 138*
Hesychius of Miletus s.v. 'Thoosa' *133*
Homer *See also Margites*

Il.

1. 1 *147*
1. 49 *152*
1. 70 *146*
1. 90 *186*
1.165 *149*
1.201 *156*
2. 23 *142*
2. 45 *154*
2. 92 *186*
2.123-8 *158*
2.201 *151*
2.284-93 *157*
2.509-10 *158*
2.529 *186*
2.559-68 *184–86*
2.562 *185*
2.565 *185*
2.567 *186*
2.570 *184*
2.591-600 *126*
2.678 *174*
2.719-20 *158*
2.734-7 *185*
2.761-2 *157*
2.830 *186*
2.862-3 *150*
2.864 *174*
3. 17 *150*
3. 64 *145*
3.150 *186*
3.192 *142*
3.328 *154*
4. 96 *186*
4.370 *142*
4.391-400 *124*
4.539-44 *166*
5. 18 *185*
5. 53 *152*
5. 60 *134*
5. 87 *154*
5. 96 *154*
5.330-2 *151*
5.349 *151*
5.629 *153*
5.646 *143*

5.813 *185*
6. 20-8 *185*
6.152 *184*
6.210 *184*
7. 31 *160*
7. 47 *142*
7. 89 *153*
7.419 *156*
7.451 *169*
7.458 *169*
8.153 *151*
8.562-3 *158*
9. 35 *151*
9. 41 *151*
9. 63-4 *155*
9. 89-91 *152*
9. 96 *152*
9.154 *186*
9.177 *155*
9.202 *142*
9.296 *186*
9.381-4 *127*
9.485 *143*
9.561 *151*
10.384 *157*
10.431 *150*
10.525 *186*
11. 67-71 *26–27*
11.527 *154*
11.700 *169*
13.130-1 *37*
13.664 *184*
14.126 *151*
15.713 *154*
16. 21 *142*
16.347 *153*
16.419-683 *153*
17.398-9 *166*
18. 23 *153*
18.569-70 *133*
21. 85-6 *129*
21.136-60 *154*
21.213 *154*
21.405 *186*
22. 51 *129*
22. 96 *185*

22.164 *169*
23. 71 *143*
23.252 *153*
23.259 *169*
23.464 *154*
23.677-99 *185*
24.605-6 *152*
24.793 *153*
Od.
  1. 71-3 *133*
  1.122 *156*
  1.325-6 *144*
  1.339-40 *144*
  2.343 *156*
  3.342 *155*
  3.375 *151*
  3.464 *127*
  4.541 *149*
  6.12 *142*
  6.30 *151*
  7.3 *185*
  8. 63-4 *166*
  8.263 *186*
  8.500 *156*
  9. 6-11 *143–44*, *145*
  9. 63 *154*
  9. 73 *154*
  9.126 *186*
  9.156 *154*
  9.566 *154*
  10.134 *154*
  10.137 *155*
  11.268 *160*
  12.182 *154*
  12.258 *156*
  14.347 *150*
  15.263 *157*
  15.363 *175*
  15.415-84 *129*
  15.473 *154*
  16. 51 *154*
  16.235-6 *157*
  16.295 *154*
  16.424 *150*
  17.103-4 *157*
  19.182-3 *157*
  19.258 *156*
  21.273 *155*
  22.74 *154*
  24.114 *157*
  24.117 *156*
  24.316 *153*
Scholia
  Il. 2.595 *127*
  Il. 2.744 *126*
  Il. 6.152 *184*
  Il. 13.197 *127*, *182*
  Il. 21.12 *125*
  Il. 22.51 *129*
  Il. 23.79 *33*
  Il. 23.79b *127*
  Od. 1.71 *133*
  Od. 3.464-9 *128*
Hymni Homerici
  2 (*h.Dem.*)
    14 *155*
    495 *147*
  3 (*h.Ap.*)
    172 *181*
    172-3 *119*
    451 *156*
    546 *147*
  18 (*h.Merc.*) 561 *160*
  27 (*h.Art.*) 9 *119*
  28 (*h.Ath.*) 11.5 *164*
Inscriptiones Graecae
  12.845.5 *172*
  22.99 *172*
  1623.5 *172*
  1926.130 *172*
Inscriptions de Délos 443 Bb 1. 146-7 *189*
Isocrates *Hel.* 65 *122*
Lexicon des frühgriechischen Epos
  s.v. διὰ χρυσῆν Ἀφροδίτην *151*
  s.v. Καλλιστώ *152*
Libanius *Defence of Socrates* (*Decl.* 1) 65-6 *34*, *37–39*
Lucian
  Alex. 53 *131*
  Dem. Enc. 9 *124*, *135*
  VH

226 Index of passages

2.20 *119*
2.20-22 *31–34*
Lucretius 3.12-13 *145*
Margites fr. 1 West *119, 122*
Melisseus 402 *FGrHist* 1 *133*
Musurus, Marcus MS
  Vienna, Österreichische
  Nationalbibliothek, Phil. gr. 187
  48r (**M**) *52–60*
Nicander
  fr. 14 Schneider *122*
  Scholia
    Ther. 400 *174*
    Ther. 472 *174*
Nonnus, *D.*
  39.293 *133*
  40.366 *135*
P.Ath.Soc.Pap. inv. M2 *75–77, 171*
P.Duk. inv. 665 *80–82, 188*
P.Freib. 1.1 b (inv. 12) *77–79*
P.Mich. inv. 2754 *67–75*
  15-18 *145*
  17-19 *145*
  22 *145*
P.Oxy. 3537 r. *136*
P.Petr. I 25 (1) (P.Lond.Lit. 191)
  60–67 *140–41, 145*
  12-15 *143*
  21-28 *144*
  31-2 *145*
Pausanias
  4.33.7 *126*
  4.5.10 *183*
  5.7.8 *135*
  9.20.1 *133*
  9.29.3-4 *133*
  9.29.6 *133*
  9.29.9 *133*
  9.31.4 *174, 190*
  9.31.6 *171*
  9.38.3-4 *173, 176*
  9.38.4 *176*
  9.9.5 *177*
  10.24.2 *139, 193*
  10.24.3 *125*

Pherecydes *See Fragmente der griechischen Historiker, Die*: 3
Philostratus
  Her.
    24.1-25.17 *30*
    43.7-10 *27–30*
  Im. 2.8 *120*
  VS 2.569 *147*
Photius *Bibl.* 319a 24 *125*
Pindar
  fr. 264 SM *119, 121*
  fr. 265 SM *125*
  N. 1.60 *160*
  P. 7.1 *188*
  Scholia
    N. 2 *188*
    N. 2.1 *121, 138*
Plato
  Grg. 449c-d *162*
  Ion
    530b *117*
    531a-535a *138*
    535d *145*
  Lg. 2.658d *138*
  Phdr.
    244a *135*
    264e *180*
  R.
    3.390a-b *144*
    10.600b-c *191*
    10.600d *138*
  Smp. 179d *134*
  Sph. 252c *175*
  Tht. 160d *159*
  Ti. 26e *187*
  Schol. *R.* 10.600b *191*
Plutarch *See also* Proclus: ad Hes. *Op.*
  Alex. 64 *146*
  Dinner of the Seven Sages 171
    151a-e *146*
    153a *141*
    153f *155*
    153f-154a *13, 14–20, 140, 141*
    162 *176*
    162c *175*

162c-e *173*
162d *175*
Lyc. 4.4 *191*
On Common Conceptions against the Stoics 1081c-1082d *20*
On the Delays of the Divine Vengeance 557a *134*
Table Talk 674f-675a *13–14*
The Cleverness of Animals
  969e *171, 173, 174*
  983e *189*
  984d *171, 173*
The Obsolescence of Oracles 431e *117*
Thes. 21 *189*
fr. 82 Sandbach *176*
fr. 84 Sandbach *140*
Pseudo-Plutarch., *Vit. Hom.*
  1.1 *118*
  1.2 *136*
  1.2-3 *119, 120*
  1.3 *124*
  1.4 *119, 129, 186, 187, 191, 192, 193*
  1.5 *75, 122*
  2.2 *119, 120, 125, 182, 187*
Pollux 5.42 *173*
Porphyrogenitus, Isaac *Praefatio in Homerum* 8 Kindstrand *129*
Proclus
  ad Hes.*Op.* 650-62 *10–13, 41*
  in *R.* 1.174.4-5 *23*
  Vit. Hom.
    2 *118, 119*
    3 *120, 121, 124*
    4 *132, 134, 135*
    5 *191, 192, 193*
    6 *20–23*
    9 *122*
Protagoras
  80 B 1 DK *159*
  80 B 4 DK *162*
Sappho fr. 16 Voigt *141*
Seneca *De brevitate vitae* 13.2 *181*
Simonides fr. 19 West *121*

Sophocles
  OC 1225-7 *142*
  Scholia *OC* 1375 *177*
Stephanus of Byzantium
  s.v. 'Ios' *139*
  s.v. Οἰνόη *172*
Stesimbrotus 107 *FGrHist* 22 *120*
Stobaeus
  3.3.45 *162*
  4.52.22 *143*
Stoicorum veterum fragmenta, vol. 1 (Arnim) fr. 593 *124*
Strabo
  7.3.6 *174*
  14.1.18 *191*
  14.1.35 *122*
Suda
  s.v. 'Aesop' *134*
  s.v. 'Alcyonids' *133*
  s.v. 'Hesiod' *135, 136, 174, 175*
  s.v. 'Homer' *183*
    1 *120, 123, 125, 127, 128, 129, 132*
    2 *119, 125, 127, 182*
    3 *121*
  s.v. 'Museus' *135*
  s.v. 'Stesichorus' *135*
  s.v. τὸ Ἡσιόδειον γῆρας *176*
Supplementum Hellenisticum
  374 *126*
  376-7 *126*
  378 *126*
Syncellus *Chronography*
  202.21-2 *137*
  206.9 *137*
Tatianus *Ad Graec.* 31 *174*
Themistius *Or.*
  15.184c-d *36–37*
  30.348c-349a *34–36*
Theocritus
  Id.
    7.47 *121*
    22.218 *121*
Theognis
  1.144-8 *163*

1.831-2 *164*
425-8 *142–43*
Thrasymachus
  85 B 6a DK *161*
  85 B 8 DK *162*
Thucydides
  1.10.3-5 *157*
  1.15.3 *140*
  3.104 *9–10, 119*
  3.96.1 *169, 171*
Tzetzes
  ad Hes.*Op.* 40
    652 *40–42*
  ad Lyc. 831 *134*
  Alleg. (Boissonade)
    Prol. 59-66 *123*
    Prol. 60 *127*
    Prol. 62 *125*
    Prol. 64 *126*
    Prol. 89-92 *44–45*
  Exeg. in Il. 37.22 *191*

H. 125
  13.658 *191*
  13.660 *191, 192*
  13.663-5 *193*
Vita Hesiodi (Colonna)
  1 *136*
  80-1 *118*
  123-42 *42–44*
  126 *139*
  127 *141*
  141 *145*
  154-5 *172*
  155 *175*
  155-6 *171*
  166-70 *169*
  171-2 *171*
  174-5 *173*
  175 *171*
  177-85 *176*
  179-82 *176*
  184-5 *176*
Xenophanes fr. 2 West *140*

www.ingramcontent.com/pod-product-compliance
Lightning Source LLC
Chambersburg PA
CBHW032058230426
43662CB00035B/591